W9-CFO-451

UNDERSTANDING LANGUAGE STRUCTURE, INTERACTION, AND VARIATION, SECOND EDITION

An Introduction to Applied Linguistics and Sociolinguistics for Nonspecialists

Steven Brown
Salvatore Attardo

Youngstown State University

THE UNIVERSITY OF MICHIGAN PRESS

Acknowledgments

Grateful acknowledgment is made to the following authors, publishers, and journals for permission to reprint previously published materials.

Blackwell Publishing Ltd. for "Kaplan's representation of the development of argument in the essays of different cultures" from "Cultural Thought Patterns in Inter-Cultural Education," by Robert Kaplan, from *Language Learning, A Journal of Research in Language Studies* Vol. 16, #1, copyright © 1966.

Cambridge University Press for *DIALECTOLOGY* by J. K. Chambers and Peter Trudgill. Reprinted with the permission of Cambridge University Press.

Pearson Education Limited for adaptations of table, "The Domains of English in East African States," and map, "The Position of English in African Nation-States," from *English in Africa: An Introduction* by Josef J. Schmied, © 1991.

Taylor & Francis Group Ltd. for figures from *A History of the English Language* by Albert C. Baugh, copyright © 1957; "Isoglosses for Various Ways of Saying 'Aren't'" from *The Linguistic Atlas of England* by Harold Orton, Stewart Sanderson, and John Widdowson, copyright © 1978.

University of Adelaide, South Australia, for material from *Encyclopedia of Bilingualism and Bilingual Education* by Smolicz and Secome.

University of Illinois Press for figure, "The Global Diffusion of Language," from *The Other Tongue, Second Edition,* by Braj B. Kachru, copyright © 1992.

University of Michigan Press for pronunciation of "water" from *The Pronunciation of English in the Atlantic States* by Hans Kurath and R. McDavid, copyright © 1960; Dialectical Regions of the United States map from *American Regional Dialects: A Word Geography* by Craig M. Carver, copyright © 1987; the isogloss for "You-All" from *A Word Geography of the Eastern United States* by Hans Kurath, copyright © 1949.

Every effort has been made to contact the copyright holders for permission to reprint borrowed material. We regret any oversights that may have occurred and will rectify them in future printings of this book.

Contents

How to Use This book   xvii

Preface to the Second Edition   xxi

List of Figures   xxiii

1. Introduction to Linguistics   1

1.1. Preliminaries   1

     1.1.1. The Subfields of Linguistics   1

1.2. Approaches to Language   2

     1.2.1. Prescriptive vs. Descriptive   2

     1.2.2. Diachronic vs. Synchronic   6

     1.2.3. Competence vs. Performance   7

     1.2.4. Linguistics as a Science   9

1.3. Exercises   10

     1.3.1 Words to Know   10

     1.3.2. Review   10

     1.3.3. Research Projects   10

1.4. Further Readings   11

2. The Building Blocks of Language   13

2.1. Overview   13

2.2. The Sounds of Language   13

     2.2.1. The Phonetic Alphabet   14

     2.2.2. How Are the Sounds Produced in the Mouth?   18

     2.2.3. Sounds and Meaning   23

2.3. Words and Their Parts   26
   2.3.1. Morphemes and Words   26
   2.3.2. Free vs. Bound Morphemes   27
   2.3.3. Affixes   27
   2.3.4. Inflectional vs. Derivational   28
   2.3.5. Where Do New Words Come From?   29
   2.3.6. Idioms and Phraseology   32
2.4. The Way Sentences Are Put Together   32
   2.4.1. The Double Articulation of Language   32
   2.4.2. Syntax   35
2.5. Types of Sentences   43
   2.5.1. Recursion and Embedded Sentences   47
   2.5.2. Syntax, Universal Grammar, and the   49
       Chomskian Program
2.6. Beyond the Sentence   51
   2.6.1. Coherence and Cohesion   51
   2.6.2. Conversation Analysis   53
2.7. Exercises   56
   2.7.1. Words to Know   56
   2.7.2. Review   56
   2.7.3. Research Projects   58
2.8. Further Readings   59

3. How Do We Mean Things?   60

3.1. The Meaning of Words   60
   3.1.1. Breaking Down Words   61
   3.1.2. Meaning Relationships   63
   3.1.3. Denotation and Connotation   64
   3.1.4. Getting Rid of Ambiguity   66
3.2. The Meaning of Sentences   67
   3.2.1. Pointers to the Context of Sentences 67
   3.2.2. The Influence of Context   68
   3.2.3. How Do We Mean What We Say?   68
3.3. Exercises   77
   3.3.1. Words to Know   77
   3.3.2. Review   77
   3.3.3. Research Project   78
3.4. Further Readings   78

4. Sociolinguistics   80

4.1. What Do We Say?   80
4.2. How Do We Say Things?   82
    4.2.1. Face   82
    4.2.2. Forms of Address   83
4.3. Whom Do We Speak To?   88
    4.3.1. Language Contact   88
    4.3.2. Bilingualism/Diglossia   88
    4.3.3. Language Planning   90
    4.3.4. Code Switching   91
4.4. Exercises   92
    4.4.1. Words to Know   92
    4.4.2. Review   92
    4.4.3. Research Projects   93
4.5. Further Readings   93

5. Language Variation   95

5.1. Language and Dialect   95
    5.1.1. Dialectology   97
5.2. The Notion of Standard English   103
    5.2.1. Why Do Dialects/Accents Persist?   105
5.3. Exercises   106
    5.3.1. Words to Know   106
    5.3.2. Review   106
    5.3.3. Research Projects   107
5.4. Further Readings   109

6. Language and Social Groups   110

6.1. Social Class Dialects   110
    6.1.1. Labov's Studies   111
    6.1.2. Social Networks   112
    6.1.3. Restricted vs. Elaborated Codes   113
    6.1.4. Caste   114
    6.1.5. Age   114
6.2. Register   116
6.3. Jargon   118
6.4. Slang   119

6.5. Exercises   120
    6.5.1. Words to Know   120
    6.5.2. Review   121
    6.5.3. Research Projects   121
6.6. Further Readings   121

7. Pidgins and Creoles   122

7.1. Languages of Wider Communication   122
7.2. Pidgins   123
    7.2.1. Characteristics of Pidgin Languages   123
    7.2.2. Types of Pidgins   124
7.3. Creoles   125
7.4. Theories of Pidgin and Creole Origins   126
    7.4.1. Superstrate Theories   126
    7.4.2. Substrate Theories   126
    7.4.3. A Universalist Theory: The Bioprogram   127
7.5. Pidgins and Lectal Variation   127
7.6. Decreolization   128
7.7. Exercises   129
    7.7.1. Words to Know   129
    7.7.2. Review   129
    7.7.3. Research Projects   130
7.8. Further Readings   130

8. African-American Vernacular English   132

8.1. Origins of AAVE   132
    8.1.1. Dialectologist Hypothesis   132
    8.1.2. Creole Hypothesis   134
    8.1.3. Recent Debate about the Origins of AAVE   136
    8.1.4. Divergence Hypothesis   138
8.2. A Grammatical Sketch of AAVE   139
    8.2.1. Phonology   139
    8.2.2. Tense and Aspect   140
    8.2.3. Relative Clauses   142
    8.2.4. Summary of Differences between AAVE and SAE   142
8.3. AAVE and Education   142
8.4. Exercises   144
    8.4.1. Words to Know   144
    8.4.2. Review   144
    8.4.3. Research Projects   144
8.5. Further Readings   146

9. Language Policy 148

9.1. Multilingualism 148
  9.1.1. Introduction 148
  9.1.2. National and Minority Languages 149
  9.1.3. Diglossia 151
  9.1.4. Successful Minority Languages 152
  9.1.5. Language Rights 153
9.2. Language Planning and Policy 154
  9.2.1. The Situation in Some Nations 155
  9.2.2. Language Maintenance, Shift, and Death 160
9.3. Exercises 162
  9.3.1. Words to Know 162
  9.3.2. Review 162
  9.3.3. Research Projects 162
9.4. Further Readings 162

10. Language and Gender 164

10.1. Early Studies 164
10.2. Men, Women, and Conversation 166
  10.2.1. Characteristics of Women's Discourse 169
  10.2.2. Language and Power 169
10.3. Gender in Playgrounds/Classrooms 169
10.4. Language and Men 170
10.5. Lesbian and Gay Male Language Use 171
10.6. Sexist Language 171
10.7. Exercises 172
  10.7.1. Words to Know 172
  10.7.2. Review 172
  10.7.3. Research Projects 172
10.8. Further Readings 173

11. Literacy 174

11.1. The Written Word 174
  11.1.1. Literacy and Orality 174
  11.1.2. Writing Systems 175
11.2. Reading 176
  11.2.1. Reader, Text, and Meaning 176
  11.2.2. Reading Development in a First Language 177
  11.2.3. Spelling 178
  11.2.4. Teaching Methods 179

11.3. Writing	181
11.3.1. Product Approaches to Writing	181
11.3.2. Process Approaches to Writing	182
11.4. Contrastive Rhetorics	185
11.5. Computer-Mediated Communication	186
11.5.1. Genres of CMC	187
11.5.2. Synchronous vs. Asynchronous CMC	188
11.5.3. Writing and Speech Features	188
11.5.4. Jargon of CMC	189
11.5.5. Sociolinguistics of CMC	191
11.5.6. How Different Is CMC from Non-CMC?	191
11.6. Exercises	192
11.6.1. Words to Know	192
11.6.2. Review	192
11.6.3. Research Projects	192
11.7. Further Readings	192
12. First Language Acquisition	**194**
12.1. Three Theories	194
12.1.1. Behaviorism	194
12.1.2. Innatism	196
12.1.3. Interactionism	196
12.1.4. Summing Up the Theories of Language Acquisition	198
12.2. Learning a First Language	198
12.2.1. The Preverbal Stage	198
12.2.2. The Role of Conversation	199
12.2.3. Stages	200
12.2.4. Babbling	200
12.2.5. First Words	201
12.2.6. Under- and Overextension	202
12.2.7. Development of Vocabulary	202
12.2.8. Later Vocabulary Development	204
12.2.9. The Two-Word Stage	204
12.2.10. Learning Grammar	205
12.2.11. Later Developments in Grammar	207
12.2.12. Pragmatics	207
12.3. Atypical Language Development	208
12.3.1. Hearing Impairments	209

12.3.2. Mental Retardation   209
12.3.3. Autism   210
12.3.4. Stuttering   210
12.3.5. Aphasia   211
12.3.6. Dyslexia   211
12.4. Exercises   214
12.4.1. Words to Know   214
12.4.2. Review   214
12.4.3. Research Projects   214
12.5. Further Readings   215

13. **Second Language Acquisition**   **217**

13.1. Transfer and Interlanguage   217
13.1.1. Developmental Sequences   219
13.1.2. Order of Acquisition   220
13.2. L1 = L2?   221
13.3. Krashen and the Monitor Hypothesis   221
13.3.1. Acquisition and Learning   222
13.3.2. Monitor Hypothesis   222
13.3.3. Natural Order Hypothesis   223
13.3.4. Input/Comprehension Hypothesis   223
13.3.5. Affective Filter Hypothesis   223
13.4. Instructed SLA   224
13.5. Input and Interaction   225
13.5.1. Interaction   225
13.5.2. Interlanguage Talk   226
13.5.3. Output   226
13.6. Individual Differences and SLA   227
13.6.1. Intelligence   228
13.6.2. Aptitude   228
13.6.3. Motivation   228
13.6.4. Attitude   229
13.6.5. Personality Factors   230
13.6.6. Learning Styles and Strategies   231
13.7. Exercises   232
13.7.1. Words to Know   232
13.7.2. Review   232
13.7.3. Research Projects   232
13.8. Further Readings   232

14. Language and Literature   **234**

   14.1. Casual vs. Elaborated Language   234
          14.1.1. Arrangement of Sounds   235
          14.1.2. Figures of Thought   239
   14.2. Narrative   243
          14.2.1. Narrative Functions   244
          14.2.2. Narrator, Narratee, and Their Implied Relatives   244
          14.2.3. Points of View   245
   14.3. Exercises   249
          14.3.1. Words to Know   249
          14.3.2. Review   249
          14.3.3. Research Projects   250
   14.4. Further Readings   250

15. Linguistics in the Professions   **252**

   15.1. Language and the Law   252
          15.1.1. Legal Language   252
          15.1.2. Language in Court   253
          15.1.3. Legislation on Language   254
          15.1.4. Forensic Linguistics   255
   15.2. Language and Medicine   256
          15.2.1. Discourse   256
          15.2.2. Social Factors   257
   15.3. Translation   258
          15.3.1. Quality of Translation   258
          15.3.2. Testing Translation   260
          15.3.3. Problems with Translation   261
          15.3.4. Machine Translation   263
   15.4. Language in Education   263
          15.4.1. Teacher Talk as a Register   263
   15.5. Lexicography   264
          15.5.1. Dictionaries   264
          15.5.2. Types of Dictionaries   265
          15.5.3. Issues in Lexicography   268
   15.6. Speech Pathology   269
   15.7. Exercises   270
          15.7.1. Words to Know   270
          15.7.2. Review   270
          15.7.3. Research Projects   270
   15.8. Further Readings   272

16. The Nature of Language   274

16.1. Features of Language   274
   16.1.1. The Double Articulation of Language   274
   16.1.2. Productivity   274
   16.1.3. Arbitrariness   275
   16.1.4. Interchangeability   275
   16.1.5. Displacement   275
   16.1.6. Discreteness   276
   16.1.7. Specialization   276
   16.1.8. Cultural Transmission   276
16.2. The Birds and the Bees   276
   16.2.1. The Bees' Dance   276
   16.2.2. Birds' Vocalizations   277
   16.2.3. Apes   277
16.3. Language and Culture   278
   16.3.1. Language and Thought   278
   16.3.2. Critical Discourse Analysis   281
16.4. Sign Language   282
   16.4.1. Introduction   282
   16.4.2. Sign vs. Gesture   282
   16.4.3. Universality of Sign Language   282
   16.4.4. Arbitrariness of the Sign   283
   16.4.5. Sign as a System of Language   283
   16.4.6. Language Variation   285
   16.4.7. Language Acquisition   285
   16.4.8. Conclusion   286
16.5. Exercises   286
   16.5.1. Words to Know   286
   16.5.2. Review   287
   16.5.3. Research Projects   287
16.6. Further Readings   287

17. Historical Linguistics   289

17.1. The History of English   290
17.2. Old English (OE): AD 450 to 1100   291
   17.2.1. OE Phonology   292
   17.2.2. OE Morphology and Syntax   292
17.3. Middle English (ME): AD 1150 to 1500   295
   17.3.1. The Grammar of ME   296

17.3.2. The Literature of ME   297
17.3.3. Dialects of ME   297
17.4. Modern English: AD 1500 to Present   299
17.4.1. Additions to the Lexicon   299
17.4.2. The Great Vowel Shift   299
17.4.3. Morphology in the Renaissance Period   301
17.4.4. The Augustan Age and the Move   301
          toward Standardization
17.4.5. Recent Morphological and Lexical Developments   302
17.5. English as a World Language   302
17.5.1. American English   303
17.5.2. World Englishes   306
17.6. Diachronic Linguistics   312
17.6.1. The Comparative Method   312
17.6.2. Language Families   314
17.6.3. The Indo-European Family   314
17.6.4. The Language Families of Africa   315
17.6.5. Asia and the Pacific   316
17.6.6. The Americas   318
17.6.7. Isolates   319
17.6.8. Nostratic/Proto-World   319
17.7. Exercises   320
17.7.1. Words to Know   320
17.7.2. Review   320
17.7.3. Research Projects   320
17.8. Further Readings   321

18. Pedagogical Grammar   323

18.1. History of Grammar   323
18.1.1. The Greeks   323
18.1.2. The Romans   325
18.1.3. The Middle Ages   326
18.1.4. The Renaissance   326
18.1.5. Scientific Linguistics   327
18.2. Pedagogy of Grammar   330
18.2.1. Types of Grammars   330
18.2.2. Grammar Pedagogy   331
18.2.3. Cognitive Grammar   334
18.3. The Reed-Kellogg Diagramming System   336
18.3.1. The Diagramming System   336

18.4. Exercises   339
    18.4.1. Words to Know   339
    18.4.2. Review   340
    18.4.3. Research Projects   340
18.5. Further Readings   340

19. **English Grammar**   **342**

19.1. The Basic Components of Sentences   342
19.2. The Verb   342
    19.2.1. Types of Verbs   343
    19.2.2. Voice   344
    19.2.3. TMA System   345
    19.2.4. Number   350
19.3. The Noun   351
    19.3.1. Number   351
    19.3.2. Gender   352
    19.3.3. Case   352
19.4. Minor Parts of Speech   353
    19.4.1. Modifiers   353
    19.4.2. Pro-forms   354
    19.4.3. Determiners   355
    19.4.4. Conjunctions   356
    19.4.5. Prepositions   357
    19.4.6. Interjections   357
    19.4.7. Particles   358
19.5. Phrase-Level Grammar   358
    19.5.1. Noun Phrases   358
    19.5.2. Verb Phrases   358
    19.5.3. Other Phrasal Constituents   359
19.6. Sentence-Level Grammar   359
    19.6.1. Complex Sentences   360
    19.6.2. Marked Sentential Patterns   363
19.7. Exercises   364
    19.7.1. Review   364
    19.7.2. Research Project   365
19.8. Further Readings   367
19.9. Answers to Research Project   368

Glossary   **369**

Bibliography   **403**

Index   **425**

to Renee Repetto

to Gaia Attardo

How to Use This Book

The purpose of this book is to provide more than enough material for a one-term introduction to the study of language and linguistics for students whose primary educational goal lies outside of the discipline of linguistics. In other words, this is an introduction to linguistics for people who do not plan to be linguists. There are two types of students who fit our target audience: (a) students who plan to pursue a career in the educational field and need to be acquainted with the ways language works so as to be effective teachers; and (b) students who need some background in linguistics because their discipline is adjacent to, but not overlapping with, linguistics. Among these we may list as examples psychologists, sociologists, and anthropologists. Since this is a large and diverse target audience, we have included a wide variety of topics and teachers will need to choose chapters based on class goals, as we will make clear in the pages that follow. This text is also suitable for practicing ESL/EFL teachers, among others, who need a reference volume about language.

We have assumed a minimum of knowledge, particularly about language. In our experience, high school graduates often do not have a firm grounding in English grammar. For this reason, we have provided Chapter 19, which provides the basics of English grammar. We have also provided a glossary of linguistic terms.

This text does not claim to be an introduction to linguistics, which would require a much more technical discussion of theoretical linguistics; most notably it would make it necessary to cover X-bar syntax and the GB/PP/minimalism developments of Chomsky's standard theory (as well as other offshoots, such as HPSG, LFG, etc.). Our choice has been to cover the standard theory (with a few additions, justified pedagogically) since its knowledge is assumed in the field (unlike minimalism, say). This makes it unsuitable, as the sole text, for those students who need more than a passing acquaintance with the methods and findings of linguistics, i.e., those students whose future professional activities will require work with and about language, such as linguistics majors and ESL/EFL teachers in training. However, this is not to say that they wouldn't benefit from reading this book.

As the title of the book tries to make clear, the text has three foci: language itself, in its systematic organization; language as a tool for interaction among speakers; and language as an object of variation, i.e., how language reflects the differences in its speakers, the situations in which they use it, and the goals to which they put it.

In our choices of subjects, we have been guided by what we saw as practical applications in the classroom and in the world of the knowledge we presented. We have tried to present knowledge that our students will be able to put to use when they leave school.

The organization of the book is cyclical: a subject is first introduced in very general terms in one of the initial chapters and is then taken up again in more detail in one of the later chapters, thus allowing the teacher to select which topics he/she wants to focus on, while retaining the all-important comprehensiveness of the presentation, which tries to provide a representative panorama of linguistics and applied linguistics. The cyclical organization is also a feature for the students: it provides repetition, which facilitates learning.

Throughout, we have conceptualized our audience as current college students, people who are comfortable with hypertext/cybermedia. For that reason, and for reasons of good pedagogy, we have sought to provide as many links inside the text as we can. We begin by providing a general discussion and then apply the terms to a specialized field. We also want the students to see (and hopefully make) connections between old and new material, and we hope that by providing them something like buttons on a Web page, we allow and perhaps even encourage them to remind themselves of the concepts throughout the course. Whether that is called reinforcement, spiraling, or strengthening connections, it remains the clearest path to learning we know. Needless to say, one does not need to be computer literate to read this book!

Other features that students will find helpful are that new and significant terms are bolded in the text, and many are listed at the end of each chapter (under the heading Words to Know). Most in-text bolded words appear in the more than 600-entry glossary, which provides more examples and definitions for the key words. Other general terms important to studying linguistics are also included in the glossary. Exercises and activities as well as references to the sources used in the text and other sources for further reading complement each chapter. The Further Readings at the end of the chapters use the customary author/year-of-publication system to refer to the comprehensive bibliography at the end of the volume.

> Interspersed in the text the reader will find "fun boxes" (such as this one), which are not strictly required reading but contain material that may stimulate discussion or may be of additional interest.

> Occasionally a very important definition will be shaded. Those should probably be memorized.

We do not expect that any single course will cover all the chapters in the book (although we would like to hear of such feats!). The abundance of material is intended to give options to the teachers. We would expect a typical course for students without prior background in linguistics to cover Chapters 1–6, which introduce the background material on linguistics and broadly cover sociolinguistics; teachers would then pick chapters according to the course's goals. For example, a course for English majors may want to cover Chapters 1–6 and then Chapters 7 and 8 on African-American Vernacular English (AAVE), 10 on gender issues, 14 on literary language, 17 on the history of English, and perhaps spend time on Chapters 18 and 19 on grammar. A course for education majors may want to cover Chapters 1–6, 7, and 8 on AAVE; 10 on gender issues; 11 on literacy; 12 and 13 on first and second language acquisition; and 18 and 19 on grammar. A course for non-majors, particularly for social scientists, may want to cover Chapters 1–6, the sections on international English (17.5) and on language planning (Chapter 9), plus some of the chapters on the social use of language (e.g., 8 or 10). A course for the humanities, such as a general-education introduction to language, could work selectively with Chapters 1–3; cover Chapters 4–6; move on to 12; and then read Chapters 7 and 8, 10, 14, 15, and 9 or 17.

The chapters have different lengths, and so one should not plan one-week-per-chapter courses. Probably Chapters 2 and 3 will be the toughest, requiring more than a week of class time, whereas all the other chapters can be covered in a week or less.

Although we tried to write this book as clearly as possible, not all parts are equally as accessible. There are sections that students will find more difficult. Teachers should keep this in mind and direct their students accordingly. The sections on articulatory phonetics (2.2.2), the mathematical foundations of Chomskian syntax (2.4.2), the theories of pidgin and creole origins (7.3), the more technical discussion of AAVE (8.2), and the comparative method in historical linguistics (17.6.1) may be left to the attention of motivated students without hindering too much the progress of the argument.

This book came out of our experiences teaching "Introduction to Language" and "Principles of Linguistic Study" at Youngstown State University and elsewhere. We thank the chairs of the English Department, Sandra Stephan and Gary Salvner, for their support. We also thank the Dean of the College of Arts and Sciences, Barbara Brothers (now retired), for her support, most concretely in the form of reassigned time. Thanks also go to Dean Peter Kasvinsky of the Graduate School for funding our research assistants during the summer of 1999: Christian Hempelmann (who did the graphics, wrote the first draft of some items of the glossary, indexed the book, and produced the camera-ready text) and Cynthia Vigliotti (who compiled and proofread the bibliography, filling in our sometimes cryptic notes). Some parts of Chapters 2 and 3 were originally developed as part of a project with the University of Maryland. A particularly heartfelt word of thanks for those who read all or parts of the text and suggested improvements: Donalee H. Attardo, Paul Baltes, Rebecca Barnhouse, Jodi Eisterhold, Patricia Dissosway, Michael Finney, Dallin Oaks, Stacy Hagen, Ndinzi Masagara, Tom McCracken, Christina Bratt Paulston, Gunther Radden, Marina Raskin, Victor Raskin, Dorolyn Smith, and Tim Vickers. While we have incorporated many of their suggestions, much doubtless remains that they would disagree with. Melina Champine, Randall Hogue, Gillian Wilkinson, and others contributed in one way or another to this effort. Special thanks to Douglas Faires, who helped with the production of the final text of the first edition. It was a pleasure working with Kelly Sippell and the University of Michigan Press staff. Last, but certainly not least, those who deserve the most thanks are our students.

Preface to the Second Edition

The genre of the preface to the second edition of a book requires to some extent self-congratulations: indeed the very existence of a second edition implies that the book itself was, if not well received, at least reasonably so. We are very gratified that so many people have found our work useful, and we are thankful to all those who provided us with much needed feedback. We have tried to integrate suggestions and requests in this second edition, without however radically changing the nature of the textbook, which was and remains a simple, straightforward introduction to linguistics and sociolinguistics.

Our work in the second edition has consisted of correcting any formal and factual errors (much to our surprise, there were still a few) and updating our figures and data, whenever possible (e.g., we now reflect the data of the 2000 census for the United States), as well as the bibilography. Elsewhere we have added a few paragraphs clarifying some areas that we found to be unnecessarily obscure. In a few cases we have added new material, most significantly about pedagogical objectives for prospective teachers, computer-mediated communication, and the glossary, which has now about 100 more entries. Perhaps the most notable change is that we have expanded significantly the treatment of English grammar, one of the most frequent requests/suggestions from our readers. We have at the same time simplified the treatment and presented more information in visual form, to aid memorization. Finally, the format of the book has changed significantly. All syntactic trees were redone using qtree, a (La)TeX utility by Jeffrey Mark Siskind and Alexis Dimitriadis. Another change is that the second edition of *Understanding Language*

Structure, Interaction, and Variation is accompanied by a workbook (ISBN 0-472-03068-X), which collects a wealth of exercises and activities that teachers can draw on to help their students familiarize themselves with the contents of the book. It should particularly help students in areas where more practice is beneficial: phonetics, morphology, syntax, and semantics.

We would like to thank all those who provided feedback, particularly Keith Folse, Randall Hogue, Virginia Ludwig, and Cynthia Vigliotti; the editorial team at the University of Michigan Press, particularly Kelly Sippell; as well as Cynthia Carter, our research assistant, and the Youngstown State University Office of Equal Opportunity and Diversity, whose Work Experience Program funded her time with us.

List of Figures

Figure 2.1 The International Phonetic Alphabet: English Consonants
Figure 2.2 The International Phonetic Alphabet: English Vowels
Figure 2.3 The Vocal Tract
Figure 2.4 Main Places of Articulation
Figure 2.5 The Organization of a Generative-Transformative Grammar

Figure 3.1 The Meaning of Some English Deictics.

Figure 5.1 The Isogloss for "You-All"
Figure 5.2 Areas of Usage of Various Terms for Carbonated Nonalcoholic Beverage
Figure 5.3 Isoglosses for Various Ways of Saying "Aren't" in England
Figure 5.4 Langue d'oil (North) and Langue d'hoc (South)
Figure 5.5 Dialectal Regions of the United States
Figure 5.6 Pronunciation of "Water" in the Eastern United States

Figure 9.1 Languages in Switzerland

Figure 11.1 Kaplan's Representation of the Development of Argument in the Essays of Different Cultures

Figure 15.1 Bei Jing/Pei King
Figure 15.2 Ho te ru = hotel

Figure 17.1 The Area Inhabited by the Anglo-Saxons
Figure 17.2 The Germanic Language Family
Figure 17.3 OE Dialects
Figure 17.4 ME Dialects
Figure 17.5 The Great Vowel Shift
Figure 17.6 The Global Diffusion of the English Language
Figure 17.7 English in Africa

Chapter 1

Introduction to Linguistics

1.1 PRELIMINARIES

Linguistics is the science that studies language. Someone who studies linguistics is a **linguist.** Note that there is a common understanding of the word *linguist* as meaning "someone who knows many languages." While it is often true that linguists know several languages, being a **polyglot** (i.e., someone who knows many languages) is not a requirement for being a linguist.

Note that in the definition above we have talked about "language," not a specific language (say, English) or a group of languages. To a large extent, all languages in the world are based on similar principles. Part of our goal will be to outline such principles. The other purpose of this book (and of this course) is to make you appreciate the complexity (and the beauty) of language as well as the complex relations among the speakers, their societies, and their languages.

1.1.1 The Subfields of Linguistics

The fields into which linguistics is traditionally divided are these:

Phonetics deals with the sounds of language.

Phonology deals with how the sounds are organized.

Morphology deals with how sounds are put together to form words.

Syntax deals with how sentences are formed.

Semantics deals with the meanings of words, sentences, and texts.

Pragmatics deals with how sentences and texts are used in the world (i.e., in context).

Text linguistics deals with units larger than sentences, such as paragraphs and texts.

There are several other fields within linguistics that look at language from the perspective of another discipline:

- Sociolinguistics (language in society)
- Psycholinguistics (psychology of language)
- Anthropological linguistics (anthropology of language, aka ethnolinguistics)
- Historical linguistics (the history of languages)
- Neurolinguistics (language and the brain)
- Language pedagogy (how to teach languages; its best-known field is English as a second/foreign language)
- Computational linguistics (computers and language)
- Many others, such as forensic linguistics (language and the law) and translation

1.2 APPROACHES TO LANGUAGE

The following sections will outline different ways in which a linguist, or a knowledgeable amateur, may approach language. The sections will cover the prescriptive and descriptive approaches, the historical approach (with a few hints at the origins of linguistics as a historical discipline), and the very important competence versus performance distinction. The last section rounds the chapter off with a discussion of the scientific method as it applies to the study of language.

1.2.1 Prescriptive vs. Descriptive

Task: What grammar rules do you remember from school? Make a list. After you have read this section, try to decide whether they are prescriptive or descriptive rules.

We can look at language from two points of view:

- **Prescriptive.** This approach consists basically of stating what is considered right and wrong in language. Prescriptivism passes judgments, e.g., "Splitting infinitives is wrong." *To boldly go where no one has gone before...* is therefore a bad sentence because it "splits" the infinitive *to go*.

- **Descriptive.** This approach, on the other hand, consists of describing the facts. For example: "Some people split infinitives; some don't. Which kind of people split infinitives? When do they do that? What can be used to split an infinitive?"

A common misunderstanding is that descriptivists "have no rules" and that they have a permissive "anything goes" attitude. In fact, nothing could be further from the truth. Descriptive linguistics is dedicated to describing the rules of the language, and language is seen as essentially rule governed (i.e., made of rules). So what is the issue? Don't descriptivists and prescriptivists agree?

In fact, prescriptivists and descriptivists disagree deeply: descriptivists seek to find the rules that govern the languages spoken by people (i.e., English, French, Chinese, Swahili, and all others), while prescriptivists, for the major part, seek to impose arbitrary rules that come from outside the language and/or seek to preserve a stage of the language that has been left behind by the evolution of the language itself.

For example, the prescription of the avoidance of the split infinitive was based on the fact that Latin avoided doing so, when Latin was thought of as a "better" language than English. Often prescriptivists are merely clinging to a past state of the language. For example, the distinction between *who* and *whom* is now lost on most speakers. There isn't anything anyone can do, practically speaking, to restore this distinction.

What prescriptivists say is often not supported by linguistic data. Example: banning the "double negative" (*I don't want no fish*). English has always had the double negative. Shakespeare uses it in *Romeo and Juliet, act 3, scene 1* (Mercutio: "I will not budge for no man's pleasure").

So why do people get so upset about prescriptivism? Perhaps because following certain grammatical rules is a social "shibboleth." A shibboleth provides information about the group to which individuals belong.

The word *shibboleth* comes from the Bible (Judges, 12:6), where it is used by the Gileadites to distinguish themselves from the Ephraimites, who pronounced it *sibboleth*. Once the Gileadites sorted themselves out from the Ephraimites, they killed their rivals.

Linguistic usage helps gather information about someone. If you do or say something in a certain way, you belong to a certain group. Following or not following certain linguistic forms may be used to identify social class or ethnic group. For example, African-American Vernacular English (AAVE) eliminates the copula in certain syntactic constructions, roughly whenever informal English allows contractions (in *It's*, *'s* is the contracted form of *is*, the third person singular form of the copula). So, *They're home* would be *They home* in AAVE (see Chapter 8 for a fuller discussion). This elimination of the copula and other features of AAVE may be perceived as unprofessional or as ignorant, while in fact, they are signs of a speaker speaking a different dialect. Because of various historical reasons (essentially, the history of discrimination against African-Americans), the AAVE dialect is considered less prestigious than other dialects; therefore, speakers will associate negative impressions, such as those noted previously, with it. In other words, the dialect a speaker uses marks him or her socially. This is why the use of a particular dialect (or some features of a dialect) may be used as a social shibboleth.

What are then the most egregious examples of prescriptivism? The following are some examples that you may have unwittingly been exposed to.

Double Negatives

The double negative " rule" was invented by Robert Lowth, a British priest, who eventually became the bishop of London. In his book, *Short Introduction to English Grammar* (1762), he states the rule that two negatives affirm *(I am not unaware = I am aware)*; see 18.1 for more information. Lowth didn't like the fact that English, a Germanic language, didn't look like Latin, which was considered the most clear and logical language.

The "rule" that two negatives equal a positive is not true. English has always had double negatives. Lowth's grammar enjoyed enormous success, but even still, his rule never made it past written English. Double and triple negatives are found in spoken English, but they are not tolerated in written English, which is typically more formal.

On occasion, even in written English, we use double negatives that do not affirm. The sentence *He couldn't sleep, even with a sedative* has the same meaning as *He couldn't sleep, not even with a sedative.* In the second sentence, the second *not* reinforces the first. In other words, we use two negatives and the sentence does not affirm, thus showing that Lowth's rule does not always work.

In some cases, Lowth's rule must be broken to obtain a grammatically correct sentence. If the sentence *No one thought so, not even you* is changed to read *No one thought so, even you,* it creates a weird sentence. The two negatives are necessary for the sentence to be correct, and yet the two negations do not affirm.

In essence, the double negative rule doesn't make sense historically, and it doesn't always apply where it should. Rather, this rule is an issue of social class and good manners. If you follow this rule, you belong to the "educated" people.

Split Infinitives

The traditional rule concerning **split infinitives** states that one should not put something between the *to* and the rest of the verb in an infinitive; in other words, don't split the infinitive. If we try to change the sentence *I have tried to consciously stop worrying about it* to make it follow this rule, we would change the meaning of the sentence: *I have tried to stop consciously worrying about it,* or *I have consciously tried to stop worrying about it.* The rule and the sentence can't both be right; therefore, we must split infinitives in some cases when necessary.

Split infinitives are also used by careful writers for special stylistic effects. Witness the following quote:
"(...) when I split an infinitive, G*d damn it, I split it so it will stay split, (...) this is done with the eyes wide open and the mind relaxed but attentive."
Raymond Chandler *Letter* (in MacShane 1981).

Postponed Prepositions

A question such as *What are you looking at?* comes from a statement having the rough form of *You are looking at what.* If the indirect or direct object is moved to the beginning of the sentence to form a WH-question, a preposition ends up being left at the end of the sentence, hence the term **postponed preposition.**

WH-questions, relative clauses, and exclamations *(What a fine mess you've gotten us into!)* will always have postponed prepositions; there's no way to avoid them. Sometimes using the passive voice can also result in sentences that end with a preposition, for example, *She was sought after.*

Infinitive clauses are also difficult to change. Consider the sentence *He's impossible to work with.* Where could one move *with* to make it "grammatically" correct, short of changing the sentence altogether? Note that if you reword the sentence as *It is impossible to work with him,* you are shifting the emphasis from *he* to *impossible.*

> "This is the sort of English up with which I will not put."
> *Winston Churchill*

Language Planning

Not all prescriptivism is wrong headed, though; for example, language planning may have positive effects. **Language planning** is when the government (or any other public body) decides which languages will be taught in schools, what languages public employees must know, etc. The revival of biblical Hebrew in modern Israel is one example of when language planning has been used. Biblical Hebrew had been a dead language for centuries, but with the new Israeli state underway, the government needed to decide upon a language. They chose Hebrew for various religious and political reasons. Among the other contenders were Yiddish and English, both spoken by many people. Naturally, the speakers have had to invent many new words that were not in the Bible (e.g., telephone). Other examples of language planning are the campaign against sexist language (see Chapter 10) and government and school board decisions about which languages should be used for instruction, which books, and so on. More discussion of language planning may be found in Chapter 9.

1.2.2 Diachronic vs. Synchronic

There are two views as to what linguistics can have as its focus.

- **Diachronic (historical) view**

  - It studies how language changes through time.

  - It traces a word back to its origins (**etymology**).

  - It reconstructs languages that are no longer spoken, by comparing several languages that descend from them (this is known as the comparative method; see 17.6.1).

- **Synchronic view**

  - It describes how language works for us today or at any given moment in time. For example, we might study classical Latin, how Latin was spoken roughly between the first century B.C. and the first century A.D., synchronically. Once we start looking at how Latin changed, our view becomes diachronic.

  - It is not concerned with the origin of words or languages.

The distinction between synchronic and diachronic approaches is not absolute. There are points that overlap: in each generation new words are created, or already existing words change their meaning, and speakers perceive them as **neologisms** or new words. At the same time, old words die out as they are no longer used (i.e., they become **archaisms**) and eventually are no longer understood and are forgotten (see Chapter 17). Clearly, in order to label a word as a neologism or an archaism, one must refer to the diachronic aspect of language, even when one is describing language synchronically.

1.2.3 Competence vs. Performance

In the past, linguistics was primarily concerned with the diachronic approach. Today, the study of language is no longer considered a purely historical task. Most of linguistic study is synchronic. There are two ways of looking at language synchronically: we can look at the actual sentences that a speaker says (or writes or signs) or maybe that a number of speakers say or write or sign. This is what **corpus linguistics** does, for example. Or we can try to abstract away from the actual production of any given speaker at any given time and try to describe the speaker's knowledge about his or her language. This is what the opposition of **competence** and **performance** tries to achieve.

- **Competence**

  1. The ability to produce a word (or sentence)

  2. What you know about a word (or sentence)

- **Performance**

  1. Actually saying the word (or sentence)

  2. The sounds you articulate and make

So, **competence** is what speakers know when they know how to speak a language, whereas **performance** is what speakers actually do. Note that competence is *not* what speakers know *about* their language (e.g., that English is spoken in England and that it used to be called Anglo-Saxon, among other facts) but rather the skills that they have acquired, without having an explicit understanding of what they know. Recently, competence has been referred to as **i-language** (for internalized language, which is language that the speakers have in their brains) and performance as **e-language** (for externalized language, which is spoken, written, or signed language).

> Think of riding a bicycle: could you describe how you do it? It's harder than you may think. Try to do so.

Some linguists say that only competence is important. This is somewhat overstated. Competence is the idealization of performance. The competence of a speaker is his or her performance not affected by such factors as fatigue, the need to eat, or other such problems. Stuttering is a performance problem, not a competence problem. Slurring words when drunk is another performance problem.

What does the competence/performance distinction do for us? Let's look at some examples. Can a sentence be infinite? Performance wise, no. (You'd eventually die!) Competence wise, yes. You could always come up with different clauses and adjectives to continue a sentence. For example:

(1.1) The man who I met yesterday at the party where I was invited by the woman who...

Consider the following sentence. Do you think it is a good sentence, one you would use, given the right circumstances?

(1.2) The mouse the cat the boy loved chased died

Chances are your answer was "no." That is fine. Consider now how (1.2) was produced: we take the sentence, *The mouse died,* then we embed (put) a sentence in it and that gives us

(1.3) The mouse [the cat chased] died

which is perfectly fine. We then embed another sentence inside the embedded sentence and get

(1.4) The mouse [the cat (the boy loved) chased] died

In other words, by applying a perfectly good grammatical rule (you can embed a sentence in the middle of another sentence) we end up with a sentence that is clearly at odds with our intuition of what is acceptable. The reason is that our brains are incapable of handling that much information. We are waiting for the first sentence to conclude, and instead we keep opening new sentences. After a while our brain simply shuts off and gives up on the sentence. This is a performance problem, not a competence one. Using paper and pencil we can demonstrate that the sentence (1.2) is perfectly grammatical. Aliens with better brains would have no problem handling these kinds of sentences.

1.2.4 Linguistics as a Science

We began our presentation with the claim that linguistics is the science that studies language. Another way to express this is to say that linguistics is the scientific study of language. This means that linguists need to follow certain procedures to make sure that their conclusions are appropriate. This is the **scientific method.** Essentially, this consists of formulating a hypothesis on the basis of the available data and then checking the validity of the hypothesis against new data. If the data do not match the hypothesis, the hypothesis is proven wrong and the linguist will need to formulate a new hypothesis. This implies that a theory can never be proven right but that it can be proven wrong any time a new observation (a new datum) contradicts it. This is called the **principle of falsification.**

Consider the following example. On the basis of the following data, a linguist is trying to formulate a hypothesis on how questions are formed in English:

(1.5) Does Mary love John? / Mary loves John.

(1.6) Did Mary meet John? / Mary met John.

(1.7) Do you want more coffee? / You want more coffee.

On the basis of these data, the linguist could produce the hypothesis that to make a question in English it is necessary to put the auxiliary *do* at the beginning of the sentence, in the right tense and person, and change the main verb of the sentence to the bare infinitive form. However, the next piece of data the linguist encounters is the following:

(1.8) Is Mary a well-known woman? / Mary is a well-known woman.

This example clearly does not follow the previous hypothesis (there is no *do* at the beginning of the sentence and the verb has been moved and not put in the infinitive) and thus falsifies it. The linguist will then have to formulate a new hypothesis on how questions are formed that will take into account the new data.

> Try to work out a better hypothesis for making questions in English.

Educational Implications

This chapter has provided some tools for teachers to think about the relationship of school to language. Children come to school with nearly complete competence in one or more languages. The purpose of school is to teach one or more standard languages and literacy. Differences between home and school languages or dialects, if any, reflect social processes.

1.3 EXERCISES

1.3.1 Words to Know

prescriptive	descriptive	double negative
split infinitive	postponed preposition	diachronic
synchronic	competence	performance
corpus linguistics	principle of falsification	i-language
e-language	neologism	archaism
scientific method	language planning	

1.3.2 Review

1. Identify the difference between prescriptive and descriptive approaches to language.

2. How do the diachronic and synchronic views of language differ?

3. Identify how competence differs from performance.

4. How is linguistics a science?

1.3.3 Research Projects

1. Compile some statements of prescriptivism and descriptivism in language. Good sources for prescriptivist claims are works by William Safire (1980) and John Simon (1980). Good sources

favoring descriptivism are works by Jim Quinn (1980) and Steven Pinker (1994).

2. In a dictionary with etymologies, or in Ullman (1957), find some words that have changed in meaning over the years.

3. Read and summarize Saussure (1916) on *langue* and *parole*.

4. Read Quinn (1980). Find the most amusing example of a wrong-headed claim by a prescriptivist and prepare a presentation for your class.

5. Do you recall any experience in which you were taught a rule that now you see makes no sense? How do you feel about it? Write a short essay documenting your experience and share it with your classmates/colleagues.

1.4 FURTHER READINGS

The reader may find dictionaries of linguistics useful. Among the best are Matthews (1997), with broad coverage and clear explanations; Richards, Platt, and Weber (1992) oriented toward applied linguistics; Trudgill (2001) on sociolinguistics; and Crystal's text (1997), in its fifth edition, oriented toward theoretical linguistics. Bussman (1983) has finally been translated in English (1996). Ducrot and Todorov's (1972; translated 1979) work is a bit older but also of interest. Two massive encyclopedias are available for further research: Bright (1992), published in its second edition as Frawley (2003), in four volumes and Asher (1994) in ten volumes. These require serious effort. Crystal's one volume *The Cambridge Encyclopedia of Language* (1997) is very accessible, user friendly, and packed with interesting tidbits. Spolsky (1999) is good for educational linguistics issues.

Etymological issues can be addressed with the *Oxford English Dictionary,* which any serious research library should carry. *Webster's* current edition also lists etymologies of words and is more accessible for homework. A good source is also McArthur's (1992) *Oxford Companion to the English Language,* also available in a more compact edition (McArthur and McArthur 1996).

General introductions to the subfields of linguistics can be found in Bolinger and Sears (1981); Fromkin, Rodman, and Hyams (2002); O'Grady, Dobrovolsky, and Aronoff (1997); Akmajian et al. (2001); Aitchison (1992); Hudson (2000); and Stewart and Vaillette (2001).

Classical introductions to the field are Bloomfield (1933), Sapir (1921), Saussure (1916), and Martinet (1966).

On prescriptivism, see Hall (1960), which offers a "militant" discussion of the linguistic reasons against prescriptivism. The spirit of the book is best summed in the original title *Leave Your Language Alone.* Another great source on prescriptivism is Quinn (1980). On the history of linguistics, a short introduction is Robins (1997). On historical linguistics, a good reference work is Hock (1991). On linguistics as a science, the only book-length treatment is Botha (1981), which is not for beginners.

Chapter 2

The Building Blocks of Language

2.1 OVERVIEW

This chapter will introduce the basic tools of linguistic analysis. We use language in order to communicate with others all the time, without thinking about it. However, the fact that using language is such a natural thing does not mean that it is a simple and straightforward matter. Think of the skills required in playing the violin. A good player makes it look very easy, but in fact it is a very complex activity. So is language. It is only because each of us has been using language in one way or another since right after we were born that we fall under the impression that language use is simple and uncomplicated.

Traditionally, linguists describe a language starting with the smallest units (the sounds) and move up building larger and larger units (words, sentences, paragraphs, complete texts). We will follow this organization here as well.

2.2 THE SOUNDS OF LANGUAGE

At the simplest of levels, language is made of sounds. In other words, we communicate using sounds that somehow carry meanings. How this is accomplished is fairly complex. We will start by looking at how we produce these sounds. **Phonetics** deals with the sounds of a language, in a physical sense. Sound is the motion of air in waves. When we speak, we move the air inside and around the mouth and the waves of the movement spread in the air.

Sounds have four components:

- quality or timbre (the frequency of the vibration of the sound waves, what makes an "a" different from an "o")

- volume (how loud the sound is)

- length (how long the sound lasts)

- pitch or tone (high or low)

We will study phonetics using an articulatory view, which looks at how sounds are produced by our body organs, as opposed to an acoustic approach, which describes the way the sound waves actually look. By articulatory description, we mean the movements made by the phonatory organs to produce the sound waves.

2.2.1 The Phonetic Alphabet

> Take a minute to make an estimate. How many sounds do you think there are in English? Pick one sound and try to describe it.

The **International Phonetic Alphabet** or **IPA** (see Figures 2.1 and 2.2) is used by linguists to represent the sounds in the languages of the world. The English sound system is listed in Figures 2.1 and 2.2. Do not worry about the articulatory descriptions; they will be explained in what follows.

Traditionally in linguistics, spoken language has been considered the language and writing a derived, secondary way to represent (imperfectly, at that) spoken language. Many sophisticated and fully developed cultures never invented writing (on writing, see Chapter 11). Spelling may have very little to do with the pronunciation of a word: for example, *through* is pronounced [θru] and *laugh* is pronounced [laf], although they both end with "gh." Note that sounds transcribed in the phonetic alphabet are always surrounded by square brackets. This is a convention followed by linguists all over the world.

We have used the American symbols for ž, š, ǰ, and č, but it is necessary to remember that the IPA symbols for the same sounds are respectively ʒ, ʃ, dʒ, and tʃ. Where two characters are given, the rightmost is the received IPA character, while the leftmost is the usual American symbol. We use [r] for simplicity, but technically it should be [ɹ].

Figure 2.1: The International Phonetic Alphabet: English Consonants

Symbol	Manner of Articulation	Examples
[p]	bilabial voiceless stop	pit, sip, apple
[b]	bilabial voiced stop	bit, sob, about
[t]	alveolar voiceless stop	tap, sot, about
[d]	alveolar voiced stop	dip, sod, adult
[k]	velar voiceless stop	car, tack, acorn
[g]	velar voiced stop	go, log, agog
[ʔ]	glottal voiceless stop	button, mutton
[f]	labiodental voiceless fricative	fluff, rough, ruffian
[v]	labiodental voiced fricative	vest, love, lover
[θ]	interdental voiceless fricative	thin, death, ether
[ð]	interdental voiced fricative	then, rhythm
[s]	alveolar voiceless fricative	snake, bass, decent
[z]	alveolar voiced fricative	zoo, roses
[š] [ʃ]	palatal voiceless fricative	shell, rush, ashes
[ž] [ʒ]	palatal voiced fricative	jejune, rouge, closure
[h]	glottal voiceless fricative	have, hill, house
[č] [tʃ]	palatal voiceless affricate	child, reach, hatchet
[ǰ] [dʒ]	palatal voiced affricate	judge, ridge
[m]	bilabial voiced nasal	man, mom, lamp
[n]	alveolar voiced nasal	nasty, run, ant
[ŋ]	velar voiced nasal	hanger, ringing
[l]	alveolar voiced (lateral) liquid	love, hill, plate
[r]	alveolar voiced liquid	ring, floor, crow
[w]	bilabial voiced glide	wood, awash
[y]	palatal voiced glide	young, canyon

A Chart of the English Consonants

	Bilabial	Labiodental	Interdental	Alveolar	Palatal	Velar	Glottal
Stops	[p] [b]			[t] [d]		[k] [g]	[ʔ]
Fricatives		[f] [v]	[θ] [ð]	[s] [z]	[š] [ž]		[h]
Affricates					[č] [ǰ]		
Nasals	[m]			[n]		[ŋ]	
Liquids				[l] [r]			
Glides	[w]				[y]		

Figure 2.2: The International Phonetic Alphabet: English Vowels

Symbol	Articulation	Example
[i]	front high tense	beat, feet
[ɪ]	front high lax	bit, pit
[e]	front mid tense	day, pey
[ɛ]	front mid lax	pet, net
[æ]	front low lax	cat, mat
[u]	back high tense	loot, you
[ʊ]	back high lax	put, foot
[ʌ]	central mid lax	but, mutt, bus (stressed)
[ə]	central mid lax	sofa, a, the (unstressed)
[o]	back mid tense	row, low
[ɔ]	back mid lax	cop, not
[a]	back low lax	pasta, father

The sound called **schwa** [ə] is the sound that is produced when the muscles in the mouth are relaxed and the tongue is in a central position. When a vowel is not stressed in English it becomes a schwa; thus, in *about* the [a] at the beginning is pronounced [ə] as in *the, but, among.* But what happens if the schwa sound is stressed? Then it's pronounced lower and further back than the schwa and is transcribed with the symbol [ʌ], known as a **wedge.** This is the sound in *bus* or *but* pronounced in isolation.

Note that your pronunciation of the vowel sounds of English may be very different from the examples chosen here and even from that of your instructor. The issue here is one of geographical variation (and will be dealt with in more detail in Chapter 5). To put it concisely, people from different areas where English is spoken pronounce certain sounds differently. For example, in America, there are two varieties of English that are distinguished by the loss of distinction between the sound [a] and the sound [ɔ] so that the words *cop* and *father* are pronounced with the same first vowel sound: [kɔp], [fɔθə]. The area where this is the case includes the western United States, some areas of the Midwest, and Canada. The following chart reflects what is called Northern Inland pronunciation. If your variety of English differs from this one, you will want to adjust the examples accordingly.

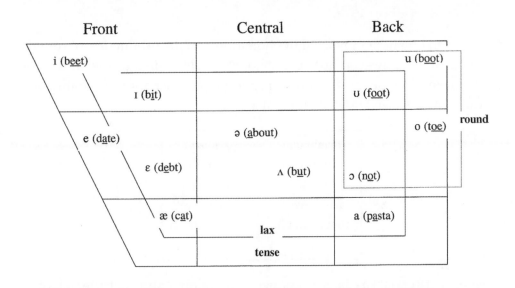

Diphthongs

The following three sounds are **diphthongs**, i.e., a vowel followed by either [y] or [w] (a **glide**). Diphthongs can be considered as one vowel. This way of marking glides is used in the American tradition. An alternative notation, used by the IPA, is to mark diphthongs as [oi], [ai], etc.

[oy]	*boy, toy*
[ay]	*buy, bye*
[aw]	*bow, now*
[ey]	*bait, gay*
[ow]	*goat, boat*
[uy]	*buoy, gooey*

2.2.2 How Are the Sounds Produced in the Mouth?

Articulatory Phonetics

Eleven organs are involved in phonation, i.e., the production of sounds for speaking; however, note that phonation also refers to the activity of the larynx (see below and on p. 19), a potentially confusing ambiguity! These organs (see Figs. 2.3 and 2.4) are:

diaphragm	lungs
trachea	larynx
velum	uvula
nasal cavity	tongue
roof of mouth	teeth
lips	

Note that the larynx is also known as the glottis and that the velum is the soft part that opens and closes the nasal cavity. None of these organs originated as speech organs. For example, the function of teeth is that of chewing our food; however, they are also used in speaking. Since the time that our ancestors started speaking, we have developed several speaking-specific muscles, which are shown in Figure 2.3.

Figure 2.3: The Vocal Tract

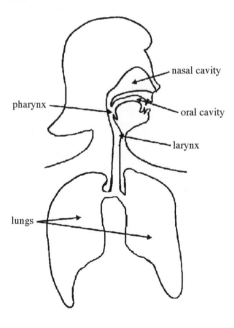

Figure 2.4: Main Places of Articulation

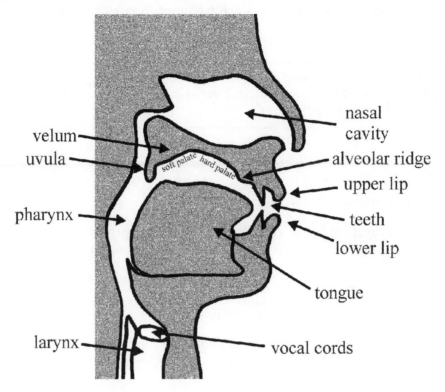

There are four processes by which we produce sound:

1. airstream

2. phonation

3. nasalization

4. articulation

Airstream

The **airstream** includes lungs, diaphragm, and trachea. Most speech sounds are produced with the airstream; this is the case for all the sounds of English. The flow of air in the **vocal tract** may be interrupted or restricted in the process of articulation (see the following section); this is referred to as occlusion or obstruction (partial occlusion). Not all sounds are produced with the airstream (e.g., **clicks**). To produce clicks, a temporary chamber of resonance is created in the mouth, and then the occlusion (obstruction) is released. Examples are *tsk! tsk!* or the sound of kissing. Clicks are frequent in African and Australian languages.

The film *The Gods Must Be Crazy* features a speaker of a clicks-rich language. Rent the movie (which is very funny) and pay attention to the speech of the main character.

Phonation

Phonation analyzes what the larynx is doing:

- open vocal cords (no vibration) = **voiceless sound**

- vibrating vocal cords = **voiced sound** (vibration = very fast opening and closing)

- small opening in the back = whisper

- closed = glottal stop (the sound between the two "a's" in *aha!*)

Nasalization

The nasal cavity may or may not be involved in the phonation process. This is determined by the opening or closing of the **velum** (aka soft palate). If the velum is closed, no air flows through the nose; if the velum is open (lowered), then air flows through the nose, producing **nasalization.**

If we have an open velum, we produce the three nasalized sounds in English [m, n, ŋ]. If we have a closed velum, we produce non-nasalized stops [p/b, t/d, k/g]. All nasals are voiced in English. Notice that nasals are continuants. Other languages (e.g., French, Polish, Portuguese) have nasalized vowels [ã, ẽ, õ], marked by the superimposed tilda ~.

Articulation

Articulation is the modification of the sounds produced by the other three processes. It deals with the way the tongue, lips, and teeth are positioned (see Fig. 2.4).

There are three types of articulations in the vocal tract

- **Vowels:** no obstruction, air flows freely through the vocal tract

- **Stops:** complete obstruction somewhere along the vocal tract, for example, [p] in *puck*

- **Fricatives** (which are continuants or sounds that can be pronounced continuously): here there is a partial occlusion; air rubs against the walls of the vocal tract and the sound waves are broken up, which produces the characteristic "hissing" sound of fricatives, for example, [s], [z]

Each sound can fit only into one type of articulation—i.e., if [p] is a stop, it is not at the same time a fricative.

Where do these **occlusions** (or obstructions) take place? Note that these places of articulation work for both stops and fricatives.

- Bilabial: putting your lips together

- Labio-dental: putting your lower lip and upper teeth together

- Tongue

  - Tip

    - interdental: placing tip of tongue between teeth

    - dental: placing tip of tongue against upper teeth

    - alveolar: placing tongue slightly higher than the dental region (the gums)

  - Body: the body of the tongue articulates against the palate
    - alveopalatal

    - palatal—hard palate

    - velar—soft palate

    - uvular—back of tongue against uvula

  - Pharyngeal: creating an occlusion using the back of the tongue and the upper pharynx

- Glottal: closure or narrowing of the space between the vocal cords

Glides, Affricates, and Liquids

We now turn to three small classes of sounds that are slightly more complex.

Glides

Glides are articulated as [i] and [u] but with the tongue higher. In English, glides occur after long vowels, e.g., [gluw] = *glue*, and in diphthongs.

Affricates

Affricates are articulated like stops but the release of the occlusion is slow, not sudden. An affricate begins as a stop but is released as a fricative, e.g., [čərč] = *church*.

Liquids

Liquids are also produced by a partial occlusion of the vocal tract, but the occlusion, unlike with stops or fricatives, is neither complete nor narrow enough to cause friction of the airflow. [l] is called a lateral liquid because it is produced by laying the tongue flat in the mouth, with the tip in the alveolar region and the sides (hence, lateral) of the tongue raised. The airflow escapes from both sides of the tongue. [r] is a very complex sound; there are several varieties of [r]. In the United States, most [r] sounds are pronounced with the tongue in the alveolar region and with the tip of the tongue bent backwards (retroflex). Other pronunciations of [r] include the uvular [r] of French. All English liquids are voiced.

Suprasegmentals

So far, we have considered the segmental aspects of sound. Now we will look at the **suprasegmental** aspects, at units beyond individual sounds. In English, we are familiar with stress and intonation. Stress is found at the syllable level and is sometimes called accent. In a word, the loudest syllable, the one said with the most energy, is stressed. English stress is unpredictable, for the most part, and must be learned with each new word. Other languages have predictable stress. Czech stresses the first syllable of each word. Welsh stresses the next-to-last syllable. But stress also plays a part in meaning within sentences. Consider the sentence *I didn't go to the store.* Depending on which word you stress, you can deny it was you who went to the store, you could deny going to the store, or you could deny it was the store you went to.

Intonation refers to the rise and fall of sentences. In English, statements and WH-questions fall at the end. Yes/no questions rise. Choice questions *(Would you like coffee or tea?)* rise and then fall.

A number of languages in the world rely on **tones** to differentiate meaning. The most famous example is probably the word *ma* in Mandarin Chinese. Said with a high level tone, it means *mother.* With a high-rising tone, it means *hemp.* A falling-then-rising tone signals the meaning *horse. Ma* said with a high-falling tone is the word *scold.* Of course, context within the sentence provides meaning. In written language, the Chinese character for each word is different, so the reader immediately understands.

The last unit of suprasegmental information we will consider is **length.** In the Italian phrase *una rosa rossa* (a red rose), *rosa* (rose) sounds different from *rossa* (red, feminine). These lengthenings are almost impossible for a native speaker of English to hear because such a process has no meaning in our language.

2.2.3 Sounds and Meaning

Consider the fact that different people pronounce the "same" sound differently; for example, a man and a woman will pronounce the word *dog* differently: a man usually has a deeper, lower voice, whereas a woman usually has a higher-pitched voice (the differences depend on the size of their phonatory organs). Often a very short sample of language *(It's me)* is sufficient for people to recognize a speaker, which tells us that the differences are noticeable. And yet the same speaker will pronounce the same word differently if stressed or sad. How can we say then that the sound at the beginning of the word *dog* is the same sound at the end of *road*?

The answer to this question lies in the concept of phoneme. People have in their minds a mental image of the sound [d]. This mental image of a sound is called a **phoneme.** A useful analogy is the score of a musical piece: different musicians will all play a given concerto differently and yet they all played that particular piece of music. Exactly in the same way, no two productions of the phoneme /d/ will be exactly alike, and yet we recognize that they are examples of /d/. Note that phonemes are written between slashes, to distinguish them from sounds.

Take, for example, the sound [p]. Do you recall the articulatory description of [p]? It is produced by blocking the flow of air from the lungs by closing the lips. When the airflow is released (by opening the lips again) and the vocal folds are still, we articulate a [p] sound. When it is pronounced at the beginning of a word and followed by a vowel (such as in *pit*), it is actually followed by a puff of air. This is called an **aspirated** [pʰ]. When a [p] sound occurs at the end of a word (such as in *tip*), it is articulated without releasing the airflow at all (this is called an **unreleased** [p]). In other words, [p] at the beginning of a word sounds different than a [p] in the middle of a word or at the end. And yet you probably never realized that you pronounced these sounds differently.

All the ways that a given phoneme is articulated are called **allophones.** So, the unreleased [p] and the aspirated one are both allophones of the phoneme /p/.

Another example involves the sound [t]. When it occurs between vowels, such as in *butter* or *Betty,* it is in fact pronounced as a short tap of the tongue against the alveolar region. This is transcribed as [ɾ] and is known as a "tap" (also as a flap, sometimes transcribed as [D]). Both [t] and [ɾ] are allophones of /t/.

Your brain recognizes phonemes by matching the allophones it actually hears (sounds) to mental images of sounds (phonemes) and then compensating for the differences.

However, we can look at phonemes from a different point of view. Thus there are two received definitions of *phoneme:*

> • Psychological: a phoneme is the mental representation of a sound.
> • Distinctive: a phoneme is the smallest unit of language that helps distinguish meaning.

We have examined the first definition. Let us focus now on the second one. The "smallest" part of the definition is not problematic. When you hear a speaker talk, you hear a long chain of different sounds one after the other. If you start cutting the chain in pieces at some point you will have to stop, because there's nothing left to cut: that is the smallest unit. For example, [ðədɔg] *(the dog)* can be segmented as [ðə] and [dɔg]; these can be further segmented as [ð], [ə] and [d],[ɔ],[g], respectively. After this, there's nothing left to segment. We have reached the smallest units of language.

Let us turn to the "distinctive" part of the definition. By distinctive we mean that the unit identified through segmentation must convey a difference in meaning. Note that we did not say that the units must have meaning but that they must cause a difference in meaning. The two are quite different claims. Clearly, [g] has no meaning. However, [dɔg] *(dog)* and [dɔk] *(dock,* or *doc,* short for *doctor)* differ in meaning. Thus, the presence of a [g] or a [k] at the end of the string [dɔ] is meaningful, in the sense that it conveys a difference in meaning.

Two words such as [dɔk] and [dɔg] are a **minimal pair.** A minimal pair is two words of different meaning that differ in only one phoneme, e.g., /bit/ and /pit/. Note that the definition of minimal pair is a twofold one:

- two words with different meanings

- that differ in one sound

So, *pit* and *bit* are a minimal pair because the two words differ in meaning and in one sound. How about [pit] and [pʰit]? Here, while the two words differ in one sound, they do not differ in meaning in English, which makes them a challenge for nonnative speakers (see 13.1). Hence, these are *not* a minimal pair (again, in English). In other languages, aspirated [pʰ] and unreleased [p] may well cause a difference in meaning so that [pit] and [pʰit] would be two different words, a minimal pair. Minimal pairs are very important, because they allow us to identify the phonemes of a language. If we find a minimal pair in the words of a language, we know that the two sounds involved in the minimal pair are the allophones of two different phonemes. So, in the previous example, since *dock* and *dog* are a minimal pair in English, it follows that /g/ and /k/ are phonemes in English. On minimal pairs in second language learning, see 13.1.

2.3 WORDS AND THEIR PARTS

If we combine phonemes we get a larger unit, called a **morpheme.** For example, if we put together the phonemes /d/, /ɔ/, and /g/, we get the morpheme /dɔg/ spelled *dog*. Note that morphemes are written between slashes, like phonemes.

Recall the definition of phonemes as the smallest distinctive units in language. An important aspect of their nature is that they have no meaning: a sound has no meaning in and of itself. On the contrary, morphemes have meanings. *Cat* means something, for example.

> Definition of **morpheme:**
> The smallest unit of language with a distinct meaning.

2.3.1 Morphemes and Words

So a morpheme can be /kæt/ *cat* but also /putɔf/ *put off* and /-z/ as in *dogs* (i.e., it marks the plurality of the dogs, meaning there's more than one dog). We notice immediately that morphemes may or may not coincide with what we think of as words.

The term "word" is not a technical term of linguistics. Usually by word we mean any sequence of letters divided by blank spaces. Thus in the sentence

(2.1) Mary has two dogs

we would say that there are four words. However, there are a number of problems: to begin with, *dogs* is two morphemes (/dɔg/+/-z/); on the other hand, as we saw previously, there are "words" that consist of more than one "word" *(put off, do away with, fly off the handle):* these are called phrasal verbs and idioms (see 2.3.6). Thus, in order to avoid these problems, linguists have decided to use the word **morpheme** to indicate any unit of meaning that cannot be broken down any further (think of them as "semantic atoms") and to use the word **lexeme** to indicate any entry in the lexicon (the vocabulary) of a speaker/language. Lexemes may be plurimorphemic (i.e., have more than one morpheme). The following section deals with the classification of morphemes.

2.3.2 Free vs. Bound Morphemes

Free morphemes can appear alone. Take for example the morpheme /cat/ (for simplicity, we will not use the IPA transcription of morphemes, unless significant); we can find this morpheme used independently in speech. Consider now the following words:

cat   -s

carriage   -s

despot   -s

criminal   -s

elephant   -s

/cat/, /carriage/, /despot/, /criminal/, and /elephant/ are all free morphemes. They can occur alone in discourse. This is not true for the /-s/ morpheme. This morpheme marks PLURALITY. Note that semantic features will appear in capital letters. PLURALITY means that there is more than one cat, dog, and so on. However, the PLURALITY morpheme cannot show up alone in speech or writing; thus it is called a **bound morpheme.** Free morphemes are often called **root morphemes** or **stems.** Bound morphemes are called **affixes** because they need to attach to another morpheme.

2.3.3 Affixes

Affixes are classified according to their position. If they come before the root, they are called **prefixes;** if they occur after the root, they are called **suffixes.** If they attach in the middle of a word, they are called **infixes.** The following chart gives you some examples:

prefixes	infixes	suffixes
un-believable	a-*whole*-nother	proud-*ly*
in-credible	un-*f**king*-believable	love-*s*
super-ordinate		walk-*ed*

Infixes are very rare in English but extremely common in other languages. Tagalog, spoken in the Philippines, uses *-um-* as an infix to indicate the infinitive of the verb: *kuha = take; k-um-uha = to take.*

2.3.4 Inflectional vs. Derivational

Some morphemes can be used to create new words from old ones; they are called **derivational morphemes.** For example, the name for the person who performs an action (agent) is often formed with the "agentive" derivational morpheme *-er* as in

(2.2) to buy → buy*er*

to sell → sell*er*

On the other hand, **inflectional morphemes** simply mark such grammatical categories as PLURALITY, TENSE (past, continuous present), comparatives *(tall-er)*, superlatives *(tall-est)*, and THIRD PERSON SINGULAR *(walk-s)*.

The principal differences between derivational and inflectional morphemes are as follows.

- **Derivational morphemes**

  - Derivationals change the meaning of the word, or change the word's part of speech.

  (2.3) adjectives → adverbs (e.g., *quick-ly*)

  - Syntax does not require the presence of derivationals. They are optional, whereas inflectionals are required by rules (see the following section on inflectional morphemes).

  - Individually, derivationals are less productive. You cannot attach them to as many words as inflectional morphemes. *Example:* *-hood,* as in *childhood, adulthood,* as opposed to /-s/. Note the dash (-), which means that the morpheme cannot appear by itself, i.e., it is a bound morpheme. Thus one should not confuse it with the free morpheme *hood,* as in *the hood of the car.*

  - In English, derivationals are located closest to the root.

  - In English, they can be either prefixes or suffixes.

- **Inflectional morphemes**

  - They do not make a significant meaning change in a word or change the word's part of speech.

  - They are required by syntax.
    Example: Mary eats lunch. The /-s/ marker for the THIRD PERSON SINGULAR is required by a grammatical rule.

  - They are very productive. You can attach them to several words. *Example*: The morpheme for PLURALITY in English (/-s/) can attach to virtually all nouns (with very few exceptions, such as irregular nouns like *ox, goose, woman, man*).

  - In English, they are located after derivational morphemes, farthest from the root.

  - In English, they are suffixes only.

Inflectional morphemes carry meaning, just like roots. Read the beginning of *Jabberwocky*.

Jabberwocky by Lewis Carroll

'Twas brillig, and the slithey toves
Did gyre and gimble in the wabe:
All mimsy were the borogroves,
And the mome raths outgrabe.
"Beware the Jabberwock, my son!
The jaws that bite, the claws that catch!

Just like Alice, you probably cannot figure out what the poem is about. However, take a word like *slithey;* we can tell that it is an adjective by its *-y* ending (as well as its position close to a noun). This means that whatever *slith* may be, the *tove* has that quality (naturally, that leaves an open question, namely, what is a *tove?*).

2.3.5 Where Do New Words Come From?

The English language has roughly 500,000 words, but new words are being invented every day to match the ever-changing needs of the speakers, such as the new words required by the rising importance of computers in our lives. Derivational morphemes are only one way to get new words from old ones. The following are some of the ways that speakers can create new words in English.

Derivation

New words can be created by using derivational morphemes. For example, after we invented the fax machine, we needed a verb to describe the action of *faxing*—hence, *to fax.*

Compounding

Another technique is that of putting two old words together to make a new one, e.g., *railway, department store.*

Clipping

New words can be constructed by shortening a longer word, e.g., *(tele)phone, prof(essor), auto(mobile).*

Acronyms

A rich source of new words is the practice of using the initial letters of a set of words, e.g., *NAFTA, NASA, NFL, PTA, REM.* **Acronyms** are different from abbreviations in that acronyms use initial letters of words or parts of words. Abbreviations shorten the word, as in *amt* for *amount* or *pres* for *president.*

Blends

New words can also be created by the blending of two existing words, e.g., *motel (motor+hotel), brunch (breakfast+lunch).*

Backformation

New words are unconsciously created by speakers when they no longer analyze a word in its constituent morphemes and instead break it down according to the way it "looks." From the word *inflammable* came *flammable,* when people perceived *in-* as the NEGATION morpheme; from *swindler* came *swindle* (when the *-er* suffix was perceived as the agentive, i.e., the person doing the action); from *burglar* came *burgle.* This phenomenon is also known as **reanalysis.**

Other examples:

alcohol-ic →	alco-holic →	worka-holic, choco-holic
hamburg-er →	ham-burger →	cheese-burger, veggie-burger
entertain-ment →	enter-tainment →	info-tainment, edu-tainment
marathon →	mar-athon →	walk-athon, phon-athon

Invention

When speakers want, they can always invent new words from scratch (e.g., *googol*, meaning a very large number). This is often done in advertising, e.g., *Kodak, Xerox, Kleenex®*. Often words start out as proper nouns (e.g., *Kodak, Kleenex*) and end up being used as common nouns *(a xerox, a kleenex)*.

Borrowing

Languages in contact borrow words from each other. It may be that one language does not have a word for a new product or concept. Thus, when coffee became popular in Europe, the Arabic word *kawatin* was used in various forms: *coffee, cafe, Kaffee*, and so on. Japan in turn borrowed *kohi* from the European languages. Borrowing is a two-way street; English gave French *weekend* and took *bon vivant.* Japanese took *game* from English and gave it *sushi.* Indeed, Japanese is full of English loan words:

Japanese	English
keiki	cake
steiki	steak
boifurendo/garufurendo	boyfriend/girlfriend
basubaru	baseball

You will notice that a language typically changes the phonology of the borrowed word. Japanese does not allow syllables to end with a consonant (except in certain cases *n*). Therefore, borrowed words need to change to fit Japanese phonology and an [i] gets added to the ends of *cake* and *steak* and a [u] finds its way into the middle of *baseball.* This happens with any borrowing, not just those from English; *arubeito* was taken from German *arbeiter* to mean not just any worker but a part-time or temporary worker. "Regular" workers are *sarariman* from "salary men" and "OL" (office ladies).

Calque

A **calque** is a special kind of loan. In a calque, parts of words are translated. A good example is *Fernsprecher,* German for *telephone.* As *telephone* is taken from the Greek *tele* (distant) and *phone* (voice); *Fernsprecher* means *distant speaker.* Other examples are *big man* in Nigerian English (see 17.5.2) for an important person, which comes from Yoruba *enia nia* (big man); *bush meat* is Nigerian English for game, as opposed to poultry. It comes from the Akan phrase *ha nam* (bush meat).

2.3.6 Idioms and Phraseology

Some units of language span more than one "word" and thus cause all sorts of problems to lexicographers (dictionary writers). For example, *kick the bucket* means *die* but consists of three words, none of which has much to do with death. It turns out that **idioms,** i.e., multiword units the meaning of which is not the sum of its parts, are quite frequent, especially if we count as idioms most **phrasal verbs.** Phrasal verbs are verbs such as *put off, do away with, get on, start up,* and *deal with,* which are composed of a verb and a preposition or an adverb. Often their meaning is idiomatic or cannot be derived by the sum of its parts. See, for instance, *put up* as in *I won't put up with your excuses anymore!* where the meaning of *tolerate* cannot be derived from *put* and *up.* Other units that are often treated as idioms are stock phrases *(How are you?)* and proverbs *(A rolling stone gathers no moss).* A related topic is **collocations,** i.e., the way that two or more words are associated, such as *bread and butter, get away with murder, salt and pepper,* and *rock and roll.* On collocations, see also 3.1.3.

> What collocations can you think of? Make a list of collocations.

2.4 THE WAY SENTENCES ARE PUT TOGETHER

We now turn to considering the way sentences are put together. In a nutshell, sentences are formed by putting together morphemes of the right kind, in the right order. How this is done is the topic of this section.

2.4.1 The Double Articulation of Language

The **first articulation** of language is the breakdown of a sentence into morphemes; the **second articulation** is the breakdown of morphemes in phonemes.

The reason the two articulations of language are so important is that they allow us to express an infinite number of thoughts, in an infinite number of different sentences, with a finite and in fact quite small number of sounds. There are roughly 43 different sounds in English. If we had to have a different idea for each sound, we would need many thousands more sounds. That would make it very difficult to remember which sound goes with which idea. So using sounds, which are not associated with any given meaning, to make morphemes, which are given a meaning, is a pretty clever way of getting around that problem. But even that would not be sufficient for the purposes of communication. Consider the fact that every day we may produce sentences that we have never produced before. If we only had the second articulation of language, we would be stuck with however many morphemes we would have produced. By putting together morphemes to form sentences (first articulation), we acquire the power to produce an infinite number of sentences, capable of accommodating any needs for communication that might arise, now or at any time in the future. The double articulation of language is also called *duality* (see 16.1.1).

ALL THE GRAMMAR YOU NEED TO KNOW TO DIAGRAM SENTENCES

The purpose of this chart is to remind you of the basic notions of grammatical analysis that you will need in order to diagram sentences. A fuller treatment of English grammar will be found in Chapter 19.

PARTS OF SPEECH

Let us consider how to identify the parts of speech in English:

- Nouns can be recognized because they can be made plural (i.e., more than one) by adding an /-s/ morpheme to them (there are some exceptions: *mice, oxen, women, children, men*, etc.).

- Adjectives can be recognized because they may add the /-er/ and /-est/ morphemes to indicate the degree of a quality *(pretty, prettier, prettiest).* Adjectives modify (are attached) to nouns, as in "pretty (adj) girl(N)."

- Verbs may appear with tense markers: these are the third person singular present (/-s/), the past tense (/-ed/), and confusingly a zero (unmarked) morpheme:

  I walk = zero morpheme
  She walks = third person singular
  I walked = past tense

- Adverbs often, but not always, end in /-ly/ (e.g., *quickly*) and can modify verbs and adjectives but not nouns: "very(adv) smart(adj) girl(N)" "laughed(V) repeatedly(adv)."

- Prepositions (e.g., *on, with, by*) cannot be modified by any morpheme (so you can identify them by exclusion) and are listed in 19.4.5.

- Articles are also not modified but are easy to remember, because there are only two: *the* and *a/an* (note the two allomorphs: *a* before consonants, *an* before vowels).

- Finally, conjunctions are function words that connect two elements of a sentence (or two sentences) such as *and, or, but, so, either...or, neither... nor, because, although, if, that.* These too cannot be modified.

IDENTIFYING THE PREDICATE (MAIN, TENSED VERB)

You are now ready to analyze sentences. The fundamental distinction in sentences is that between the subject and the predicate. So, the first thing you should do is identify the main verb (aka tensed verb) of the sentence. This is relatively easy: a main verb carries tense morphological markers, as we saw.

Things are complicated by the presence of auxiliary verbs (*to do, to be, to have*; see a complete chart of their forms in 19.2.1) and modal verbs (*can, could, may, might, shall, should, will, would,* plus a few others, see 19.2.1) that may appear before a main verb. When they do, auxiliaries take the tense inflectional markers as in "Elvis *has* left the building" where *has* is marked for third person singular present. When a main verb appears with a modal, it appears in the bare infinitive form, and the modal is considered tensed: "Mary *will* defend her dissertation tomorrow." "Will" is the modal, indicating future time, and "defend" is the bare infinitive; an infinitive usually appears with a "to" before it (e.g., "To be or not to be.") and the bare infinitive is without the "to." A further complication is that some "irregular" verbs (aka strong verbs, see 17.2.2) such as *sing, put, choose*, etc., mark the past with other morphological markers than the /-ed/ morpheme (i.e., *sang, put, chose).*

PHRASAL CONSTITUENTS

The main tensed verb and all the rest of the sentence, excluding the subject, are the predicate of the sentence, aka the verb phrase (VP).

The subject of a sentence is the noun phrase (NP), which is the subject of the main verb of the sentence (i.e., the predicate). The subject is (usually, but not always) the entity doing the action described in the verb. An NP can consist of several parts (see 19.5.1) but must always have a noun in it. Unless a sentence has had some transformation applied to it, everything to the left of the tensed verb is usually an NP (except possibly an adverb modifying the verb).

NPs can be modified by prepositional phrases (PPs). VPs can be modified by PPs as well and also by adverbs. PPs consist of a preposition followed by an NP (there are other cases, as well, see 19.5.3). Adverb phrases (and adjective phrases) are more advanced, and we do not require you to diagram them at this level.

COORDINATION AND SUBORDINATION

Finally, conjunctions may connect two sentences (or two phrasal constituents, i.e., NPs, VPs, PPs). The nature of the connection may be either coordination or subordination. In either case, the presence of a second tensed verb should alert you to the presence of a subordinate or coordinate clause. See 19.6.1 for details, but let's point out that some subordinate clauses lack a main verb, so you cannot rely on that feature for identification.

2.4.2 Syntax

Putting together morphemes to form sentences is the area covered by **syntax.** Syntax is based on the idea of **grammaticality.** A sentence is said to be grammatical if the speakers of the language agree that it is a sentence that they would produce under the appropriate circumstances. Thus

(2.4) The book is on the table

will be accepted as grammatical by all speakers of English, while

(2.5) *Table the on is book

will not. Accordingly, the ungrammatical sentence is marked with an asterisk (*), which shows that the sentence is unacceptable. The goal of syntax is to describe all the grammatical sentences of English, or any other language, and show why the ungrammatical sentences aren't acceptable. By doing so, syntax eventually hopes to explain how people's capacity to use language works. Incidentally, the grammar of a language is the entire description of the language (from sounds to sentences, including meaning), not just its syntax, as some believe. Try not to confuse the grammar of a language and the grammaticality of sentences; grammaticality is only part of the overall grammar. If you feel you need a little help remembering basic English grammar, we offer Chapter 19.

You will probably recall sentence diagramming from high school. Syntax provides linguists with a similar, but more effective, tool. Consider

(2.6) Bob eats broccoli.

This sentence can be broken down into [Bob] and [eats broccoli]. These are called the sentence's **immediate constituents;** [eats broccoli] can be further broken down into [eats] and [broccoli]. In conclusion, [Bob], [eats], and [broccoli] are the **constituents** of our sentence. Consider now that the sentence could have been

(2.7) Bob eats his lunch.

In (2.7) the immediate constituent analysis gives [Bob] and [eats his lunch], which is further analyzable as [eats] and [his lunch]. The latter can be finally analyzed as [his] and [lunch].

Note how [his lunch] and [broccoli] have the same function in the sentence (the direct object). Thus, we say that since [broccoli] is a noun, [his lunch] is a **noun phrase** (NP). Along the same line, we can find that since *eats* is a verb, [eats broccoli] is a **verb phrase** (VP). There are other types of phrases, the most significant being the **prepositional phrase** (PP), which requires a preposition, such as *on, in,* and *by.* Incidentally, the part of speech without which a given "phrase" could not exist is called the "head" of it. So the noun is the head of an NP.

Recapitulating, we have introduced the immediate constituents of a sentence, which are the parts in which a sentence can be broken down. Its constituents are the parts in which it ultimately is analyzable (i.e., the morphemes). We further introduced the concept of **phrase,** which is any constituent, either immediate or not, that is not a **clause.** A clause is a full sentence that has a subject and a verb. Somewhat confusingly, phrases may consist of only one constituent, as will be seen later.

Table 2.1 gives a list of what can appear in a phrase structure grammar, with examples.

Table 2.1: Lexical and Phrasal Categories

Major Lexical Categories

Noun	(N)	*John, rock, table, idea*
Verb	(V)	*run, kiss, kill, speak*
Adjective	(Adj)	*old, beautiful, large*
Adverb	(Adv)	*quickly, madly, yesterday*

Minor Lexical Categories

Determiner	(Det)	*the, a/an, this, those*
Auxiliary Verb	(Aux)	*do, be, have, can, may, must*
Preposition	(P)	*in, on, up, near, at, by*
Pronoun	(Pro)	*he, she, it, him, her, they*
Conjunction	(C)	*and, or, but, however*

Phrasal Categories

Noun Phrase	(NP)	*the young man, books, John*
Verb Phrase	(VP)	*runs, opened the door*
Prepositional Phrase	(PP)	*in the dark, in open contest*

It is traditional to represent the structure of the sentence with a **tree diagram** that shows with branching lines the process illustrated of breaking down the sentence. A simple example follows:

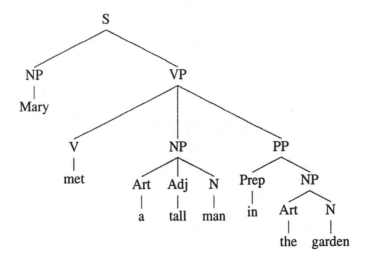

Types of NPs in English

Let us look at some other examples that will show the various configurations of an NP in English. An NP may be very simple or have a fairly complex structure:

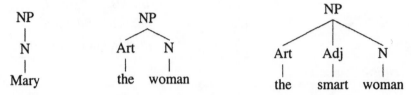

Notice the increasingly more complex structure, going from a simple noun, to an article plus noun, then an article plus adjective, and so on.

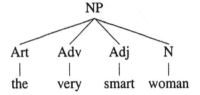

Finally, notice that an NP may be modified by a PP, as in the example *the woman at work*. Note that modification takes the form of attaching under the NP node. This will become quite significant when we discuss PP attachment.

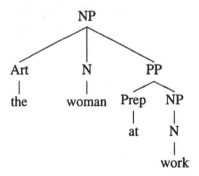

Let us add that VPs can be similarly complex, except nothing ever comes before the verb (we will not deal with auxiliaries in this text, but even those do not come out of the VP node, but rather out of S).

Configurational Definitions

Tree diagramming offers a clear and simple solution to problems that had plagued grammar for centuries. Take the issue of how to define the subject and/or direct object of a sentence. You are probably familiar with such "nondefinitions" as "the person or thing doing the action," which can be defeated by a few well-chosen examples (just to name one, in *It rains*, who or what is doing the raining?).

Generative grammar, as discussed later in this section, notes that when labeling sentence structures, there is no need to label subjects and direct objects. The subject of a sentence is a nontechnical name for the first noun phrase located immediately below the S in a tree diagram. The direct object is simply the noun phrase located immediately below the verb phrase (NP, VP). This is what is called a **configurational definition.** It only relies on positions within the tree.

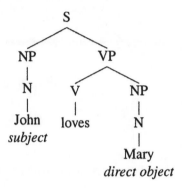

Syntactic Ambiguity

Sentences can often be ambiguous. Tree diagrams can exemplify this fact. Note that phrases can be attached to more than one spot. This can lead to differences in meaning.

Consider this joke: *A woman walks in a store and says to the clerk, "I'd like to try on the red dress in the window." And the clerk says, "But, Ma'am, we have dressing rooms for that."* The woman means that the dress is in the window, while the clerk understands that the trying on will take place in the window. Here's how this ambiguity is represented in a tree diagram (simplifying the sentence a little); first the clerk's interpretation:

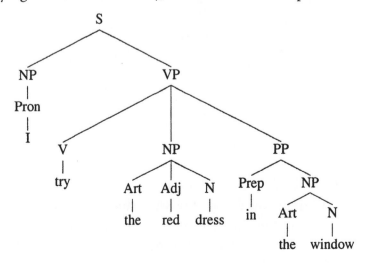

And now the woman's intended interpretation:

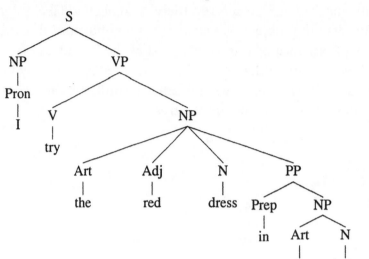

There are many other kinds of syntactic ambiguities. Another example of ambiguity: *Flying planes can be dangerous.* You could interpret this sentence in more than one way. For instance, you could take it as planes that are flying can be dangerous or actually piloting planes is dangerous.

A Notational Shortcut

Sometimes linguists do not need the detail of a complete analysis of a syntactic tree for a sentence or are in a hurry. It is a convention that a constituent of a sentence, or an entire sentence, may be represented by a triangle, as in the following tree. Needless to say, students should not use triangles in tree diagramming unless so directed by their instructors.

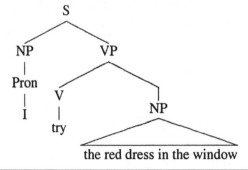

Generative Grammar

This kind of grammar, associated with the groundbreaking work of Noam Chomsky in the mid-1950s, is called a **generative grammar.** Why generative? Chomsky wanted to design a model (a grammar) that would produce all the sentences that a native speaker would agree are grammatical and none of the sentences that a native speaker would reject as ungrammatical. The main idea is that the sentences of a language are *generated*. In mathematics, from which Chomsky was inspired, generation means that given a symbol and a rule one can produce new (sequences of) symbols, based on the rule. For example, a mathematical system that generates even numbers can be defined as:

$$n_{even} = \text{n} \cdot 2$$

This system, known as a function, is extremely simple. If you plug in any number (n) and multiply it by 2, the result is an even number. A similarly simple formula generates odd numbers:

$$n_{odd} = (\text{n} \cdot 2) + 1$$

If you take an even number and add one, you get an odd number.

Notice also that, in their misleading simplicity, the two systems defined previously are quite powerful. In fact, they can both generate an infinite set of even and odd numbers. Any formal system will have rules and "objects" to which the rules apply; these formal systems are also known as "grammars."

What do the rules used to generate sentences of a language look like? They are called **rewriting rules.** Rewriting rules are all of the same form. You take element A and rewrite it as B or in symbols: (A → B). A can only consist of one symbol (item), but B can be any number of items. This is very significant, as the following discussion of transformations will show.

However, we still have not touched upon the specifics of a grammar capable of generating sentences of English. The rewriting rules that generate sentences are called **phrase structure rules.**

Phrase Structure Rules

Phrase structure rules are simple instructions for building larger constituents from smaller ones. They also give us information on the order in which their components appear and their grammatical categories.

For example, the following rule will immediately look familiar:

S → NP + VP

It can be paraphrased as follows:

A sentence may be rewritten as "noun phrase " plus "verb phrase"

or more formally as

To build a constituent of the category S, take a constituent of the category NP and combine it with another constituent of the category VP, in that order.

Thus what the rule says is merely that a sentence is made up of an NP and a VP and in that order. Tree diagrams can also be used to represent the structure of this sentence. In fact, phrase structure grammars (PSGs) are equivalent to tree diagrams. The only difference is that in tree diagrams, you are unable to tell which "branch" was generated first. But for our purposes, they are the same.

A PSG for a Subset of English

The following simple phrase structure grammar generates all the sentences used as examples or in the exercise questions in this book.

S	→	NP + VP
NP	→	$(Art) + (Adj)_n + N + (PP)_n$
VP	→	$V + (NP) + (PP)_n$
PP	→	Prep + NP
Art	→	*the, a, an*
N	→	*girl, house, book ...*
V	→	*eat, run, laugh ...*
Prep	→	*up, above, with ...*
Adj	→	*big, small, green ...*

Note the following conventions:

- Items in parentheses (...) are optional, i.e., either zero or one instance of the item is permitted.

- The notation *n* following an item in parentheses indicates that any number of the item may occur (zero, one, or more than two).

- The ... notation indicates that the items are too numerous to be listed, but any noun, for example, could be used.

2.5 TYPES OF SENTENCES

We traditionally distinguish different types of verbs and corresponding types of sentences. In English, verbs must always have a subject, but some verbs do not take a direct object; these are called **intransitive** verbs.

(2.8) Mary laughs.

Mary sleeps.

Verbs that have a direct object are called **transitive.**

(2.9) Mary won the race.

Mary kissed John.

Some verbs have two objects, a direct and an indirect object (see Chapter 19). These are called **ditransitive** verbs.

(2.10) Mary gave John a book.

Mary sent Ann a letter.

Other types of sentences do not have an NP as their direct object, but rather an adjective is their complement. A **complement** is anything that follows the verb. Usually this happens with **copular verbs** (such as *to be, to seem, to look*):

(2.11) Mary is tired.

Mary seems happy.

Naturally, we can add all sorts of adverbs or adverbial clauses in various positions to modify the sentence or some of its parts. So, for example, we can have:

(2.12) Mary won the race yesterday.

Luckily, Mary won the race.

Mary easily won the race.

Mary won the race without much effort.

Finally, **transformations** can be used to move parts of a sentence into different positions, for emphatic purposes. For example:

(2.13) It's in the garden that John lost his glasses.

This wreck of a car you want me to drive?

A good student he is not.

In a now somewhat old-fashioned terminology, sentences before transformations have been applied to them are in **deep structure** (see Figure 2.5) and after the transformations have been applied in **surface structure.** Deep and surface structure were originally used to capture the fact that two sentences such as

(2.14) Mary loves John.

(2.15) John is loved by Mary.

are clearly related. The idea was that the two sentences (2.14/2.15) share the same deep structure but undergo different transformations, resulting in different surface structures. Thus, sentence (2.14) is in the **active voice**, while sentence (2.15) is in the **passive voice. Voice** is a technical term indicating that the verb is either active or passive. An active sentence to which no transformation has been applied is called a **kernel sentence.**

Figure 2.5: The Organization of a Generative-Transformative Grammar

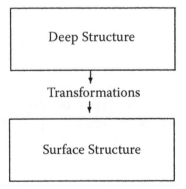

Syntacticians, or people who study syntax, used to believe that there were many more transformations, even in simple sentences. Today we

tend to believe that there are few, if any at all. For example, take **subordination**. A clause is called a subordinate if it is "inside" another clause. By inside, we mean that a higher-order sentence has as one of its components another sentence (the subordinate clause). For example, a sentence may have its direct object replaced by a subordinate clause, which will appear under the *comp* node (comp stands for *complementizer*, i.e., a word that introduces a complement/subordinate clause; see 19.6.1):

(2.16) Mary believes that John is the culprit.

In this sentence, *Mary believes* is the **main clause** while *that John is the culprit* is the subordinate clause.

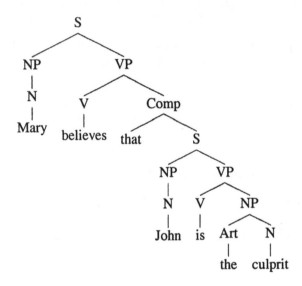

Another way to join sentences, besides subordination (aka hypotaxis), is **coordination** (aka parataxis). In coordination, unlike subordination, the two sentences, or phrases, are on the same level. Consider the following example

(2.17) Mary left and John went to bed.

in which the two sentences *Mary left* and *John went to bed* are on the same level (i.e., neither is a subordinate of the other). This can be seen very clearly from the phrase structure tree.

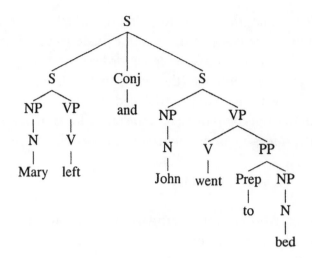

The joining together of sentences (through coordination or subordination) was handled by transformations in the early versions of the theory. Nowadays, syntacticians think that transformations are mostly unnecessary, although they still use the concepts of deep and surface structure.

The following are some further examples of transformations.

- **Particle hopping:**

  Mary stood up John. ⇒ Mary stood John up.

  NP + V + part + NP ⇒ NP + V + NP + part

  Note the detachment of the particle of the phrasal verb *(stand up)*.

- **Question:**

  Mary stood up John. ⇒ Did Mary stand up John?

  NP + V + NP ⇒ Aux + NP + V + NP

  Note the "appearance" of the auxiliary *(did)*.

- **Negation:**

  Mary stood up John. ⇒ Mary did not stand up John.

  NP + V + NP ⇒ NP + Aux + Neg + V + NP

  Note the "appearance" of the auxiliary, followed by the negation *(not)*.

- **Passive:**

  Mary stood up John. ⇒ John was stood up by Mary.

  $NP_1 + V + NP_2 \Rightarrow NP_2 + BE + V\text{-}en + by + NP_1$

  Note that *BE* is the verb *to be* and the notation *-en* indicates the past participle form of the main verb.

- **Dative movement:**

  Mary gave a book to John ⇒ Mary gave John a book.

  $NP_1 + V + NP_2 + Prep + NP_3 \Rightarrow NP_1 + V + NP_3 + NP_2$

  Note that "John" is called an indirect object.

Besides the way yes/no questions are formed in English, there is another way of asking questions, i.e., the so-called WH-questions. It consists in taking the complement phrase (in the following example, the direct object NP) and moving it to the beginning of the sentence, in the empty node under the "comp" node (marked by a circle). Note that we are ignoring the presence of the auxiliary ("Who *does* Mary know?") for the sake of simplicity.

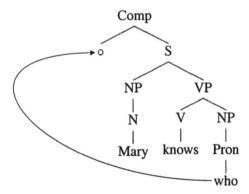

2.5.1 Recursion and Embedded Sentences

Recursion is a syntactic phenomenon that occurs in some sentences. Essentially, it consists of the occurrence of a given constituent within a constituent of the same kind. This definition is a bit abstract, so let's look at a concrete example, followed by the relevant PSG rules:

(2.18) The boy with the hat with the logo of a company...

PP → Prep + NP; NP → Art + N + PP; PP ... etc.

In example (2.18), we see an NP *(The boy)* modified by a PP *(with the hat)* that has the peculiarity of being itself modified by another PP *(with the logo)* that, in turn, is itself modified by yet another PP *(of a company)*. The suspension dots at the end of the sentence indicate that this sequence of modifying PPs could continue indefinitely, precisely because there is no theoretical reason to stop the recursion of the PP constituents within the PPs. Of course there are practical, performance-related (see 1.2.3) reasons to stop (i.e., your sentence will become too long to be uttered or understood), but theoretically (i.e., competence-wise) the sentence could continue adding PPs recursively an infinite number of times. Hence, the conclusion that, potentially, competence-wise English sentences are infinitely long, since they can keep adding PPs infinitely many times.

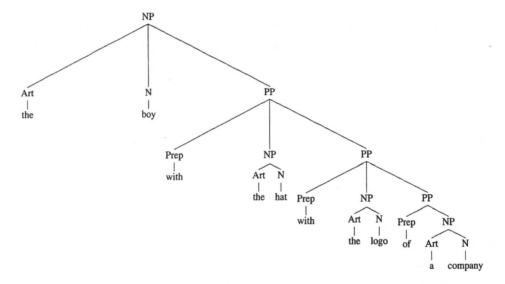

Another way of having recursive components in a sentence is to have an **embedded sentence** inside another sentence. In this case, the constituent that recurs is a sentence. As in the case of PPs, there is no theoretical limit to how many sentences can be embedded into one another, although, of course, the practical limits remain. In the following example, the embedded sentence is italicized.

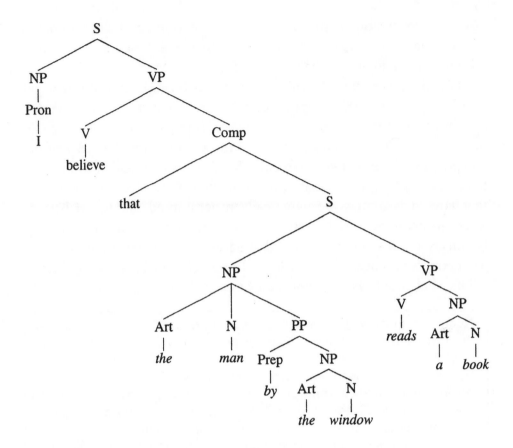

Note how the embedded sentence could itself have another sentence embedded in it, and so on (e.g., *I believe that the man by the window reads a book about a woman who thinks that...*).

2.5.2 Syntax, Universal Grammar, and the Chomskian Program

Syntax, and indeed most of linguistics, has been influenced deeply by the work of Noam Chomsky, one of the geniuses of the 20th century. Even those who disagree with him have to recognize that his influence has been momentous. Chomsky is largely responsible for the central role of syntax in most of theoretical linguistics' work in the last 40 years. Chomsky's grammatical theory has a very significant and controversial psychological and even biological underpinning.

Note that to this point we have presented Chomsky's standard theory. The theory has been heavily revised several times (see the box on p. 50);

however, discussion of the more recent notations and developments would be far too complex for a beginners' text. See the *Further Readings* section at the end of this chapter for references.

Chomsky claims that the rules of grammar (syntax, morphology, and phonology) are governed by principles that are universal, in the sense that all languages of the world obey them. For example, no language would negate or deny the sentence *John is not tall* by reversing the order of the morphemes of the sentence to form *tall is John* (meaning that John is not tall). Chomsky says that that is no coincidence, because the principles that govern grammar are genetically programmed in human beings. These principles are called **universal grammar (UG).** In other words, Chomsky and his followers claim that part of our genetic makeup tells us what counts as a possible grammatical/linguistic rule, just like our genes tell us what counts as a possible hair or eye color.

Noam Chomsky was born on December 7, 1928. He received his Ph.D. from The University of Pennsylvania in 1955. By 1965, when he published *Aspects of the Theory of Syntax,* which is his "classical" book, he was the established leader of a new approach to linguistics, based on such mathematical concepts as *generation* and on *transformations,* a linguistic concept introduced by Chomsky's mentor, Zelig Harris. This is why the "standard theory," as Chomsky's theory became known, is called *transformational-generative grammar.* Since then, Chomsky has significantly revised his theory, in fact altering it very deeply. The standard theory became government and binding (GB), principles and parameters (PP), and, lastly, minimalism. Besides writing more than 20 books in linguistics, Chomsky is also a political intellectual, and his critique of the foreign policy of the United States, as well as the media treatment thereof, has been quite influential in leftist circles. Significantly, in a survey of academic journals conducted in the early 1990s, Chomsky was the most frequently quoted living individual, bested only by Karl Marx, Vladimir Lenin, Shakespeare, Aristotle, the Bible, Plato, and Freud (in that order— and note that they are all dead). Chomsky is probably the most significant living linguist. Books have been written about his life and work, and even a documentary film has been realized about him, titled *Manufacturing Consent: Noam Chomsky and the Media.*

Each individual specification toward the nature of universal grammar is called a **parameter.** Parameters are very abstract, but **PRO-DROP** can be used as an example; in Italian, the following sentence is perfectly grammatical:

(2.19) Piove.

while in English

(2.20) *Rains.

is clearly ungrammatical. Spanish, German, Chinese, Latin, and many other languages behave like Italian in this respect, while French and other languages behave like English. What we have here is a parameter that says roughly that in a given language one either can or cannot have an empty subject position (cf. the grammatical *It rains*). Parameters can be thought of as yes/no switches. A parameter allows either one thing or the other.

2.6 BEYOND THE SENTENCE

Sentences do not occur in isolation (except in grammar books!). Sentences may occur in paragraphs or as part of a conversation where two or more speakers talk to each other. The disciplines of linguistics that look at these units larger than the individual sentence are called **text linguistics** and **discourse analysis;** also, **contrastive rhetoric** is interested in paragraph structure (see 11.4).

2.6.1 Coherence and Cohesion

This area owes a lot to the work of M. A. K. Halliday and R. Hasan. Generally, we distinguish between textual cohesion, which happens at the level of the surface of the text, and coherence, which happens at the level of the meaning of the text.

Cohesion

Cohesion, generally speaking, is the property of the surface structure of the text to "hold together." Consider the following example:

(2.21) *The boy* came in the room. **He** was wearing a red coat.

In sentence (2.21) the italicized NP *the boy* is referred to by the bolded pronoun *he*. Technically, we say that the pronoun is an **anaphoric** item, i.e., a linguistic item that refers to another (part of a) text, and what it refers to is called its **antecedent.** So, the relationship between any anaphoric item and its antecedent is a cohesive relationship.

Pronouns are not the only type of cohesive devices found in texts. Articles are cohesive too, as well as some adverbials (e.g., *on the one hand...on the other hand; however*) and conjunctions *(and, but)*. Other cohesive devices include lists, parallelisms, explicit markers such as chapter and section titles, and tables of contents. NPs can be cohesive too:

> (2.22) *Napoleon* was a great general. *The winner of Marengo* was proud of his reputation. *Bonaparte* was also known for his habit of keeping his hand on his stomach. It is believed that *the emperor's* digestion problems are the reason for his well-known pose.

In this paragraph, the italicized NPs are all co-referential and are therefore cohesive.

Coherence

Coherence is the overall meaning of a text. You may think of it as its "point," or "main idea," or as the part of its meaning that makes it all fit together. Coherence happens at the semantic level. As such, it may, but does not have to be, explicitly expressed in the text itself. Besides by cohesion, coherence may be established by any of the following means:

- the setting up and fulfillment of expectations in the text, e.g., we start talking about a couple engaged to be married and then we describe them getting married;

- the **cooperative principle,** i.e., by implicature (see 3.2.3), for example, one asks for walking directions to a given address, only to be told that that address is five miles away; the answer assumes the implicature that the question is being asked with the purpose of going to the address;

- reasoning, i.e., by inference, for example, if we say that John wants to go to the swimming pool and he asks to borrow Mary's car, we infer that he is doing so in order to reach the swimming pool;

- by the activation of our knowledge of a common situation (see 3.2.2), e.g., if we are discussing a trip to the restaurant we will expect to find mention of food, whereas if we are discussing an IRS audit, any mention of food would be considered unexpected and/or out of place; certainly, the text would have to work hard to explain why there is a mention of food in the audit at all.

The presence in a text of cohesive devices does not guarantee that it is also coherent, although usually coherence and cohesion go together. To show that cohesion is neither a sufficient nor a necessary component of coherence, consider the two following paragraphs:

(2.23) John likes to swim. Mary is fond of skydiving. Ann is a pro golfer. What athletic children I have.

(2.24) John likes to swim. It is a very good sport, from an exercising point of view. Exercise is a good way to lose weight. Weight loss is the number one reason for dieting.

In paragraph (2.23) there are no cohesive ties (unless you count the fact that John, Mary, and Ann are potentially children's names), and yet coherence is easily achieved by invoking the frame for *family*, which tells us that one may have three children.

In (2.24) there are cohesive ties between each sentence and the following one, yet the paragraph fails to be coherent because there is no unifying theme, no one thought that is expressed by the text.

2.6.2 Conversation Analysis

Conversations occur when two or more people talk together and are coherent (if everything goes well, obviously!). Coherence in dialogue is achieved by all the means discussed previously (especially the cooperative principle). There are, however, also conversation-specific tools, such as adjacency pairs.

Adjacency Pairs

An **adjacency pair** is the succession of two linked turns, by different speakers, which make sense only taken together. The following are some examples of adjacency pairs:

- greetings

    (2.25) A: How are you?
           B: Fine. How about yourself?

- question and answer

    (2.26) A: What is your name?
           B: Bond, James Bond.

- offer and acceptance/refusal

  (2.27) A: Would you like to go to the movies?
  B: Yes/No.

- leave taking

  (2.28) A: Good-bye.
  B: See you later.

- apology /acceptance or refusal

  (2.29) A: I am sorry I missed the final.
  B: Tough.

Note that a speaker may choose not to complete the adjacency pair immediately but instead delay it by introducing another adjacency pair.

(2.30) A: When are you going on vacation? [question]
B: Why do you want to know? [question]

A: I have to write a report for the boss. [answer]
B: Ah. The second week of July. [answer]

In this example, we see speaker B refusing to complete the adjacency pair and instead opening another adjacency pair. Note that when the second adjacency pair (turns 2 and 3) is complete, B does eventually complete (in the last turn) the adjacency pair opened in the first turn.

However, conversations are quite different from written texts. To name the most obvious differences, they are spoken, as opposed to written, and they have more than one speaker, as opposed to written texts, which usually have one author.

Turn Taking

One of the central issues in the analysis of conversation is how to regulate **turn taking,** i.e., who is to speak. In general, people tend to avoid **overlapping** turns, because it is fairly complex to follow what someone is saying while someone else is speaking too. People have developed strategies to ensure that speakers who **have the floor,** or are speaking, will not be interrupted. In middle-class American culture, the convention is that whoever is speaking is entitled to keep the floor until he or she arrives at a **transition relevance place (TRP)** (for example, the end of a sentence or a pause in speech). Then, unless the speaker signals with appropriate means that he or she is not done speaking (for example, by making a hesitating sound), the floor is up for grabs. The speaker also has the option of selecting the next speaker, for example, by asking a question.

This is not to say that speakers never interrupt. However, interruptions are viewed as "rude" (not following the conventions of proper behavior) and disruptive. Not all interruptions are rude or disruptive, either. Speakers may interrupt to agree or to express interest in what the speaker currently holding the floor is saying. These kind of overlapping turns are called **backchannel,** here exemplified by B's turns.

(2.31) A: I went to the store...

> B: Uh-huh.
> A: ... and bought milk...

> B: Right.
> A: ... because they were out of cream.

Educational Implications
Teachers need to be aware of the structure of language. Knowledge of phonetics and phonology helps in the teaching of reading, as well as in the teaching of other language arts. Knowledge of morphology allows the teacher to confidently teach the structure and formation of words. Knowledge of syntax helps the teacher to more deeply appreciate sentence structure. Knowledge of discourse is useful in analyzing student production of texts, both written and spoken.

2.7 EXERCISES

2.7.1 Words to Know

phonetic alphabet	phoneme	first articulation
morpheme	free morpheme	bound morpheme
root	stem	affix
prefix	infix	suffix
derivational morpheme	inflectional morpheme	derivation
compounding	clipping	acronym
blends	backformation	borrowing
calque	invention	second articulation
syntax	grammaticality	constituent
phrase	tree diagram	universal grammar
parameter	kernel sentence	allophone
collocation	phrasal verb	idiom
lexeme	phonetics	diphthong
articulatory phonetics	airstream	voiced
voiceless	velum	nasalization
glides	affricates	liquids
aspiration	unreleased	minimal pair
configurational definition	syntactic ambiguity	generative grammar
rewriting rule	phrase structure rule	intransitive
transitive	ditransitive	deep structure
surface structure	active voice	passive voice
subordination	coordination	main clause
recursion	embedding	coherence
cohesion	contrastive rhetorics	anaphor
antecedent	conversation	adjacency pair
overlap	TRP	backchannel

2.7.2 Review

1. Why is the International Phonetic Alphabet (IPA) useful?

2. Transcribe the following words in IPA. It may be helpful to say the words out loud before you do so.

plush	bet	bleak	do
chop	but	nit	bough
church	boat	jump	new
down	bought	boy	fruit
fluff	through	sing	plain
cough	knight	child	poach
beep	push	judge	flinch
bit	chirp	flash	beat
heap	hurt	bait	hip
dew	hat	heat	hit

3. Break these words into morphemes:

   a. indecision, cheaters, broadcasting, conferences, childishness

   b. Unconstitutional laws are unusually common lately.

   c. The reemergence of nationalisms is worrisome.

4. Look at the list of ways new words are made. Can you think of other examples for each process?

5. Try your hand at diagramming sentences:

   a. The pretty boy likes the smart girl.

   b. Mary loves pizza with anchovies.

   c. John ate the pizza with his hands.

6. Compare the trees of the last two sentences. Is the place where you attached the PP the same? Why? See if you can explain your choice.

7. Draw the syntactic trees for the following kernel sentences:

   a. The tall woman complained about the noise.

   b. John loves the warm feeling of an open fire.

   c. The book is on the table with the white tablecloth.

d. A hardworking student passes a tricky exam without any trouble.

e. The woman with the red dress closed the door with a kick.

f. I ate a slice of pizza with my friends from college.

g. The man with red hair ate a slice of pizza with his fingers.

h. The man with the red umbrella in his hands laughs.

8. Draw the syntactic trees for the following sentences. Note that all of the following have undergone a transformation, so you need first to find out what transformation has applied, apply it backwards to find the kernel sentence, and then draw the tree diagram.

a. The old table was repaired by a good craftsman.

b. Mary was given a flower by John.

c. John was hit on the head by Mary.

d. Is the book on the table?

e. The book was put on the table by Mary.

f. Clinton was elected by the American people.

g. Is the car with the flat tire in the garage?

h. The lazy students were flunked by the righteous professor.

i. Is Mary in the blue car with John?

j. The game was canceled by the tall umpire.

k. Mary gave John a piece of cake with many candles.

2.7.3 Research Projects

1. Make a list of words you think were invented in your lifetime. Use a dictionary to check your intuitions.

2. Transcribe some English words into IPA. To check your answers, use a dictionary with IPA pronunciation. English as a second language dictionaries like the *Longman Dictionary of Contemporary English* use IPA. If you know a language other than English, you might want to try transcribing some words you know.

3. Tape a five-minute piece of conversation and identify adjacency pairs and turns. For an example of transcription conventions, see Brown and Yule (1983, x–xi).

4. Select a newspaper article and try to identify all markers of cohesion. Use colored highlighters to mark different types (e.g., pronouns, repetitions of words, synonyms, conjunctions).

2.8 FURTHER READINGS

More detailed, but nonetheless introductory, treatments of phonetics, phonology, morphology, and syntax can be found in the relevant chapters of the general introductions to linguistics listed in the previous chapter. The treatment of phenomena above the sentential level is spotty, at best. A good introductory text in that area is Stubbs (1983).

For a more advanced look at the various subfields, the following sources may be helpful. A complete description of the IPA can be found in Pullum and Ladusaw (1986). Clark and Yallop (1995) is an in-depth look at phonetics and phonology. Matthews (1991) is a good introduction to morphology. Syntax is a difficult area to keep up with, given the dizzying pace of change in the theories. A recognized, excellent all-purpose introduction to mainstream syntax is Radford (1997). Other options are the relevant chapters in Napoli (1996) and Culicover (1997). Introductions to the variety of theories of syntax are Sells (1985) and Horrocks (1987). The "ideology" of the Chomskian program is spelled out in the very readable Pinker (1994) and in Cook (1996). Lyons (1977a) is an excellent introduction to Chomsky's standard theory. A book on Chomsky's life and politics is Barsky (1997). On the double articulation of language, see Martinet (1966), translated by E. Palmer.

On cohesion and coherence, the fundamental reference is still Halliday and Hasan (1976). On discourse analysis, the relevant chapter in Levinson (1983) is a good synthesis. Brown and Yule (1983) is also excellent. Schiffrin (1994) provides a broad survey. Tracy (2002) and Gee (1999) are good recent introductions to discourse analysis, Hutchby and Wooffit (1998) to conversation analysis. The Nigerian English examples come from Ahulu (1998).

Chapter 3

How Do We Mean Things?

In the previous chapter we saw how words and sentences are put together to form texts. In this chapter we will look at how sentences mean things and how the same sentence may mean different things in different settings. Finally, we will look at how settings affect language in general. We now turn to the semantics of words.

3.1 THE MEANING OF WORDS

Words have meanings. When you read the word *dog* in a sentence you think of a dog. The mental representation of the dog is the **meaning** of the word *dog*. The animal in the world that you can see, touch, hear, or smell is the **referent** of the word *dog*. The word *dog* is a **sign** that allows us to connect the meaning and the referent, which would be otherwise completely unrelated, as they belong to different spheres: thoughts and real objects, respectively. The sign (word) *dog* is made of a **signifier** (the sequence of sounds that make up that word) and of a **signified** (the meaning of the sign).

The signifier and the signified are unrelated because there is no special reason for a dog to be called *dog*. As proof of this fact, consider that if there were a good reason to call a dog *dog*, this reason, whatever it may be, should hold true for French and any other language. But a dog is called *chien* in French. Thus, there seems to be no good reason for words to be what they are. It is a matter of convention. The fact that the connection between a word's phonological shape and its meaning is arbitrary (i.e., lacking a motivation, other than convention) is called the principle of the **arbitrariness of the linguistic sign.**

3.1.1 Breaking Down Words

Compare the following pairs of words: *rooster/hen, man/woman, boy /girl,* and *boar/sow.* All pairs differ by one feature: they are female/not female animals. To put it differently, they differ in one feature, [female] or [male]. We can choose arbitrarily [female] and then say that *sow* is a [+female] pig while *boar* is a [-female] pig.

Compare now the following pairs: *sow/boy, rooster/woman, hen/man,* and *boar/girl.* All pairs differ in another feature: [animal] (or [human]). Now we can represent the eight words with a grid:

	man	woman	boy	girl	rooster	hen	boar	sow
[female]	-	+	-	+	-	+	-	+
[animal]	-	-	-	-	+	+	+	+

Ideally, we could continue until we describe the entire meaning of each word by breaking it down into **semantic features,** i.e., meaning components. In reality, things do not work out entirely this way, because the **lexicon,** or all the words of a language, is a very complex part of how a language works. When one tries to apply this system to the lexicon, one soon realizes that one needs roughly as many features as there are words. Not only that, but there are words, such as *father,* that define relationships rather than simple meanings, so to define *father* we need to say something like "parent of someone" (the someone is the other term in the relationship). Finally, many words have "fuzzy" boundaries, and so it is hard to decide how to define words like *tall:* Should it be above 6 feet? Above 7 feet? This makes it hard to assign features.

The Semantics of Scrambled Eggs

Consider the following example: there are many ways to prepare eggs for breakfast (at least, in America, many people do not eat eggs for breakfast, but let's ignore this cultural issue). A list, incomplete but representative, would include hard-boiled, poached, scrambled, sunny-side up, over easy, and, of course, omelet. Let's ignore for convenience sake additions to the bare eggs, such as omelet with cheese, eggs Benedict, etc. And also we will ignore the practice of eating eggs raw.

Our problem is to provide a feature analysis of the semantic field of "egg preparation techniques." We will do so by introducing a few features. The first feature is [± intact shell], meaning that the eggshell is not broken for cooking. This differentiates hard-boiled eggs from everything else. The next feature is [± boiled], which differentiates poached eggs from all the other types. Note that we could have used [± fried] to the same effect (this is due to the restricted domain of egg-cooking procedures; in another field, this would not be true). The next feature is [± scrambled], which takes care of scrambled eggs and of omelets. Omelets may be distinguished from scrambled eggs by a further feature [± in pan], which indicates that the egg in an omelet is scrambled prior to cooking, whereas scrambled eggs are scrambled while being cooked, or at least scrambled *more* while being cooked. The category of unscrambled, fried eggs is further subdivided by the feature [± flipped], which distinguishes sunny-side up from "over" eggs (over easy, over medium, over hard). Finally, the three-way distinction of "over" eggs may be described by the two features [± hard] and [± runny] as follows: eggs over easy are [- hard], [+ runny], over medium are [+ hard], [+runny], and over hard are [+ hard], [- runny]. Note how we could also have introduced a graded feature, say [hard] with three levels of "hardness": easy, medium, and hard.

Our analysis is summed up in the following diagram:

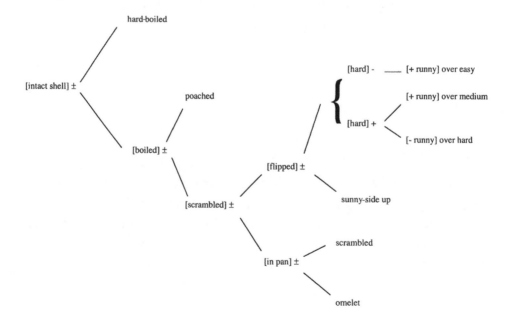

or, alternatively, in the following chart:

	[intact shell]	[boiled]	[scrambled]	[flipped]	[in pan]	[runny]	[hard]
hard-boiled	+	+	-	-	-	-	+
poached	-	+	-	-	-	-	-
omelet	-	-	+	+	-	-	+/-
scrambled	-	-	+	+	+	-	+
sunny-side up	-	-	-	-	n/a	+	-
over easy	-	-	-	+	n/a	+	-
over medium	-	-	-	+	n/a	-	+
over hard	-	-	-	+	n/a	-	+

Note how, with the features we have introduced, we could theoretically have analyzed 128 (2^7)* words, while we have used them to analyze only eight words. Ideally, only three features would have been necessary (2^3).

3.1.2 Meaning Relationships

Besides the problems with feature assignment, words may change their meaning: when we say that *Bob is a pig,* we do not mean literally that Bob is a swine, but rather that Bob has some significant feature in common with such (for instance, that of being dirty). This is a **metaphor,** or figurative use of meaning.

In other cases, words shift their meaning slightly. When we say that we will *drink a glass of water,* we really mean that we will drink the *contents* of a glass, not the glass itself. Or when we say that we cannot *place someone's face,* we do not mean that we remember very well the rest of the person's body. This kind of shift in meaning (from the container to the contained, from a part to the whole) is called **metonymy.**

Yet in other cases words may have similar or almost identical meanings: What is the difference between *freedom* and *liberty?* Between *pillage* and *plunder?* Between *immaculate* and *unsoiled?* These pairs of words that have similar, if not identical, meanings are called **synonyms.** Other pairs of words have opposite meanings and are called **antonyms;** examples are *hot* and *cold* or *alive* and *dead.*

---

*Two to the power of seven, i.e., $2 \times 2 \times 2 \times 2 \times 2 \times 2 \times 2$, which comes to 128.

3.1.3 Denotation and Connotation

How do near synonyms such as *freedom* and *liberty* differ? One way to look at this is to say that their connotations are different. Then what is the connotation of a word?

A big distinction that underlies the problem of defining meaning is that between the denotation of a sign and its connotation. The **denotation** of a sign is commonly assumed to correspond to its sense or **intension.** **Connotations** are assumed to be all aspects of meaning that go beyond its sense. For example, the words *bachelor* and *spinster* can be both analyzed as

[+ adult]

[- married]

[± female]

but the connotations are radically different, namely that a bachelor is someone who chooses not to marry and lives a life full of entertainment, while a spinster is someone who cannot get married and lives an unpleasant life as a result. (Needless to say, these connotations reflect the sexist assumptions of the culture and are not endorsed by the authors or publishers.)

We can distinguish between a core meaning (the denotation/intension) and an outside nebula of meaning (the connotations) along the lines of the following picture:

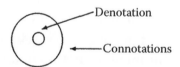

The situation is however complicated by the fact that connotations cover a broad, indeed indefinite, range of meanings, covering such disparate areas as those listed in the following section.

Sources of Connotative Meaning

There are different sources of connotative meaning, which we will review next.

- **Affective connotations:** The aspects of meaning having to do with the feelings or attitudes of the speakers. Compare, for example, *resistance* *fighter* versus *terrorist:* labeling someone who fights a government as a *resistance fighter* implies that one agrees with the goals of that person, whereas labeling her or him *terrorist* implies the opposite.

- **Collocative connotations:** The aspects of meaning having to do with the linguistic environment in which an expression usually occurs. For example, by uttering the word *cease* or *liberal*, one evokes (connotes) *desist* and *bleeding heart,* respectively.

- **Social connotations:** The aspects of meaning having to do with different levels of formality. For example, the following synonymous expressions have increasingly more formality (see Chapter 6.2):

The door!

Shut the door!

Please shut the door.

Would you shut the door?

Could you shut the door?

Would you mind shutting the door?

Would it be inconvenient to shut the door?

- **Reflected connotations:** The aspects of meaning concerning other meanings of a linguistic expression that may be activated even when they are irrelevant in the situation. Consider the word *cock*, which has several perfectly innocent meanings, including that of *rooster* and that of *hammer of a firearm.* Nevertheless, speakers avoid the word because of its well-known sexual reflected connotation.

- **Individual or restricted connotations:** The associations that an individual speaker or a small group of speakers (e.g., a family or a group of coworkers) may develop out of everyday experiences. For example, if your cousin Bob is an unpleasant person, you may come to associate his name and the idea of unpleasantness; if your boss always uses a stock phrase, such as *another day, another dollar*, that phrase may evoke your boss. The significant issue is that these connotations are valid only for the individual or the small group of people who are exposed to the conditioning environment (cousin Bob, the monotonous boss).

- **Coded connotations:** The aspects of meaning that are evoked by cultural or literary codes, e.g., lilies evoke purity, chastity, and innocence; elephants evoke lasting memory; pigs evoke dirt and unpleasant manners. Obviously, meanings change with cultures. The color white in some cultures connotes not purity, but death.

A very significant issue is that the previous categories are not clear-cut distinctions; connotative meaning is notoriously very difficult to identify, let alone classify. A good working approach is to consider connotative meaning as a nebula of associative and evocative meaning that surrounds the denotative "core" of the more "stable" meaning of a word.

Another significant issue concerning connotation is that all words, syntactic turns of phrase, pronunciations, and, in short, all aspects of a linguistic expression have some connotation. It is a common mistake to think that *dog* has no connotation, while *doggie* connotes "child talk." In fact, both words have connotations. *Dog* connotes mature, nonchildish language.

3.1.4 Getting Rid of Ambiguity

Most significantly, words are very often ambiguous. **Ambiguity** is the property of having more than one meaning; this is also known as **polysemy.** Take the polysemous word *coat*, for example. In it we can distinguish several meanings: a garment, the fur of an animal, or a layer of paint on a wall. Notice that these various meanings share some common features; for example, all three meanings are related to external coverings of objects. In some cases words have meanings that are entirely unrelated, such as *bank* (which can refer to the place where you cash checks or the place where you fish by the river). These are called **homonyms.**

If words are often ambiguous, how can we make sense of sentences? Consider the verb *to get.* This verb has more than 25 meanings. How do we know which one is being used in a sentence?

Actually, it is the very fact that the word is being used in the context of a sentence that makes it easy to get rid of the ambiguity. This fact is called **disambiguation.** When we say *Did you get the money?* there is no doubt that we mean *get* as in *receive,* while when we say *Did you get the joke?* we mean *get* as in *understand.* The context of the other words of the sentence in which the word *get* occurs tells us which of the many meanings of *get* is actually being used. In other words, disambiguation is the process whereby the various meanings of a word are discarded under pressure from the other meanings of the words in a sentence and its context. We turn now to the semantics of sentences.

3.2 THE MEANING OF SENTENCES

Words lose their ambiguity in the context of the sentence. Once words have been disambiguated and a sentence has a clear meaning, the sentence acquires a **truth value.**

3.2.1 Pointers to the Context of Sentences

If you consider the sentence

(3.1) It is raining outside.

carefully, you will notice that its truth-value is dependent on "where" *outside* is. Consider now the sentence

(3.2) I am here, now.

While this sentence is clear, its truth-value depends on who "I" is, where "here" is, and when "now" is.

I, here, now, and other similar words are known as **deictics** (i.e., words that depend on the context of the sentence for [large] parts of their meaning). **Deixis** is the branch of pragmatics that studies deictic words. Figure 3.1 presents the meaning of some common deictics in English.

Other deictics are concerned with the social status of the speakers. They will be analyzed in a later chapter (4.2.2).

Figure 3.1: The Meaning of Some English Deictics

I	the speaker
you	the person the speaker is talking to
he/she	neither the speaker nor the hearer
we	both the hearer and the speaker
here	the place where the speaker is
there	a place distant from the speaker
now	the time of speaking
today	the day in which the sentence is uttered
yesterday	during the day before today
go	move away from the location of the speaker
come	move toward the location of the speaker

3.2.2 The Influence of Context

Deictics are only the most obvious influence of the **context,** or the situation in which a sentence is uttered, on that sentence. The context participates actively in the entire process of disambiguation. For example, in the following sentence

(3.3) In Hollywood you can see many stars.

the word *star* is most likely to be interpreted as *famous people* rather than *heavenly bodies,* whereas in

(3.4) With a telescope you can see many stars in the sky.

the context selects the other interpretation as more likely.

Context is also very important in determining how we understand sentences. Consider

(3.5) John stacked the beer in the fridge.

Beer is a liquid, so the sentence should strike us as strange, just as

(3.6) John stacked the water in the pool.

strikes us as anomalous. Yet, we do not feel that the first sentence of the pair is anomalous. This is because our knowledge of the world around us (**encyclopedic knowledge**) tells us that beer often comes in stackable containers (cans, bottles), whereas water is not as likely to come in bottles (although it can, obviously). We also know that people are more likely to stack things in refrigerators than in pools. The encyclopedic knowledge and the knowledge about the word itself are stored in the brain in what is known in psychology and artificial intelligence as a **frame** or **script.** Thus a script or frame for the word *beer* would have all the information commonly available to speakers, such as that beer is a liquid, that people drink it, that it has a variable content in alcohol, that it comes in bottles or cans, that there are many brands of beer, and so on.

3.2.3 How Do We Mean What We Say?

Context is also important from another point of view. Consider the following sentence:

(3.7) I'll take the kids and leave you alone.

This could be a thoughtful sentence uttered by a caring spouse who realizes that his or her partner has had a rough day and needs some rest. On the other hand, it could be a threat by an enraged spouse in a bitter divorce battle. Again, the context in which the sentence is uttered will determine whether this is a promise or a threat. A sentence in context is called an **utterance.** To understand the "complete" meaning of utterances, you must take into account the real-life factors of the speech event. You must consider the speaker, the time, the place, and also the speaker's opinion or belief on that topic (for example, the speaker's intonation in uttering sentence 3.7). Semantics is often done "in isolation," that is, outside of context. But, as we have seen, context is important.

In fact, in some situations, context is all important in determining what we mean. Consider the situation when a clumsy guest spills wine on your new Armani jacket at a party. You say, *That was clever.* What you mean, and your hearers will understand, is that the action of spilling was in fact the opposite of clever. This is called **irony.** How do we go about figuring out what the speakers mean, since, as we have seen, the literal meaning may well be quite different than the intended meaning? We reconstruct the nonliteral, or implied, meaning of sentences out of shared knowledge about language and the world. We will look at how people arrive at the intended meaning of utterances, but first we must consider how people manage to get things done using words.

Speech Acts

The philosophers J. L. Austin and John Searle have laid the foundations for what is called speech act theory. Speech act theory's primary interest is to distinguish three different acts in each utterance:

- **Locutionary act:** what we say literally.

- **Illocutionary act:** the fact that saying something commits you to it. Examples are betting, promising, swearing, baptizing, and naming. This is the force of the sentence; what you are trying to accomplish with it.

- **Perlocutionary act:** the effect the utterance has on its audience. Examples are becoming scared or becoming threatened.

Consider the example of *It's hot in here.* The sentence has a literal meaning, and it may be said for that meaning alone by a weather forecaster or by someone wanting to make small talk. Its illocutionary meaning may, however, may be that of a request, i.e., *Turn down the heat* or *Open a window.* If the heat is turned down, or the window opened, then that is the perlocutionary force of the utterance.

In general, a **speech act** is any utterance produced by a speaker. However, the speaker is not free to utter just anything. There are conditions necessary for speech acts; for example, one cannot promise to do something that would have happened anyway, without intervention, for example,

(3.8) I promise the sun will rise tomorrow.

or that one has no power to accomplish. Suppose you know that Mary will be promoted tomorrow by her boss. You cannot truthfully promise to her that she will be promoted (although you can tell her that she will be promoted). Finally, you cannot promise something that the hearer thinks is bad for him or her. Promising something bad is in fact threatening!

Promises and threats, as in the previous example (sentence 3.8), are an interesting kind of action because they are accomplished just by speaking the right words. If you say *I promise I'll do this,* then just by the fact that you have said it, you have also promised. This kind of action is called a **performative speech act.** Promises and threats are good examples of performative speech acts. Blessings, christenings, and pronouncements that two people are husband and wife (marrying) are all examples of performatives.

Categorizations of Speech Acts

Speech acts have been categorized into five large groups:

1. representatives (assertions, claims and reports, etc.)
2. directives (requests, suggestions, commands, etc.)
3. expressives (thanks, apologies, complaints, etc.)
4. commissives (promises, refusals)
5. declaratives (performatives: the act of speaking itself performs the act, e.g., *I sentence you to life in prison. Class dismissed.*

Every speech act has a set of realization patterns. For requests, that set may include the following, among others:

- *Could you open the window?*
- *I wonder if you could open the window?*
- *Open the window, please.*

How can you decide which speech act is which? That is, how do you know that the phrase *Excuse me* is meant as an apology instead of as an attention-getting device? Speech acts meet certain conditions. You have to know the preconditions of the act and the interactional goals of the speaker. For example, an apology would take place if the speaker believes some wrong has been done that affected another person who deserves an apology. The apologizer must also believe he or she is responsible. The interactional goal is to make amends, to smooth out the relationship.

Speech acts can be taught, rather easily in some cases, to students of foreign languages. In fact, some have organized the foreign language syllabus around the teaching of speech acts. In one study of teaching speech acts, researchers gave questionnaires to native speakers of English and native speakers of Hebrew studying English. These questionnaires asked what the students would say in a number of contexts. The researchers constructed materials targeting the problem areas in **cross-cultural communication** (the culturally inappropriate answers to the questionnaires) and then used the materials in three short lessons (Holmes 1989). They gave the students the questionnaires again. The students used more culturally appropriate strategies after being taught.

Apologies

Apologies have been widely studied as speech acts. The set of realizations for the speech act of apologizing consists of the following:

1. An expression of apology: this uses words such as *apologize, excuse, be sorry, forgive (I'm really sorry I'm late.)*

2. An explanation of the situation *(I ran out of gas.)*

3. Acknowledgment of responsibility *(I should have checked the gauge.)*

4. Offer of repair *(Can we meet later?)*

5. Promise of nonrecurrence *(This won't happen again.)*

Not all of these moves are made in each apology. Their use depends on the severity of the offense and on cross-cultural uses of speech acts. The elaborateness of apologies tends to decrease with intimacy: the closer you are to someone, the more likely it is you'll just say *Sorry*.

There are gender differences and cross-cultural differences in the use of speech acts. In one study, women used more apologies than men, apologized to women more than to men, and focused their comments on the offended/ hearer. Men apologized less overall, apologized to women more than to other men, and focused their comments on the offender/speaker. Another study found a cross-cultural difference in native speakers of English and Italian, with English speakers tending to prefer *hearer-supported strategies* such as admitting their own guilt and offering compensation or redress and Italian speakers preferring *self-supportive strategies* such as providing an explanation and appealing to the interlocutor's leniency.

Requests

Familiarity and social distance are important factors in the choice of request strategies. Hints, for example, can be used by close friends, while "needs statements" *(This has to go out by 5:00)* are used by superiors in business situations and by parents to children. Other types of requests are imperatives *(Hand me the remote)* and embedded imperatives *(Could you hand me the remote?)*.

Compliments

In American English **compliments** follow one of a handful of syntactic patterns. Five adjectives are used in most compliments: *nice, good, beautiful, pretty,* and *great*. Eighty-five percent of the compliments of one corpus (Wolfson, 1989) studied followed one of the three following patterns:

- Noun phrase *is/looks (really)* adjective:

   Your dress is beautiful.

- *I (really) like/love* noun phrase:

   I really like your dress.

- Pronoun *is (really) (a/an)* adjective + noun phrase:

   That's a beautiful dress.

Cross-cultural misunderstandings can happen over who compliments. There are two basic things that get complimented: abilities and appearance/possessions. In the United States, while anyone is deemed a good judge of appearances or possessions, only someone of higher status is seen as an appropriate judge of someone's ability.

Cooperation and Implicatures

There are some special preconditions that are common to all sentences of all languages and not just to speech acts. One such precondition is that we assume that other speakers are telling the truth. Naturally, we know that this is not always the case and that speakers lie on occasion. However, as a general rule, we assume that speakers are telling the truth and are not trying to deceive us. If we didn't, communicating would be impossible, since we could not trust anything said by the other speakers. Another assumption is that speakers are sticking to the point. Suppose that someone asks you, *What do you think of hip-hop?* The answer, *My sister just graduated from Harvard,* is not to the point and is completely irrelevant to the question. Thus, if we want to communicate, we must stick to the point of what is being said.

Principle of Cooperation

These assumptions are some of the maxims that govern conversations. These are general rules or principles that all speakers follow unconsciously. Taken together, they form the **principle of cooperation (CP),** which states roughly that a speaker's conversation should be as effective and cooperative as possible. The principle is based on four maxims:

- The maxim of **quality**

  Do not say what you believe to be false.
  Do not say that for which you lack adequate evidence.

- The maxim of **relevance**

  Be relevant!

- The maxim of **quantity**

  Make your contribution as informative as is required.
  Do not make your contribution more informative than is required.

- The maxim of **manner**

  Avoid obscurity of expression.
  Avoid ambiguity.
  Be brief.
  Be orderly.

When we do not follow the principle of cooperation, we either lie, joke, or playact. Not following the CP can also result in awkward or failed communication. For example, a speaker who is obscure, unclear, or ambiguous runs the risk of being misunderstood.

Flouting

A special case of not following the CP is flouting one of the maxims. In this case one violates a maxim but does so openly and salvages the commitment to the CP by following another maxim. For example, if two students meet outside of class and one asks, *What time is it?* and the other answers *The bell hasn't rung yet*, on the surface it may seem as if he or she is not answering to the point of the question. However, the first student can see that, given the context (outside of a classroom), the second student knows that the first one knows that a bell is going to ring to signal the beginning and the end of classes, and that this information is enough for him or her to figure out roughly what time it is. This is a kind of violation on the surface of a maxim, while one is following the CP, i.e., **flouting** the CP. The meaning that we derive from flouting is called an **implicature.** In this case, the implicature is that it is a little before class time.

Flouting is very important in figurative language, such as metaphors. For example, *Joe is a stick.* Literally this is false, since Joe is a human being, and thus this sentence violates the maxim of quality. However, we understand that this is a metaphor and that there is a relevant sense in which Joe has some of the properties of sticks, namely being thin, and therefore we can reconstruct that the intended meaning was that Joe is thin, which makes sense and is (let's assume) true. On metaphors, see also 14.1.2. Irony is another example of flouting (often of the maxim of quality).

Presuppositions, Inferences, and Implicatures

Among the preconditions that hold for a sentence, there are some aspects of the meaning of a sentence that have particular significance. In what follows we will try to tell them apart. Consider the following example:

(3.9) Mary won the game.

This sentence presupposes that there was a game (since one cannot win a game if there was no game; consider the nonsensical nature of the sentence *Mary won the game although there was no game*), furthermore, it presupposes that there was a Mary to do the winning (once more, consider the oddness of *Mary won the game, although she does not exist*). If Mary won the game, it follows that she defeated some opponent (or at least that the opponent forfeited the game, for example, by not showing up), or that Mary did not lose the game. Moreover, if Mary won the game, it is likely that she was better at it than her opponent and presumably that she's good at it.

Can we disentangle this jumble of "meanings" that surround sentence (3.9)? We begin by noticing that some facets of meaning follow necessarily from sentence (3.9), while others do not: for example, that Mary exists, or that Mary did not lose the game are necessary consequences of sentence (3.9). Conversely, that Mary was better at the game than her opponent is not necessarily true: Mary could have had a stroke of luck, or perhaps Mary bribed her opponent, who then threw the game. This tells us that the conclusion that Mary was better at the game than her opponent, or for that matter, that Mary is good at the game in absolute terms (i.e., regardless of her opponent) are merely a matter of probability, i.e., they are highly likely but not necessary conclusions, given sentence (3.9). This is the mark of implicatures: implicatures are never 100 percent certain (in fact, an implicature can always be canceled: *Mary won the game although her opponent was better at it* is a perfectly logical sentence).

We can further distinguish between those conclusions that follow from the sentence being true (*Mary did not lose the game* follows only if *Mary won the game* is true, otherwise it does not follow) from those in which the sentence's truth does not matter (*There was a game* is necessarily true whether Mary won it or lost it). We can therefore say that this last set of conclusions "resists the negation test" (i.e., is necessarily true regardless of the truth or falsehood of the sentence).

We are now in the position of being able to discriminate among all the facets of meaning surrounding the sentence in (3.9): if a conclusion follows only probabilistically, it is an implicature; if a conclusion follows necessarily from a sentence pending its truth, it is an inference; if a conclusion follows from a sentence regardless of whether it is true or false, it is a presupposition.

A **presupposition** is the set of sentences that must be true for the sentence to be true or false. Example: *John is married* presupposes:

- that John exists

- that John is above the legal age for contracting marriage

- that John meets all other requirements for contracting marriage in his society (e.g., John is not a rabbit)

An **inference** is what can be deduced from the sentence's literal meaning. If I say *John is a bachelor,* it follows that John is not married. This is an inference. We can infer from the fact that he is a bachelor that he is not married. Another way to express the same thing is to say that being a bachelor implies being unmarried.

The difference between inference and presupposition is rather subtle. Consider the following examples:

(3.10) Mary has more than one PhD.

(3.11) Mary does not have more than one PhD.

(3.12) Mary has at least two PhD's.

(3.13) Mary exists.

(3.14) Mary has a PhD.

Sentence (3.10) presupposes (3.13) and (3.14); sentence (3.11), which is the negation of (3.10), also presupposes (3.13) and (3.14) but does not imply (3.12). Hence, presuppositions are said to resist negation, while inferences do not. In other words, if you deny a statement, the inferences will change, while the presuppositions will remain the same.

An **implicature,** as we saw previously, is an inference that does not come strictly from the meaning of the sentence but from what we know about the world and how we communicate. For example, from *John and Mary are married* we can draw the implicature that they are living together or that they like one another (as we know implicatures are always sure only to a degree).

Educational Implications

Knowledge of semantics and pragmatics is especially useful for teachers because such knowledge provides a foundation for understanding communication (and miscommunication) in the classroom.

3.3 EXERCISES

3.3.1 Words to Know

meaning	referent	sign
signifier	signified	semantic feature
lexicon	metaphor	metonymy
synonym	antonym	denotation
intension	connotation	affective connotation
collocative connotation	social connotation	reflected connotation
individual connotation	coded connotation	restricted connotation
homonym	disambiguation	polysemy
truth-value	mental representation	deictics
context	encyclopedic knowledge	frame/script
speech act	maxim	deixis
flouting	implicature	irony
utterance	idiom	presupposition
inference	arbitrariness	cooperative principle
locutionary act	illocutionary act	perlocutionary act
performative	ambiguity	

3.3.2 Review

1. Why do we say that languages are arbitrary?

2. What are the connotations of *terrorist* and *freedom fighter?*

3. Why do we think of bacon when someone says *eggs?*

4. How do we know that *bank* in *I'm broke; I need to go to the bank* means a financial institution and not the side of a river?

5. Why is *Fish* an inappropriate response to *How many surrealists does it take to screw in a light bulb?* Or isn't it inappropriate?

6. How do we know whether *You think like a Californian* is an insult or not?

7. What are the presuppositions of *John married a Californian?*

8. What is an inference of *John is a bachelor?*

9. What is the implicature of *John and Mary are married?*

10. What are the four maxims on which the cooperative principle is based?

11. What are the locutionary, illocutionary, and perlocutionary acts of *It's hot in here?*

12. What are three ways you realize the speech act set for apologizing?

3.3.3 Research Project

1. Pick 10–15 common words and provide connotations (affective, collocative, social, reflected, individual, and coded) for each.

2. Look at the set of realizations for the speech act of apologies. Now think of two other speech acts. (For ideas, see the section on categorization of speech acts.) Write down similar sets of realizations for those speech acts. Be sure to include concrete examples.

3.4 FURTHER READINGS

On semantics, the best introduction remains Lyons (1977b). The section on connotation owes a lot to Leech (1974). There are several general introductions to pragmatics: a classic is Levinson (1983), more current are Green (1989) and Mey (1993), but all three are fairly technical. More accessible are Grundy (1995), Thomas (1995), and LoCastro (2003).

On signifier, signified, and arbitrariness, Saussure's (1983) course is the classic. On feature analysis of semantics, Lyons' (1977b) treatment is good. Cruse (1986) is more advanced but very thorough. On meaning relationships, see Lyons (1977a). On disambiguation, Katz and Fodor (1963) is too difficult for beginners, but any introductory textbook to linguistics will have a section easy enough to handle. On deixis, see Fillmore (1997). On frames and scripts, see Raskin (1985), Chapter 3. On speech acts, Austin (1962) is accessible; Searle (1969) is a bit less accessible, but it is a classic.

On the principle of cooperation, any of the introductions to pragmatics has a discussion of this central topic. Mey's (1993) is very good. Levinson (1983) is excellent and covers presuppositions as well, but it is challenging.

Wolfson (1989) provides an excellent discussion of speech acts, including an illuminating discussion of compliments. On the speech acts of apologies, see Cohen and Olshtain (1981). On women's and men's apologies, see Holmes (1989). On Italian/English cross-cultural differences, see Frescura (1984), and, on compliments, see Wolfson (1989).

Chapter 4

Sociolinguistics

In the late 1950s, as Noam Chomsky's program began to build up momentum (see Chapter 3), some linguists took note of all that the linguistics of the day overlooked. Rather than competence, they said, we need to take account of performance. Joshua Fishman wanted to know "who speaks what language to whom to what end?" Charles Frake said that just knowing the grammar of a language was not enough. Those who want to know a language need "a specification of what kinds of things to say in what message forms to what kinds of people in what kinds of situations." These are the sorts of questions Dell Hymes wanted to answer as part of a definition of **communicative competence.** This chapter will deal then with three questions: What do we say? How do we say things? Whom do we speak to?

4.1 WHAT DO WE SAY?

How do people arrive at common understandings? We have tended to see **communication** according to the "conduit metaphor." This widespread metaphor sees communication as the passage of thoughts, which are seen as concrete, through a conduit (say, speech), from a sender to a receiver (speaker and hearer, respectively). So we speak of *having an idea, giving someone an idea,* or of *stealing* one. We speak of *putting ideas in* someone's mind, of *getting* or *giving* the general idea of a speech or book. This is fine as far as it goes, but this metaphor has a basic flaw: it sees communication as the transfer of a formed thought from one mind to another, which is obviously impossible.

Communication is not only transmission, it's an act of construction. We need to know the context of the conversation and who the participants are to fully describe what is going on. Paradoxically, the interaction creates and also changes the message. There have been a number of ways to describe the interaction that happens when people speak to each other. Indeed, two of the pioneers of sociolinguistics, John Gumperz and Dell Hymes, spent much time describing some of the communicative "rules" we know as native speakers of a language. These rules are not grammatical rules, but rules of interaction in continuous speech or "discourse." Before we begin, take a look at this exchange.

(4.1)   Mary: Hi John, how are you?
        John: Fine, Mary. Going to Stan's party?
        Mary: Gotta work.
        John: Know what you mean.

Describe what you see going on as far as interaction is concerned.

You might have mentioned that in North American culture, we expect a person to reply *Fine* when asked *How are you?* A response detailing our hay fever—or at least a long, detailed response—is probably not what our friend wants to hear. In fact, some people under some conditions would not even answer the question, but would instead greet the other person. You might have seen the conversation as two pairs of exchanges, A and B, or you might have seen it as one unit. You might have said that John's question about Mary's going to the party was a real question, or you could have seen it as "something to talk about." These sorts of issues are central to analyzing talk. **Interactional sociolinguistics** is a rather broad field that centers on the interplay among speakers (interlocutors).

Interactional sociolinguistics uses a number of the tools and ideas we learned in Chapters 2 and 3. Prominent among these ideas are adjacency pairs and turn taking. As you will recall, an **adjacency pair** consists of two utterances that cannot be interpreted without each other (see 2.6.2). **Turn taking** is the process by which speakers negotiate who is to speak next (see 2.6.2). Sometimes, people talk all at once and nobody seems to "have the floor." "Having the floor" (see 2.6.2) is a concept used to describe who is controlling the conversation. This tends to be the person who is doing the talking at any given time, but there can be several floors going on at once and a person can have the floor without speaking. For example, if you can influence the choice of topic of conversation, although you may not be speaking, you still "have the floor."

Another example of conversational rules is **contextualization cues** that we give each other in speech; these are signals using intonation, word choice, or speed of speech. We know, for example, that a certain intonation signals we are joking because of our background knowledge or **contextual presuppositions.** When groups do not share contextual presuppositions, there may be misunderstandings. This can, and does, happen frequently in schools when children from other cultures come with one set of contextualization cues and presuppositions and the teacher has another. For example, Native American children may seem shy and even uninterested to Anglo teachers because silence is valued in most Native American cultures. Hawaiian children may work better in groups than alone; their culture values cooperation (Tharp and Gallimore 1988). Contextualization cues and presuppositions are aspects of our communicative competence.

We use our communicative competence within our speech community. A **speech community,** in Hymes's words, "is defined as a community sharing rules for the conduct and interpretation of speech, and rules for the interpretation of at least one linguistic variety"(1986, 54). A speech community may then have more than one language, and people may be part of more than one speech community. The linguist Neustupny has differentiated between a **language area** (Sprachbund) and a **speech area** (Sprechbund). A language area is a place where a common language is spoken, while across a speech area, people may well not share a language but may share rules for speaking. They may agree on what sorts of questions are appropriate and how to address strangers. One example of a speech area is central Europe. Germany, Hungary, and the Czech Republic share a number of speech rules, such as greetings and acceptable topics of conversation, though different languages are spoken in each country.

4.2 HOW DO WE SAY THINGS?

4.2.1 Face

An important part of interaction is the idea of **face.** Face can be defined as the image of oneself that a speaker presents to others. Think of the expression *to lose face;* that is the meaning of face in this context. If you lose face, then the image you had been projecting to others is damaged (i.e., you don't look as good, smart, or sophisticated as you'd hoped.)

We distinguish between positive and negative face. **Negative face** is the desire to be left alone, not to be imposed upon, and to be able to act as we please. **Positive face** is building someone's ego, the desire to be liked. Some aspects of negative face are apologies and deference. We know people want not to be imposed upon, so if we bother them, we apologize. Some aspects of positive face are compliments and showing interest. People want to be liked and feel important, so we tend to these needs. People are more polite when the threat to face is great. Of course, they are also polite to people of higher status and to those who are socially distant (those they do not know very well).

Brown and Levinson talk about face as part of a universal theory of politeness: to a large extent politeness can be seen as a tool to save face, both for the speaker and for the hearer. Consider this situation: if you ask someone for a favor and he or she turns you down, you have lost face (since your hearer was not willing to do as you wanted); moreover, your hearer has also lost face by appearing selfish or ungenerous. Thus, to avoid this potentially embarrassing, if not disastrous, situation, when you ask for a favor, you do so politely. **Politeness,** in this case, consists of building into your request ways out for the hearer. In other words, you allow the hearer a chance to refuse the favor without having to lose face. This is accomplished, for example, by providing the hearer with a ready-made excuse to refuse. Consider the following example:

(4.2) I know you are a very busy woman, but could you find a minute to look at this proposal?

Here, not only is the speaker providing the hearer with an excuse to refuse the favor *(you are busy),* but the speaker is also minimizing the imposition *(find a minute).*

4.2.2 Forms of Address

Forms of address are an important and very frequent form of **social deixis** (see 3.2.1). Choice of form of address is also influenced by such aspects of interaction as familiarity, solidarity, and respect.

In the United States, people are usually either on a first name basis or they use a person's title and last name (for example, Dr. Smith). The two choices are abbreviated as **FN** (first name) and **TLN** (title, last name), respectively. The choice of form of address is governed by a number of factors. Let us consider a few examples to get an idea of the breadth of variation involved. In the United States, if two adults have just been formally introduced, they are likely to use TLN mutually. However, after only a few minutes of casual conversation, the TLN frequently changes to a mutual FN. Among younger people, there is a tendency to use only FN. There are also situations where the use of FN is unlikely: think of your doctor; chances are that you address her or him as TLN, unless there happens to be a special friendship between the two of you.

Social Conventions Governing FN and TLN

In the United States, the patterns that govern the use of FN and TLN are usually based on age, occupation, gender, and class. Generally, the younger person will address the older person by TLN and will be called by FN in return. An interesting pattern is that parents, when they want to indicate displeasure with a child's behavior, will often address the child by his or her full name *(Gaia Christine Attardo, come here this moment!)* to indicate (temporary) lack of intimacy.

Occupational status operates in a similar manner; the person with the higher occupational status is addressed by TLN and addresses the person with the lower occupational status by FN. It is important to remember that this is not always age related. For example, in a restaurant even a server much older than the patrons will be referred to by FN and the patrons will expect to be referred to as *Ma'am* or *Sir,* or at least by some polite form of address. In business situations in which the boss is younger than many of the employees, the boss will still be referred to by TLN and he or she will address the employees by FN. The employees cannot alter the use of TLN unless instructed to do so. This pattern is changing, however, and informality and consequent use of FN is increasing in business encounters.

Gender is no longer a socially acceptable determinant for forms of address, but men are in fact called by TLN more often than women. Furthermore, women often receive FN in return.

Class status plays a part in how people are addressed; the person of the higher-class status is called by TLN and uses FN to the person of lower-class status. As a general rule, TLN is used to mark formality or politeness while FN indicates casualness or intimacy.

An interesting fact is that two persons may use different forms of address depending on the situation. For example, colleagues in offices or schools are often on an FN basis among each other but will switch to TLN in public, when other people (such as clients or students) are involved. For example, a professor may call his department chair *Linda* when they are talking privately or with other colleagues but address her as *Dr. Smith* in front of a student.

Formal vs. Informal Personal Pronouns

When it comes to choosing the pronoun with which to refer to someone, the English language does not have the same dilemma as many other languages. There is now only one form of *you* in English, but in French, German, Italian, and in many other languages there is a formal *you* and an informal *you*. These are called **T and V pronouns.** The T is from *tu,* the Latin for you singular (also considered informal), and the V is from the Latin *vos,* or you plural (formal). The use of T and V pronouns today follows a similar pattern to that of FN and TLN in English.

The Development of T and V Pronouns

The manner in which T and V pronouns are used has varied a great deal through the centuries. In medieval Europe people belonging to the same class used reciprocal pronouns. Equals from the upper class used V pronouns with each other while members of the lower class used T pronouns with each other. From this followed people from the lower class addressing the higher classes with the V pronoun and receiving T in return. Families often used T and V pronouns as well; of course, the children were addressed by T and the adults were addressed by V at all times.

Pronouns of Power

A nonreciprocal use of T and V pronouns indicates unequal power. **Power** is indicated by many different things such as usage, wealth, profession, sex, and even strength. The person in power is always the one to determine which pronoun will be used. If the person of lower status attempts to use the informal, or intimate, pronoun without having been instructed to do so, he or she will receive the V pronoun in response. This is a clear remonstration and shows that the distance between the speakers is to be maintained. The division between T and V remained strict well into the 19th century. This meant that employees, servers, and children were called T, while employers, patrons, and parents were called V. Then there was a move away from these **pronouns of power** to pronouns that indicated solidarity.

Pronouns of Solidarity

The move to **pronouns of solidarity** meant that there was a more widespread use of T pronouns. The T pronoun was used to show a feeling of equality. Some countries that have made a conscious change to the use of T pronouns are Sweden, China, and Russia.

Solidarity in China

The change in the Chinese language is particularly interesting because it was caused by political change. After the Revolution of 1949, the Chinese stopped using their form of the V pronoun to mark higher status. Instead the word *comrade* became very popular because it was a term used by revolutionaries. (In fact, the term had been used by both sides in the war between the communists and nationalists.)

Indeed, *comrade* shows how changes in word meanings often follow changes in society. A standard Chinese dictionary in 1936 defined *comrade* as the term for individuals with the same beliefs. In 1965, the dictionary defined the term as applying to members of the same political party, who presumably shared beliefs. In 1979, *comrade* was defined as the appropriate general term of address for China's citizens. In the 1999 edition of the dictionary, the term was no longer defined as the preferred general term of address. The word fell out of favor because it is so strongly associated with the Cultural Revolution, which is now criticized as having been too radical a movement. *Comrade* is used in contemporary China as a euphemism for *gay* or *lesbian*. Older Chinese terms of address such as *Master Worker* (used to address a worker who is unknown to you), *Sir,* and *Madam* have replaced *comrade*.

Use of V Pronoun Today

In many societies the V pronoun is looked upon negatively today and is even considered somewhat insulting. One reason for this is that the V pronoun is still connected with the higher class, which represents wealth and power. The use of the solidarity pronoun is prevalent today. Some cultures do more than merely differentiate between FN and TLN or the T and V pronoun. The Japanese, for example, use an entire system of honorifics.

Honorifics

In many languages there are several ways to address one's interlocutor. The choice of form of address is regulated by complex rules, for example, in Japanese one would address one of us as

(4.3) Attardo-sama = extremely formal/superior/outsider
Attardo-san = formal/neutral
Attardo-kun = friendly/lower

Clearly, the acceptability of these forms, called **honorifics,** will vary drastically with the context.

Honorifics can be prefixes, suffixes, and even infixes. The Japanese use separate markers depending upon what or who is being honored. The first type reflects the higher status of the person being addressed. For example, in the next two sentences the first one is neutral and the second one contains the markers (the honorifics are bolded). Note that HON = honorific.

Yamada ga musuko to syokuzi o tanosinda.
(4.4) yamada   son   and dinner   enjoyed
Yamada and son enjoyed the dinner.

*Yamada-**san** ga musuko-**san** to **o**-syokuzi   o   tanosim-**are**-ta.*
(4.5) yamada-HON   son-HON   and HON-dinner   enjoyed-HON
Yamada and son enjoyed the dinner.

A second type of honorific marker is more indirect; the speaker honors the addressee by "lowering" himself or herself with linguistic markers. In this example *musuko* becomes *gusoku* as a marker of humility. *Gusoku* is a humble word for *son* that deprecates the person being spoken about. Note that HUM = humility marker.

*watashi ga gusoku   to **o**-syokuzi   o tanosim-**are**-ta.*
(4.6) I   HUM-son   HON-dinner   enjoyed-HON.
I and my unworthy son enjoyed the honorable dinner.

Here, because English and Japanese are very different languages, a translation does not really capture the flavor of the original. By translating in this manner, we risk making Japanese seem strange, even archaic. A Japanese reader or hearer of these sentences would understand the humility being conveyed but might not necessarily "translate" the words as we would.

Obviously the Japanese need to have a clear understanding of what the relationship is between the speakers as well as the subject of the sentence. An individual's social status and the culture determine which markers he or she will choose.

Conclusion

The rules governing forms of address are based on cultural considerations, as was shown by the changes in China. In order for a person to be able to speak in a manner that is socially acceptable, he or she must absorb the culture's rules. Most of these rules are absorbed without any conscious training. Forms of address are an important part of behaving correctly within a culture, and native speakers are skilled at using them.

> The use of the general *you* in English releases English-speaking people from the dilemma of choosing between a formal or informal *you*. Does this make the decision to use FN or TLN pointless? Should there be one form of address for everyone? Why or why not?

4.3 WHOM DO WE SPEAK TO?

4.3.1 Language Contact

Of particular linguistic significance are those situations in which more than one language is used by some or all the members of a given community. These situations are covered by the broad term of **language contact.** An important fact, which often comes as something of a surprise, is that the majority of people in the world are in a situation of language contact and, in fact, speak more than one language. Speakers of only one language are called **monolingual,** while speakers of two languages are called **bilingual.** Speakers of many languages are called polyglots or multilinguals.

4.3.2 Bilingualism/Diglossia

When only an individual speaker or a group of speakers happen to be bilingual in an otherwise monolingual community, we speak of bilingualism. However, when the bilingual situation extends to an entire community, we may speak of **diglossia.**

Bilingualism

The fact that speakers may be able to speak more than one language should not surprise us. In fact, even monolingual speakers are to a certain extent bidialectal (or polydialectal), i.e., have mastered different varieties or dialects of their native language. Studies have shown that children as young as two or three years old can adjust their register according to whether they are speaking to an adult, to a peer, or to a younger child.

Four central issues around bilingualism are time of acquisition of the languages, representation and storage of the languages, extent of the balance between the languages, and relative status of the languages.

Simultaneous vs. Sequential Bilingualism

Are the two languages learned at the same time, or are they acquired one after the other in childhood? If the languages are learned at the same time, for example, by the mother speaking one language and the father the other, the child is said to have acquired simultaneous bilingualism. If the child first acquires one language, then the other, the child is said to have acquired sequential or consecutive bilingualism. Some researchers differentiate between childhood bilingualism and adolescent or adult bilingualism. The first process follows a path similar to the one a child follows in learning one first language while the second follows a different path (see Chapter 13).

Coordinate vs. Compound Bilingualism

An early theory of bilingualism claimed that individual bilingual people might store word meanings in the brain (and by implication have them available for use) in two different ways. A **compound bilingual** would have two words but one unified meaning for a concept. The words *dog* and *chien* (French for *dog*) would generate the same meaning for that person. A **coordinate bilingual** would have slightly different mental representations for the two individual words. Practically speaking, foreign language learners are often coordinate bilinguals. There are problems with this distinction as a model of bilingualism, but the labels are often used in studies of vocabulary learning.

Balanced Bilingualism

A very controversial issue is whether there exist speakers who are equally fluent in two (or more) languages and are therefore **balanced bilinguals.** This is very hard to answer, although it is clear there is a continuum of bilingualism, starting at one extreme with a person who is merely learning a few words to be able to communicate with a cab driver and gradually building up, to the individual who was brought up speaking two or more languages and who is equally fluent in either in reading, writing, listening, and speaking in all registers and in all situations. When a speaker is more comfortable in one language, that language is said to be **dominant.**

Additive vs. Subtractive Bilingualism

In general, studies have shown that the acquisition of bilingualism has a positive effect on children. However, we must distinguish between additive bilingualism, in which a second language is added with no thought of replacing the first language, and subtractive bilingualism, in which the attempt is to replace the first language with the second. Greater cognitive benefits have been found for additive bilingualism.

Diglossia

A diglossic situation occurs when an entire community has two or more varieties of language at its disposal and the languages are arranged along a scale, so that we have a high and a low variety. This is true for example in the Arab world, where classical Arabic, the language of the Quran, is the variety of culture and learned interaction, whereas the local variety (e.g., Lebanese Arabic, Tunisian Arabic, Egyptian Arabic, and so on) is the variety used for everyday interaction. See 9.1.3 for more on diglossia.

4.3.3 Language Planning

Usually, when bilingualism and/or diglossia take place, one of the two languages is "under attack" by the other. What we mean is that one of the two languages is perceived by the younger members of the community as more attractive (financially, socially, or in other ways) than the other. In a situation like this, bilingualism is usually the first step toward **language shift,** i.e., the process whereby a group of people will move from one language to another. If the entire community which speaks a given language shifts to another, the original language may face **language death.** When the last native speaker of a language dies, that language is dead, just like Latin or Greek. Language death is an all too real threat for many of the Native American languages, the Aboriginal languages of Australia, and the Celtic languages of Europe (Irish, Breton). On the retreat of the Celtic languages in the face of the Anglo-Saxon invaders in England, see 17.2.

However, a community may fight language death by setting up a campaign of **language maintenance,** for instance by declaring a language the **official language** of the region, teaching it in the schools, and promoting its use in cultural and artistic events. Many successful instances of language maintenance have been recorded, for example, Basque in Spain. Any such planned activities aiming at affecting the language a community speaks, either locally or nationally, fall under the banner of **language planning.** Language planning may range from the choice of textbooks in the local high school to laws forbidding the use of a language or making a language the official language of a state. On language planning, see Chapter 9.

4.3.4 Code Switching

When speakers are bilingual, they seldom segregate the two languages absolutely. When they mix the two languages, we speak of **code switching,** i.e., the alternation between two different languages, dialects, or styles within one sentence or indeed within a conversation. The reasons people code switch are complex, but it is often the case that people use a particular language or dialect to announce their identity. For example, a regional or social dialect may be considered friendlier than a standard language. Two people talking may switch from the standard language to the dialect to affirm their friendship.

Teachers who teach English as a foreign language often have students who all speak the same first language. If the teacher shares that language with the students, it may be used instead of English, the object of study, to organize the classroom, to provide explanations of difficult words, or to create a sense of solidarity and warmth. This use of two languages in the same discourse may be frowned upon by the principal or school board because it seems disorderly, but in fact it models the way many bilinguals use their two languages in the real world.

Numerous newspaper articles have commented on the rise of "Spanglish" in the United States. Spanglish is simply Spanish-English code switching. Often, Spanish words are inserted in English sentences and vice versa. Sometimes, especially in the case of verbs, Spanish morphology is added to English words, such as in the word *nerdear,* to act like a nerd. Ilan Stavans has collected a number of Spanglish words and offers this translation of the first sentence of *Don Quixote:*

> In un placete de La Mancha of which nombre no quiero remembrearme, vivía not so long ago, uno de esos gentlemen who always tienen una lanza in the rack, una buckler antigua, a skinny caballo y un geyhound para el chase.

or, in English:

> In a village of La Mancha, the name of which I don't care to remember, there lived not so long ago one of those gentlemen that always keep a lance in the rack, an old shield, a skinny horse, and a greyhound for the chase.

Educational Implications
This chapter, like Chapter 3, has addressed the bases for communication, enabling a better understanding of what goes on in interactions.

4.4 EXERCISES

4.4.1 Words to Know

sociolinguistics	interactional sociolinguistics	communication
positive face	adjacency pair	face
language contact	negative face	code switching
diglossia	monolingual	bilingual
language planning	language shift	language death
additive bilingualism	language maintenance	turn taking
contextual presupposition	subtractive bilingualism	contextualization cue
coordinate bilingualism	speech community	language area
dominant language	compound bilingualism	balanced bilingualism
pronouns of solidarity	T and V pronouns	honorifics
speech area	pronouns of power	communicative competence
FN	TLN	

4.4.2 Review

1. Why is knowing only the grammar rules of a language not enough to speak it?

2. Why do people code switch?

3. What is diglossia?

4. Do you believe that the manner in which you choose to address someone is based on your sense of power?

5. The introduction of the term *comrade* in China instead of using other titles was intended to create a feeling of equality. Did this work? Why or why not?

6. Obviously terms of address have been of great importance to every language since most countries have at some point made an effort to change the use of the terms. Why are they of such importance?

7. Define honorifics and explain how the system is used and what language uses it.

8. How are T and V pronouns considered pronouns of power and solidarity?

9. Explain the patterns for the use of FN and TLN in the United States.

4.4.3 Research Projects

1. Write a short narrative based on the following situation. Suppose you were hired as an assistant in a company. You, of course, call all of your superiors by TLN. After working there for some time you are promoted to a position in upper-level management. How would you deal with the transition of suddenly having to treat your former superiors as equal while your former coworkers are now to treat you more formally? What forms of address would you use and expect to receive?

2 Find a bilingual speaker (you may be one yourself!) and prepare a set of questions, trying to elicit the contexts in which he or she uses both languages. Do you find a pattern?

3. If you have access to a bilingual community (a family, a group of friends, a market, and so on), tape a conversation and search for cases of code switching. Try to explain why the speakers may have switched in each instance. Do not worry if you cannot classify all cases. (If you yourself are not bilingual, you may have to ask for someone else's help in taping the conversation, as your being part of it may limit the instances of code switching.)

4.5 FURTHER READINGS

Good introductions to sociolinguistics are Trudgill (2000), Fasold (1990), and Wardhaugh (2002). An excellent anthology of important articles is Paulston and Tucker (2003). Useful very early collections of articles are Giglioli (1972) and Gumperz and Hymes (1986). Fishman, Frake, Gumperz, and Hymes are all found in Giglioli (1972) and in Gumperz and Hymes (1972). The conduit metaphor is discussed in Reddy (1979). An introduction is Saville-Troike (1989).

Neustupny (1970) is an outline of his theory on speech and language areas. Brown and Levinson (1987) is the classic account of face and politeness. The classic article on pronouns of power and solidarity is Brown and Gilman (1960), reprinted in Giglioli (1972). Paulston's (1976) work on Swedish pronouns in flux is a widely quoted piece of research on language change. For China, see Fang and Heng (1983). The examples for Japanese honorifics are from Yamanashi (1974).

Edwards (1994) is a good introduction to multilingualism. Romaine (1995) is a good introduction to bilingualism, as are Grosjean (1982) and Hamers and Blanc (2000). Wei (2000) is a very useful collection of classic articles on bilingualism. Ferguson coined the term *diglossia*. His article is reprinted in Giglioli (1972). For Native American and Hawaiian children, see Tharp and Gallimore (1988).

For language maintenance, shift, and death, see Fishman (1992), Dressler (1988), Paulston (1994), Dressler and Wodak-Leodolter (1977), and Dorian (1981). More recent books on endangered languages and language death are Nettle and Romaine (2000) and Crystal (2000). Stavans (2003) offers a brief introduction to Spanglish as well as a significant dictionary of Spanglish.

Chapter 5

Language Variation

5.1 LANGUAGE AND DIALECT

Do you live in a part of the country where people have a distinctive way of speaking? How would you describe it?

Most people think their way of speaking is natural, the best way, perhaps the only way. It's other people who "talk funny." Language attitudes are powerful things. We are likely to make judgments of people based on what they say and sometimes, most importantly, how they say it. Think of the stereotype of the southern North American White male "Bubba" who speaks in a drawl. Many people hear the voice, and, without even having met the person, think him probably stupid and even racist, even though he is likely neither. Similarly, we have stereotypes of the brash speaker of Brooklynese or the Valley Girls of California. These people have an accent, we say. When we hear someone talking using a different pronunciation but the same words we would have used, we say that that person has an accent. Note that it's always someone else who has an accent! In this chapter, we will discuss geographical dialects, and in Chapter 6 we will discuss social dialects.

Accent is one aspect of **dialect.** Dialect is a variety of language that may certainly include accent, but dialect also may be defined through its vocabulary; that large item in your living room may be a *sofa, couch, davenport, chesterfield,* or *divan.* People say *pop, soda,* or *coke* depending on where they live. Grammar is another aspect of dialect. The *y'all* of the South, the *youse* of the Bronx, and the *yunz* of Pittsburgh are attempts to give English a second person plural.

Everyone has a dialect, despite the language he or she speaks. What are the differences between **language** and dialect? It's frequently said that a language is a dialect with an army and a navy. There is considerable truth in that. There is never a good way to differentiate between language and dialect. The largest difference between a language and a dialect is that a language is spoken in a state that has chosen to give it some power. Dialects become languages for political and social reasons, not for linguistic ones.

Trudgill's notion of **autonomy** (independence) versus **heteronomy** (dependence) is helpful here. German and Dutch are considered autonomous languages and the various dialects of both heteronomous. Autonomous languages are languages that have been politically defined as different, whereas heteronomous languages are languages/dialects that have been defined as falling under a common language. Autonomous languages are independent of each other: they have different models and different political, cultural, and economic centers of prestige. Heteronomous languages, on the contrary, look to the same centers of prestige, perhaps to a capital or to a national academy.

It is important to note that heteronomous language/dialects may be full-fledged languages of their own. Consider the linguistic situation of Italy, where the many regional "dialects" of Italian have a literary tradition going back many centuries and, in some cases, were used in legal and political transactions, not to mention being used in the economic arena. However, after the reunification of Italy at the end of the 19th century, Italian (actually the dialect of Tuscany) was chosen for political reasons (as well as literary prestige, since it was the dialect of Dante, Petrarch, and Boccaccio) as the standard language. It was felt that a national language was needed in part because languages such as Sicilian and Milanese were mutually unintelligible; that is, speakers of Sicilian and Milanese could not readily have a conversation. (Things have changed lately, due to the influence of the mass media, and now dialects are dying out all over Italy and are being replaced by regional varieties that are mutually intelligible.) Thus, it was a political decision dictated by the needs of the new unified Italian state that made Sicilian, Milanese, Roman, and Napolitan all heteronomous languages under the umbrella of Italian.

Variation tends to lie along a continuum, i.e., there is a gradual passage from one dialect to the other. This is called a **dialect continuum.** Usually, linguists in creole studies (see 7.4.2) distinguish three basic levels, which also apply here:

- **acrolect:** the most prestigious form, used in formal situations, by educated speakers, often of the upper classes

- **mesolect:** an intermediate variety, used in less formal situations, by a majority of speakers, from all classes

- **basilect:** the low variety, used in most informal situations, by the least educated speakers, often from the lower classes

Moreover, people slide up or down the scale, depending on the situation. This is an example of code switching (see 4.3.4).

Finally, we must remember that not all speakers speak alike. As a matter of fact, no two speakers speak exactly the same. Each speaker has his or her own individual variety of language, called an **idiolect.**

5.1.1 Dialectology

Dialectology is the study of dialects.

Isoglosses

An **isogloss** is an imaginary line that marks the boundaries of areas where a particular form is used by speakers. One form is used on one side of the line and another form on the other. See Figures 5.1–5.3. This can include features at all linguistic levels:

- phonological, such as [aw] and [ay] becoming [a] in western Pennsylvania (*towel* is pronounced [tal] as is *tile*)

- morphological, such as the plural for the second person pronoun (*y'all, youse, yunz*)

- syntactic, such as the alternation

(5.1) My car needs washed (eastern Ohio and western Pennsylvania)

and

(5.2) My car needs to be washed/needs washing (Standard English)

- semantic, such as the alternation between *pop* (Midwest and western United States), *soda* (eastern United States), and *bottle(d)/cold drinks* (southern United States), as shown in Figure 5.2

Figure 5.1: The Isogloss for "You-All"

Source: Kurath 1949.

Figure 5.2: Areas of Usage of Various Terms for Carbonated Nonalcoholic Beverage

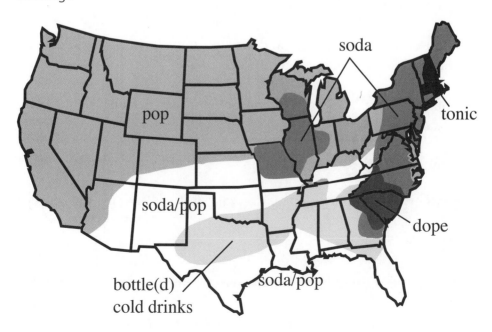

Figure 5.3: Isoglosses for Various Ways of Saying "Aren't" in England (note that area 3 is "ain't")

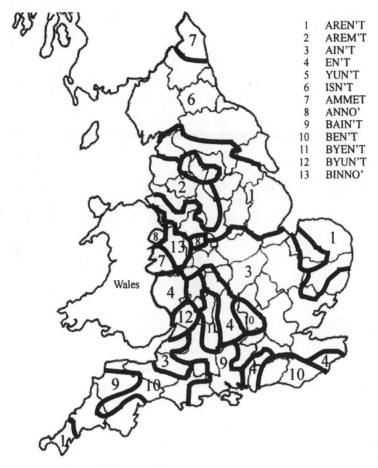

1	AREN'T
2	AREM'T
3	AIN'T
4	EN'T
5	YUN'T
6	ISN'T
7	AMMET
8	ANNO'
9	BAIN'T
10	BEN'T
11	BYEN'T
12	BYUN'T
13	BINNO'

Source: Orton, Sanderson, and Widdowson 1978.

Note that an isogloss represents only a single item. A given isogloss alone does not mark a dialect boundary. However, when many isoglosses surround or separate the same group of people, this indicates that the speech of that group is different in a number of ways from the other groups around it. Therefore, a **bundle of isoglosses** may mark a dialect/ language boundary.

As an example, consider the bundle of isoglosses that separates France into two distinct major dialects (see Figure 5.4), called in medieval times *Langue d'hoc* and *Langue d'oil*, after the way one said "Yes" (*hoc est*, this is [the case]).

Figure 5.4: Langue d'oil (North) and Langue d'hoc (South)

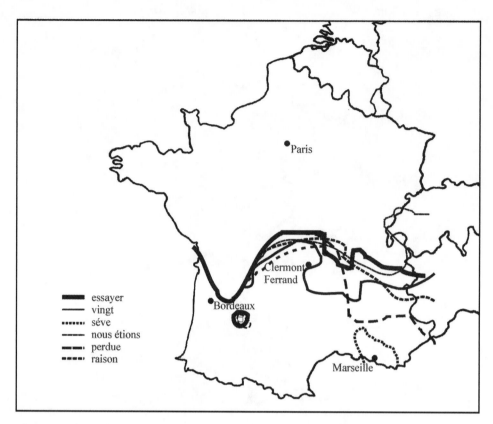

Source: Chambers and Trudgill 1998.

Dialectology of the United States

Up to the 1960s, dialect studies used rural informants almost exclusively. The idea was that regional words tend to stay longest among professions like coal miners, wheat farmers, and tobacco growers in the country. These people have been called **NORM:** nonmobile, older rural males.

These early studies divided the United States into

• North: People here made a distinction between the pronunciation of *horse* and *hoarse* but used the same vowel in *root* and *wood*. A typical grammar feature was the use of *hadn't ought* as a negative.

• Midland: There was no distinction in this area between *horse* and *hoarse*. People characteristically said *warsh* for *wash*. The vowels in *due, new,* and *food* were the same and did not sound like the vowel in *fuel*. Other features were *seen* for *saw, all the further,* and *I'll wait on you.*

- South: This area, like New England, had no [r] after vowels. It also used *might could* and *may can* (African-Americans took these north after World War II).

In the 1960s, there was more effort made to conduct urban (see 6.1.1) as well as rural fieldwork. One thing that this urban fieldwork found was a rise in a number of regionalisms for highways:

- **parkways:** eastern New York, Connecticut, Rhode Island

- **turnpikes:** Pennsylvania, New Jersey, New Hampshire, Massachusetts, Ohio, Indiana

- **thruways:** New York

- **expressways:** Michigan

- **freeways:** California

Despite this, and despite the maintenance of many dialects throughout the country, some linguists theorized the rise of a neutral "Network Standard"' as television became more important in people's lives. Dialect uniformity is fostered by mass media such as radio, television, and newspapers. These mass media have national audiences that go beyond any dialectal region, thereby contributing to a common dialect by providing prestige varieties that people imitate.

The earliest mention of what was later called Network Standard was the adoption of Inland Northern, the dialect from the Great Lakes area, as what was considered in the 1930s "general American." This dialect area is characterized by, among other things, the presence of postvocalic /r/ [kar] versus [ka] (as in some Boston pronunciations) and the pronunciation of *cot* the same as *caught*. Why did this dialect become "standard"? One theory is that the Great Lakes region was a commercial and industrial center and people moved in and out of the area from company headquarters to branch offices, spreading the variety.

Another is that several of the movie stars of the day used this variety. They provided prestige models for speech. Yet another theory, related to the second, is that media pronunciation guides of the time were based on this variety, and radio announcers would have used the guide's recommended pronunciations, providing another prestige model.

Figure 5.5: Dialectal Regions of the United States

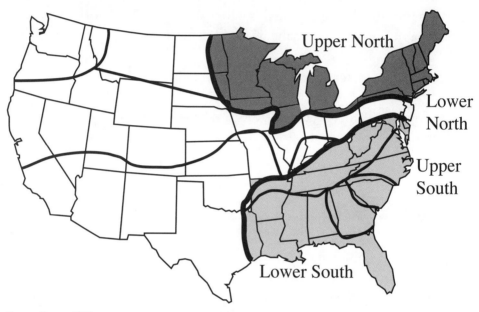

Source: Carver 1987.

Notice that in the western United States, as shown in Figure 5.5, dialect differentiations to some extent disappear; there are no bundles of isoglosses. The farther west you go, roughly after the Mississippi, the differences break up and are lost by the time they reach the Pacific. This took place because of the vast settler migration to the west from so many different parts of the country. Western English developed from a mix of language influences, including English dialects, Scandinavian languages, Spanish, and dialects of North American English. Recent changes occurring in some areas of the West show some dialect differentiation, challenging both the older notion of American dialect boundaries and the notion that dialects are becoming even more homogenous as the culture itself becomes more homogenous.

Recent work by William Labov (1991, 1996) and others has shown that there has been a fairly rapid evolution of sound changes in the urban areas of the United States and Canada. These changes go against the idea that dialects are disappearing. The main changes that are taking place are the following:

- [o]/[ɔ] merger: In the western United States, Canada, and parts of the Midland (western Pennsylvania, Ohio, Indiana, Illinois), there has been the loss of distinction (i.e., a merger) between the two sounds, so that *cot* and *caught* are pronounced alike.

- [ɪn]/[ɛn] merger: In this case, the difference between the words *pin* and *pen* is lost (both are pronounced [pɪn]). This feature was originally southern, but is spreading north and west.

- The "chain shifts": These are broad phenomena that involve many of the vowels of the vowel system of American English. They are similar in scope to the Great Vowel Shift (see 17.4.2). There are southern and northern shifts. The southern shift includes several sound changes, the best known of which is probably the monophtongization of dipthongs, such as [ay] becoming [a] (so that a word like *fight* will be pronounced [fat]). The northern shift takes places primarily in the big industrial cities around Chicago, Celeveland, Detroit, Buffalo, and so forth. It too involves several vowels. An example is the shift from [kod] *(cod)* to [kæd].

The United States is unusual in that it has no major differing dialects. The reason behind this is that the United States is a fairly new country with a short history. Contrast this with areas in Asia or Europe, where populations speaking the same language have lived in a given area for millennia. See for example Figure 5.3, which shows the much richer variety in England.

5.2 THE NOTION OF STANDARD ENGLISH

Many languages are shaped by the presence of national academies that codify the language, make up new words when necessary, rule on dictionary entries, and so on. However, both the United States and Great Britain have resisted the calls for national language academies. Despite this, the status of English as a national language has not been questioned in either country.

Standard languages rose in Europe between the 15th and 19th centuries for a number of reasons. The invention of printing standardized spelling and usage, and as more people attended school with the rise of mass education and learned to read, the standardized forms spread. Standardization was also helped by the sociological and geographic mobility associated with industrialization and urbanism.

In England, beginning in the late 15th century, the East Midlands dialect was widely diffused throughout the country through printing. Standard English in Britain has come to be known as **RP,** or **received pronunciation.** There are now two kinds of RP: an **unmarked,** i.e., normal and unexceptional form used by announcers, teachers, secretaries, and educated people in general, and a **marked** form used by the royal family and aristocracy. Most educated people now keep some part of a regional accent, and commentators have also noted the rise of **Estuary English,** an educated London-based variety.

Braj Kachru has claimed that it makes no sense to speak of a monolithic Standard English (cf. 17.5). He sees English falling into three circles:

- **inner circle:** Great Britain, the United States, Canada, New Zealand, and Australia

- **outer circle:** Bangladesh, Ghana, India, Kenya, Malaysia, Nigeria, Pakistan, the Philippines, Singapore, Sri Lanka, Tanzania, and Zambia

- **expanding circle:** China, Egypt, Indonesia, Israel, Japan, Korea, Nepal, Russia, Saudi Arabia, Taiwan, and Zimbabwe

There are three nonnative speakers of English for every one native speaker, and this is obviously having an effect on the language. Who decides what is "correct" English? What is measured as "standard"? Is it accent, grammar, or pragmatics? Perhaps three-quarters of Indian English speakers use indirect requests such as *Could you close the window?* when trying to speak politely, while the other one-quarter are likely to use something closer to what is appropriate in their other native languages such as *Close the window, please.* This may strike an American English speaker, for instance, as abrupt. Which is correct? Both, actually. Nobody owns English.

Finally, it is useful to remember that because dialects are more than just accent, including grammar and vocabulary as well, it is possible to speak Standard English in any accent.

5.2.1 Why Do Dialects/Accents Persist?

Given the trend to uniformity in everything from television shows to hamburgers, why do some people keep their accents? Part of the answer is **solidarity.** A study of Martha's Vineyard (Massachusetts) showed that young men, who would be expected to speak more "standard," actually spoke in an "old-fashioned" manner of pronunciation to differentiate themselves from the summer visitors to the island. The same phenomenon has happened in Ocracoke, North Carolina, where younger men have retained the pronunciation of [hoy toyd] for *high tide,* for example, to differentiate themselves as "old-timers" from recent arrivals. There may then be **covert prestige** in speaking in older ways. There is covert prestige in forms that normally are considered nonstandard; for example, use of profanity makes one sound "tough" and toughness may be valued in certain groups.

Another answer lies in **accommodation theory,** which says that people adapt their speech to their conversation partner. Their speech may converge to minimize distance or diverge to show distance. In some cases, people maintain their speech style. This may be seen as a form of divergence, depending on their interlocutor. Accommodation theory is based on a number of theories from social psychology, among them similarity attraction theory, which basically says that "Birds of a feather flock together"; social exchange theory, which says that we tend to weigh the costs and benefits of any behavior; and intergroup distinctiveness theory, which says that people make comparisons across groups, look at socially valued factors, and may try to set themselves or their group apart through language or other means.

Attitudes

Perceptions of dialects may ultimately be more important than measurable features. People may hear a particular dialect and form opinions about the speaker based on the dialect alone. One way to measure attitudes toward other dialects or languages is called the **matched-guise** technique. In this technique, a person who speaks two dialects or languages is taped saying the same thing, once in the first dialect and then again in the second. Listeners, who are not told they are hearing the speakers twice, rate speakers on a list of qualities (*This is an intelligent person* or *This is someone I'd like to know*) using a numbered scale. If a person speaking English with a French accent is rated highly in intelligence by other French speakers but not by monolingual English speakers, for example, researchers are given some insight into language attitudes. Of course, researchers need to see this pattern repeated by a significant number of people before they can make any claims about attitudes in the larger community.

Educational Implications
Teachers need an understanding of the regional and social varieties of language in order to more fully respect differences.

5.3 EXERCISES

5.3.1 Words to Know

dialect	idiolect	accent
autonomy	heteronomy	unmarked
isogloss	received pronunciation	inner circle
outer circle	expanding circle	dialect continuum
solidarity	covert prestige	accommodation theory

5.3.2 Review

1. What is the difference between a language and a dialect?

2. In what ways can dialects differ?

3. Why do some people argue that there is no one standard English in the world today?

4. Why do dialects/accents persist?

5.3.3 Research Projects

Dialect Survey

How many words can you think of for these definitions? Work with a partner or partners. Do they have the same words?

1. to put a single room of the house in order = *clean up*

2. paper container for groceries = *bag*

3. device that gives water, found on outside of house or in yard or garden = *hose*

4. window covering on rollers = *blind*

5. large open metal container for scrub water = *tub*

6. web hanging from ceiling of a room = *cobweb*

7. metal utensil for frying = *pan*

8. thing over the sink that gives water = *faucet*

9. vehicle for small baby = *carriage*

10. to—the baby in such a vehicle = *stroll put place*

11. furry stuff that collects under beds or on closet floors = *lint*

12. immediate family =

13. of a child (she/he—her/his mother) = *mom*

14. grass strip in the middle of a divided road = *divider blvd*

15. grass strip between sidewalk and street = *grass strip between*

16. call to hail a taxicab =

17. wet roads are often = *slippery*

18. dog of no special breed =

19. a carbonated drink =

20. large sandwich designed to be a meal in itself =

21. call to passerby to return a ball to the playground =

22. to be absent from school =

23. where swings and play areas are =

24. holds small objects together, might hold a newspaper =

25. someone from the country =

Isoglosses

Try your hand at drawing isoglosses. In Figure 5.6, the empty dot represents /ɔ/, while the black dot represents a special type of /a/. The little "umbrella" represents a tense schwa (wedge).

Figure 5.6: Pronunciation of "Water" in the Eastern United States

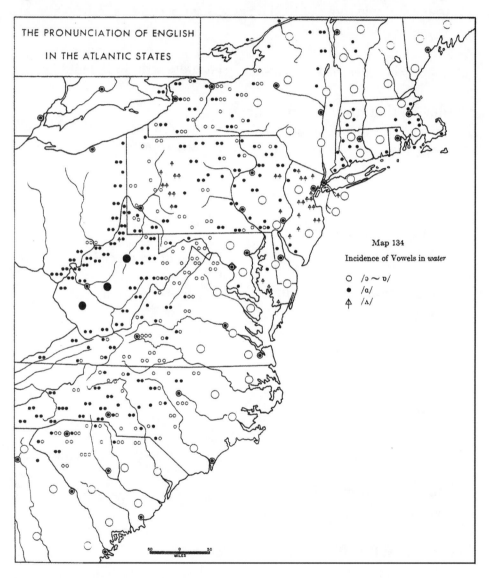

Source: Kurath and McDavid 1961. Courtesy of Virginia G. McDavid.

5.4 FURTHER READINGS

General introductions to dialectology can be found in any introductory text to linguistics. On American dialects, see Carver (1987), Wolfram and Schilling-Estes (1998), and MacNeil and Cran (2005). Lippi-Green (1997) is an excellent look at language attitudes in the United States. On autonomy versus heteronomny, see Trudgill (1995). Kachru (1992) is the standard treatment of the "circles" of English.

On Inland Northern, see Donahue (1993); on Martha's Vineyard, see Labov (1972b). On attitudes toward dialects in Canada, see Gardner (1985). The map of the *y'all* isogloss is taken from Kurath (1949). The map of French dialects is from Chambers and Trudgill (1980, 111). The map of the bundles of isoglosses and the North/Midland/South division of the eastern United States is from McDavid (1979). The English map is from Orton, Sanderson, and Widdowson (1978).

On the linguistic atlases of the United States, see a review in Carver (1987, Chapter 1). There are several collections of essays: a representative one can be found in Allen (1964). More recently, the *Dictionary of American Regional English (DARE)* began to appear in 1985 (Cassidy and Hall). An example of the linguistic atlases developed in the 1950s is Kurath and McDavid (1961).

On language attitudes, see Skehan (1989). Beebe (1988) provides a nice summary of accommodation theory. The dialect survey is adapted from R. W. Shuy (1967). Recent changes in American dialects are described in Labov (1991) and (1996).

Chapter 6

Language and Social Groups

This chapter reviews some of the principal forms of language variation in relation to social groups. It begins with relatively large units of analysis like social class and caste, moves on to age groups, and finishes with occupational groups, very broadly considered. It does not, however, cover all types of language variation, because more extensive treatments of particular topics, such as gender- , ethnicity- , and geography-related variation will be found in other chapters of the book.

6.1 SOCIAL CLASS DIALECTS

Americans simultaneously declare themselves free of class and are very conscious of class. Many have remarked on the "Genteel Tradition" in America. This is a widespread feeling that people should be ever vigilant about the "correct" use of language. Some have claimed this tradition comes from the Puritans, while others have said that the relatively fluid class system in America has encouraged middle-class anxiety and therefore great attention to "the proper way of speaking." For whatever reason, American English has given the world such status-conscious words as *mortician* and *beautician* (on the analogy of *physician*) as well as *engineer* (sanitation, extermination). A home is never a house; there are home-builders, -owners, -appliances, and -makers. There are funeral homes and nursing homes. The bathroom is a restroom, comfort station, powder room, or washroom.

6.1.1 Labov's Studies

One of the pioneering studies of language and social class was Labov's department store study. Labov wanted to test the hypothesis that the pronunciation of postvocalic (after vowel) and final /r/ is a reflection of social class differences, with the upper-middle class producing more /r/ because it is a prestige feature (saying [kar] is more prestigious than saying [ka]). Labov was aware that people tend to use more careful speech (in this case, use more /r/) when they are focused or aware of their language.

He investigated the pronunciation of clerks in three New York City department stores: Klein's (lower class), Macy's (middle class), and Saks Fifth Avenue (upper-middle class). He assumed the speech of clerks would be representative of the speech of customers. Labov first found out what was sold on the fourth floor of each store. He then asked a clerk who was distracted *"Where are the toys?"* After the clerk answered *"Fourth floor,"* Labov pretended he had not heard and repeated his question. The clerk, this time more focused on language, repeated in what Labov hypothesized would be a careful style, *"Fourth floor."* When busy or preoccupied, the clerks gave few instances of /r/. When Labov asked for help, the clerks' use of /r/ increased.

Social class also made a difference. At Saks, there was more /r/ in casual speech. Macy's was closer to Klein's in casual speech, but Macy's clerks actually were more "correct" than Saks' clerks in careful speech. The tendency of middle-class speakers to pay a lot of attention to prestige (standard) forms is called **hypercorrection.**

Labov also investigated the **social stratification** of English in New York at large. He took New York as a speech community because he claimed that there were agreed-upon norms for the evaluation of speech that all New Yorkers shared; they could agree on what was prestigious and what was wrong in speech. Labov studied the Lower East Side in detail. Again, his first hypothesis was that the more careful the speech, the more prestige forms would be exhibited. His second hypothesis was that, depending on social class backgrounds, speakers have different frequency with which they use prestige forms.

Labov used a wide range of data-collection devices or tasks to get at attention to style. He asked people to read a minimal-pair word list (in which words would sound the same if people dropped off the final /r/), another word list, and a short passage. He also interviewed them, and, in order to get a casual spoken style, asked them, in the course of the regular interview, about emotion-laden events in their lives. Labov was looking at the frequency of five sounds [/r/, /e/, /o/, /θ/, and /ð/], not their absence or presence, because variation in language is a matter of percentages. What is interesting is how often sounds are used, in what circumstances, and in doing what sorts of tasks. Labov found that his hypotheses were correct. There were more prestige forms in careful speech, and social class had an effect on speech.

The lower-middle-class participants used both standard and non-standard forms. In the careful speech tasks, they used excessive standard forms (hypercorrection), while in casual speech they used nonstandard forms. Labov also asked people to evaluate the correctness of various forms. The lower-middle class showed the greatest sensitivity to, or dislike of, nonstandard features, even though they themselves used them. Labov saw hypercorrection and dislike of nonprestige forms as examples of linguistic insecurity. He saw language change as happening through this linguistic insecurity of the lower-middle class: hypercorrection leads to the spread of prestige norms through the speech community.

William Labov received a Ph.D. from Columbia University in 1964. He is rightfully considered the father of quantitative sociolinguistics, since he made this method of research extremely popular. Besides his work on social stratification, Labov wrote extensively on African-American Vernacular English (AAVE) (see 8.2.4 and 8.1.4) and was instrumental in the Ann Arbor case (see 8.3), which is a groundbreaking case for equality in teaching. His article "The Logic of Nonstandard English" (1969a), in which he shows that AAVE is not any less logical than Standard English, contrary to common stereotype, is rightly famous and has been widely anthologized. More recently, Labov published an important article on U.S. dialectology (1991) in which he finds that the vowel system is changing in the northern cities (Cleveland, Detroit, Buffalo, Chicago, etc.) and in the South. A third region, which corresponds roughly to the Midland region (cf. 5.1.1), is characterized by the merger (loss of distinction) between [ɔ] and [a]. Labov teaches at the University of Pennsylvania.

6.1.2 Social Networks

Some have critiqued "class" as a rarefied concept alien to the way people describe their own lives. Perhaps it is more fruitful to look at the social networks that people live in, to look at the individual before looking at variation within and across groups. There is a link between networks and social class, however, so much of the same information is available to researchers.

Many cities of the world resemble urban villages. People stay in a set locality and have all their primary interactions within that space. Some people live their whole lives in that community. Milroy's pioneering study investigated three communities in Belfast in order to investigate the ways lower-prestige groups see their variety of language as a symbol of group identity and solidarity. These communities were found to be characterized by high-density **networks,** clusters based on kinship, occupation, and group membership. These were frequently multiplex networks in which one person served multiple roles (e.g., uncle, coworker, pub mate). These networks were taken as the unit of analysis. Network strengths were computed on an index of 0–5, with one point each for strong neighborhood kinship ties, working in the same place as at least two others in the same area, working at the same place with at least two others of the same sex from the area, and voluntary association with workmates during leisure hours. Men scored higher for network strength than women in all age groups. Overall, presence of certain linguistic features like characteristic pronunciation of /a/ (no difference between *Sam* and *psalm*) was correlated with network strength (the higher the network strength, the higher use of the vernacular).

Many see the Milroy study as showing that people are constantly constructing their identities. It is not that people are essentially working class or middle class, but that they are together deciding what it means to speak like a person from the working class or middle class. Networks reinforce those largely unconscious decisions.

6.1.3 Restricted vs. Elaborated Codes

Basil Bernstein's work on language and social class, begun in the 1960s and continuing for 30 years, remains extremely controversial. Since the work is often cited in educational circles, we need at least to touch on its outlines. Bernstein postulated two codes (varieties of language), one restricted and the other elaborated. He tried to tie these codes to social class and family type. **Restricted codes** are rooted in localities where there are strong communities that center on physical work. The emphasis is on "we" over "I." Because people share a subculture, the need to make meanings explicit is not great. Lots of information (and understanding) is shared. Bernstein saw this type of social organization leading to a code that was inflexible, with fixed syntactic patterns. Language is predictable. **Elaborated codes,** on the other hand, are a result of families and communities where things are not taken for granted. Therefore, people have to make themselves clear to negotiate meaning. Explicitness is valued. However, elaborated code speakers, of course, also use restricted code in situations of intimacy or familiarity. Bernstein went on to further characterize families as based on "positional" appeals to authority *(Because I'm your father. Little boys don't do that)* and "personal" appeals to authority *(I really like it when you behave like that)*. He correlated the positional with restricted codes and the personal with elaborated.

6.1.4 Caste

Another type of social stratification is the notion of **caste.** While there are opportunities for people to change classes in a class-based society, in a caste-based society social position is inherited and fixed throughout life. Caste-based societies often assign different lexical items and grammatical structures to a given caste. Here are some examples from one area of India:

		Brahmin	Non-Brahmin
Vocabulary			
	sheep	tungu	orangu
	water	jalo	tanni
Phonology			
	haircut	krafu	krappu
	sugar	jini	cini
Grammar			
	it	-du	-ccu
	it came	vandudu	vanduccu

The Kirundi in Burundi have a caste system in which seniority and gender are important. When people meet, the older person speaks first; the male speaks first. (If no men are present, then an older woman speaks first.) In fact, women do not speak to strangers unless spoken to. Members of the upper caste never raise their voices or show emotions. Upper-caste boys are given speech training as part of preparation for manhood.

6.1.5 Age

Penelope Eckert's "jocks and burnouts" study of a Michigan high school links concerns about social class with a focus on a particular age group. As in many American high schools, middle-class students in the study organized their lives around extracurricular activities.

These middle-class students are frequently called *soshes* (from *socials*), *preppies,* and at this school, *jocks.* As in all high schools, there were other students who will probably not go on to college, people who tend to stay with the friends they grew up with in the neighborhood. These students are often called *hoods, greasers, stoners,* and in this school, *burnouts* or *jellybrains.* Yes, there are in-betweens, but those caught in the middle often report some discomfort. For jocks in this study, burnouts represent "drugs, trouble, hedonism, lack of ambition." Burnout women are seen as sexually promiscuous. For burnouts, jocks represent "competition, hierarchy, elitism, ambition." Jock women are considered "phony." Eckert discovered that this all starts in junior high school. At the beginning of junior high, burnouts can still be cheerleaders and play on the football team. By high school, however, the groups are all but frozen.

So far, you may wonder why we needed a study to tell us this. Your high school might well have been similar. What is of interest is Eckert's finding of a correlation between social group and pronunciation, with the burnout women leading a change in pronunciation. They were beginning to pronounce the /u/ in *fun* like the sound in *bought.* The sound in *file* was beginning to be pronounced like the sound in *foil.* All speakers used both conservative and these innovative pronunciations, but the percentage is what matters. Remember that Labov said that language change starts in the lower middle class and moves upward, with women often in the lead. That seems to be the case here.

Age is a notion that has not received much attention in sociolinguistics. The field has tended to take middle age as the norm, though dialectology has tended to choose older, conservative speakers (see 5.1.1). One problem is that it is very hard to study age carefully. When you see language change, for example speakers becoming more conservative/correct in their usage or using less slang, you do not know if the language itself is changing or the speakers themselves are changing as they age. In general, older people tend to speak a more archaic variety, and younger speakers tend to use more neologisms and slang terms (see 1.2.2 and 6.4). Recent studies have found that female Japanese secondary school students are changing their use of pronouns from a conservative "female" variety to an innovative "masculine" variety (see Chapter 10). The question is: will these speakers, when they become adults, go back to using the more conservative forms? To answer this question, you can follow individuals over the years or you can sample the target group at different times (looking at teenagers at five-year intervals, for instance).

Age-based variation seems to begin as early as age ten, when boys start to use nonstandard "adult" forms. For example, Japanese boys of this age will start to use (and even overuse, since subject pronouns are optional in Japanese) the masculine pronouns *boku* and *ore* in order to show they are "grown-up men." American boys may start to use taboo words about this age.

Despite their best efforts, parents are not the child's primary linguistic role model. Children learn from their peers on the playground. Generally, if children move to an area before the age of nine, they are able to "pick up" the local dialect, which their parents do not. This may result in parents and children having different dialects.

Baby talk is another aspect of age-variation: baby talk is used by and with children under the age of five, in general. After that age, it is abandoned. This brings us to the idea of register (see 6.2 and Chapter 12).

6.2 REGISTER

A **register** is another variation of a language, similar to a dialect, but determined by the subject matter, rather than geographical and social issues. Examples are:

Baby talk, motherese, or child-directed speech: the language caretakers use with children, e.g., *itsy-bitsy* = small, *boo-boo* = small cut, diminutives such as *blankie* and *doggie* (see 12.1.3).

Newspaper English, e.g., the dropping of articles *(President orders withdrawal of troops)*.

Sports announcer talk, e.g., *She shoots! She scores!*

Can you think of other registers?

Most of the discussion around register has been in the fields of stylistics, sociolinguistics, and, more broadly, in pragmatics. Interestingly a large amount of the discussion on register comes from language pedagogy, where register identification is quite important for successful mastery of a second language.

A register is commonly defined as a set of choices among linguistic features. The set of features must be recognizable because the concept of register is a distinctive one, that is, a register is identifiable insofar as it opposes itself to another kind of register. For example, one can talk of child-directed speech only if one is willing to claim that it is possible to look at a text and tell whether the text is in child-directed speech or in, say, Standard English.

There have been attempts to define register prevalently or even exclusively in terms of "linguistic features." An example of a purely linguistic definition can be the "language of instructions": recipes, and the like, use the so-called "object drop" as in the following example:

(6.1) Skin and bone chicken, and cut [ ] into slices.

In this example, the [ ] marks the place where the object pronoun *it* would occur in Standard English. These observations are interesting but do not lend themselves to generalization (i.e., one cannot generally come up with a feature dividing all registers into classes, with regard to this feature).

A recent influential approach has been proposed by Biber. By tracking with computers a large number of variables, one can show that statistically certain features tend to be associated with particular registers. Biber is able to distinguish written from spoken language on the basis of these clusters of features (called "dimensions").

The concept of register is also often defined as "related" to contextual factors because among the various parameters that have been proposed as determining register are:

- **subject matter:** what the text is about; what speakers are talking about will determine, to a certain extent, their choices in the various linguistic levels: lexical, syntactic, and so on. Chemistry or physics, for example, will have their own registers.

- **social roles/situations:** who the speaker is and what he or she does.

- **discursive function:** what the speaker is using the text for, such as discussing, insulting, and so forth, such as the "field of discourse."

Joos distinguishes five styles primarily based on the speaker and hearer roles, the situation, and the purposes of the exchange; linguistic features follow from these constraints, as outlined here.

- **consultative:** the speaker provides background information and the hearer participates as it is a public mode; no familiarity is presupposed or established.

- **casual:** the speaker may be elliptical and use slang as it is also a public mode; familiarity is presupposed or established.

- **intimate:** the speaker may take ellipsis to its ultimate degree: single-word utterances; jargon may be used (as this is an in-group only style).

- **formal:** the speaker provides background, the hearer(s) do not participate; the text must be very cohesive, to make up for the distance between speaker and hearer; feedback is regulated.

- **frozen:** this is a written mode; speaker and hearer are not in contact, so there is no feedback (unlike in the other styles); it is a sophisticated style, associated with literature (see Chapter 14).

Finally, a caveat: the distinctions between registers as well as those among register, jargon, slang, and **argot** (the special, exclusive language of a group; originally of thieves in medieval France) are not watertight. At times it is difficult to decide if a certain text is in one or another register or if a given expression is jargon or, say, slang.

6.3 JARGON

Jargons can be seen as occupational varieties. For example, postal workers need to talk about their job using specific, clear, specialized, unambiguous terms and thus they develop some special terms that refer to their activity. The same is true for every profession. This type of specialized variety is called a **jargon.** Another example of extremely developed jargon is the one used by computer programmers and other computer experts.

The police and postal workers have well-developed, well-defined jargons (there even exist booklets collecting the terminology), but CB users, chat-room users, restaurant workers, drug addicts, and college students all have jargons. In fact, any occupation, hobby, association or organized group is likely to develop its own jargon.

Note that jargon is also used for purposes of not letting others understand you, to show off, or to establish in-group membership. The fact that people of the same profession converse about their work topic using words and sentences that people outside of that profession would have trouble understanding is jargon. For example a "rhinoplasty" is just a doctor's jargon for "nose job."

Thus, summing up, jargon has two main functions. It

- provides speakers of specialized domains with clear, unambiguous terms to refer to their activities, and

- provides speakers of a subgroup with a means of marking in-group membership and excluding outsiders.

Needless to say, both functions are not exclusive, i.e., both may be accomplished at the same time.

> How many wrenches do you own? How many do you think an auto-mechanic owns? What do you think would happen if you asked an auto-mechanic to "hand you the wrench"?

6.4 SLANG

Finally, a variety of language that is very well known but often misunderstood is **slang.** Slang is a variety of language that is used by a restricted part of the population, often younger or "less respectable" than the majority, and is based on a very informal or very innovative lexicon that often replaces other words available in the general lexicon. Thus the word *buck* for *dollar* is a slang term, as well as *cool* for *good.* Slang often ages very quickly. For example, it is now very "uncool" to use the words *hip, groovy,* or *dough,* but this was not always the case. The primary function of slang is to mark its speakers as different or unconventional. This is why such disparate groups as teenagers and criminals are some of the most active creators and users of slang.

Because of the informal nature of slang, many people confuse dialectal varieties, such as AAVE, with slang. The principal difference between a dialect and slang is that slang is used only by a small part of the population. Thus there is an African-American English slang, just as there is a wider English slang.

An interesting feature of slang is that it may use a high number of **taboo** words. The word *taboo* comes from the Tongan language and means roughly things that violate the standards set by society for proper behavior. Picking your nose in public is a social taboo. There are certain words that are considered too crude or offensive to be uttered by a proper person. Needless to say, there is a certain degree of hypocrisy in the fact that most people will use taboo words when the circumstances are right (e.g., when you stub your toe, expletives may fly). When the transcripts of the Nixon administration tapes were released, people were shocked to see the frequency of "expletive deleted" found in the conversations.

The primary sources of taboo words in most societies are:

1. sexual and/or reproductive organs and behavior
2. excretory organs and/or fluids
3. taboo-breaking behavior (incest, extramarital relationships, etc.)
4. racial/ethnic slurs
5. blasphemy

To avoid taboo words, speakers use:

1. euphemisms ("down there" for the genitals)
2. child language (pee pee, ca ca)
3. medical/technical language (urination, defecation)
4. zero/avoidance (blankedy-blank, the symbols that indicate swearing in the comic strips)

What is the difference between slang and jargon, then? Slang is a public variety, and it is meant to be understood by all the hearers (those in the know, obviously); on the contrary, jargon is primarily an in-group variety, meant to be understood only by the members of the group. Let us note, however, that the two terms (as well as *cant, argot,* and the like) are often used loosely and interchangeably.

Educational Implications

This chapter has shown another aspect of language variation, the social. It also has given teachers tools to more carefully talk about variation, allowing them to distinguish between register, jargon, and slang.

6.5 EXERCISES

6.5.1 Words to Know

hypercorrection	(social) networks	multiplex networks
speech community	restricted code	elaborated code
caste	jargon	register
argot	slang	taboo

6.5.2 Review

1. What were Labov's findings in the "department store" studies?

2. Why is hypercorrection significant?

3. How does studying people in networks differ from studying people in classes?

4. What are the differences between restricted and elaborated codes?

5. What are the differences among jargon, register, slang, and argot?

6.5.3 Research Projects

1. Prepare a dictionary of slang (50 words/expressions, with definitions of their meaning). You may interview other speakers or use your own knowledge.

2. Prepare a dictionary of a given jargon you have access to (50 words/ expressions, with definitions of their meaning). You may interview other speakers or use your own knowledge. (You may want to use your workplace experience or your hobbies as sources.)

3. Collect taboo words and ask some people to rate them on a scale of "taboo-ness." What are the most taboo words today? What does this say about society?

6.6 FURTHER READINGS

Labov's work has been collected in two volumes (1972a, 1972b). Milroy's work on networks can be found in Milroy (1980, 1987). Bernstein's early work is summed up in his 1973 book and his entire career in his 2000 book.

The caste example is from Crystal (1997). The "jocks and burnouts" study is from Eckert (1989). On Japanese women's dialect, see Brown (1994).

On register, see Biber's work (1988). Joos's (1961) five "clocks" is worth reading (at least the first five chapters) as it is nontechnical. On journalese, see also Ferguson (1996), Ghadessy (1988), and Weizman (1984). On sports announcer talk, see Ferguson (1983). On newspaper English, see Zwicky and Zwicky (1982). The "recipe" example is from Haegeman (1987, 236). On slang, see Partridge (1934). For slang among college students, see Eble (1996).

Chapter 7

Pidgins and Creoles

7.1 LANGUAGES OF WIDER COMMUNICATION

Languages of wider communication (LWC), lingua francas, or **auxiliary languages**, as they are also called, are languages that are used to facilitate communication among speakers of different languages. One example is English in Ghana, which has many indigenous languages. Rather than choose one, the leaders of Ghana decided on English as a neutral language that would give an advantage to no one group. LWCs are also used to communicate internationally. An example is the use of English as the language of air traffic control throughout the world. The widespread adoption of a language as a means of international communication is not a new phenomenon.

Latin was one the first auxiliary languages, having been used in the western part of Roman Empire. Greek and Aramaic were also important auxiliary languages in the ancient world. Latin was adopted by many of the people conquered by the Romans and survived the fall of the empire in Italy, France, Spain, Portugal, Romania, parts of Switzerland, and the former Yugoslavia where it evolved into the various Romance languages.

Other countries such as England and Germany did not maintain Latin as a spoken language but continued to use Neo-Latin as the means of scientific, religious, and otherwise "cultivated" interaction until well after the Renaissance, as did all the countries in which Romance languages were spoken.

In the 18th century, French replaced Latin as the language of diplomacy and was itself replaced by English with the increasing importance of England and later the United States in the world economy and politics.

Auxiliary languages spring up when they are needed, often for trading or political purposes. During the Middle Ages the original *lingua franca* (Sabir; see 7.4.2) was used across the Mediterranean Sea, and classical Arabic is currently an auxiliary language among the Islamic countries.

The desire for one language that would allow people from across the world to communicate with each other is a very strong human trait that is illustrated by the biblical myth of the tower of Babel, and more recently by the hundreds of attempts at creating an artificial auxiliary language. Some of these attempts have been quite successful, the most significant of which is **Esperanto,** created by Dr. Zamenhof in 1887. But, in general, artificial languages have never really gained widespread acceptance because of the large number of native speakers of languages such as English and Chinese, which gives these languages a "head start" against artificial languages.

LWCs are very similar in function to pidgins, which arise from a mix of different languages rather than from the adoption of one particular language.

7.2 PIDGINS

A **pidgin** is a language that comes about as a result of contact between two groups who speak different languages and do not understand each other. Often, the reason for this contact is trade where there is a need for a simplified language. In Hawaii, for example, in the 19th century, a pidgin developed that allowed speakers of Philippine languages, Portuguese, Japanese, Chinese, and English to communicate for trade and on the plantations.

Most often, the words of the **superstrate** (aka lexifier) or dominant language are spoken in and used inside the syntax of the **substrate** or less dominant language. Here is an example from Tok Pisin, spoken in Papua New Guinea:

(7.1) tupela bikpela pepa = two big newspapers

Here is another example from Cameroon pidgin (West Africa):

(7.2) di tu big pepa = two big newspapers

7.2.1 Characteristics of Pidgin Languages

Pidgins are commonly thought of as "simplified" languages, but, as the following example makes clear, "simplification" is not the only process governing the formation of pidgins. In this case, Tok Pisin uses the plain form of the verb throughout, but it is more complex than Standard English in that it has pronouns for second person *you* (*y'all* in southern dialect, *yunz* in Pittsburgh dialect): *yupela* from "you fellows." It also has two forms of "we"—what is called **inclusive** (you and I = *yumi*) and **exclusive** (someone else not you and I = *mipela*).

English	*I go*	*you go*	*she goes*	*we go*	*you go*	*they go*
Tok Pisin	*mi go*	*yu go*	*em go*	*yumi go* *mipela go*	*yupela go*	*ol go*

Singular nouns and verbs in the plain form are characteristic of pidgins as is the use of adverbs instead of morphology *(-ed, -ing)* to mark time or duration in Pacific pidgins:

(7.3) baimbai = future (baimbai i kam = *By and by, he will come.*)

pinish = past (i go, pinish = *He went.*) [*pinish* comes from English *finish*]

The following are some other typical features of pidgin languages:

1. Simpler phonology. Pidgins tend to have five or seven vowels; compare that to English (which has twelve). On the other hand, Italian has five vowels and Samoan and classical Arabic have three.

2. Smaller vocabulary, primarily drawn from the lexifier language (superstrate).

3. Large number of polysemous words. In Tok Pisin, *gras* is used for hair, *gras bilong fes* = moustache; for fur, *gras bilong dog* = dog fur; and for plants, *gras nogut* = weed.

4. Words can function as nouns, adjectives, adverbs, or verbs. In Tok Pisin, *askim* can be the verb *to ask* or the noun *question.*

5. Few prepositions.

6. Few inflectional morphemes.

7.2.2 Types of Pidgins

Pidgins can be separated into restricted and extended, aka elaborated. **Restricted pidgins** die a relatively quick death. One example is the pidgins that developed around U.S. army bases in Korea and Vietnam during the wars in those countries. **Extended pidgins,** aka **elaborated pidgins,** are used in a wide variety of circumstances in a multilingual area and thus grow through their use into creoles (see 7.3).

A pidgin can result from any two languages. Russenorsk was a Russian/ Norwegian pidgin used by fishermen. Sranan is an English/West African creole used in Surinam. Sango is a combination of Ngbandi and other central African languages.

Pidgins are divided into Atlantic and Pacific pidgins, but all English-based pidgins share a core vocabulary:

English	Krio	Kamtok	Jamaican creole	Sranan
arm/hand	an	han	han	ana
ask	aks	aks/as(k)	(h)asks	aksi

Many English-based pidgins have some Portuguese words, such as variants of *saber* (to know) and *pequeno* (small or child). This is certainly due to the dominance of the Portuguese in the early maritime environment. It may also be due to words left over from Sabir (see 7.4.2).

Pidgins and creoles also typically share more structures with each other than they do with their source languages. Haitian creole has French as a superstrate and Kamtok has English, but their sentence structure is similar:

(7.4) Haitian creole: li pa te kone (= *He doesn't know you*)

Kamtok: i no bin sabi (= *He doesn't know*)

Here is another example:

(7.5) mi kol tumas (Tok Pisin, Pacific) = *I am very cold*

mi, a kol tumos (Kamtok, Atlantic) (= *I am very cold*)

7.3 CREOLES

Pidgins are used in contact situations. If they no longer are useful, they die. If they are useful, they become a lingua franca and in the process become nativized (acquire native speakers) and become creoles.

Creoles are mother tongues. Children grow up using them as their first language. This happens when the mother tongue of the children is not available, as when people from many language groups were put together on Hawaiian plantations, or when a pidgin becomes a useful lingua franca. It is difficult to separate pidgins and creoles in actual use, however. Cameroon pidgin, for example, is not a native language, yet it is used in all domains for all reasons. It is the most frequently heard language in its part of West Africa. Krio, the English creole of Sierra Leone, is the sole language of many people.

7.4 THEORIES OF PIDGIN AND CREOLE ORIGINS

A number of theories have been advanced for the origins of pidgins and creoles.

7.4.1 Superstrate Theories

Superstrate theories explain pidgin and creole origins by putting the emphasis on the acquisition of the superstrate, or more powerful, language by speakers of the substrate language.

The foreigner talk theory points out that when people speak to individuals trying to learn their language as a second language, they speak slowly, in short, simple sentences (see 13.5.1). This is similar to the strategy parents employ when speaking to very young children (see 12.1.3) Thus, pidgins and creoles take on aspects of this simplified language.

A related theory is the imperfect second language learning hypothesis. This theory says essentially that pidgins and creoles are the result of failed attempts at learning the superstrate language.

Both of these theories are **polygenesis** (i.e., they claim that they derive from multiple sources) theories. They say that individual pidgins and creoles developed independently of each other.

A superstrate theory of the origin of African-American Vernacular English (AAVE) was maintained by some dialectologists, who claimed that much of the difference between AAVE and American English came from the influence of various dialects spoken by English settlers on slaves learning English. (See Chapter 8.)

7.4.2 Substrate Theories

Other theories have said that pidgins and creoles are similar because they derive from (similar) Indo-European and West African languages. This is known as **monogenesis,** from a single source.

One theory, now largely discarded, claimed that all pidgins came from **Sabir,** a 15th century Portuguese-based trade language that was the lingua franca of the Crusades. The Portuguese spread this pidgin through their exploration and colonization. It became relexified, or changed, as a result of further contact. Another theory claims that a West African pidgin should be considered the original substrate.

7.4.3 A Universalist Theory: The Bioprogram

Yet another theory says that pidgins and creoles are alike because they share underlying processes; everyone is hardwired for language in the same way. We all have **universal grammar (UG)** (see 2.5.2). In some cases, says this theory, the only input available to children may have been a relatively unstable pidgin and thus, in a sense, the children must have developed their own language with the help of UG.

7.5 PIDGINS AND LECTAL VARIATION

What is the difference between pidgins, creoles, and dialects? Pidgins are contact languages by definition, whereas dialects are not. Dialects are usually mutually intelligible, while pidgins are not intelligible to a speaker of either the superstrate or the substrate. In some countries, the differences between creoles and dialects are slight. In Jamaica, there is a continuum from creoles to creole-influenced English dialects to Standard English, which is nicely mapped by the concepts of **acrolect, mesolect,** and **basilect** (see 5.1):

(7.6)

I didn't get the ball	acrolect
mi no get di ball	mesolect
mi din get di ball	mesolect
a din get di ball	basilect

We should not think that the boundaries between acro-, basi- and mesolects are sharp. In reality, we face the so-called **creole continuum,** i.e., the presence of a number of intermediate varieties that bridge the gap between the three **lects.** Consider the following example, from Guyana:

English	I gave him	acrolect
	a geev him	
	a geev im	
	a geev ii	
	a giv him	
	a giv im	
	a giv ii	
	a did giv hii	
	a did giv ii	
	a did gi ii	mesolect
	a di gi ii	
	mi di gi hii	
	mi di gi ii	
	mi bin gii ii	
	mi bin gi ii	
	mi bin gii ii	
	mi bin gii am	
Guyanase creole	mi gii am	basilect

Observe that the lower you move on the chart, the further away you go from English. Mesolect would be somewhere between the acro- and basilects. No one speaker controls the entire range of the creole continuum.

7.6 DECREOLIZATION

Once creoles come into contact with a standard version of one of their constitutive languages, they become decreolized, more like the standard. This often happens at school, where children learn the standard language, such as English in Jamaica. The children can then choose to speak, at different times and in different circumstances, either creole or standard. The creole may then change as a result of having such speakers.

The process of **decreolization** starts when a creole subsists alongside the **lexifier language.** In that situation, the lexifier language is usually the acrolect. That gives to the speakers of the creole a very good reason to adapt their language to the model provided by the lexifier. By speaking standard languages, people have access to better employment prospects, enjoy more social prestige, and often have access to a broader audience for their language. For example, in the many creoles whose lexifier is English, the pressure to adapt to Standard English is very strong because if one writes a book (for example) in English, one's audience is of hundreds of millions, whereas the speakers of a given creole may number in the mere hundreds of thousands or in the low millions.

   Good examples of decreolization can be seen in Hawaii and throughout the Caribbean. Some people see evidence of decreolization in AAVE, where the process has erased much of the West African traces in AAVE, though this is controversial, as we shall see in the next chapter.

Educational Implications
Teachers of children who speak creole languages will now understand their students' home languages better. Teachers of children who speak African-American Vernacular English will benefit from information that will be more fully developed in the next chapter.

7.7 EXERCISES

7.7.1 Words to Know

LWC	lingua franca	auxiliary language
pidgin	superstrate language	substrate language
lexifier	superstrate language	extended/elaborated pidgin
creole	restricted pidgin	decreolization
inclusive	creole continuum	Esperanto
Sabir	exclusive	

7.7.2 Review

1. Why are LWCs necessary?

2. What is an auxiliary language? How and why do they develop?

3. How are pidgins typically constructed?

4. What are some characteristics of pidgins?

5. What is the difference between restricted and elaborated pidgins?

6. What is the most prominent theory of why pidgins are alike?

7. How does a pidgin differ from a creole and a dialect?

7.7.3 Research Projects

1. Consider the following text (taken from the Cameroon pidgin version of the New Testament). Underline or highlight pidgin features discussed in the chapter.

John 1

Jesus He First Disciple

(35) When that day been pass, as John be stand and the talk with he two disciple

(36) then see Jesus. John look Jesus fine fine, then he talk say, for true, na this one be God He pikin.

(37) When John he two follow back them be hear the thing way John he talk, then turn strat follow Jesus.

(38) Jesus want turn back. He say two disciple of John the Baptist start for follow he. Jesus ask them say na which thing owner want? The two disciple for John answer Jesus say, "Papa, we want follow you for see place way you the stay."

(39) Jesus take them for place way he the stay. And he talk for them say, na place this way I the stay. The two disciple stay with Jesus from four o'clock for evening till night begin the came.

(40) (This two follow back for John one he name been na Amdrew, Simon Peter he brother.)

(41) Quick, quick, Andrew go tell he brother Peter say "came we dong see that God he pikin."

(42) Andrew be take he brother make he meet up Jesus. When Jesus see Peter He talk for he say, "You be Simon pickin' for John, but I go give you new name. Your new name na Peter way mean say, "Stone."

2. How easy do you find reading the previous text? Try to translate it in English and then compare it to a recent translation of the Bible.

3. Research the changes that occurred in Tok Pisin after it became the official language of Papua New Guinea.

7.8 FURTHER READINGS

Todd (1990) is a short clear introduction to pidgins and creoles, as is Singh (2000). Good general works on pidgins and creoles are Hall (1966), Muhlhausler (1986), Romaine (1988), and Holm in two volumes (1988–1989)—and more recently in one (2000). Thomason (2001) looks at language contact more broadly. The Guyanese example is from Macaulay (1994, 176); the Jamaican one, from Todd (1990, 7); and the Tok Pisin ones, from Todd (1990, 15). The list of typical pidgin features comes from Todd (1994). On the bioprogram theory, see Bickerton (1981) and Todd (1990). On the creole origins theories, see Mufwene (1995). For the creole continuum, see Rickford (1987). The pidgin translation of the New Testament was from *www.unomaha.edu/* (last consulted 2000).

Chapter 8

African-American Vernacular English

African-American Vernacular English (AAVE) is the name for the variety of language that has also been called **Black English** and Ebonics. The first thing to say about **AAVE** is that not all African-Americans speak it; those who do speak it may not speak it all the time and not all of its speakers are African-American (people who grow up in areas that are majority African-American may well learn the language, e.g., Italian-Americans and Puerto Rican–Americans in some areas of New York City may be fluent in AAVE). The second thing to say is that AAVE is not a monolith; there are regional varieties. However, there is a core set of generally agreed-upon features common to all speakers of AAVE.

8.1 ORIGINS OF AAVE

There were originally two main theories about the origin of AAVE. They can be labeled the dialectologist and the creole hypotheses. Research since the 1980s seems to be arriving at a synthesis, a middle way between the creolist and the dialectologist theories. Furthermore, a new issue has arisen very recently, about the fact that AAVE may be in fact diverging from Standard American English (SAE) (see 8.1.4). We will look at these issues in the following section.

8.1.1 Dialectologist Hypothesis

There have been a number of attempts to explain AAVE as an archaic form of British dialects. In this thinking, because East Anglia dialect has no third person singular *s* in the present tense as in *He go* (which AAVE also does not have), AAVE is a carryover from settlers from that part of Britain. Similarly, Anglo-Irish has *He be working every day* and Scottish dialects have *He done worked,* and therefore they too had a hand in the construction of AAVE. In its clearest formulation, this approach is tantamount to claiming that there are no differences between the speech of African-Americans and the speech of the SAE speakers of the region; witness the following quote, from dialectologist Hans Kurath (1949):

> By and large the Southern Negro speaks the language of the white man of his locality or area and of his level of education.

A major weakness in the theory is that southern Whites haven't also kept these features in their dialect; in fact, they have all disappeared. There seems to be no reason to think that African-Americans were more attached to their dialect than Whites. Also, why would AAVE choose features from a variety of British dialects (and not just one)? Today, this theory has been largely abandoned by modern researchers; however, a synthesis between the dialectologist and the creolist approach has been proposed.

One recent piece of evidence for the dialect hypothesis is the finding that older southerners, black and white, who live in isolated rural communities speak more like each other than younger people do. African American young people in these communities tended to adopt the urban vernacular of hip hop music and other entertainment as their prestige variety, using more AAVE than their grandparents. This is also an argument for the existence of divergence (see 8.1.4)(Wolfram 2003).

An interesting issue is that a closer look often shows that the match between expressions and the way they are used by SAE speakers and African-Americans is not exact. This has been called **camouflage.** Consider the following sentence:

(8.1) She come acting like she was real mad.

This AAVE sentence looks like an SAE construction of the type

(8.2) She came running

where *come* is a verb of motion (i.e., *She arrived running*). However, the AAVE sentence (8.1) has a meaning of *She had the gall to act as if she were mad* with a clear, and AAVE-specific, sense of moral indignation on the speaker's part. Another example of camouflage is the use of *been.* Most AAVE speakers when presented with the sentence

(8.3) She been married

will say that the person is still married, while SAE speakers will conclude that she no longer is.

8.1.2 Creole Hypothesis

AAVE is thought by many linguists to have come from a West African pidgin. As we have seen in 7.2, pidgins came out of contact situations. West Africa in the late 1500s saw the rise of a pidgin that arose out of maritime contacts between West Africans and the early explorers and merchants and then the slave traders. At the same time, this pidgin was competing with **Wolof,** which was an African language used as a lingua franca in the area. This pidgin and Wolof were both carried to the New World by Africans, beginning with the first slaves brought to Virginia in 1619.

Some have seen the rise of a pidgin as occurring later in the New World, as people from different ethnic and language groups were mixed. Apparently, at least at first, there were instances where groups were not mixed; this became a common strategy later to lessen the chance of well-organized slave revolts. Most feel now, however, that many Africans came to the United States already speaking an English-based pidgin. They certainly could have transmitted this pidgin to speakers of other languages as groups did mix on plantations. As children were born and raised on the plantation, a creole developed.

During slavery, as people continued to be brought from Africa, African languages, pidgin English, plantation creole English, and Standard English were all in competition. As there was frequent contact between speakers of Standard English and creole English, the creole gradually became **decreolized,** more like the standard form. It is this decreolized language that is thought to be the base for AAVE.

Creole and Standard English were also in competition in the North. There are documented cases recorded by early American colonists Cotton Mather, Benjamin Franklin, and others of what seems to be a creole. Because contact between the races was somewhat greater in the North, decreolization probably took place faster, contributing to the mistaken impression that AAVE was really just a form of southern dialect.

Gullah

Gullah is a variety of AAVE spoken on the coastal islands of South Carolina and Georgia, in particular in the region around Savannah. Given the isolation of the islands, the language spoken by their inhabitants has remained very conservative (this is a general rule: the language of outlying areas is less prone to change than the language of central areas). This is a boon for linguists, because it allows us to see a variety of AAVE that has decreolized much less than the others. The similarities between Gullah and West African languages are striking.

Among the African languages that are believed to have influenced Gullah are Wolof, Malinke, Mandinka, Mende, Twi, Yoruba, Hausa, Igbo, Efik, Kongo, Kimbundu, and others. The similarities between these languages and Gullah were first recognized by Lorenzo Turner.

Lorenzo Dow Turner was born in North Carolina in 1895. In 1919 he enrolled at Howard University. He supported himself by being, among other things, a professional baseball player. In 1914 he received his B.A. and his M.A. in English in 1917. While teaching at Howard he pursued his Ph.D. at the University of Chicago. He then taught at South Carolina State College, where he came in contact with speakers of Gullah. He set out to study the hypothesis that Gullah showed an African influence. To do so, he acquired knowledge of the following languages (besides Latin, Greek, and Italian): Portuguese, Arabic, German, French, Dutch, and several African languages (Kongo, Igbo, Yoruba, Krio, and Mende). His book *Africanisms in the Gullah Dialect,* published in 1949, established without question the African nature of the Gullah creole.

The examples of West African influence on Gullah range from the phonology of the language to its semantics. For example, English phonotactics (phonological rules that describe which sounds may occur after one another) forbid the cluster of consonants *gb* at the beginning of a word.

Are there any words than begin with *gb*? Look it up in the dictionary.

Gullah, however, does have words that begin with *gb-*, e.g., *gban,* meaning *tightly,* as does Mende (a language spoken in Sierra Leone): *gbaa,* meaning *to sigh.* At the semantic level, Turner found hundreds of words that had been borrowed from West African languages, down to the system of naming children after the day of the week on which they are born.

The important issue, in relation to the origins of AAVE, is to know whether Gullah is a remnant of a broader plantation creole, which extended to the south of the United States, or rather an isolated phenomenon.

The following are some grammatical features of AAVE that are generally used to show that it is an African-based creole. That is, its rules are rules found in other creoles and in West African languages:

- Repetition of subject *(John, he live in New York.)*

- *Do* questions (*What it come to?* = What does it come to?)

- Same form for singular and plural *(one girl, two girl)*

- No tense on verb *(I know it good when he ask me.)*

- Verb not inflected for person *(I know, he know.)*

- *Done* to indicate completion *(I done go.)*

These similarities to other creoles and to West African languages led the creolists to say that AAVE had creole origins.

8.1.3 Recent Debate about the Origins of AAVE

New Evidence

Since the 1980s new evidence has emerged that has led linguists to reevaluate both the dialectologist and the creole hypotheses. These new data include the following.

- Studies on the historical and social conditions of the slaves in the plantations. For example, studies have shown that the average plantation in the United States was relatively small and had few slaves; therefore, the conditions for the development of a pidgin/creole were not optimal, since presumably the slaves would have significant contact with speakers of SAE.

- The emergence of written and audio recordings of AAVE speakers. These include interviews of former slaves (32 volumes, published between 1972 and 1979), tape recordings for the Archive of Folk Songs, and recordings of interviews with 1,605 AAVE speakers conducted between 1936 and 1942 about "hoodoo" (vodoo).

- "Diaspora" recordings. On several occasions African-Americans migrated to areas outside of the United States. The most significant ones are:

  1. The Samaná region (1820s), in the Dominican Republic, where the general population speaks Spanish

  2. Liberia (1822–1910)

  3. Nova Scotia (1750–1850)

  The issue, of course, is how much these varieties have preserved the AAVE the speakers spoke when they migrated. While it may seem that a century may bring about too much change, one has to remember that isolated varieties are often very conservative (i.e., do not change much).

- Other creoles, especially the English-based Atlantic ones. More studies on creoles allow us to better understand the nature of AAVE, by comparing it to creoles.

From these new data, it appears that AAVE may not have developed from a creole in the United States, as we saw was believed. It may, in fact, have been imported, for example, by the many slaves brought to the United States from Jamaica and other areas where Atlantic creoles were spoken.

The differences between AAVE and SAE are not primarily categorical (i.e., all or nothing phenomena) but more a matter of degree. For example, AAVE speakers do not always delete the verb *to be;* moreover, the copula deletion phenomenon turns out to be present in some varieties of southern American English, but to a lesser degree than in AAVE, and in broader grammatical contexts. It is absent from other varieties of English. Moreover, by and large, all the features listed in 8.2 are also found to a lesser degree in other varieties of English, with the notable exception of the habitual *be.*

Studies of other creoles and of the available recordings of AAVE speakers have shown substantial similarities with Atlantic creoles, which would lend credit to the creole hypothesis. However, the study of ex-slave interviews, both written and audio, has shown that those varieties of AAVE do not differ from the SAE of that time, thus weakening the creolist hypothesis. The same goes for the "diaspora" varieties of AAVE that have been found to resemble SAE, more than a common creole ancestor.

Finally, it has been noted that the creole and the dialectologist hypotheses do not exclude one another: there is nothing to prevent us from thinking that there was a (British) dialect influence on a prior creolized variety.

8.1.4 Divergence Hypothesis

Very recently work by Labov and others has led to the formulation of a daring hypothesis that reverses the emphasis on the difference between SAE and AAVE: up until now we have considered different historical explanations of the differences that try to explain them by relating them to its origins (be it from a creole or from the remnants of British dialects). The common assumption has been that AAVE and SAE are converging, i.e., that AAVE has undergone (and still is undergoing) a process of decreolization.

However, it has been noted that there are some features of AAVE that have appeared relatively recently and that are clearly distinct from SAE. The most significant are the following:

- *be done* (resultative):

    (8.4) My ice cream's gonna *be done* melted by the time we get there.

    (8.5) Don't do that 'cause you *be done* messed up your clothes! (said to children playing)

- *-s* (narrative present):

    (8.6) The lil' boy, he *comes* and hit me right? I *hits* him back now.

    Note the alternance within a single sentence of the uninflected "hit" with the narrative forms in italics.

- *be V-ing* (habitual):

    New research has shown that this feature (discussed in more detail in 8.2.1) has emerged in the second half of the 20th century and as such is an example of divergence, rather than a relic of a creole (the habitual *be* is found in creoles).

The reasons for the divergence between SAE and AAVE are to be found in the effective conditions of segregation and socioeconomic disparity between speakers of AAVE and speakers of SAE, which leads to the formation of a specific African-American identity that is then reflected in a separate linguistic variety.

When all is said and done, AAVE is best considered a dialect of English because it is mutually intelligible with SAE. However, an African influence is probable, if not certain. Needless to say, you should recall that this does not mean that AAVE is somehow therefore "inferior" to SAE.

8.2 A GRAMMATICAL SKETCH OF AAVE

The following sections provide a short sketch of the principal differences between SAE and AAVE.

8.2.1 Phonology

Phonological rules for AAVE:

- no consonant pairs: *jus* (for *just*) *men* (for *mend*)
- few diphthongs: (aka monophthongization) *rat* (for *right*)
- no /r/ in middle or final position: *mow* (for *more*)
- *th* goes to *d* in initial position and to *f* in final position:

  dem (for *them*)

  souf (for *south*)

Why does AAVE phonology have these features? You could make the case that these are features of some southern dialects. The clearest example that AAVE is not the same as southern English is consonant cluster reduction. *Test* reduces to *tes* in southern English as well as in AAVE. However, when there is a suffix, southern English (SE) cannot reduce. *Tester* is still *tester* in SE but *tesser* in AAVE. The same is true for *testing*, which gets reduced to *tessing* and for *tests* reduced to *tesses* in AAVE.

However, the following features are apparently unique to AAVE:

final nasals reduce to nasalization	[man]→[mã]
final consonant deletion (especially nasals)	[faiv]→[fa:]
devoicing of final stops	[bæd]→[bæt]
devoiced final stop + glottal stop	[bæd]→[bætʔ]
loss of *y* after consonants	computer→[kəmpurə]
t becomes *k* in /str/ cluster	street→[skrit]

8.2.2 Tense and Aspect

The clearest grammatical evidence that AAVE is a system following its own rules is aspect. In Standard English, **aspect** is an optional way of describing whether the action of the verb is continuing or completed.

(8.7) I was watching TV when the phone rang. (continuing)

I have been to Disneyland twice. (completed)

Tense is obligatory in Standard English (you must put -ed on regular verbs to show past action).

Aspect: Habitual *Be*

In AAVE, aspect is obligatory and tense is optional. In AAVE, you might have the sentence,

(8.8) You making sense, but you don't be making sense.

This means roughly, *What you say makes sense in this context, but usually you are not so intelligent (you don't be making sense).* Here, the first clause has no *be* and the second does. The absence of *be* in the first clause (known as **zero copula**) shows that we're talking about the present, about right now. Similarly,

(8.9) The coffee be cold.

is an everyday complaint while

(8.10) The coffee cold.

means it's only today that it is a problem.

All grammar is complex and so is AAVE's grammar. *Be* can also be used in the future:

(8.11) She be there later.

I be going home tomorrow.

Some think that this is an example of the decreolization of AAVE, the influence of Standard English. Note also that *be* deletion does not work in the past or with tag questions:

(8.12) He was my teacher last year.

You ain't sick, is you?

Aspect: Completive *Been*

Been indicates recently completed action (perfective). (Note: An *
indicates an ungrammatical sentence in a particular language.)

(8.13) She been tardy twice this semester.

(8.14) * She been tardy twice last semester.

Been works something like Standard English *have/has/had been:*

(8.15)   He been there before.

They been there and left before I even got there.

It can be used for emphasis when time doesn't matter:

(8.16) He been there.

Aspect: Completive *Done*

Done alone also indicates recently completed action:

(8.17) I done my homework yesterday/today.

When used with other verbs, *done* focuses on the recentness of the
action:

(8.18) I done finish my homework (today).

(8.19) * I done finish my homework yesterday.

This last example should be in AAVE:

(8.20) I finish my homework yesterday.

So *done* too works a little like Standard English *have* because *James done
seen the show* means *James has seen the show.*

8.2.3 Relative Clauses

Relative clauses look like this in AAVE:

(8.21) He got a gun sound like a bee.

I had an uncle was one of the world's heavyweight contenders.

My youngest sister, what live in Georgia, ...

In SAE, a relative clause is introduced by *which, that, who, whose,* and *whom,* as in the bolded part of the following phrase:

(8.22) The woman **who won the prize**

8.2.4 Summary of Differences between AAVE and SAE

Labov (1982, 192) summarizes the findings of linguistics about AAVE in this way:

1. AAVE is a dialect of English with its own set of phonological and syntactic rules that are similar to the rules of other dialects.

2. It shares features with the southern dialect, and AAVE in turn has affected the dialects of the South where there has been contact (see 9.1.4).

3. It has a distinctive aspect system, which makes it different from other dialects of English.

8.3 AAVE AND EDUCATION

In an attempt to integrate neighborhoods, Ann Arbor, Michigan, placed a number of public-housing units throughout the city during the 1960s. One such unit was in the area served by Martin Luther King, Jr. Elementary School. The school was 80 percent White, 13 percent Black, and 7 percent Latino and Asian. African-American children were observed not doing well in school and were labeled as being learning disabled, having behavioral problems, and being mentally retarded as a result of the use of culturally and linguistically biased tests and evaluations.

In 1977, parents brought suit in federal court, charging that the children's sociocultural and economic backgrounds had not been taken into account and that these factors were causing a lack of progress in school. The parents wanted both better instruction for their children and better teacher training to help teachers understand the children's needs. The judge hearing the case, Judge Charles Joiner, ruled that the plaintiffs would have to specifically show that this was a linguistic question. The economic disadvantages and cultural differences the African-American students had compared to the majority were deemed irrelevant because the judge saw the need to base the case on the precedent of *Lau v. Nichols*, the San Francisco ruling that said that Chinese-speaking students could not get an equal education unless their language needs were addressed. *Lau* also said that there was no need to prove an intent to discriminate, only that previous discrimination had lead to the current problem.

Several linguists, including Geneva Smitherman, J. L. Dillard, and William Labov, testified for the plaintiffs. Smitherman, director of the Center for Black Studies at Wayne State University in Detroit, compared speech samples from the Ann Arbor children to the speech of children in Harlem, Detroit, Los Angeles, and Washington, D.C. She found agreement among all the samples and thus showed that AAVE was a widely spoken variety. She was also able to articulate the difference between home and school languages, which was important because when the children went to court the judge found that they "spoke like his grandchildren." Joiner found for the plaintiffs and ordered the board of education to draw up a plan to remedy the situation, including identifying AAVE speakers and training teachers.

The role of AAVE in education continues to be controversial. African-American children continue to be placed in developmental classes and in speech therapy because their language variety is not the same as Standard English. When educators call for training teachers to recognize (and to value) AAVE, self-appointed guardians of English protest vehemently, claiming that this will lead to teaching AAVE instead of Standard English in the schools.

An excellent example of this occurred in 1996 in Oakland, California. The school board announced a plan to recognize "Ebonics" (AAVE) as the home language of most of the students in their majority African-American district. The board felt that declining achievement among African-American students could be helped by essentially treating AAVE speakers the same as bilingual students, that is, as students whose home language was not the same as the school's language. News reports made it seem as if Oakland was "teaching Ebonics" rather than standard English. The U.S. Department of Education, fearing it would have to increase bilingual education funds to Oakland, almost immediately declared that

Ebonics was not a language but a dialect of English. The controversy eventually died down when the school board essentially abandoned much of its original position, but before it did there were numerous examples of mean-spirited parodies of AAVE in the news, virtually all of them getting the rules of AAVE completely wrong.

Educational Implications
Teachers of children who speak African-American Vernacular English will now better appreciate the complexity and rule-governed nature of the variety.

8.4 EXERCISES

8.4.1 Words to Know

AAVE	Wolof	Gullah
dialectologist hypothesis	creole hypothesis	divergence hypothesis
camouflage	zero copula	the *Lau* decision
decreolization	aspect	the Ann Arbor case

8.4.2 Review

1. What are the theories of the origins of AAVE?

2. What is the divergence hypothesis?

3. Why is Gullah important to linguists?

4. What kinds of new evidence has led to a reconsideration of the creole hypothesis?

5. What are some of the phonological and grammatical characteristics of AAVE?

6. What is the significance of the zero copula in AAVE?

7. What was the Ann Arbor case about?

8.4.3 Research Projects

1. If you are yourself an AAVE speaker, or if you have access to an AAVE speaker (friends, relatives, coworkers, etc.), test some of the constructions discussed in the chapter and summarize your results.

2. If you have access to software that can play sound clips, do as in the first research project, but look for recordings of actual speakers.

3. Using a novel that includes AAVE passages, locate the features that mark AAVE in relation to the SAE of the novel. (Good texts are Alice Walker's *The Color Purple*, Toni Morrison's *Beloved* or *The Bluest Eye*, Sapphire's *Push*, Pat Conroy's *The Water Is Wide*, etc.)

4. Read *The Water Is Wide* by Pat Conroy, an account of teaching on the coast of South Carolina, and note the features of Gullah in the book.

5. View the video *Daughters of the Dust*, Julie Dash's beautiful film about the Gullah region.

6. You will find a sample AAVE text below. What features of AAVE can you find in the text?

Search the Internet for other AAVE texts (ex-slave narratives, interviews, etc.) and see what features of AAVE you can find in these texts.

The following are a few sentences in AAVE, taken from an interview from the narratives mentioned above. The narrative is in SAE, but interspersed in the English text are some sentences in AAVE. Note the non-IPA transcription, which gives a good idea of the pronunciation.

Project #-1655
Mrs. Genevieve W. Chandler
Murrells Inlet, SC
Georgetown County

EX-SLAVE STORY
(Verbatim)

"My old man can 'member things and tell you things and he word carry. We marry to Turkey Hill Plantation. Hot supper. Cake, wine, and all. Kill cow, how, chicken and all. That time when you marry, so much to eat! Finance wedding! Now—

"We 'lamp-oil chillum'; they 'lectric light' chillum now! We call our wedding 'lamp-oil wedding'. Hall jam full o' people; out-of-door jam full. Stand before the chimbley.

"When that first war come through, we born. I don't know just when I smell for come in the world.

"Big storm? Yinnah talk big storm hang people up on tree? (Noah!) Shake? I here in house. House gone, 'Rack-a-rack-a-racker!'

"My husband run out – with me and my baby left in bed! Baby just come in time of the shake.

"When I first have sense, I 'member I walk on the frost bare-feet. Cow-belly shoe.

"My husband mother have baby on the flat going to Marion and he Auntie Cinda have a baby on that flat.

"From yout (youth) I been a Brown and marry a Brown; title never change.

"Old timey sing?

1. "Wish I had a hundred dog
   And half wuz hound
   Take it in my fadder field

Source: Born in Slavery: Slave Narratives from the Federal Writers' Project, 1936–1938.

7. Read up on the Ann Arbor and the Oakland "Ebonics" cases. Compare and contrast the two cases. Try to explain the media frenzy in the Oakland case.

8.5 FURTHER READINGS

The differences between SAE and AAVE are described and analyzed in Labov (1969a), Wolfram and Fasold (1974), Smitherman (1977), Rickford (1999), and Morgan (2002). The latter is exceptionally readable. Labov (1969b) is an impassioned argument for the inherent value of AAVE as a linguistic system. It has been widely anthologized, for example in Giglioli (1972).

The creolists' position is powerfully argued for in Dillard (1972). For a critique of the theory of the origins of AAVE from English dialects see also Dillard (1972, Chapter 1). The position of the dialectologists can be found in the publications of the American dialectologists (see 5.1.1) and has been recently put forward in Schneider (1989, Chapter 1). A state-of-the-art review of the literature on the synthesis between creolists and dialectologists can be found in Mufwene et al. (1998, Chapters 4–6), which is unfortunately at times too technical for beginners. Mufwene (1993) has a number of excellent articles. A simpler discussion can be found in Wolfram and Schilling-Estes (1998, Chapter 6).

It is too early to have pedagogical expositions of the more recent developments in the research on AAVE. The list of new evidence is taken from Rickford (1998) where some discussion can be found. Some relevant discussion will be found in Wolfram (2003), Mufwene et al. (1998), and Mufwene (1993). The same goes for the divergence hypothesis, for which see Labov (1998) and Butters (1989). Camouflage was proposed in Spears (1982) and is discussed in Labov (1998, 135) and Rickford (1998).

On the pedagogical implications of AAVE's nature, see Labov (1982) on the Ann Arbor case, Baugh (1998, 2000), Smitherman (2000), and Adger et al. (1999). Perry and Delpit (1998) is a good anthology on the Ebonics controversy.

The data on consonant cluster deletion are from Trudgill (2001). The data on the phonology of AAVE are from Bailey and Thomas (1998). Turner's biographical data come from Holloway and Vass (1993). Most of the examples of aspect, tense, and the relative clause come from Smitherman (1977). The Mende example is from Innes (1969).

Chapter 9

Language Policy

This chapter is divided in two main parts: the first one, multilingualism, and the second, language planning/policy. In the first section we will look at the situation of a number of countries in which more than one language coexists. In the second, we will consider (mostly) governmental policies toward languages, again in a number of countries.

9.1 MULTILINGUALISM

9.1.1 Introduction

Most countries in the world are at least bilingual, and most of them are in fact multilingual. Before looking at some of the consequences of multilingualism, we will go on a brief tour, highlighting the situation in a very few countries in order to give some sense of the landscape. First of all, we should define "national" and "minority" languages. **National language** may be defined as the official or unofficial **superordinate language,** that is, the language whose speakers have the most power, the language that someone who wanted to be upwardly mobile would have to know. **Minority language** is frequently used as a kind of shorthand, but in reality a minority language has nothing to do with numbers. More properly, we should speak of **subordinate languages,** with "subordinate" meaning "subordinate in terms of power." An example is the former administration of South Africa, which conducted the affairs of the country in Afrikaans, the superordinate language, while the majority of the country spoke one or more subordinate African languages.

The French Revolution outlawed dialects as feudal. Ever since, regional varieties have been frequently seen as dangerous in that they are a threat to a unified nation. National languages are good, goes the argument, for unifying the country under one linguistic banner and also simultaneously setting it off from other countries.

9.1.2 National and Minority Languages

North America

One of the world's most famous multilingual countries is Canada. The use of French and English in Quebec has been debated for years, but Canada also has many indigenous languages and a large immigrant community. Canada has thus been at the forefront of work on bilingual education. The United States has had a long history of immigration, and recent increases in numbers of immigrants have fueled debate on the place of English in the country. We will take up the question of Official English in a separate section (see 9.2.1). Indigenous language policy in Mexico and Central America has changed recently, with the indigenous languages receiving more attention as they become endangered.

South America

Indigenous languages share official status with Spanish in several countries. Spanish and Quecha, for example, can both be used for official purposes in Peru. In Paraguay, Spanish and Guarani share official status. The two languages have very different uses, with Guarani being used to show solidarity and Spanish being considered the language of formality. The example is often given that two young lovers would start their courtship in Spanish and then shift to Guarani as they became more serious. Some of the indigenous languages of the Amazon are among the most endangered in the world.

Europe

European countries have always been multilingual, but during the 19th and 20th centuries there was an attempt to raise one national language over all others. Paradoxically, as Europe has recently become more unified, the regions have been given more power and the regional languages have been given more resources. Welsh, Irish, and Scots Gaelic have lost native speakers to English in the United Kingdom, but the situation shows signs of revival as the languages are taught in schools and, perhaps equally important, are used in media. They thus gain in prestige. The United Kingdom also currently has about 100 minority languages as a result of immigration. Since the 1980s, Spain has given more control to its regions and their languages, Catalan, Basque, and Galician. In 1993, the Belgian constitution devolved greater control to its regions. There are now four distinct language areas: the Flemish northwest; the Walloon (French) southeast; the bilingual capital, Brussels; and a small German-speaking area in the east.

Perhaps the greatest change that has taken place since the 1960s in Europe has been the arrival of "guest workers" in northern Europe. Germany has had more than seven million guest workers to date, two million of them Turks. Others have come from Greece, the former Yugoslavia, and several other places in Europe. The original intent of the program was to hire temporary industrial workers for a booming economy. Many Turks are now third-generation residents of Germany, but because of German nationality/immigration laws, since amended, they are not citizens. Sweden has also had a large number of similar immigrants and now offers **mother-tongue** education in 60 languages.

With the expansion of the European Union (EU) eastward comes the question of the roles of French and English in the EU. Citizens (and hence bureaucrats) of the newer member states are more likely to know English as an additional language than French. This has caused worries among the French at the possible dilution of the importance of their language for internal discussions within the EU.

The Former Soviet Union

The 21 ethnic republics of the former Soviet Union are home to speakers of 175 languages, about 20 of them endangered. For 70 years in most places, Russian was the official language and the local languages were written in Cyrillic. Since the breakup of the Soviet Union, most of the local languages with large numbers of speakers have been given official status and many of them are changing from Cyrillic to the earlier alphabets. Yet Russian remains a home language for approximately 90 percent of the people regardless of ethnicity. One issue is the large number of ethnic groups in any republic. Kazakhstan, for example, has 100 languages. A recent law requires everyone to be able to speak, read, and write Kazakh. This will take some time to implement.

Asia

India has two main language groups, Indo-European languages in the north and Dravidian languages in the south. There are more than 380 languages in India alone. China is similarly, though not as spectacularly, linguistically diverse. We think of "Chinese" as a language, but most of the languages of China are mutually incomprehensible, united only by the written Chinese characters. Some Chinese languages like Hokkien and Cantonese are important languages in overseas Chinese communities in Southeast Asia. Malaysia and Singapore are examples of places where multilingualism and harmony exist side by side. In both countries, several varieties of Chinese, Bahasa Malaysia, Tamil, and English are all important languages.

Africa

The boundaries of African countries were drawn by European colonialists without regard to the rich variety of languages within each. This led to a situation after independence in which a number of languages vied for the status of national language. In many cases, the status quo was chosen and the language of colonial administration, most often French or English, was chosen as the national language. Swahili was used for a number of years as a lingua franca in eastern and central Africa, and it continues to be an important language as well as one of the official languages of Tanzania. (The other is English.) The recent democratization of South Africa has led to language policy questions as Afrikaans, the language of the old regime, falls in status and is replaced by several official languages.

9.1.3 Diglossia

A special form of "bilingualism" is **diglossia.** In diglossia, two varieties of one language are used in what linguists call "functional distribution." That means that the varieties are specialized, with one being used, for example, for *high* (H) functions like sermons and the other used for *low* (L) functions like conversations with friends. Examples of diglossia include classical (H) and colloquial (L) Arabic across the Arab world, French (H) and Haitian creole (L) in Haiti, and Kathaverusa (H) and Dhemotike (L) Greek.

Such is the separation between the high and the low that you would read a newspaper aloud in classical Arabic but discuss it in colloquial Arabic. You would lecture in French but answer questions in Haitian creole. The high language is (erroneously) considered more beautiful, more logical, and more expressive. The very existence of the low variety is sometimes in fact (erroneously) denied: *We never use that. That's ignorant.* Editorial writers may be judged good stylists if they use words that are incomprehensible.

Diglossia is not bilingualism because there are no native speakers of high varieties; these must be learned in school. Children grow up speaking the low varieties. In bilingualism, children may grow up speaking either language, either French or English in Canada, for example. In fact, the high form is not used in conversation. It is a language of public speaking. Diglossia and bilingualism are also different in that bilingualism has no functional distribution; both languages can be used for any purpose.

High varieties are standardized. There are dictionaries and grammars of the language. The low variety may not be standardized (though it may), and when it is described, it may be outsiders who finally write it down, because the local community does not value it.

The low variety may have fewer grammatical categories than the high. It is simpler (though remember that does not mean that the high variety is "better.") There are many paired vocabulary items, so that the verb for *see* might be different in the two varieties, as it is in high and low Arabic:

(9.1) ra'aa (high)

       shaaf (low)

Some researchers would extend the meaning of diglossia to any two languages in functional distribution, that is, that occupy different domains. For example, Spanish is the formal language in Paraguay, while Guarani is the informal. Another development since the first description of diglossia has been the increased use of low in public, on television talk shows and sports commentary.

Speakers faced with a diglossic situation often cope by code switching (see 4.3.4), which allows one to jump from one variety to the other to mark emotional and social meanings.

9.1.4 Successful Minority Languages

> What language or languages did your great-grandparents speak? Do you remember any of the words? Do your parents remember any words from the language of your great-grandparents?

There are three possible outcomes of contact between languages: language maintenance, bilingualism, and language shift. If there are economic incentives to shift languages and opportunity to learn the superordinate language, speakers of a subordinate language will likely shift their language within three generations, as was the case with immigration to the United States. One successful example of maintenance of a subordinate language is Catalan. Catalan is spoken in the Catalonia region of Spain as well as in Valencia, the Balearic Islands, parts of Sardinia, the Roussillon area in France, and in Andorra. Catalonia had been a mercantile nation until the merger of Castile and Aragon in 1469. Catalonia was first a dependency and then a province of Spain. In 1716, Catalan was outlawed and, with the exception of the period of the Second Republic in the 1930s, remained outlawed until the death of Franco in 1975. Yet, in 1979, 97 percent of native Catalans spoke the language. It is now an official regional language. Catalan survived for a number of reasons. Perhaps most important was the Catalans' sense of identity based on their territory. It was also helped by a strong regional economy that was frequently better off than the capital's. There was no economic incentive to switch to Spanish.

In Tanzania, an African language became the official language while in most of the rest of Africa the old colonial languages became official languages. Tanzania chose Swahili, a Bantu language used as a lingua franca in eastern Africa. That long tradition of language use doubtless helped the acceptance of Swahili. It was already being used as a medium of instruction in schools and it was related to many other languages used in the area, so it was comparatively easy to learn. Perhaps most important, it was not the language of any one dominant group, so it could be seen as a compromise.

9.1.5 Language Rights

Several businesses in the United States have passed work rules prohibiting workers from speaking their home language at work. Spanish-speaking workers in factories and Tagalog-speaking nurses in hospitals have sued for the right to speak to their friends in a familiar language. Public officials, like police officers, in the Southwest have complained that their rights have been violated by their having to learn Spanish to get or keep a job. What linguistic rights do people have?

Minority language rights have come to be seen as a form of human rights. The issue is complicated. Should the rights be assigned to territories, to individuals, or to groups? Individual rights can be a threat to collective rights or territorial rights, as when English speakers are given the right to buy weekend houses in Welsh- or Gaelic-speaking areas. Giving rights to a group institutionalizes that group; individuals need the right to be perceived as something other than a member of a (potentially stigmatized) group. Yet group rights are useful for gaining political action. UNESCO has spoken of linguistic rights as universal; everyone should have the right to speak his or her own language privately and publicly.

In reality, most countries weigh a number of factors when granting language rights, including the number of speakers of the language, its territorial concentration, the level of services required, and the material resources available.

9.2 LANGUAGE PLANNING AND POLICY

Language planning is a relatively new field within sociolinguistics. Its central question is "What language is to be used?" There are two kinds of language planning, corpus planning and status planning. **Corpus planning** is concerned with standardization and codification of the language (i.e., grammar, spelling, new words, script). The French Academy, for example, decides what new technology should be called in French. Governments in the former Soviet Union decided to switch from the Cyrillic alphabet to a variety of other alphabets including Latin and Arabic. **Status planning** is concerned with the choice of languages and the attitudes toward dialects. Included in status planning are decisions about which languages should be taught in schools.

Many of these decisions are made on the governmental level, but the private sector also plays a part. Publishing houses and universities have teamed, for example, on dictionaries of Australian English and South African English. They have decided the corpus of those two varieties just as Noah Webster's spellers and dictionaries told Americans how to spell without intervention from a government academy. Writers like Dante and Chaucer who chose to write in the **vernaculars** of their countries rather than in the status languages of their times were involved in language planning of sorts.

As with language contact, there are typically three outcomes for language planning: language maintenance, language shift, and bilingualism. Languages tend to be maintained when there are boundaries around the language, either self- or externally imposed. Diglossia may help language maintenance by building boundaries and setting up rules for when varieties may be used. Shift takes place when there is less enclosure of languages and when there is access to resources and education. Speakers who shift away from their own language typically shift to the dominant language. Many immigrants to the United States have followed this pattern. The mechanism of shift is bilingualism. Second-generation immigrants become bilingual, but their children usually shift to the dominant language and often become monolingual. Language shift may ultimately lead to language death (see 9.2.2).

A number of stages in language planning have been identified. The first is *selection* of a variety or varieties as the new norm. The second is *standardization* of the new norm (script, phonology, morphology). The third is *diffusion or implementation,* usually through the schools. The fourth and last is *modernization.* In this last stage, the language is spread and updated as necessary. One example of modernization is unification of technical vocabulary. When British soldiers in World War II thought that *inflammable* meant the same thing as *unflammable,* the labels on chemicals and ammunition had to be changed to *flammable* (see 2.3.5). Another example is the periodic effort to get the government to write its documents in a clear style that everyone can understand (see 15.1).

9.2.1 The Situation in Some Nations

The United States

The 2000 U.S. Census found that of the 262.4 million people aged five or older, 47 million (18 percent) spoke a language other than English at home. These figures increased from 31.8 million (14 percent) in 1990 and 23.1 million (11 percent) in 1980. The census asked how well these individuals speak the language other than English. The 2000 figures show that most people (55 percent) said they spoke English "very well"; they just did not speak it at home or at least spoke it relatively little at home.

Spanish is the largest non-English language spoken in the United States. There are 28.1 million Spanish speakers who reported speaking Spanish at home, according to the 2000 U.S. Census. Their numbers rose by about 60 percent from 1990 to 2000. Chinese is the second most frequently spoken non-English language, followed by French, German, and Tagalog. States with the largest numbers of non-English speakers are California, Texas, New York, Florida, Illinois, New Jersey, Arizona, and Massachusetts.

Because of this increase in immigration, there is a belief that English is threatened. Notice, however, that a majority of the people who said they spoke a language other than English at home said they spoke English well. Most people are bilingual. On the other hand, there are growing numbers of people who are what the census calls "linguistically isolated." The census defines a "linguistically isolated household" as one in which no one over the age of 14 speaks English "very well." There are 11.9 million people living in such households, according to the 2000 U.S. Census.

Some people still push for a constitutional amendment to the U.S. Constitution that would declare English as the official language of the United States. The first state constitutional amendment declaring English as the official language was Nebraska's in 1920. Illinois followed soon thereafter, and Hawaii has declared both English and Hawaiian official languages. It was not until the 1980s that momentum gathered across the country for official language laws. Official English amendments have been offered at every session of Congress since 1980. An organization called U.S. English has been the principal lobby group. Members argue that language ties a country together and that the United States could be split into factions if bilingualism increases. More ominously, a former chair of U.S. English made clearly racist statements about Hispanics when arguing the need for an official language. Twenty-seven states now have laws that declare English the official language of their state. Arizona's official English amendment was struck down by the state Supreme Court in 1998.

The climate of official English has led to a number of lawsuits about language in the workplace. People have been fired from their jobs for speaking a language other than English. Court opinion has been mixed. In *Guiterrez v. Municipal Court,* an appeals court ruled in 1988 that requiring a person to speak English in the workplace was not a valid rule, while similar rules in *Dimaranan v. Pomona Valley Hospital* were upheld.

English Plus is an organization formed to encourage pluralism. It says that English is the primary language of the United States and will remain so, but those citizens who speak a native language other than English should be encouraged to keep their home tongue. English Plus maintains that bilingualism is an economic and cultural asset. It also contends that Official English laws have the potential of denying people a voice in their government.

Other aspects of language policy in the United States revolve around bilingual education, Native American language rights, the status of Puerto Rico, foreign language education, and gender neutrality.

The Bilingual Education Act (Title VII of the Elementary and Secondary Education Act) was passed in 1968. Originally, it was a program to help Spanish speakers. When the bill was finally passed, "Spanish speaking" was changed to "limited English proficiency." This seemed to suggest that the children's language was a problem, not a resource. It put the emphasis on what they did not know. Later amendments and reauthorizations shifted the focus away from maintenance bilingualism, in which both of the children's languages are cultivated in school, to a transitional model that supports English monolingualism. The Bilingual Education Act expired in January 2002 and was not renewed. There are continuing efforts to include deaf education in bilingual education.

A 1992 law was aimed at protecting Native American languages that were dying out. This new approach contrasted sharply with the former approach that encouraged language shift to English.

Puerto Rico has at various times in its history been spoken of as a potential 51st state of the United States. The island, while officially bilingual, is Spanish dominant. Many wonder whether Congress will invite Puerto Rico into the union given this fact. There has been legislation, in fact, that would give Puerto Rico statehood only if it declared English its official language. A large number of people in Puerto Rico do not care to see Puerto Rico become a state, in fact. Some would prefer independence while others like the current commonwealth relationship.

Language policy also addresses which languages should be taught in public schools. There are periodic cries that the United States cannot compete in global markets without a better foreign language capability. In this view, high school and college students need to study foreign languages to a higher level of proficiency than is typical now. Several states have passed laws defining foreign language ability as a basic skill necessary for high school graduation, and many are beginning elementary school programs in foreign languages.

Australia

Australia had a language policy stressing multilingualism from the 1980s to the 1990s. Almost 15 percent of Australians use a language other than English at home. In Melbourne, the figure is 26 percent. One of the national television channels offers programming in eight languages with English subtitles, and private stations broadcast in Italian and Greek. Schooling is the responsibility of state governments, and some states teach up to 22 languages. If their home language is not offered, children have the opportunity to go to government schools after school or on Saturdays.

Recent policy has focused on codifying both Australian English and aboriginal languages. While there had also been an emphasis on teaching languages useful for economic development, such as Chinese and Indonesian, support at the higher levels of government has waned in light of recent efforts to limit immigration and some backlash against immigrants.

Hong Kong

The return of Hong Kong to China as a special administrative region has been an interesting window on superordinate and subordinate languages. Ninety-eight percent of the citizens of Hong Kong speak Cantonese as a first language. Since Hong Kong built its wealth on international trade, English was and still is an important language. In the 1990s, approximately 6 percent of the population was fluent in English but about 30 percent could use English in limited domains such as on the job. Because Hong Kong was a British colony, Cantonese was not made an official language until 1974. Beginning in July of 1997, when Hong Kong rejoined China, the official administrative language of Hong Kong became Mandarin. Cantonese, English, and Mandarin are all mutually unintelligible, though Cantonese and Mandarin speakers can understand perhaps 60 percent of the other language.

Education is obviously important to Hong Kong's future, and the region has autonomy to make its own educational policies. In the past, Cantonese was the medium of instruction for elementary schools, but there was a two-track system for secondary school. There was a Chinese school track in which English was taught as a subject and an "Anglo-Chinese" track in which English was the language of instruction and Chinese was taught as a subject. The English-medium schools were more popular because parents wanted their children to be able to speak English. Beginning in 1984, Mandarin was taught as a subject or as an after-school extracurricular activity, but it may well take some time before it can be used as a medium of instruction because of a shortage of Mandarin-speaking teachers. Hong Kong is now trying to see which languages are studied when and in what manner, but there have been recent attempts to limit the teaching of English in favor of Mandarin. For example, English is no longer the main language of instruction in most schools; it is mandatory for secondary school teachers to use Cantonese in the classroom, unless an official waiver is given. The goal of the educational system remains trilingualism, however.

Singapore

Singapore has four official languages: Malay, English, Mandarin, and Tamil. Until 1957, however, 80 percent of the population did not speak any of these languages at home. Several Chinese languages were spoken. In the past 50 years, education in English and use of English at home has greatly increased, so much so that recent figures show that almost one quarter of the population speaks English at home. Indeed, "bilingualism" in Singapore is defined as English plus one other official language. The country has had a policy of encouraging the ethnic Chinese population to speak Mandarin rather than another Chinese language. Children are typically educated in English and another official language. Typically, the second language is the mother-tongue language (based on ethnicity) but sometimes ethnic Malays and Indians take Mandarin as their second language because of its utility as a language in Asia. Moral and religious education and language and literature classes are given in the second language; the rest of the curriculum is in English. A recent issue in Singapore is the use of "Singlish," or colloquial Singaporean English. The government has launched a campaign to encourage people to speak Standard English.

Switzerland

Switzerland also has four official languages: French, spoken in the western part of the state; (Swiss) German; Italian (spoken in Ticino); and Rhaeto-Romansh, spoken in a small area around St. Moritz (see Fig. 9.1). Children typically grow up speaking one language while being educated in two or three others. Most speakers remain monolingual within their regions, which are almost all monolingual. Most public officials are trilingual or have some proficiency in the three major languages (German, French, Italian).

Figure 9.1: Languages in Switzerland

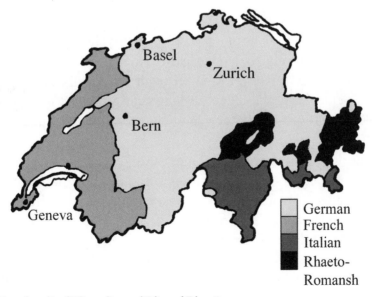

Source: Encyclopedia of Bilingualism and Bilingual Education.

Italy and France

Both Italy and France have one national language (Italian and French, respectively). However, both nations have provisions for groups of speakers of other languages within their borders. Speakers of Breton (related to Welsh) in Brittany (Western France) are free to use their language and have newspapers and other media in Breton. Italy has two "special status" regions where French (Val d'Aosta) and German (Trentino Alto Adige) are recognized as official languages as well. There is even a very small political party (Südtirolervolkspartei) that has representation in the national parliament.

9.2.2 *Language Maintenance, Shift, and Death*

We have seen that given an opportunity, the minority language in a bilingual situation tends to shift to the dominant language over generations. This is called **language shift.** An example of minority **language maintenance** is Spanish in the southwestern United States. Spanish and English exist there on a continuum from Spanish retention to English assimilation. The language a person chooses to speak depends on factors such as residential segregation, economic mobility, proximity to the international border, and the influx of immigrants. The closer a person is to the border and the more contact he or she has with recent Spanish-speaking immigrants, the more likely it is that Spanish is important in life.

In other language contact situations, a language may die. Individuals may lose language as a result of a biological or psychological episode, or someone may lose a foreign language learned in high school. But language death may occur collectively, either through bilingualism and shift or through genocide. Several indigenous languages were lost in El Salvador in the 1930s as a result of military campaigns against local populations, for example.

Language death is a continuum. Fluent speakers keep a language alive. Younger fluent speakers may sometimes speak in ways that older fluent speakers consider a mistake. Other speakers understand the language almost perfectly, but they do not use it often in speech. Their children will almost certainly be monolinguals. Other categories of speakers are passive bilinguals, who know a lot of words but little else about the language, and "rememberers," who may have been fluent in their early life or may have been fluent only in certain domains. Language death follows a basic pattern of simplification. Very often, words in the language get replaced by words from the dominant language. Syntax is simplified in most cases; certain elements like relative clauses may disappear. In some cases, like Breton, the formal register has disappeared and people are only able to speak casually. In other cases, only formal chunks of language like prayers are remembered.

Languages are sometimes, though not very often, brought back from the edge of death. Irish Gaelic had almost disappeared by the end of the 19th century. Now it is the "first official language" of Ireland. Thirty percent of all Irish people have a working knowledge of the language if that ability is defined as being able to follow parts of a conversation. Relatively few Irish people speak it as their first language (perhaps 10 percent nationally), mostly in an area in west Ireland called the Gaeltacht, though recent trends seem to indicate an eastward shift in Irish use. The government supports Gaelic. A television channel broadcasts in Gaelic. Children must take 3,000 hours of the language before graduating from high school. Gaelic is tested and required for entrance into university or the civil service. In these ways, Gaelic is being revived. Still, once people leave school, Gaelic does not play a large part in daily life for most. Perhaps its most important function is that of a symbol of the nation of Ireland.

Recently there has been a lot of interest in **heritage languages,** i.e., the pockets of language maintenance associated with immigrant communities. The term *heritage language,* which was first used by Canadian researchers, stresses the positive attitude of scholars and government agencies toward these (often bilingual) speakers who are no longer considered a liability to get rid of by acculturation and schooling but rather are considered an asset to the country they live in, since they can be easily trained as translators, teachers, and other social services personnel, thus allowing better delivery of services to the multilingual community or employment in international trade or relations.

Educational Implications

Basic knowledge of the issues of language policy is useful in order for teachers to contextualize policy debates within states and districts. Teachers of students from other countries will now also have a better understanding of the contexts in which some of the students acquired their first languages.

9.3 EXERCISES

9.3.1 Words to Know

national language	minority language	diglossia
corpus planning	status planning	language maintenance
language shift	language death	

9.3.2 Review

1. Why are *majority language* and *minority language* not always a good labels?

2. Select a country or area of the world and be prepared to talk about its language situation.

3. What are the three possible outcomes of language contact? How does each come about?

4. What are the differences between status and corpus planning?

9.3.3 Research Projects

1. Research the maintenance of the Gaelic language. Try the library and also the Internet. Are there Gaelic websites?

2. Research an endangered language.

3. Research an extinct language of your choice. Why did it die out?

4. Research a recent debate about language policy in the United States, at the state or federal level.

5. Research the language policy of any nation you choose.

6. Go online to the Modern Language Association (MLA) website. There you will find a map showing 2000 Census data on the top 30 languages spoken in the United States, displayed by county. Use the interactive map to gather information about your area or an area that interests you.

9.4 FURTHER READINGS

A good overview is Spolsky (2004). Two *Annual Reviews of Applied Linguistics* edited by Grabe (1993–94) and (1997) have published useful review articles on the issues surrounding language planning in a number of countries. The data on the United States is from the 2000 U.S. Census. Historical comparisons can be made by consulting McKay (1997) and Ruiz (1993–94). Good sources for the Official English/English Only/ English Plus debate are Crawford (1992) and Baron (1990). Lippi-Green (1997) is very good on language discrimination issues in the United States. The data for Canada are from Carey (1997) and Edwards (1993–94). For Mexico, see Patthey-Chavez (1993–94). A good source for South America is Hornberger (1993–94). For Europe, see Beardsmore (1993–94). An excellent source for Central and Eastern Europe is Paulston and Peckham (1998). For the former Soviet Union, see Haarmann and Holman (1997), Kreindler (1997), and Landau and Kellner-Heinkele (2001). On the linguistic minorities in Italy, see Grassi (1977). India is covered in Kachru (1982). See Platt (1982) for Malaysia and Singapore. Johnson (1993–94) is a good source for Hong Kong. For Japan, see Carroll (2001). Pierce and Ridge (1997) and Webb (1993–94) cover South Africa. For Australia, there are Clyne (1997) and Eggington (1993–94). Issues of educational language planning in Asia are addressed in Kam and Wong (2002) and Silver, Hu, and Iino (2002).

The classic article on diglossia is Ferguson (1959), reprinted in Giglioli (1972) and in Ferguson (1996). For successful languages, see Fishman (1985) and Paulston (1994).

The field of linguistic human rights is complex. It is probably best to begin with a review article like Riagain and Shuibhne (1997) to get an overview. A recent collection is Skutnabb-Kangas and Phillipson (1994). On corpus and status planning, see Haugen (1983).

For language maintenance, shift, and death, see Edwards (1997), Marshall (1993–94), Fishman (1992), Paulston (1994), Dorian (1981), Nettle and Romaine (2000), and Crystal (2000).

Chapter 10

Language and Gender

10.1 EARLY STUDIES

> Based on your experience, what are the differences between male and female speech?

The linguist Robin Lakoff was a pioneer in the field of language and gender. She claimed that there were several distinctive features of women's language. Women's speech, she said, used a number of words *(mauve, divine, lovely)* that men's speech did not. Women often sounded like they were asking questions when they were really making statements; their sentences ended with a rising intonation. In fact, women asked more questions, especially tag questions like those ending in *you know?* As a result, they seemed less certain than men. Women often tended to use more hedges like *sort of.* Lakoff also believed that women used emphatic modifiers like *so, very, such* as well as a distinct intonation that used a lot of emphasis. She believed that women used hypercorrect grammar and pronunciation (see 6.1.1) and made hyperpolite requests *(Would you please open the door, if you don't mind?).*

Robin Tolmach Lakoff received her Ph.D. in linguistics from Harvard University in 1967. In 1973 she published an article on language and gender that she expanded in 1975 into *Language and Woman's Place,* a slender booklet (84 pages) that sparked more than two decades of research on language and gender. Her central thesis was that there was a "language of women," which she identified with nine features. Soon a large debate, involving hundreds of scholarly articles, was sparked in which scholars tried to check whether Lakoff was right. The number of features had grown to 35 by 1986, and some of the results were not consonant with Lakoff's hypothesis, but it remains the case that Lakoff effectively set the agenda for a significant part of the research on language and gender in the last quarter of the 20th century. Lakoff is also interested in the language of psychoanalysis, legal language, and in language in literature. She currently teaches at the University of California, Berkeley.

Lakoff's beliefs basically confirmed a folklinguistic tradition. For years, people had believed that women use words like *immensely* and *horribly* more than men. The otherwise excellent linguist Otto Jespersen, in fact, said that women have a tendency for hyperbole or exaggeration. Women were also thought not to use taboo or off-color expressions. Some people had even gone so far as to talk of separate languages for men and women. Mostly what they mean by this is that in some languages, men and women have different words for the same thing. Here's an example from Japanese, where men and women in fact have a different set of pronouns.

	Men	Women
formal first person	*watakushi/watashi*	*watakushi/atakushi*
informal first person	*boku*	*watashi/atashi*
very informal first	*ore*	—
formal second person	*anata*	*anata/anta*
informal second	*kimi/omae*	*anta*

Historically, women have been seen as both innovative and conservative. That is, some said that women's speech was different from men's because women were innovative, the first to use new words. Other theories said that women were in fact the more conservative speakers, that they kept alive the old words. Actual data from dialect surveys (see 5.1.1) differed as to whether women are conservative or not, but the surveys rarely got their input from women. One of the problems was that most of the researchers were male, and male researchers at that time could not decently speak to women alone. Another was that the surveys were interested in older, even obsolete, terms that often included farm gear, terms that men would be more likely than women to know.

Another explanation for the difference between men's and women's language is concerned with **language attitudes.** Gender reflects attitudes toward language varieties. If a researcher asks people, *Do you ever say* *this?* women tend to overreport their prestige language use. That is, if the researcher asks about a grammatical form or a prestige pronunciation, women are more likely than men to say that they use that form (even though they may in fact use a nonprestige variety). Conversely, men underreport prestige forms. They say they use more nonstandard forms than they really do. There is considerable covert prestige (see 5.2.1) involved in speaking like "one of the guys."

When researchers actually observed people talking, for example in a study done in England, women did indeed use more prestige variants for all tasks (see 6.1.1 for tasks). Lower–working class women shifted their style of speech; in the most informal task, they used a high number of nonstandard forms, but when doing the more formal tasks, they behaved like the class above them. In a Scottish study, women in each social class spoke like the men in the class above them. We have seen that men may well attempt to speak less "correctly" than they can because of covert prestige. Another explanation along these lines is the dichotomy of **status** and **solidarity.** Those who strive for more correct language want status, while those who seek solidarity may often value relationships more than correctness. From this point of view, women may, for whatever reason, be more concerned with status in language than men are, or at least a more conventionally defined sort of status.

10.2 MEN, WOMEN, AND CONVERSATION

While earlier insights into gender and language were important, the explanations that drove research over the next 20 years were the dominance and difference approaches. The **dominance approach** is associated with Lakoff and her followers. The dominance approach sees the differences in men's and women's languages as developing from or reflecting the power differential between men and women in society. The **difference approach** sees men and women coming from two distinct cultures with different rules of speaking. This approach is associated with Deborah Tannen, who has written a number of best-selling books. The approach, however, had its origins in the work of Maltz and Borker. Both approaches tend to be criticized by those linguists who adopt a community of practice model. A **community of practice** consists of people who share participation in an activity and thus also share certain beliefs and ways of behaving and talking. People join this community through doing shared activity but may in the process change the way they mark their linguistic identity, for example by pronouncing words a certain way. A community of practice approach says that people do not speak in a given way because they are born male or female, but rather they construct their identities through talk. Thus, we should study the who, what, when, where, and why of language use, at how people actually use language in specific ways. Much of this work has been ethnographic, focusing on language as an activity in specific settings.

Despite the theoretical orientation of the researchers, much of the research on language and gender has concerned itself with the analysis of conversations. "Men" and "women" are abstractions, but what we report here are some findings from studies of conversation that make some broad statements about the behavior of the two genders. Such studies have been criticized because they attempt to generalize from very specific instances, so any conclusions that get drawn from the research should be taken with the proverbial grain of salt. It is also important to note that most of the research has been done within the context of Western culture and its conversational rules.

One early study of conversation, language, and gender was done on coffee shop conversations. The researchers were interested in overlap versus interruption. **Overlap** is a facilitating aspect of conversation. Good friends finish each others' sentences, for example. **Interruption** is a violation of good conversational practice. Same-sex conversational pairs (male-male or female-female) tended to overlap about three times as much as they interrupted. In mixed-sex (male-female) pairs, there were five times as many interruptions as overlaps. The overlaps were all by men, and all but two of the almost 50 interruptions were by men. While men rarely interrupted each other, they frequently interrupted women. Note that's not a gross generalization; in this case, at least, the numbers of overlaps and interruptions were counted. Of course, it is another matter to decide the significance or the generalizability of the study.

Another finding about mixed-sex conversations is that men often delay their responses or backchannel behavior (see 2.6.2). They paused and then said *Mm* or *yeah*. Within the general conversational "rules," this is supposed to signal lack of comprehension or lack of interest because, though it is a response, it is a minimal one. In general, women do more of the work of keeping the conversation going. Men give little feedback. One way that women tended to smooth out conversations in one study was by using *you know*. It was used by women when they expected a response from men but didn't get it. Women used *you know* five times more than men did. You'll remember that hedges like *you know* were seen by Lakoff as characteristic of women's speech and that hedges were seen as a form of powerless language, at least in Western culture. It seems, however, that we cannot arbitrarily decide what certain linguistic forms mean, but instead we must see their actual use in conversation. For example, here *you know* served the function of saying *Hello out here!*

Hedges can be of several different kinds, and we need to see how the phrase is used in context. *You know* can be confident *(all that baloney, you know, we've heard before)* or tentative, said with rising intonation *(I didn't know what to say, you know?)*. In at least one study, while women and men both used *you know* with about the same frequency, women used "confident" *you know* more than men, who, when they used *you know*, meant it as a way to signal tentativeness. Here, we see some evidence for the difference approach; men and women are using the same form to mean different things. Another study found, for example, that women in same-sex groups used hedges when they were talking about sensitive topics. They used *sort of* and *I mean* when criticizing a friend, as a way to soften the criticism, while the men in that sample tended to avoid sensitive topics, so they used fewer hedges.

Similarly, the assumption has been that tag questions function as an indicator of tentativeness but tags may well have different meanings. One meaning of a tag question is uncertainty *(The movie's at 8, isn't it?)*. Another use of a tag question is an attempt at smoothing the flow of the conversation; this sort of tag question can be seen in the language of caretakers *(The cat's pretty, isn't it?)* or in friendly criticisms where the attempt is to soften the negative *(That was pretty dumb, wasn't it?)*. It may well be that there is a gender difference in use of this language form.

Silence is another aspect of language (and it is an aspect of language) that has been studied from the point of view of language and gender. Silence can be a form of conversational dominance in Western culture. Silence breaks Western conversational rules. In studies of married couples, women tend to talk more and introduce more topics, but their topics are often not taken up, or followed up on, by their husbands. Men will say they "didn't feel like talking." Yet men do talk more. When asked to describe a picture, women took on average a little over 3 minutes while men took an average of 13 minutes. In conversation, men seem to feel no need to link the conversation to what has been said before, so their topic shifts are more abrupt. Women feel they must refer to what has been said, to make the conversation as cohesive as possible. Women often use questions to do this. For men, questions are to be answered. It has been frequently commented on that men are likely to respond to a question like *What should I do?* with a plan rather than the sympathy the speaker is eliciting.

10.2.1 Characteristics of Women's Discourse

The picture of women's speech that emerges from the studies on discourse is that women tend to build on each other's conversations more than men do. They tend to talk more about people and relationships, not things. Compared to men, women use a lot of backchannel devices, giving more feedback to their conversational partners. There is a lot of overlapping but little interruption in women's speech. Hedges are used in conversation to respect the face needs of others, and tag and other questions are used to bring people into conversations. Questions may also be used to make sure that everyone agrees, that the conversation does not become too confrontational.

10.2.2 Language and Power

Lakoff's notion was that women's speech was powerless. That notion has been tested in courtrooms, hospitals, and businesses. In some studies it turned out that "women's language" was not characteristic of all women. Some women expert witnesses in court, for example, speak very "powerfully." Conversely, women's speech was not restricted to women. In one study, a young male ambulance driver witness spoke in the way Lakoff characterized as female. Perhaps what we have is a continuum, with more women speaking in "powerless" language than men but with social status and experience being important factors. Other research has shown that even when women are in positions of authority and power, such as doctors, they often speak in "powerless" language. Women doctors are also interrupted by their male patients, and men frequently dominate the conversation at work whether or not they are the boss.

10.3 GENDER IN PLAYGROUNDS/CLASSROOMS

It seems that gender roles in language can be seen at least as early as elementary school. Again, what we are summarizing are averages, but many have commented that the play and friendships of boys tend to be activity based while girls value talk-based friendships. When eight-year-old boys were filmed talking, they shifted topics, squirmed, made faces at the camera; girls could talk for 20 minutes. Older boys could do the task but didn't look at each other and avoided personal details; they talked about things rather than relationships.

Studies through the early 1990s found that teachers spoke more to boys, including giving boys more praise and blame than they did girls. Teachers also asked boys a wider range of question types; girls were asked fewer open-ended questions that called for lengthy responses. Teachers gave boys the advantage of more wait time when answering questions, reprimanded girls and not boys for calling out answers without being called upon, and directed their gaze to boys more often than girls. Boys stood out more in a class (if you asked teachers what happened during a class, they tended to remember the boys' contributions). Teachers often played the boys and girls off against each other. Both men and women teachers acted in the same way. Later in the 1990s, there was less research of this nature, perhaps because there was less interest in gender differences in general. As we have noted, many scholars have suggested that setting up gender-based oppositions is not helpful because doing so erases individuality. While some accept the picture of the older classrooms as remaining basically true, others are beginning to challenge the conventional wisdom. Still, there is no new definitive picture to take the place of the old one thus far. One problem is that measured classroom differences are often the results of averages, all the girls, all the boys. If just a couple of boys stand out, the average for all boys increases, thus giving perhaps an unreal picture of the classroom.

10.4 LANGUAGE AND MEN

Since men were perceived unthinkingly as the norm in sociolinguistics at the beginning, few specific studies of men's language were made early in the research on language and gender. Implicit in several of the studies, however, was the notion that men are men and women are women and there's not much that can be done about that. Several of the more interesting recent studies of men's language have denied this premise. These studies have focused on construction of male identity within society, looking at the ways that boys and young men learn to talk "like a man" while simultaneously showing that there are many ways to talk like a man. These studies, and recent studies of women's language as well, show that we need to look at factors like race, class, and sexuality in combination with gender.

10.5 LESBIAN AND GAY MALE LANGUAGE USE

The area of gay and lesbian speech has been studied comparatively less than other areas of linguistics. One early mention of gay and lesbian speech can be found in Lakoff. She briefly touches on the idea that homosexuals adopt the language of the opposite sex. That is to say that gay men speak more like women and lesbians adopt a more masculine manner of speaking. How much truth is there to this claim? Studies on phonology and grammar have not supported this assertion. Research on discourse has attempted to compare the conversational styles of gay men and lesbians with findings from the language and gender studies of conversation, but no solid findings have emerged.

One area of gay and lesbian speech that has received a considerable amount of attention is lexicon. One way in which any community differentiates itself from the larger society is by constructing new words and giving new meanings to already existing words that will better define their experiences (see slang 6.4). Gay and lesbian slang has, over the years, been the subject of several books and dictionaries. One aspect of the lexicon is the debate over labels for lesbians and gay men, for example, whether *gay* is in fact an appropriate label; some gay men feel it trivializes them. Another controversy is the use of the word *queer* as self-identifying

10.6 SEXIST LANGUAGE

Many have pointed out the sexist assumptions of English grammar and of the lexicon (see 15.5.3), particularly the use of *he* for both *he* and *she*. Sexism can also be found in naming conventions (laws that require a woman to take her husband's name at marriage) and in terms of address (women tend to get called by their first names at work more than men do). Women workers still get called by more terms of endearment than male workers *(Honey, can I get another cup of coffee here?).*

Things have changed, however. In fact, the removal of sexist language as an option in publishing is one example of successful nongovernmental language planning (see 9.2). Any book or article that gets published will have to defend its use of *he* as an all-purpose pronoun, and the author will probably lose the argument and be required to use *he/she* or another device. Occupational titles have also changed in the United States, for the most part, with actresses, for example, now being called *actors;* waitresses being called *servers;* and stewardesses being called *flight attendants.*

Educational Implications
Differences in language use by gender have an impact in both classrooms and staff rooms as well as in the outside world.

10.7 EXERCISES

10.7.1 Words to Know

taboo	dominance approach	difference approach
status	solidarity	overlap
interruption		

10.7.2 Review

1. What were some common folklinguistic descriptions of women's language?

2. How has language changed recently to become less sexist?

3. How are the difference and dominance approaches distinct?

4. What does current feminist theory say about the two approaches?

5. How do the ideas of status and solidarity explain men's and women's speech behavior?

6. What are the main findings about conversation between men and women?

7. What are the main findings about language and power?

10.7.3 Research Projects

1. Tape a conversation involving speakers of opposite genders. Analyze your transcript to see if the claims made in the text fit your sample. Why do you think you got the results you got? What factors may have influenced your speakers?

2. Gather the transcripts of a newsgroup, chat room, or another Internet discussion forum. Identify the contributors based on gender. Can you draw conclusions on features of the messages each gender composes?

3. If you have access to young children, try to investigate at what age gender differentiation in language has its onset. If you had to guess, what would be your time frame? Check your results against against your guesses.

10.8 FURTHER READINGS

Excellent starting points are Coates (1993) and Talbot (1998). Both are comprehensive and readable. Eckert and McConnell-Ginet (2003) is also good. Coates and Cameron (1989) is a good collection. Roman, Juhasz, and Miller (1994) broaden the field to include psychology and psychoanalysis and should therefore be read with caution.

Lakoff (1975) was foundational. On Lakoff's influence on gender studies, see Crawford (1995) and the revised edition of Lakoff (Bucholtz 2004). Jespersen's much quoted passage is in (1922). The Norwich study is by Trudgill (1974). The Glasgow study is by Macaulay (1978).

Tannen's popular work is (1990c); her (1994) collection is scholarly, if less fun. Her 1984 book, while more general, provides valuable information on gender differences in communication. Maltz and Borker (1982) laid the foundation for the difference approach. A survey of the "miscommunication" debate can be found in Henley and Kramarae (1991) and is also anthologized in Roman, Juhasz, and Miller (1994).

A very good collection of articles in the communities-of-practice tradition is Hall and Bucholtz (1995). See also Eckert and McConnell-Ginet's (1992) widely quoted article and Ehrlich's (1997) article.

The "coffee shop" study was Zimmerman and West (1975). They also address silence. Fishman (1980) discusses *you know* and minimal responses. On women working harder at conversations, see DeFrancisco (1991). On politeness, see Holmes (1995).

On hedges, see Holmes (1984, 1987) and Coates (1987, 1989). With the exception of Coates (1989), they may be hard to find. There is a good discussion of hedges in Coates (1993). For tag questions, see Coates (1993), Holmes (1984), and Cameron (1985). On men talking a lot when describing a picture, see Swacker (1975).

The research on court cases and powerless language is O'Barr and Atkins (1980). See West (1990) on women doctors and Woods (1989) on work settings. On gender in playgrounds, see Tannen (1990a, 1990b). Swan (1992) and Sunderland (2000) are good sources for the role of gender in education. For a good collection of articles on men's language, see Johnson and Meinhof (1997). Good review articles on lesbian and gay male language use are Jacobs (1996) and Kulick (2000). See also *www.ling. nwu.edu/~ward/gaybib.html* for a useful bibliography.

On the sexist bias in the lexicon, see references in Chapter 15; on nonsexist language, see Frank and Treichler (1988), who provide guidelines and some discussion. See also Pauwels (1998).

Chapter 11

Literacy

11.1 THE WRITTEN WORD

11.1.1 Literacy and Orality

Linguists in the early 1900s were not very interested in writing. Only speech was considered true language; writing was speech written down. Through the years, however, as sociolinguists taped and then transcribed speech, it became clear that writing is something other than speech written down. Speech is aural. It needs to be understood in real time; the listener cannot go back and rehear the sentence without asking the speaker's indulgence. Speech is full of hesitations, false starts, pauses, and errors. Writing is permanent, visual, and free of disfluencies. The listener, if confused by the degenerate output, can get extra clues from intonation and body language of the speaker. Deixis (see 3.2.1) is a little easier because speaker and hearer can agree immediately on terms such as *here/there* and *this/that*. Overall, speech has simpler grammar, with an emphasis on coordination *(then, and)* rather than the common pattern of subordination *(which/when clauses)* used in writing.

However, perhaps too much has been made of the differences. There is, after all, no structure that is found in writing that is wholly absent from speech and vice versa. Researchers suggest writing and reading are separated not sharply but by continua of formality (formal to informal), planning (more to less), explicitness (explicit to implicit), and meaning (objective to interpersonal). Finally, the conclusion must be that both writing and speech are aspects of language, two different modalities.

Ideas about speech and writing are implicated in arguments and misunderstandings about teaching writing to speakers of nonstandard social dialects. Speakers of nonstandard dialects may be put at a disadvantage early on in their schooling because they must learn a new modality of a new language variety while their peers are simply learning a new modality of their home language.

11.1.2 Writing Systems

There are three main types of writing system: logographic, syllabic, and alphabetic. The best modern example of a **logographic system** is Chinese. In Chinese, the character is the unit of meaning. Some characters are icons in the sense that they look like their meaning. The character for tree looks like a tree. Most, probably about 80 to 90 percent, of characters, however have little iconic value. Most characters are made up of a radical and a phonetic. There are about two hundred radicals that give clues to meaning. For example, three lines arranged in a certain way will give the reader a clue that the character has to do with water. The phonetic part of the character will help with its pronunciation. Despite the fact that this system sounds cumbersome, it is well suited to Chinese because there are so many homonyms in the language. (See an example of Chinese characters in Figure 15.1. A quick look at the character clarifies meaning.) Incidentally, English-speaking children first read logographically. They know that the stop signs read *stop* because stop signs are, in the United States, octangular and red. They "read" the arches at McDonald's® as *McDonald's* without accessing the words. One child "read" the McDonald's® sign as *Old McDonald* because she had overextended (see 12.2.6) the character from the nursery rhyme to the fast food restaurant.

A good example of **syllabic systems** are the kana of Japanese. There are about 40 hiragana and 40 katakana. The two systems of kana encode the same sounds (e.g., *ka, ki, ku, ke, ko*). Hiragana is used to write some words of Japanese origin and all grammatical morphemes. Katakana is used to write foreign loan words. For historical reasons (the esteem in which Chinese civilization was held by the Japanese), Chinese characters are also used extensively to write Japanese and a high school graduate must know at minimum close to two thousand. The well-educated person knows many more. Finally, Japanese also use the Roman alphabet extensively. For an example of katakana, see Figure 15.2.

Readers of this book are well acquainted with the **alphabetic system.** It is one based on sounds. English has poor sound-symbol correspondence and is therefore very difficult to spell. Children in the United States routinely spend a great deal of time each week learning the spelling of words and being tested on them. George Bernard Shaw satirized this fact when he jokingly noted that *fish* could be spelled in English as *ghoti* (with the *gh* of *rough*, the *o* of *women*, and the *ti* of *initial*). Incidentally, Shaw was, technically speaking, wrong, as initial *gh* is actually never pronounced [f] and no English word ends in *-ti*.

Ultimately, writing systems are arbitrary. Closely related languages such as Hindi and Urdu or Serbian and Croatian are written in different systems. Scripts such as Chinese and Arabic are used to write unrelated languages because Chinese and Arabic have been important cultural and political languages across wide areas of the world.

11.2 READING

11.2.1 Reader, Text, and Meaning

Reading is an active process, a meaning-making activity. Readers bring to reading a lot of experience and background knowledge. Since each individual has different life experiences, no one will read the same text the same way. Texts, too, have histories. They "speak" to other texts across time. If a character in a novel says *To be or not to be,* we know she's quoting Hamlet. She might even be quoting Hamlet if she leaves off the first part of the quotation and says something like *Ah, that's the question.* At some level, the author may even be "quoting" Hamlet if she decides to write about a contemporary family in which a child is unhappy with a mother's remarriage. Or she may be quoting an old American television quiz show when she says *That's the $64,000 question* (see 14.1.2).

This way of looking at readers and reading has been very influential lately. Researchers love to disagree, however, and many would define reading in a very different way. Fundamental to research in education, psychology, and linguistics has been the idea of top-down and bottom-up processing. Some researchers, psychologists primarily, see reading as largely a **bottom-up process** in which letters are matched to sounds, sounds are blended together, and finally meaning is made. This seems plausible until we consider the speed at which print is processed. Some estimates say that this bottom-up way to read would take a remarkably long time, yielding a speed of about 60 words per minute (wpm). This is significantly fewer words per minute than the average 200–300 wpm a native speaker can handle. Yet research also shows that when we read, we focus our eyes' attention on 80 percent of the text, indicating some bottom-up processing. We are probably reading a lot of chunks. Humans seem to process information by "chunking" it, and we can retain seven chunks of information in working memory.

Goodman looks at reading as a very **top-down process.** He called reading "a psycholinguistic guessing game." In his view, based on miscue analysis, print serves to confirm our guesses based on our schematic or background knowledge. Miscues are mistakes in oral reading like *Dad picked up the children from school* when the reader meant to say *Father picked up the children from school.* No one, Goodman claims, says this incorrectly as *Feather picked up the children from school* or *Father packed up the children from school.* To Goodman, this shows that people process meaning and not letters. However, if we accept Goodman's view of reading, it's hard to see how anything new could be learned through print. How do we understand ideas not already in our schema? Finally, relying too much on a hypothesis-testing model such as Goodman's would be even slower than a bottom-up approach.

Stanovich's **interactive-compensatory model** seems to make the most sense. We read along in a top-down mode until we get to things that are confusing. Then we stop and process bottom up. Weaker readers thus tend to rely more on bottom-up processing. For second-language learners, there are any number of potential problems lurking in text: syntax, vocabulary, and background knowledge, especially culture-specific knowledge, are all snares, and beginning second language students are frequently tied to **bottom-up processing.**

11.2.2 Reading Development in a First Language

We have already noted in the previous section that, even in an alphabetic language, children begin reading by recognizing shapes and configurations of letters as wholes. For example, they memorize *stop* by remembering the shape of stop signs. At this level, children are aware that print represents speech. As they enter school, or are coached by their parents, children begin to see that individual letters represent segments of speech. They begin to sound out words and invent spellings based on what they hear. For example, they might write KR for *car.* As their alphabetic literacy develops, children increase their ability to match letters on the page with individual sounds. They also learn more "sight words," words that are read as wholes and that are crucial for rapid, fluent reading. They learn to recognize chunks of words as well, two- and three-letter combinations. Finally, they become increasingly attuned to the spelling system and its rules; they recognize what a silent *e* at the end of the word does to pronunciation, and they learn that *-ed* usually means the past tense of a verb but that it is pronounced in different ways. They can compare unknown words to known words to figure out pronunciation. Some children are better at these segmenting or "awareness" skills than others. Let us take a moment to break down the kinds of awareness necessary for reading skillfully. Basically, children need to be able to break down a word and build it back up.

Consonants cluster around vowels to produce **syllables** (see 14.1.1). The central part of a syllable is its rime. The **rime** consists of a vowel and what follows it; the part of the syllable after the vowel is the **coda.** Sometimes, there is a consonant or consonants before the vowel in the syllable and this is called the **onset.**

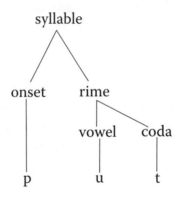

Beginning readers need to know how many syllables there are in a word and how to divide the syllable into its parts. Being able to recognize syllables helps fluency in reading because recognition of chunks leads to more automatic processing. Beginning readers also need phonemic awareness, that is, the ability to discriminate sounds. They need to be able to judge whether two initial (or final) consonants have the same sound. They need to be able to judge which vowels are the same. Children need to know that the word *cat* consists of three phonemes and to be able to blend the phonemes together to say the word. Finally, they need to recognize rhymes like *cat* and *hat*.

11.2.3 Spelling

Obviously, there is some level at which reading skills as they have been defined here and spelling skills overlap. Several researchers have tried to bring order to what appears to be the chaos of English spelling. They have posited three ordering principles for English spelling. The first principle is that English spelling is alphabetic; this means that letters match sounds, often very roughly indeed as a result of sound changes over time. Still, there is a system in place.

There is a second principle of English spelling, within-word patterning. For example, as native speakers, we know that *gh* is pronounced as /f/ at the end of a word *(rough)* and /g/ at the beginning *(ghost)*. This idea that spelling has within-word patterning has led to some books listing six or so basic syllable/spelling formulas. Two of these have a "silent" *e* at the end of the syllable. The first formula is vowel + consonant + e, in which the silent *e* at the end of the syllable changes the pronunciation of the vowel *(mat/mate)*. The second formula occurs in unaccented final syllables and takes the form consonant + *l* + silent *e (apple, little)*. In this formula, the silent *e* does not change the pronunciation of the vowel. Some researchers advocate teaching these sorts of patterns to learners.

The third principle says that English spelling conserves meaning. By this, we mean that words like *serene/serenity, improvise/improvisation,* and *impose/imposition* have similar spellings to show that they are related, even though the sounds of the vowels change in each case.

11.2.4 Teaching Methods

The teaching approach that emphasizes developing these skills, and specifically the matching of letters to sounds (**sound-symbol correspondence**) is **phonics.** Phonics works on the matching of real-world knowledge to printed form. Phonics assumes that beginning readers already know the pronunciation of words (and therefore should be used with caution when teaching second language speakers). Most children know that *bee* and *boy* start with the same sound and that *cat* and *hat* rhyme. Teachers then use that information to teach that the initial sound of *bee* and *boy* is realized by the letter *b*. Remember that according to the interactive-compensatory model of reading, most of the time people read top-down but they use bottom-up strategies when they get "stuck" on a word. Phonics is a way of giving children these bottom-up skills. Much of the criticism of phonics is based on the boring worksheets that have been used to teach sound-symbol correspondences. Phonics can be taught well. It is best not used 100 percent of the time because there is more to reading than sound-symbol matching.

Phonics is often paired with a **skills-based approach** to reading. A skills-based approach to reading would take into account the following:

- **Flexibility:** Students need to know their reason for reading and how to most efficiently address that need. They need to know how to skim for the gist or main idea of the passage or scan for specific information.

- **Utilization of nontextual information:** Students learn to use titles, subheadings, pictures, and charts to better understand the text.

- **Word skills:** Students learn to use predictable morphology like prefixes and suffixes to guess unknown words, as you did when reading part of *Jabberwocky* (see 2.3.4).

- **Discourse skills:** Students learn to use **discourse markers** like *next, then,* and *after that* and rhetorical patterns like comparison/contrast and cause/effect to make sense of texts.

- **Comprehension questions:** Comprehension questions are often at the core of the skills approach to reading and have tended to give the approach a bad name among those who think that these sorts of questions test more than teach. Teachers need to be aware that there are different levels of comprehension. Here are four levels of comprehension questions:

  1. Literal comprehension: The answers are in the text. Students pick them out.

  2. Recombination: These questions still ask for literal comprehension but their answers require combination of literal information from two or more parts of the text.

  3. Inference: The answers to these questions are implied.

  4. Personal responses: Some possible questions of this sort are *Did you enjoy the story?* and *What did you think of the behavior of character X?*

Phonics and skills-based approaches to reading are **intensive reading** approaches. They look at reading from the bottom up. **Extensive reading** is an approach that believes that students learn to read by reading. One of its forms is *sustained silent reading,* when the whole school stops for 15 minutes a day to read. In many programs, children are encouraged to read whole books, not just short pieces in an anthology. One type of extensive reading program is **whole language.**

Advocates of whole language say children learn best if they read whole texts. But advocates also say that reading and writing should not be separated and that language should be approached as a whole. Often in whole-language classrooms, learners tell stories to teachers or aides, who then write down the stories exactly as the learners tell them. These stories then become the texts that students learn to read. The texts have meaning because they are the children's stories. Eventually, children write their own texts. Spelling and grammar are not emphasized in whole-language classrooms (although there is no reason a teacher could not include them, and some do). As a result, whole language has come in for some criticism by people who feel that this approach does not offer students fundamental skills.

11.3 WRITING

11.3.1 Product Approaches to Writing

In the era during which behaviorist psychology ruled, writing was a way to practice grammar. Students were taught a limited number of rhetorical modes such as comparison/contrast, cause and effect, narration, and exposition. Implicit in this approach was the belief that you probably couldn't teach writing anyway, that it was a mysterious process. The best students could do was imitate good models.

Writing was controlled so that mistakes were few. Remember that mistakes were thought to be bad. Students added punctuation, filled in blanks, and changed words in model paragraphs. Here are some typical exercises that might have been given in the 1970s:

1. Model paragraph: Mary plays tennis on Saturdays. Mary's friend plays too. John doesn't play tennis. He likes to play golf.

   Cover up the model paragraph. Copy the sentences below in a paragraph form. Add necessary punctuation.

   mary plays tennis on saturdays
   marys friend plays too
   john doesnt play tennis
   he plays golf

2. Write the present tense of the verb on the line:

   Mary _____ (live) in a big city.
   John _____ (work) at an office.

3. Mary gets up every morning at 7 o'clock. First, she takes a shower and washes her hair. Then, she goes downstairs and eats breakfast. Mary usually eats cereal and fruit for breakfast. At 8 o'clock, Mary leaves for work. She works in a big office building downtown.

Instructions: You are writing about John, not Mary. Change *Mary* to *John*. Change *he* to *she*, and make any other changes necessary.

Another form of exercise that was quite common would have students personalize the paragraph by writing a similar one about themselves *(I get up every morning at 6:30...)*.

Sentence combining was a popular teaching as well as testing device. The student would have to combine these three sentences into one:

(11.1) The dog is large.

(11.2) The dog is black.

(11.3) The dog ran down the street.

This was the **product approach** to writing. What was important was the final piece of writing produced, with the fewest errors possible. We still write this way all the time. The teacher assigns a paper, due at the end of term. The students write it on the last evening or morning, if possible, turn it in, and are given a grade for it. That's no way to teach writing, but it's a dandy way to test it. To teach writing, it is now thought that students need practice in all stages of the writing process.

11.3.2 Process Approaches to Writing

The **process approach** has deep roots in the expressive school of writing. Writing, in this view, is for discovering meaning, ideas, and personal views. Writing progresses through a process of prewriting/idea generation; drafting (first and second drafts, at least); conferencing/peer review; and editing. Students brainstorm or use other **heuristics** (i.e., discovery procedures) to come up with some preliminary ideas. They write a draft and then show it either to the teacher, who works with the student in a one-on-one conference, or to a peer or peers, who provide written feedback. The writer then considers this feedback, incorporates what is relevant, and writes a second draft. Only when the ideas are finalized does the writer sit down and edit the paper for grammar and spelling.

The process approach has been extremely influential but also extremely controversial. It has helped some people become better writers. It has also put a premium on expression. Some have wondered whether this emphasis on expression has gotten in the way of preparing students for higher education. They have argued that most writing assignments in a college or university do not ask for a personal opinion but instead center on comparing and contrasting, describing, showing cause and effect—in short, are manifestations of the most common rhetorical patterns. They want attention paid to these patterns in basic writing classes so students can use them as a heuristic. Many say, however, that this approach means that students capitulate to the discourse of the academy and forgo their own "natural" discourse.

Audience and Purpose

Two important notions that the process approach stresses are audience and purpose. You must know to whom you are writing and why you are writing. A good example to use to get this point across is that of comics. There is a wide range of newspaper comics; some appeal to children and others appeal mostly to adults. When we write, we have an image, or should have an image, of our reader in our head. The notion of purpose overlaps a bit with the notion of rhetorical mode, but as purpose is taught today, learners do not imitate models but instead work on developing a clear idea of the purpose of their writing in the prewriting stage.

Teaching the Writing Process

The process approach has devised a number of prewriting techniques. Among them are **mind maps** or **brainstorming,** in which students write down everything they can think of about a subject in a given amount of time and then try to find connections and something to write about in the mass of ideas. In the past, teachers said that outlines were necessary for good writing. They may indeed help some people, but others are helped by the freer associations of brainstorming.

Freewriting is another widely used technique. Students write in sentences. They ideally do not raise their pencils from the paper and fill in periods when their minds go blank with words on the page like *What should I write? I need to write something. Maybe I should say* . . . . They then often "loop": they read their freewriting, choose an idea, freewrite about that, and repeat the process.

Another technique that has risen out of the process approach that is widely used is the **dialogue journal.** Students write to teachers, who answer them as people, not correcting their grammar and punctuation but instead responding authentically. This is an ideal use for electronic mail. Teachers can send out assignments to the whole class and also respond individually.

Perhaps the most important technique used in process writing is having students work collaboratively in pairs or groups to critique each other's writing. Sometimes it is easier to think about good writing as a critic; then you can apply what you have learned from criticizing others to your own writing. Collaborative learning also provides a real audience for writing.

Reading/Writing Connections

The assumption in the past has been that writing is the payoff, something you do after reading, often in response to the reading. People are beginning to see that the process goes in both directions, and so it is possible to start with writing and move to reading. The writing first approach uses reading logs or journals in which students write while reading or uses writing assignments before reading assignments to activate student knowledge of the topic.

Feedback

What makes good writing? Order these from most to least important. Is there anything missing that you would like to add?

- correct grammar
- proper length
- originality of ideas
- correct spelling
- correct punctuation
- neat handwriting
- a good range of vocabulary
- complex and varied sentences
- good organization: introduction, body, conclusion
- clear idea of audience
- clear idea of purpose

Errors may come about as a result of transfer from a first language or dialect or from ignorance of the rule, overgeneralization (learning a rule "too well"), or simply through difficulty level ("not being at that stage yet"). The process approach says that errors can be put off until the editing stage.

Also consider accuracy versus fluency. Do we want students to write more or more accurately? Well, both. A focus on accuracy may lead them to play it safe, which in turn leads to a short essay with simple sentences.

Once you've decided to correct, how do you do it? Most teachers have a system of symbols they use to mark up drafts. Others use margin comments or notes, on or off the page. It makes a great deal of sense to focus comments. Give the student one or two things to watch out for and improve in the next essay. Don't overwhelm.

Portfolios are becoming more common means to evaluate students. Here, the work for the term is collected, including all the drafts and even the notes if the teacher so chooses. The grade for the course is based on the amount of work the student puts into the writing process itself, not on the products produced.

11.4 CONTRASTIVE RHETORIC

The techniques described previously are used with students whose first language is English and with students who are studying English as a second or foreign language. Those studying English as a second or foreign language have usually learned to write in their first language. However, they may need to be shown the differences between writing in their first and second languages.

It is rare for a person to invent a field **(contrastive rhetoric),** but Robert Kaplan did that with the publication of "Cultural Thought Patterns in Intercultural Education" in 1966. Kaplan's "doodles" encapsulated lines of thought that ran through the essays of various cultural/language groups (see Figure 11.1). He assumed that English was linear, while Semitic (Arabic/Hebrew) writers zigzagged and "Oriental" writers wrote in a spiral. Romance (French, Italian, Spanish) and Russian writers were a mix of the linear and the zigzag.

This had the unfortunate result of setting English up as the logical model, leaving the others needing remediation. There are aspects of Kaplan's theory (since modified) that deserve attention. Clearly, prior experiences with writing in school do influence how people write in English. Students

Figure 11.1: Kaplan's Representation of the Development of Argument in the Essays of Different Cultures

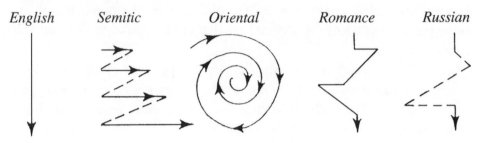

English   Semitic   Oriental   Romance   Russian

Source: Language Learning 1966.

need to see the acquisition of English as additive bilingualism, as getting another resource on top of the language they learned in school.

Recent developments have seen follow-up research, focusing on other languages, often but not always compared with English, but also significant criticisms and revisions of the original ideas of contrastive rhetorics, some by Kaplan himself. Among the current trends we can identify a growing influence of first-language writing pedagogy on contrastive rhetorics, with a related push to move in the direction of examining not only linguistic differences among writers but also cultural, educational, and sociological differences. Similarly, there have been claims for extending contrastive rhetorics to include among the variables gender, ethnicity, and sexual orientation. In a different direction, critics of contrastive rhetorics have pointed out the cultural stereotyping implicit in the idea of reducing the behavior of millions of writers to one scheme and in some cases have even rejected the idea that the nonnative speaker should be acculturated into the English writing tradition.

11.5 COMPUTER-MEDIATED COMMUNICATION

The 1990s have seen the rise of a new field of study: **computer-mediated communication (CMC).** This is due to the sudden rise of the personal computer (computers have been around since World War II, but they were too big to be used by many people) and the Internet, essentially a network of computers. These technologies allow computer users across the world, or sitting across a room, to interact via the technological medium. Similar in significance to the telegraph and the telephone, CMC has "happened" much faster, over a period of a mere 10–15 years. Because of the speed with which CMC has spread, and the fact that it is so recent, its impact on communication, access to information, and more broadly the socioeconomic situation worldwide has not yet been fully evaluated. We will therefore limit ourselves to describing some of the principal issues raised by CMC that are of significance to linguists and language teachers.

11.5.1 Genres of CMC

The first observation, even before we start trying to characterize the nature of CMC, is that CMC has created a large number of new genres of communication. The following is a list of some of the most common ones.

Hypertext

Hypertext is a text that includes connections (links) to other texts, so that one can access very easily the other texts referenced by the links. Footnotes in a printed book are hypertext links, except that in hypertext, the footnotes can have another footnote and so forth. This is the idea that made the Internet so popular, since it allows extremely easy and fruitful connections across ideas, people, services, businesses, etc.

E-Mail

E-mail tends to differ from letters in that it is less formal, shorter, and closer to speech patterns than to written ones. It often includes direct quotes of previous e-mails to provide the context of responses.

Web Pages

Information on the Internet is presented in "pages" (the term is, of course, a metaphor), which can be significantly long given the capacity of the computer to "scroll down" to reveal more information than can fit on one screen. Web pages range from the very formal business or academic work-related presentations to personal spaces where the main goal is to express the user's personality.

Listservers

These are e-mail discussion groups in which a central computer has a list of addresses to which all e-mails are forwarded after receipt. It is a many-to-many model of communication. Listservs can range from the academic to the frivolous and can be very different in nature. For example, some are "moderated," which means that there is someone who decides what is allowed to be sent to all the users and what it not. This form of benign censorship is necessary due to the large amount of unwanted or off-topic messages often posted in unmoderated groups.

Chatting

Chatting is the practice to have a "conversation" with one or more other computer users by typing one's turns into the computer. The various turns are displayed either in separate parts of the screen or as a scrolling sequence.

Blogging

Blogging is essentially keeping an online diary, although blogging ranges from personal introspection to serious news and media coverage. Originally, blogs consisted of little more than collections of links to other web pages, but they quickly acquired a more textual (and visual) nature.

11.5.2 Synchronous vs. Asynchronous CMC

Computer and Internet technology is changing so fast that by the time this book will have been printed it is safe to assume that part of what we could say about it would be out of date. We will make no attempt at describing cutting-edge technology, such as video and audio conferencing, which are beginning to take hold, nor will we address the possibility of easily documenting with pictures and sounds one's ideas and equally easily sharing them. We will restrict ourselves, in other words, to linguistic CMC that takes place via keyboard input. Most research on the subject is concerned with this modality.

A fundamental difference exists between synchronous and asynchronous CMC: asynchronous CMC are cases like e-mail, in which the participants need not attend to the interaction at the same time. In synchronous CMC, the participants must operate simultaneously. Writing is asynchronous, while speech obviously is synchronous.

11.5.3 Writing and Speech Features

There is a broad consensus that CMC occupies an intermediate position between speech and writing. CMC retains some features of the written register, thus the fact that CMC lacks the suprasegmental (word stress and intonation) and visual clues of face-to-face communication makes it an impoverished form (such as writing). Conversely, the shortness of turns, the informal nature of the messages, and the use of slang point toward spoken interaction.

Users adapt to the written nature of CMC by using a series of strategies. For example, spelling a word in ALL CAPS is considered the equivalent of yelling and the use of *stars* around a word signifies emphasis. CMC has developed a series of emoticons, which are used, for example, to indicate that one is joking, thus replacing a knowing wink, or a smile, or laughter pulses—indicated conventionally in conversation by :-)—interspersed in speech ("Mary :-) went :-) home :-)"), which indicate the humorous intention of the speaker in face-to-face communication. Other strategies include "addressivity," such as the practice of prefacing a turn with the name (or handle) of the addressee. This is necessary in chat rooms where many users may be interacting at the same time, and therefore one would not be able to identify who the addressee of a given turn is. Along the same lines, quoting a part of the text in an e-mail response achieves the effect of approximating a question/answer conversational strategy.

CMC does display some features that are unique to the medium, including turn-adjacency disruption and topic decay. Because of the presentation of turns in chat rooms, which is done in strict chronological order in a scrolling window, it is often the case that a pair of turns in an adjacency pair, such as question and answer, will be several turns apart in CMC. Studies have shown that this is indeed the case but that users do not seem to be bothered by this feature. Conversely, topic decay indicates that discussions in CMC abandon topics brought up by participants more often than face-to-face conversations. This is due once more to the presentation of turns and to the collective nature of chat rooms. Since, unlike in face-to-face conversations, the user of CMC does not know who else is responding to a given turn, several conflicting responses or new bids for topics may appear after a turn. As a result there is topic fragmentation in CMC.

11.5.4 Jargon of CMC

Users of CMC have generated a very large number of slang terms, especially acronyms (such as CMC), that are used both to facilitate the use of the technological medium in the communicative situation (e.g., making typing faster and easier) and to show in-group membership (if you know what RTFM means, you are a member of the group) (see 6.4).

The following list presents some of the most common slang terms and acronyms of CMC, as well as a small sample of emoticons:

- **Slang**

   e-mail: electronic mail (arguably, this word has already entered the mainstream of English)

   Web: the Internet, or World Wide Web

   Net: the Internet, World Wide Web

   flaming: abusive messages directed against someone

   spam: unwanted e-mail

   blog: clipping of the expression web log

- **Acronyms**

   DOS = disk operating system

   HTML = hypertext markup language

   FAQ = frequently asked question

   RTFM = read the f**** manual (used when someone asks a question that is in the FAQ)

   ROTFL = rolling on the floor laughing

   IMHO = in my humble opinion

   BRB = be right back

   LOL = laughing out loud

   a/s/l = age, sex, location (used in chat rooms to establish basic information)

- **Emoticons (aka smileys)**

   :-) = user is happy or is joking

   :-(= user is sad

   ;-) = user is winking

   :-)~ = user is drooling

   :-0 = user is shouting or surprised

   :-P = user is sticking his or her tongue out

There are hundreds of (mostly facetious) smileys. Lists can be found online.

11.5.5 Sociolinguistics of CMC

There have been early claims that CMC "erased" gender differences, essentially based on the assumption that the mediated nature of CMC made gender irrelevant and allowed women to escape the strictures of face-to-face communication, with its bias toward male-patterns of communication (see Chapter 10). However, more recent research has challenged this view. For example, in general, males have both more messages and words than women in CMC. Conversely, other studies show that both males and females receive the same amount of attention. So it seems clear that on the one hand the claim that gender is neutralized in CMC is too optimistic, but on the other hand gender issues do not transfer directly from face-to-face to CMC.

An interesting issue, which we cannot explore, is of course that because of the nature of CMC, gender is much more fluid online, as many users adopt genderless personae or even attempt to pass as members of the opposite sex.

11.5.6 How Different Is CMC from Non-CMC?

In conclusion, it appears that, while CMC is certainly an interesting and even important new field of communication that deserves much study and research, there might have been a certain degree of hype, probably due to the novelty of the medium, in the early claims that CMC was radically different from face-to-face communication. In fact, CMC appears to be merely a new genre, which falls somewhere between speech and writing, and that has developed interesting adaptations to overcome the limits of the written medium and approximate orality.

Educational Implications
While this chapter was not intended to teach methodology, it has tried to put literacy acquisition in a larger context and to suggest how knowledge of the ways language works may affect that acquisition.

11.6 EXERCISES

11.6.1 Words to Know

literacy	orality	logographic writing system
syllabic writing system	alphabetic writing system	bottom-up processing
top-down processing	interactive-compensatory mode	intensive reading
extensive reading	whole language	skills approaches
phonics	sound-symbol correspondence	process approach
product approach	heuristics	brainstorming
contrastive rhetoric	mind map	freewriting
speed	feedback	dialogue journal
CML	emotion	blog

11.6.2 Review

1. How do speech and writing differ?

2. Compare the three kinds of writing systems and give examples.

3. Compare top-down and bottom-up processing.

4. Compare intensive and extensive reading.

5. Compare whole language and phonics approaches to reading.

6. Compare the process and product approaches to writing.

11.6.3 Research Project

Interview two people about their views on reading instruction. Find one person who supports whole language (perhaps a college professor) and one who supports phonics (perhaps a school board member). Edit their respective arguments and report. You might also want to include other perspectives from research in the library or on the Internet.

11.7 FURTHER READINGS

On orality and literacy, the standard work is Ong (1982). An excellent overview of reading research is Adams (1990). While she does argue for the need to teach phonics, she shows that the debate is not an either/or proposition. For the opposite view, see Smith (1985).

The research on top-down/bottom-up processing is scattered in psychology and education journals over 20 years. A very good collection is Ruddell, Ruddell, and Singer (1994). See also Barr et al. (1991). Stanovich's model is articulated in (1980) and (2000).

Though it is centered on second/foreign language reading, Nuttall (1982) provides an excellent overview of the pedagogical issues in reading. Urquhart and Weir (1998) cover pedagogy and research in second language (L2) reading, as do Grabe and Stoller (2002).

For writing, a good overview is Grabe and Kaplan (1996). They cover theoretical as well as practical issues. Academic L2 writing is also covered in Ferris and Hedgcock (1998) and Canagarajah (2002). Silva and Matsuda (2001) is a very useful collection of classic articles on ESL writing. On contrastive rhetorics, see Kaplan (1966). Connor (1996) is an excellent overview of the development of the field since then.

On CMC, the seminal research can be found in Turkle (1995), and, in a linguistic perspective, Herring (2001), Cherny (1999), Crystal (2001), and Barnes (2002). The latter are introductory texts. Raymond (1996) is an updated edition of the *Hacker's Dictionary*, a tresure trove of computer-related jargon.

Chapter 12

First Language Acquisition

Have you ever watched a child learning language? What do you remember most?

12.1 THREE THEORIES

There have been three theoretical positions identified that claim to explain first language acquisition. The first is behaviorism, which was identified most closely with the psychologist B. F. Skinner. The second is innatism or nativism, most closely identified with the linguist Noam Chomsky. The third, interactionism, has many current proponents but no central figure.

12.1.1 Behaviorism

Behaviorism considers the mind a blank slate. Learning is imitation and habit formation. Children learn because their actions are "reinforced" with praise or successful communication. This is the way most people believe language is learned. The mother says a word, and the child repeats it. After enough uses of the word, the child remembers it. There is clearly some imitation involved in first language learning, particularly in vocabulary learning. However, Chomsky and others have raised "the logical problem" of **language acquisition:** children learn a complete language in about five years. This is more than could reasonably be expected, given the input they receive. The problem is known as the **poverty of stimulus** argument. Children are exposed to false starts, incomplete sentences, and odd constructions. Their grammar is seldom corrected. Their use of language with others, politeness forms, and so on may be corrected, but their grammar seldom is. Here are famous examples from the conversations of the same parent and child:

(12.1) *C:* And Walt Disney comes on Tuesdays.

   P: No, he comes on Thursdays.

(12.2) *C:* Mommy not a boy, he a girl.

   P: That's right!

Even when parents try to correct, the corrections are little heeded:

(12.3) *C:* Want other one spoon, Daddy.

   P: You mean you want the other spoon.

   C: Yes, I want other one spoon, please, Daddy.

   P: Can you say "the other spoon?"

   C: Other ... one ... spoon.

   P: Say ...other

   C: Other

   P: Spoon

   C: Spoon

   P: Other ... spoon

   C: Other spoon. Now give me other one spoon.

Yet children emerge with a more-or-less perfectly formed language. They are able to speak new sentences they couldn't possibly have heard. How is this possible? Certainly imitation cannot explain this.

Consider also the fact that all children during their linguistic development produce examples such as *I goed to school.* Certainly no adult uses that kind of form, so how could we explain that all children go through a stage that has this kind of mistake?

Ultimately, behaviorism is untenable as a theory of language acquisition. Behaviorism has no answers for the previous questions.

12.1.2 Innatism

Innatism suggests that humans are genetically programmed to acquire language. They do not have language in their brains, but they have the capacity to acquire it readily and with minimal input. Chomsky used to speak of a **language acquisition device** or **LAD** in the mind. Now the principles that are hardwired in our brains are called **universal grammar** or **UG** (see 2.5.2).

A crucial piece of evidence for innatists is the **critical period** hypothesis (CPH). The CPH in its strongest form says that children must acquire their first language before puberty if they are ever to acquire it at all. A weaker version claims that first language acquisition will be more difficult after puberty. There have been a number of feral children raised in the wild, supposedly by wolves, tigers, and other animals, who have found their way to towns. Attempts to teach them language have for the most part failed. They have been able to learn isolated words and simple structures, but their language development has never approximated children of their own age. It would seem, then, that there is something to the weak version of the CPH, but the fact that these children have been raised in harrowing circumstances leads one to believe that age is not the only factor at work. In the 1970s, linguists documented a modern case of a child raised in the most abusive of environments. "Genie" had learned no language at home; she had been tied to either a potty chair or her bed and rarely spoken to for almost 12 years. She was ultimately unable to make very much sustained progress in learning language, particularly in learning syntax (though she did learn many words). Perhaps the custody battles that swirled around her caused the progress she was making to be less than what might have been possible.

12.1.3 Interactionism

The innatist position has been challenged recently by those who see **interaction** as central to the acquisition of a first language. These researchers point to the role of what used to be called "motherese" and is now more often called **child-directed speech** (CDS) or caregiver speech. CDS is characterized by a slower rate of speech, a higher pitch, quite varied (singsong) intonation, more pauses, shorter and simpler sentences, frequent repetition, frequent questioning, paraphrase, and a focus on the here and now: what is in front of the caregiver and a child. The purpose of CDS seems to be to segment the flow of speech to make it more salient to the child. The wide pitch range seems to function as an attention getter. Keep in mind this is not an effort to teach speech. CDS is an attempt at communicating with the child.

Innatists considered CDS "degenerate." Research by those in the interactionist paradigm has shown that CDS is really much "cleaner" than adult-directed speech. It tends to be more grammatical. Fewer than ten percent of the caregivers' utterances are disfluent or run-on sentences. Caregivers pay attention to whether children understand, usually by watching faces or by seeing if children follow the conversation.

One important question is just how finely tuned CDS is: Do caregivers give children the sort of input they need? Does input vary with age? There is some evidence it does. Adults do tend to increase their production of some features just before children begin producing them. High-pitched intonation tends to disappear by the time the child is five. Simplification of syntax decreases with the child's age. The clarity of speech, like clear vowels and nonreduced consonants, increases about the time children reach the one-word stage in vocabulary acquisition.

Fathers and older siblings may play a different role in acquisition. Their speech tends not to be all that different in syntax and vocabulary from CDS, but they are more likely to have shorter dialogues with the baby, follow up less on child-initiated utterances, and be more demanding in their desire for clarification. All this leads to more conversational breakdown, which may help acquisition.

Remember that the innatists claim that children are not corrected on their grammar. They call this "getting no negative evidence" for the construction of their language. However, fathers and older siblings do seem to give at least implicit negative evidence in their impatience with negotiation and demands for clarity. Caregivers in general tend to repeat more wrong sentences than right ones. When sentences are ill formed, caregivers do ask clarification questions. They seldom stop and offer a direct correction or a "rule," but particularly when there is only one error in the child's utterance, caregivers will repeat the error or ask for clarification.

Different cultures have different notions of appropriate CDS. Some cultures, like the Quich'e, Javanese, Kaluli of Papua New Guinea, and Western Samoans consider babies unworthy conversation partners. Some cultures tend not to simplify their speech for children, instead repeating if there are misunderstandings. Other cultures do not respond to children's initiatives. Children are simply ignored. The Kaluli and Samoans do not ignore the child's speech, but any lack of clarity on the child's part is not repaired or recast in a correct form. These cultures tend to believe that you cannot speak for another. They may simply ask the child to repeat. Still other cultures recast a child's speech into something culturally or situationally appropriate, ignoring what was "really" said. In many cultures, a child's first words are conventionalized. Americans, for example, if asked, would say a baby's first word is *mama* or *dada*. Western Samoans believe that every child's first word is *tae*, which means *shit*. The community interprets this to mean *Eat shit*. Why? Samoans say it is the nature of children to be mischievous and to like to say naughty words.

Despite the differences, and the proscriptions of some cultures on aspects of CDS (the Quich'e reserve high-pitched intonation for speaking to superiors while the Kaluli associate nonsense syllables and thus baby talk with the spirits of dead children and would not use it with the living), all cultures seem to have some form of syntactic or lexical simplification and prosodic exaggeration in their CDS.

12.1.4 Summing Up the Theories of Language Acquisition

The following chart sums up the various approaches to language acquisition:

	Behaviorism	Innatism	Interactionism
imitation	essential	triggers LAD	part of the process
poverty of stimulus	—	UG	—
critical period	—	LAD shuts off	—
CDS	—	degenerate	essential
corrections	essential	useless	significant
overextension of rules	—	rule-governed UG	—

12.2 LEARNING A FIRST LANGUAGE

12.2.1 The Preverbal Stage

Children are primed to learn language. The hearing of infants is as good as that of adults. They may in fact be more sensitive to higher-pitched sounds such as those of CDS. Infants' sight at birth is not quite as good as adults', but by the time they are six months old, their vision is almost adult-like.

Early on, children prefer human beings to objects, both visually and auditorially. They like looking at faces and listening to voices. There is some preference for faces as early as two months, and this preference is established by four months. As early as three days old, children can distinguish their mother's voice from among other sounds. Children are in a sense ready to acquire language because they are focused on sounds like voices and things like faces that will serve as input for language learning.

It is useful to look at how scientists measure children's attention. The two most common methods are observation of head turning and **high amplitude sucking** (HAS). Children seek stimuli. When they become habituated to stimuli, they lose interest. When the stimulus changes, their interest begins anew. Scientists can observe the direction the baby turns and see from that the object of his or her attention. HAS operates by wiring a pacifier to an electronic system. Babies will suck at a rate that shows their interest. As they become habituated, the rate of sucking slows. As the stimulus changes, the rate of sucking goes up again. In this way, scientists can see what distinctions babies make between stimuli.

12.2.2 The Role of Conversation

By three months, utterances by the caregiver typically are attempts to get the child to coo or smile. Even burps or other "vegetative sounds" are considered attempts at communication. By seven months, caregivers tend to pay attention less to burps and more to babbling. They then frequently engage children in conversation along the lines of *You're happy today, aren't you?* They interpret the child's side of the conversation and then respond. This continues up to the point of first words, when *ababababa* might be interpreted by some as *A baby. Yes, you're a baby,* and by others as *You want a bottle? Are you thirsty?* Contrary to the behaviorists, who saw practice and quantity of speech as being important, interactionists feel it's not the quantity of speech heard that is important but the interaction between child and caregiver that matters. This interaction is the foundation for discourse.

Ochs has pointed out the discrepancy between the frequency of input and the use of certain structures by children in Western Samoa. Though these children frequently hear the word for *come* (*sau*), they seldom produce it because it is not considered acceptable for a child to order someone older to come. Similarly, forms may be infrequent in input but frequently used. Samoan has at least two words for *I*. One is *ta ita*, which means something like *poor me*. The other is the neutral *I*. Children are more likely to use *poor me* than the neutral form. They know that it will help with their requests.

12.2.3 Stages

Stages are dangerous things. Parents who think their child is lagging behind the norm tend to worry. Keeping in mind a stage is a construct, not a reality, here are the stages toward baby's first word:

- 0–8 weeks: Reflexive (undifferentiated) crying; vegetative sounds (burps, sneezes, coughs).

- 8–20 weeks: Laughing, cooing. Crying becomes differentiated. Parents can tell a call or request from discomfort.

- 16–30 weeks: Prolonged vowel or consonant sounds (a-a-a) (b-b-b).

- 25–50 weeks: Reduplicated babbling (babababa).

- 9–18 months: Nonreduplicated babbling. At this point, the child starts to play with stress and intonation and includes more consonant sounds.

12.2.4 Babbling

Children are born with the ability to discriminate and produce sounds not in their native language. They, of course, can also discriminate sounds in their own language and can do this at a young age, as young as two months. Using HAS techniques, scientists have shown that two-month-olds can tell the difference between /d/ and /g/ for example. Children lose the ability to discriminate and produce sounds not in their own language by the age of 10 to 12 months. The sounds need to be practiced if the children are to keep their ability.

Most babbling sounds are the same across languages. It is only when adults hear longer stretches of **babbling** with intonational cues that they can recognize the baby's native language. It used to be thought that adults determined sounds the baby made. Now it seems that adults can increase the amount of babbling by paying attention, but they can't change the sounds that the baby makes.

The acquisition of sounds is universal across culture and languages. Stops like /b/ and /g/ are produced early, and fricatives like /s/ and /f/ are produced later. Why? Think of how easy it is to make a stop, as opposed to a fricative. Labials, sounds produced by the lips, are very common in early babbling, as are dentals and alveolars. Here are some very common early sounds: [da], [ba], [wa].

There is no clear line between babbling and speech. Children continue to babble as they say their first words. Early words often share the earliest sounds. If children do not get a chance to work on these common sounds like /ba/ and /da/, their early words are not as likely to be made up of them.

12.2.5 First Words

> Which words do you think children learn first?

Children produce their first word typically between the ages of 9 and 12 months. They have 10 words typically by 15 months and 50 by 20 months. Of course, there is a difference in the number of words comprehended and produced. Children may well comprehend 50 words by 13 months. There is a spurt in acquisition around the time the child gets up to a 20-word vocabulary.

> Here are some common words. What do they have in common? Which of them go together?
>
> *mommy / daddy / bye-bye / all-gone / no / car / ball / dirty*

Nelson's study of the first 50 words has been influential. The study showed that words like *mommy, car, ball, bye-bye, go, big, dirty,* and *no* were all common. Among the nouns, those that were easily manipulated by children tended to be acquired faster than other nouns like *house* or *tree.* Nouns were split almost evenly between general names like *dog* and specific names for people and pets. There was, of course, a lot of individual variation, but Nelson saw children falling into two categories: expressive and referential. **Expressive** children have a high percentage of first words that were "social" like *bye-bye* and *thank you.* They tend to produce formulas. They are holistic learners. **Referential** learners learn a higher percentage of nouns early on. They have large vocabularies and tend to be analytic learners.

What's a Word?

Children's words sometimes are not "real" words. All that counts is that the child uses a combination of sounds in a consistent way. Of course, sometimes adults may give children too much credit for consistency. Sometimes children have categories that adults don't. *Uh oh* may mean any surprise, for example.

12.2.6 Under- and Overextension

> Why might a child call a ball an apple?

When children learn a new word, they may well underextend it or overextend it. An example of **underextension** is a child's confusion at hearing the color white used for paper when he or she thought it was the word for snow, or the common denial that birds are animals (animals are synonymous with mammals at first). **Overextension** happens when a child takes a property of an object and generalizes it. Thus *ball* may come to mean *ball, marble, wheel,* or anything else round. Overextension is likely to occur later rather than immediately following the acquisition of a word. Overextension is based not only on extension of categories (*apple* for all fruit) and analogies (*apple* for anything round) but also on what are known as family resemblances, as when *clock* gets extended both to *bracelet* and to the sound of dripping water, which sounds like *tick, tick, tick.*

Extension is important because it shows that children are working on their language, constructing it creatively. To get ahead of ourselves some, you can also see this in morphology when children learn irregular past tense verbs like *went* as wholes and are then confronted with the regularity of *-ed. Went* soon changes to *goed* before the whole system becomes sorted out. Extension is another important piece of evidence to support innatist theories.

12.2.7 Development of Vocabulary

The most obvious fact about vocabulary acquisition is that it goes hand in hand with the child's environment. First words are labels for things in the environment. Not surprisingly, then, nonlinguistic strategies often determine order of acquisition. For example, in the set of prepositions *in, on,* and *under, in* is likely to be acquired first because children have a preference for putting objects into other objects. They are much less likely to put objects under other objects and, to the extent they are likely to do this, put this in the category of "hiding."

A second important idea in vocabulary acquisition is semantic feature analysis. See 3.1.1. Take the word *zebra*. What are the components of its "zebraness?" You are likely to say *living/animal/wild/four-legged/ striped.* Clark proposed the theory that children begin with some of these features. So they might have "living/animal" and call a zebra a dog. As more features are added, the child will call a zebra a horse. Finally, the child approximates the adult meaning. Children may do something like this when they learn kinship terms. At first, for example, the child is likely to be unable to break down the term into component parts. Figures in parentheses give the child's age in (years; months):

Adult: What's a cousin?

Child (3;5): I have a cousin Daniel.

A: Are cousins big or little?

C: No.

After this, children may have some of the features but not those that relate the term to others:

A: What's a father?

C: (5;10): A father is someone who goes to work every day except Saturday and Sunday and earns money.

Then the child may be able to relate the terms but not see reciprocity in them:

A: What's a mother?

C: (6;6): It's a mommy. I have a mommy. It's somebody in your family.

Finally, the term is relational and reciprocal:

A: What's a niece?

C: (7;0): A niece is like a mother has a sister, and I'd be her niece.

Clark has since her earlier work abandoned semantic feature analysis for a theory of **lexical contrast,** in which the building blocks of vocabulary acquisition are contrasts rather than features. This theory says that children believe that there are conventional words for things. Overextension results when the child uses the conventional word for something else. When the proper word is found, the child contrasts it to the other word and the proper label emerges.

Other researchers are working with the idea of prototypes. Think of the word *bird.* What comes to mind? If you are an American, you probably saw in your mind's eye a sparrow or robin. You probably didn't see a penguin or ostrich. **Prototype theory** says that a child first gets a prototype and then extends its features. This theory explains underextension in that the peripheral cases like penguins get excluded from consideration. It also explains why children are likely to overextend through family resemblances in addition to categories. Unfortunately, very few prototypes have been broadly agreed upon.

12.2.8 Later Vocabulary Development

Around the age of two, children begin coining words. They start with compounds like "plant man" for gardener. They soon learn how to use morphology to make new words. One of the first morphemes they use is *-er* for "one who does something." So you have the word *sworder* for a figure with a sword. Around the same time, they can make new verbs from nouns (*Don't hair me, Mommy*, when they don't want their hair brushed). They can make adjectives with *y*: a dinosaur *looks growly.* By four, children can coin words "on demand." They can answer the question, What do you call someone who _____?

12.2.9 The Two-Word Stage

Around the age of two, children begin to produce two-word sentences like the following:

- *more car*
- *all wet*
- *bye-bye Daddy*
- *see pretty*

The speech is telegraphic (it uses only the words that are necessary and leaves out the rest), but it follows the rules of the native language: in English, adjectives before nouns, subjects before verbs, verbs before objects. Roger Brown and his colleagues also found that these two-word utterances express a limited set of "meaning relations." The meaning relations are common throughout the world, though children speaking different languages with different rules change word order as appropriate. Here are some meaning relations:

- agent + action: *Dolly kiss* (child kisses doll)

- action + affected: *Throw ball* (child throws ball)

- agent + affected: *Me ball* (child throws ball)

- action + location: *Sit bus* (child sits on the toy bus)

- entity + location: *Car table* (toy car is on the table)

- possessor + possession: *Mommy chair* (child points to mother's chair)

- entity + attribute: *Kitty pretty* (points to cat)

Two-word utterances are truly creative. Many of the sentences that children say could not have been spoken by an adult. They are simple, but they are systematic. The utterances revolve around and are dominated by content words, especially nouns. There are few functors like prepositions or articles at this stage. Some words are very frequent. These are the words that are important to the child's life. Finally, topics like people, possession, location, and recurrence are very important to children and get talked about a lot.

12.2.10 Learning Grammar

Of course, as children learn vocabulary they are also learning morpho-syntax, or grammar. Children acquire their first 14 morphemes in English in a predictable order:

1. present progressive *-ing*

2. preposition *in*

3. preposition *on* (items 2 and 3 may be inverted; children differ in which they learn first)

4. plural -*s*

5. irregular past *went, etc.*

6. possessive's

7. copula (*be*) uncontracted

8. articles

9. regular past -*ed*

10. third person present -*s*

11. third person present irregular

12. auxiliary verbs, uncontracted

13. copula (*be*) contracted

14. auxiliary verbs, contracted

Why this order? Frequency in the input would not seem to be the answer. If it were, the articles would be among the first acquired, since they are among the most common words in English. It seems to be a matter of linguistic complexity. Where the number of aspects of meaning and/or number of rules are few, acquisition comes early. Thus, the plural morpheme only marks number. The present progressive marks only duration. But auxiliary verbs have as part of their meaning number, earliness, and duration, so they are difficult.

A much commented-on feature of the acquisition of English morphology is its productivity. Children are soon able to make new words. When shown a *wug* they are able to extrapolate *two wugs*. When shown a man *ricking* they can say he *ricked* yesterday. Not only do the children get the morphological information right, they also are able to predict that the plural marker will be voiced /z/, when the root ends in a voiced consonant /g/.

Other aspects of English grammar that have been studied are negatives and questions. Negatives have been shown to be learned in three stages. The first moves *no* outside the sentence: *No go home.* The second stage is the moving of the negative next to the main verb: *I no like it, I no want juice,* and *Don't go.* The last example shows that sometimes *don't* and *can't* are acquired as unanalyzed chunks of language. The child does not treat them as verb plus negative but as a whole word. In the third stage, the child's language is like the adult's: *You can't have this. You can't do that.* Here, the argument goes, the child "has" the grammar.

Similarly, questions are acquired in predictable patterns. Children first use rising intonation, and then gradually are able to invert subject and verb to make a yes/no sentence. The WH-question words are acquired in stages, with the more concrete *(what, where, who)* developing before the more abstract *(when, how, why).* Again, semantic complexity has an effect on acquisition.

12.2.11 *Later Developments in Grammar*

Passives have been studied to show how children acquire word order rules. These sentences do not occur naturally in speech often enough to get a good sample, so researchers elicit them or test comprehension by asking children to act out sentences with dolls or puppets. A distinction is made between reversible and irreversible passives. *The boy kissed the girl* can logically be reversed to *The girl kissed the boy. The girl patted the dog* cannot be so logically reversed. Irreversible sentences are acquired first. Only four- to five-year-olds can act out reversible sentences. At ages three to four, children made the first mentioned noun the agent, basing their production on English word order, which puts the subject first in most sentences. This is not universal. In Japanese, which has a more flexible word order than English, children rely on word order plus sentences markers like the subject marker *ga* that tell the function of the sentence's components.

It used to be assumed that passives were fully acquired by age five, but recently this has been shown true only for action verbs. Five-year-olds still do not understand the passive use of verbs such as *like.*

Coordination is also acquired in stages and depends on semantics and context. Children begin with "additive *and*": *You do this and I'll do that.* Only after several months do they understand "temporal *and*" equally well: *Johnny went upstairs and played with his car.* The idea of stages will be taken up later when we talk about second language acquisition.

12.2.12 *Pragmatics*

While they are acquiring morpho-syntax and vocabulary, children are also acquiring **pragmatics,** or how to speak to others in an appropriate manner. One aspect of this is gender. Children seem sensitive to gender.

When asked to role play with dolls, and to assume either the mother's or father's perspective, children will speak differently, usually having the mother issue indirect orders like *It's time for your nap* and the father issue direct orders like *Go to bed.* In mixed-sex groups, girls tend to agree more, but most of the differences are in the topics they talk about or the quantity of talk (contrary to our stereotypes, boys talk more). Mothers tend to talk more, use longer utterances with girls, and ask girls more questions. (See Chapter 10.)

Another aspect of pragmatics is adapting to the listener. Piaget and his followers argued that children were egocentric and could not modify their messages to each other. Their speech was thought to be a series of monologues. Younger children were likely to speak the same way to a blindfolded person as to one who could see. Kindergartners simply repeated or fell silent when an interlocutor signaled a lack of comprehension. However, all these studies were done under laboratory conditions, with children talking to adults in white coats. When children are observed under more naturalistic conditions, they seem capable of building on each others' sentences. Their responses are appropriate. They do simplify their speech to younger children.

Politeness is one of the few aspects of speech that is explicitly taught by parents. By the age of three or four, children can respond to indirect requests and produce polite direct requests. By elementary school, they can produce both indirect and direct requests but can't yet hint. By seven or eight, they are able to hint as well.

12.3 ATYPICAL LANGUAGE DEVELOPMENT

In this section, we will consider cases in which the typical development of language is affected or language is lost due to trauma or injury. The first question one needs to ask is, "How many people are affected by atypical language development or by handicaps?" The estimates vary widely, anywhere between 0.5 percent of the population to 8–10 percent. Not all children achieve the same level of language development. What is important to remember is that although acquisition may be delayed, nothing the children produce is "deviant" or out of the ordinary. Deaf children who learn American Sign Language as a first language progress through all the stages hearing children do. Language is often delayed but follows the same rules of language as typical children's language. Adults who are involved in accidents or strokes that cause brain damage may lose part of their language ability.

12.3.1 Hearing Impairments

Hearing impairment varies along a continuum: it may be very slight and lead only to minor losses of language input (such as voiceless consonants), or it may be severe, leading to a total lack of hearing. Quite obviously, if a child has a severe degree of hearing loss, his or her language acquisition may be impaired because the input cannot be processed. Many deaf children are born to hearing parents and therefore the child may not be exposed to linguistic stimuli he or she can access for an extended period of time (until the hearing problem is diagnosed).

Deaf children's articulation is often affected by their lack of input. The production of some sounds by deaf children may be "off" but the sounds are approximations of typical sounds. Nothing is made up. The same is true for syntax. Deaf children have many of the same problems as hearing children do, with particular problems with modals, verb auxiliaries and infinitives, and gerunds. Their reading and writing skills are also negatively affected by their limited exposure to language due to the hearing impediment.

On American Sign Language and its acquisition, see 16.4.

12.3.2 Mental Retardation

What is mental retardation? Despite widespread criticism of IQ (intelligence quotient) tests, the most widespread definition of retardation is given on the basis of IQ scores. The following table sums up the various levels of retardation. A score of 100 is assumed as average:

IQ	Retardation
70–52	mild
51–36	moderate
35–20	severe
< 20	profound

The language acquisition of mentally retarded children is delayed but follows the same rules as other children, i.e., it is not deviant. Mentally retarded children typically match their peers of the same mental age in semantic and pragmatic abilities; thus a child of five but with a mental age of three will show language skills comparable to that of a three-year-old nonretarded child. However, there is evidence that mentally retarded children may have more problems with morphology.

12.3.3 Autism

Autistic children seem to be language-impaired from the very beginning. They seem to lack the ability or desire to establish social relations, including with their parents. Language development is very slow and includes **echolalia,** the repetition of another speaker's speech. Initially echolalia is immediate, i.e., the autistic child repeats something immediately. However, he or she may repeat something heard two days before in a pragmatically appropriate way. Autistic children often do not babble or have facial expressions. They may avoid gazes and not respond. They are unable to play cooperatively. Autism is almost certainly caused by physiological problems and not by the parents' behavior, as was previously believed.

12.3.4 Stuttering

Stuttering can manifest itself as the repetition of sounds, syllables, or phrases, or as a block, where the speaker cannot "release" the words. There are many theories about the origins of **stuttering,** which range from the physiological to the psychological. To this date, we do not know the cause of stuttering, and increasingly researchers are becoming convinced that there may not be one single cause for stuttering. We do, however, know that no link has been established between stuttering and personality factors (or in other words, that stuttering is not caused by personality traits, e.g., shyness). More significantly even, no correlation has been established between neurosis and stuttering, i.e., stutterers are not neurotic and do not need psychotherapy.

Stuttering is in fact quite common; 25 percent of all children go through a phase of stuttering and of these males outnumber females by four to one. A significant number of stutterers recover without intervention. Two-thirds of school-age stutterers will stop on their own. Parental intervention, including helping out the child or scolding, seems to have no effect, either positive or negative.

There are some facts about stuttering that seem to indicate that stuttering is related to the complexity of the speech to be produced: there is more stuttering in polysyllabic words (i.e., those having more than one syllable), in infrequent or unfamiliar words, and in connected fast speech, whereas there is less stuttering in word-by-word reading and least of all in syllable-by-syllable reading.

Modern therapies for adult stutterers include the "stutter more fluently" approach, which teaches the stutterer to become more fluent and reduce his or her avoidance behavior (the avoiding of problematic words, or being silent altogether). Another approach is labeled "speak more fluently" and consists in teaching the stutterer to speak slowly, often using the delayed auditory feedback technique (the speaker is made to listen to his or her own speech via headphones, but the speech is delayed by a tape recorder by one-quarter of a second). He or she can then substitute this slowed-down speech for the stuttering.

12.3.5 Aphasia

Damage to the brain, if it involves the areas of the brain that govern language, may lead to partial or total loss of language. This is called **aphasia.** Aphasia may be **fluent** or **nonfluent.**

Nonfluent Aphasia

This disorder is also called motor aphasia. The speech of patients with nonfluent aphasia is slow, full of hesitation, and often shows errors of pronunciation and omission of words. A type of nonfluent aphasia is Broca's aphasia, which is incurred when there are lesions to a part of the brain called Broca's region (named after the discoverer of its importance to language). Broca aphasics tend to omit function words (articles and prepositions, for example) and inflectional morphemes. This disorder has been called "telegraphic speech" since it resembles the kind of language used in telegrams.

Fluent Aphasia

Fluent aphasics have no problem producing words, but they have a hard time selecting them. A typical example of fluent aphasia (aka sensory aphasia) is Wernicke's aphasia. In this condition, speakers are fluent, they do not hesitate, and in general they sound fine. However, they make very little sense. Wernicke aphasics may show **anomia,** i.e., the incapacity to name an object, in which case they utilize a circumlocution. Often Wernicke aphasia leads to parts of utterances that are grammatically correct but pragmatically inappropriate, intermixed with grammatically incorrect and meaningless fragments.

12.3.6 Dyslexia

Dyslexia is a disorder in reading; it corresponds to **dysgraphia,** which is a disorder in writing. Both disorders can be acquired or developmental.

Acquired dyslexia and dysgraphia are the results of brain damage in adult life. Three types of dyslexia and dysgraphia are distinguished:

Phonological

In this kind of impairment, speakers can read or write familiar words but fail to apply the kind of "phonic" rules that unimpaired speakers use to spell new or unfamiliar words (such as nonsense words).

Deep

In this kind of impairment, speakers have the same traits as phonological dyslexia but with the addition of semantic "errors" (e.g., a patient will read *forest* as *trees* or write the nonsense syllable *blom* as *flower* [cf. *bloom*]). There are errors that involve both semantic and phonological/visual levels.

Surface

In this case, patients rely on phonic rules and are unable to read or spell irregular words.

The following are some features found in dyslexia:

- reading, spelling, and writing below age level, despite no mental retardation and equal or higher IQ than their peers;

- reversal of letters, reversal of ordering, confusion of letters such as *d/b*;

- confusion of left and right, poor directional ability;

- difficulty in putting things in series (e.g., days of the week);

- poor short-term memory.

Dyslexia, like other problems with writing, spelling, and language at large, may manifest itself in many ways. Usually, a child will show a performance level in a given academic area vastly below average (a rule of thumb is two years below his or her age group) while being otherwise of average or above-average intelligence. Other ways in which a problem may manifest itself is with aggressive or disruptive behavior, withdrawal, cheating, refusing to do homework, and watching a lot of television. It is easy to misdiagnose dyslexia. Possible factors that need to be ruled out before a diagnosis of dyslexia/dysgraphia can be made (Selikowitz 1998):

- vision or hearing problems

- intellectual disability

- physical disability

- lack of familiarity with the language of instruction

- lack of family support

- poor teaching

- lack of motivation

- frequent absenteeism

- brain damage

- epilepsy

- drugs that impair learning

Developmental dyslexia and dysgraphia are not acquired. There is no consensus on the causes of developmental dyslexia. There seem to be no correlations between intelligence or other intellectual factors and developmental dyslexia and dysgraphia. Unrecognized developmental dyslexia and dysgraphia may lead to poor performance in school. There is wide variation on the number of dyslexics: estimates range between 1 percent and 33 percent! It seems that there is a genetic predisposition toward dyslexia in that it may be inherited, and since boys tend to be dyslexic three times as frequently as girls, the X chromosome (which distinguishes the sexes) is probably involved. Other theories involve undetected brain malfunctions, the way the brain processes language, and failed lateralization (the left side of the brain controls language, so the theory goes that if a child fails to develop the dominance of the left side of the brain—lateralization—dyslexia occurs).

There are a number of therapies for dyslexia (see Further Readings), although since the causes remains unclear, there is no agreement on the best way to approach therapeutic treatment or intervention.

Educational Implications
This chapter has provided the basic information needed to understand how children acquire their first languages.

12.4 EXERCISES

12.4.1 Words to Know

behaviorism	innatism	interactionism
logical problem	poverty of stimulus argument	critical period
child-directed speech	babbling	overextension
language acquisition device	expressive	referential
overgeneralization	lexical contrast	prototype theory
nonfluent aphasia	dyslexia	stuttering
anomia	aphasia	fluent aphasia
interaction	high amplitude sucking	dysgraphia
underextension	semantic feature analysis	passive
echolalia	pragmatics	

12.4.2 Review

1. Contrast the three positions on first language learning. What evidence is there for and against each?

2. What is the role of child-directed speech (CDS)? Is it degenerate?

3. What is the role of culture in CDS?

4. What are the characteristics and functions of babbling?

5. How would you characterize a child's first 50 words?

6. What sorts of relationships are there between words in the two-word stage?

7. What are the explanations given for the order of morpheme acquisition?

8. What is the relationship between typical and atypical language development?

12.4.3 Research Projects

1. If you have a child at home, keep a diary of a day's worth of language. How does your child's output fit into the theories outlined in this chapter?

2. If you have access to the Internet, find out about the CHILDES Project.

3. If you have an interest in other languages, look at the several volumes of Slobin (see Further Readings).

12.5 FURTHER READINGS

A very readable introduction to first language acquisition is deBoysson-Bardies (1999). deVilliers and deVilliers (1979), is now unfortunately out of print. Foster (1990) is only slightly more technical. Clark (2003) is an excellent book that challenges the innatist perspective. Berko-Gleason (2000) is a classic collection of articles geared to beginners in the field.

Lightbown and Spada (1999) provide a short introduction to the three positions on language learning. The Disney example is from Brown and Hanlon (1970). Genie's story is told by the linguist Curtiss (1977) and the journalist Rymer (1993).

For CDS, see Snow and Ferguson (1977) and Gallaway and Richards (1994). The latter has several important chapters. For the negative evidence argument, see Sokolov and Snow in Gallaway and Richards (1994). On fathers and other family members, see Berko-Gleason (1975).

Slobin has edited five volumes containing studies of first language acquisition throughout the world (1985–1992). Ochs and Schieffelin in Fletcher and MacWhinney (1995) summarize what is known about CDS in some other cultures. Schieffelin and Ochs's 1986 volume is also important to understanding language socialization as a manifestation of culture. For Western Samoa, see Ochs (1988).

Foster (1990) has a good section on the preverbal stage and on babbling. See also the relevant sections in Berko-Gleason (2001). Nelson (1973) may be hard to find but more information on first words can be found in any of the general volumes mentioned at the beginning of this section. Those volumes will also contain information on overextension and underextension.

The examples of stages in understanding kinship terms is from Haviland and Clark (1974). Examples of later vocabulary development are from Clark (1993).

Roger Brown's work on the two-word stage and on learning grammar (the morpheme studies) is summarized in his classic book of 1973. Some of the examples in the two-word stage section are from Peccei (1994). The wugs study was Berko (1958).

For pragmatics and atypical language development, see the relevant chapters in Berko-Gleason (1989). On the number of dysfluent speakers, see Crystal (1997) and Ratner in Berko-Gleason (2001). Any introduction to speech pathology will have significant treatments of the topics briefly covered in the chapter, e.g., Hedge (1991) and Shames, Wiig, and Secord (1998). Seymour and Nober (1998) has a multicultural approach. On mental retardation, and in general on the subjects of special education, see Culatta and Tompkins (1999). On autism, see Happe (1998). Obler and Gjerlow (1999) has a treatment of aphasias in the broad context of neurolinguistics. Cordes and Ingham (1998) has surveys of recent literature. On dyslexia, a good clear introduction is Selikowitz (1998), which has the advantage of being addressed to parents but contains a serious review of the subject. It also contains a discussion of the therapeutic options. The list of factors to be ruled out is also from Selikowitz (1998, 26).

Chapter 13

Second Language Acquisition

> What do you remember about your foreign language classes in high school?

During World War II, a number of people had to be trained in languages like Japanese or Burmese that were not then commonly taught in high schools or colleges. This gave rise to a renewed scientific interest in how people learn languages. In the immediate postwar years, behaviorism (see 12.1.1) was the main explanation for second language learning. As the influence of behaviorism waned, a separate field called **second language acquisition** began to organize itself. The field has become increasingly important as large numbers of immigrants have arrived in North America and Western Europe and need to learn the languages of their new homelands. It is important to note that both adults and children learn second/foreign languages and that in many places in this chapter, we are generalizing to both groups. It is also important to note that we are not discussing here how to teach languages, except in passing, but are operating at a more theoretical level in order to provide background information on the learning process itself. We should, however, mention briefly that language teaching itself has been marked since the 1970s by a concern to teach communicative competence (see Chapter 4).

13.1 TRANSFER AND INTERLANGUAGE

Everyone has a first language, which has been acquired through a combination of innate factors and the environment. Some knowledge of language is obviously transferred from **first language (L1)** competence to **second language** (**L2**) (called perhaps misleadingly L2, because the student may in fact be learning an additional language). It used to be thought that all second language learning was transferred, and that in fact you could predict the problems learners would have based on their L1. Now we see the language learning process as being influenced by transfer but also having some unique and interesting properties of its own. First of all, however, let us consider what transfers from L1 to L2.

The student's first language may affect learning of the second in almost all areas: phonetics, phonology, morphology, syntax, semantics, and pragmatics. Perhaps the two areas of transfer you know most are what you've probably called "accent" and "vocabulary," which involve the linguistic subfields of phonetics/phonology and semantics. The two areas serve to show two sides of transfer. Languages, as we have seen, have different sounds. In Japanese, there is only one alveolar liquid, a sound represented in English transcription of Japanese as *r*. The English phonological system has two alveolar liquids, /r/ and /l/. So, Japanese students learning English have a difficult time making the distinction between [r] and [l] in English, a distinction they don't have in their L1 system. English-speaking students learning Japanese have a difficult time distinguishing between [r] and [d] in Japanese, because the sound of [r] in Japanese, what's known as a *flap r*, is very similar to that of the [d] in *steady* (alveolar stops between vowels are pronounced as flaps [D] in American English, e.g., *butter* [bʌDər]). Here transfer of the system of oppositions (cf. minimal pairs, see 2.2.3) in the L1 phonological system would manifest itself in L2 as "a foreign accent." While sounds show that transfer may happen as a result of language differences, we see in semantic transfer the problem of **false friends,** words that seem to be related but aren't. *Embarazada* in Spanish doesn't mean *embarrassed* at all. It means *pregnant* and many an English-speaking learner of Spanish has raised some eyebrows by trying to say something like *I'm embarrassed by my poor Spanish.*

While first languages are important, as we have seen, it is also true that all learners, regardless of L1, go through similar processes. Perhaps the most important process is **interlanguage (IL).** Students begin with L1, go through IL, and may or may not reach complete L2 proficiency. In IL, they may make mistakes or errors. *Mistakes* are slips of the tongue; learners know the rule but do not apply it at that time. *Errors* are windows into IL. Learners who say *No go* are showing that they are at the first stage of learning negation. No amount of correcting alone is going to make them immediately say *I don't want to go.* They will need, depending on whom you talk to, lots of input, lots of practice, or lots of time to work out the correct form. Interlanguages are natural languages, like English or French; they just have different rules. Because they are natural languages, they vary systematically in ways we have seen in the chapters on sociolinguistics. We will postpone a discussion of variability until later in this chapter. We will next address the issue of developmental sequences in IL.

13.1.1 Developmental Sequences

There are certain stages that most L2 learners go through. The first is the **silent period.** This period is necessary in L1 learning but may well be a luxury in L2 learning, especially with adult learners who must communicate immediately when posted to a new country. Some L2 children learners stay silent for weeks or even months. The function of a silent period may be to serve as an active period of listening, a period of reflection, or simply a period of incomprehension that finally gets sorted out. Silent learners may in fact speak to themselves. Some students have been recorded rehearsing: repeating, practicing, substituting, and expanding words and sentences.

The use of **formulas** is another early stage in L2 learning. Learners will often use these memorized chunks of language (like *Can I have X?*) to communicate basic needs and to get feedback. These chunks are well formed, often in contrast to other utterances. They often perform more than one discourse function. For example, one learner used *Whaduyu* as an all-purpose question word. One controversy is whether these chunks ultimately get analyzed into grammar that the learner can then build on. It may depend on age; in some studies children did indeed break down chunks while in another the adult studied never did acquire most grammar rules but instead used chunks to help his fluency, to help him communicate. Formulas serve to buy processing time during conversations and maintain conversations. One can speak the chunk while thinking of words for the next sentence. The ability to analyze these chunks and break them down into grammar that can be used is called **unpacking** and is the next step in learning. That is, *Whaduyu* becomes *What do you,* and then the learner begins to use *do* in other sentences.

As they use formulas, L2 learners will also use **simplification.** This stage is marked by the use of one or two word utterances like *Me no X.* These utterances look like sentences from pidgins: grammatical markers are dropped (see Chapter 7). Only words that are really needed are used. Some object to calling this a stage on the grounds that you cannot simplify a language you do not yet speak.

13.1.2 Order of Acquisition

ILs not only exhibit certain stages but also a certain order of acquisition of morphosyntax. In the 1970s, researchers investigated when L2 learners acquire various morphemes of English to see if there is an order of acquisition that does not change. They found at first that their learners followed this order:

- pronoun case *he/him*
- articles
- copula *be*
- progressive *-ing*
- plural *-s*
- aux *be* + V + *-ing*
- regular past
- irregular past
- plural *-es*
- possessive's*
- third person singular *-s*

The order was the same for children who were speakers of L1 Chinese and L1 Spanish learning L2 English. Other researchers confirmed the order for adults, while others claimed that there was not an exact order but rather that morphemes clustered together. Of course, because Spanish and Chinese are such different languages, if language learning is simply transfer, you would expect speakers of one to acquire grammar in a different order than speakers of the other. That they did not, and that the order of acquisition of second language morphemes was similar to the order of first language morpheme acquisition (see 12.2.10), led to a view that these stages cannot be disturbed and therefore classroom learning is unnecessary, perhaps futile. Many have questioned a view of language learning that boils down to a piling on of morphemes, and some longitudinal studies have not replicated the findings of the morpheme studies. Still, this finding impressed many and led to further research.

13.2 L1 = L2?

To what extent is the acquisition of L2 identical to the acquisition of L1? Perhaps in some early stages (the silent period, use of formulas, simplification) it is. Morpheme orders are similar but not the same: articles, auxiliaries, and the copula are all acquired earlier and the irregular past later in L2. Both L1 and L2 learners omit items and substitute nouns for pronouns (though L1 learners often use their own names instead of first person pronouns). The acquisition of syntax, particularly negation and questions, is very similar.

Many researchers see things differently. They argue that L1 and L2 learning are fundamentally different in that everyone succeeds at L1 and many do not succeed at L2. There is little variation in L1 and a lot in L2. There is **fossilization** (learners get "stuck" at a certain level) in L2 but not in L1. Instruction and negative evidence (correcting mistakes) seem to help in L2 acquisition and not in L1. Finally, affective factors (motivation, personality factors) are very important in L2 but not in L1.

The debate certainly has something to do with age. Adults and children L2 learners probably have different learning styles. Adults may be able to make better use of their memory and of strategies, while children may still have some ability to use principles of universal grammar that helped them learn their first language.

13.3 KRASHEN AND THE MONITOR HYPOTHESIS

While we do not agree with all of it, the work of Krashen has been very important in second language acquisition (SLA) research and students need to know something about that work. Krashen's model has five parts:

- acquisition/learning hypothesis

- monitor hypothesis

- natural order hypothesis

- input/comprehension hypothesis

- affective filter hypothesis

13.3.1 Acquisition and Learning

Krashen believes that acquisition is unconscious and learning conscious. Acquisition is identical to the way children learn languages. Learning results in knowing about the language and its rules. Krashen does not really define consciousness, but he does say that learning leads to an ability to make grammaticality judgments based on rules, while acquisition leads to judgments based on intuition and "feel."

In the view of many, the learning/acquisition dichotomy is problematic because it is very difficult to define "rule." Many of our "rules" of grammar are examples, prototypes, or fuzzy rules. We have a "feel" for what is right but cannot articulate it. This feeling is for Krashen acquisition and has nothing to do with learning.

In Krashen's view, learning never becomes acquisition but sometimes there is acquisition without learning. But what about those drill-induced sentences we remember from high school foreign language classes? Krashen says they only appear to be learning becoming acquisition. People only acquire language, he says, through communicative situations, through understanding messages.

13.3.2 Monitor Hypothesis

The monitor hypothesis says that learning has only one function: as an editor. Acquisition initiates the utterance and is responsible for fluency. The focus of language learning should be on communication, not rule learning, so the monitor is not very important.

There are only three conditions that Krashen feels are necessary for monitor use:

- a focus on form (the speaker must be thinking about correctness)

- the rule must be known

- the speaker must have time to think

Krashen has lately argued that the monitor is seldom applied under normal circumstances. If that is true, say many, why have the learning/acquisition dichotomy?

Krashen says that children do not use the monitor, so they are superior language learners. Other research has shown that adults in fact learn quicker but children are better in the long run (though this may be true only for phonology).

13.3.3 Natural Order Hypothesis

The natural order hypothesis came out of the morpheme studies (see 13.1.2). It says that there are predictable stages, and teachers, by implication, should get out of the way. However, subsequent studies have shown individual variation in acquisition and some effects for transfer in syntax from one language to another.

13.3.4 Input/Comprehension Hypothesis

The **input/comprehension hypothesis** says that humans acquire language in one way: by understanding messages received at a level just above their current competence. Krashen calls this *comprehensible input at i + 1.* He does not carefully define *+1* but this statement indicates that if input is understood, the necessary grammar is automatically provided. Krashen denies an important role for output, though a commonsense notion is that it can provide input. Krashen's evidence that comprenhensible input is good for language learning is an analogy to how children learn L1. Children remain silent and take in what they hear. Of course, children also babble and actively try out speech.

13.3.5 Affective Filter Hypothesis

The affective filter hypothesis says that an important reason for individual differences in L2 ability is affect (feelings, emotions, moods). Anxiety blocks language learning. According to Krashen, this is a reason children learn quickly: they have no affective filter. The affective filter determines which language models (dialects) people will adopt, which parts of language will be attended to, when attempts at acquisition will stop, and how fast a learner will acquire L2. Krashen has also suggested that there might be an output filter that prevents acquired language from being used.

Practical aspects of Krashen in the classroom are a focus on meaning at all times, no structural grading, and no error correction. The major criticism made of Krashen has been his unclear definitions of learning, acquisition, and other important terms. Most damaging is the inability to test this theory because of the vague definition of *i + 1.* White has said that perhaps it is incomprehensible input that a language learner really needs; only then can he or she get negative evidence. By that White means that learners may need to be challenged by hard input so that they can better analyze the language.

13.4 INSTRUCTED SLA

Krashen and several others have argued that it simply does no good, and maybe even harm, to teach languages. They must be acquired. There is a place for the classroom, but the classroom must be of a kind of environment that will allow acquisition to take place.

One piece of evidence that instruction is ineffective is that the order in which we learn certain structures is fixed. Evidence that order of acquisition cannot be changed was found in the ZISA Project in Germany. People learning German always learned certain pieces of morphology or syntax first. For English, it has been shown that the development sequence of instructed English L2 learners is often identical to that reported for naturalistic learners, or learners who pick up their language outside of class. One difference may be how long learners stay in certain stages.

Lightbown and her colleagues did a number of studies on the effects of classroom instruction. In one classroom study of -s and -ing morphemes among classroom learners, it was found that intensive practice of -ing led to the item "sticking" and thus being oversupplied. That is, students used -ing even when another verb form would have been more appropriate. The -ing declined in favor of the plain forms when they were taught. The same phenomenon occurred with the -s forms, but oversuppliance wore off over time.

So, order can be interrupted, at least trivially, by teaching, but the teachability/learnability thesis that came out of ZISA still is accepted by many. This says that students will not learn an item until they are cognitively ready for it. In this view, instruction will not enable students to acquire any "developmental" feature out of order. Instruction will allow learners to acquire a developmental feature if the easier features have been mastered. Instruction that is aimed at features for which the learner is not ready may in fact impede natural acquisition. However, the ZISA Project found that some features may be "variational" and not developmental. These variational features can be acquired through instruction. Just what is developmental and what is variational is not firmly agreed upon.

Others argue that instruction helps learners. Instruction can speed up acquisition within stages and helps with ultimate attainment; classroom learners tend to learn more complex structures than naturalistic learners do. Classroom learners also make certain kinds of errors, and naturalistic learners make different ones. There may also be delayed effects for instruction. Perhaps instruction in some ways primes the students so acquisition becomes easier when they are ready to acquire the structure. It raises consciousness and makes forms salient. Studying might make learners aware of forms they hear in input.

13.5 INPUT AND INTERACTION

> Think about how you talk to people who do not speak English as their first language. How would you describe your speech to them?

13.5.1 Interaction

Just as child-directed speech (CDS) is important to first language acquisition, **foreigner talk (FT)** is important to SLA. Just as CDS was once thought to be "degenerate," FT was thought to be ungrammatical. Researchers focused on the extent to which it omitted functors like the copula, articles, and conjunctions. Notice was made of the expansions in imperatives (*You give me that*), the addition of *Yes?* at the end of sentences, and the use of names instead of pronouns. FT was also characterized as pidgin-like in its use of structures like *No want* and *Him go.*

Now studies have shown that FT is for the most part grammatical. It is simplified (speech is slower, sentences are shorter, syntax is less complex, and vocabulary is easier). It is regularized: speakers use full forms instead of contractions, have fewer false starts, and put the topic at the beginning of the sentence to make comprehension easier. Speakers also use superordinate vocabulary instead of subordinate vocabulary; they say *car* instead of *sedan*. FT is also elaborated; that is, synonyms and paraphrases are used extensively.

So far, we have focused mostly on sentences, but FT discourse is different too. Topics are treated simply and briefly. Speech is about the here and now. There are lots of choice questions: *X or Y?* Topic shifts seem to be accepted more readily in FT than in native speaker/native speaker (NS/NS) speech; people feel free to change the subject as soon as it looks like communication is breaking down. Stress and pauses may be exaggerated. NSs may regulate the amount of information that they give, especially in phone conversations; they may give just the basics, whereas with other NSs they may embroider a bit. Conversations tend to follow the pattern of question/answer; new topics are initiated much more through questions than in NS/NS discourse. There are many more comprehension checks *(OK? Did you understand?).*

As is probably clear from this sketch, the purpose of FT, like CDS, is to communicate, not to teach language.

13.5.2 Interlanguage Talk

In today's classrooms, learners are as likely to be talking to other learners as to teachers. Nonnative speaker/nonnative speaker (NNS/NNS) interaction has also been termed "interlanguage (IL) talk." It is less grammatical than FT. IL talk is characterized by a lot of negotiation of meaning: *Right? No, left. OK, left.* Is this good for students? Some have claimed that ungrammatical input will lead to a pidginized variety of the target language. Those who claim that IL talk is good for students say that pair work or group work is good because it leads to a lot of negotiation of meaning (because conversations break down) and negotiation of meaning helps with acquisition.

Several studies have been done to answer the question: is it better to modify/simplify the original input (what students hear or read) or to allow for negotiation of meaning between students and/or students and teacher? Usually, three groups are used. One receives unmodified input, the other simplified input, and the third unmodified input and an opportunity to clarify the input. The task is typically to work in pairs and complete a drawing. One person communicates what a kitchen looks like, and the other person draws in the pots and pans, for example. In these studies, the groups that have a chance to negotiate their understanding do best on the task and learn more, based on later tests of target vocabulary. This is in line with other research that shows that elaborated discourse may help comprehension more than simplification. It is better to say more about a topic, within limits, than it is to use simple but disconnected speech. This may be because elaboration allows for connections within discourse.

13.5.3 Output

Of course, interaction leads to **output.** The **output hypothesis** says that output is as important as input in SLA, that when learners fail in communication they make their output better. They move from semantic processing (stringing words together) to syntactic processing (more well-formed sentences). So classrooms have to provide opportunities for students to push themselves to give better output and ways for students to capture and analyze their output. Output can help students notice the gap between what they want to say and what they do say. It is also a means of hypothesis testing, of trying out new language. Output additionally serves a metalinguistic function of controlling internal knowledge; by analyzing what they said and putting labels on it, students can improve their language.

In Canadian studies, students clearly notice gaps in their knowledge: they modify their output in response to clarification requests and confirmation checks by other students *(I don't understand. Do you mean X?)*, and they are able to apply metalinguistic knowledge to transcripts of recordings of their output such as *Oh, I should have used the past tense there.*

13.6 INDIVIDUAL DIFFERENCES AND SLA

Learners to some extent all follow the same patterns in language learning. Interlanguage is also to some extent variable. We have seen in the work of Labov (see 6.1.1) that the tasks we do have an effect on our speech. This is also true of ILs. We speak more or less carefully in a second language, and the sorts of tests or tasks we are given will bring forth different samples of language, making us at times seem more or less competent than we really are. Careful speech will be closer to target language norms than will spontaneous conversation, for example.

Our inner states and individual styles of learning also have an effect on language. Think of the word *anxiety*. What is it? Is it a general state of mind (are you a nervous person)? Is it situation-specific (do you get nervous about public speaking)? Is *nervous* really the right word—or is anxiety a bundle of thoughts and behaviors? How does anxiety relate to extroversion/introversion?

As you can see, thinking about inner states is difficult. Let's assume you answer these questions to your satisfaction. Now how do you measure anxiety or any other inner state or personality factor? You have to be very careful about the questions you write—and most of this research is done through questionnaires. How do you measure the results? Most of this work is correlational; it attempts to link one thing by another through measuring co-occurrence. A perfect positive correlation is +1.0. This means that for every measure one factor goes up, the other measure also increases. This can happen in reverse, leading to negative correlations up to -1.0. For example, high aptitude scores correlate negatively with the length of time students need to reach a certain proficiency in language. A correlation coefficient of 0 means there is no relationship at all; things are random. In research, a correlation coefficient of .30–.60 is usual, with .30 being weak and .60 and above being relatively high.

13.6.1 Intelligence

There is a folk perception that IQ is positively related to language learning ability, and indeed the correlation coefficient between language aptitude test scores and IQ test scores is .60 in some studies. What really is measured on IQ tests may be more closely related to cognitive/academic skills than the ability to communicate, however.

13.6.2 Aptitude

Researchers have shown that language aptitude is a stable, perhaps innate factor separate from, but perhaps related to, achievement, intelligence, and motivation. Aptitude is what allows people to learn easily and quickly. According to Carroll (2001), language aptitude has four factors or aspects. The first is phonemic coding ability, the ability to associate sound and symbols. In alphabetic languages, this is the ability to spell well. The second is grammatical sensitivity, being "good at" grammar. The third is inductive language learning ability, the ability to notice patterns and relationships, and to extrapolate from examples. The last is rote-learning ability, the ability, for example, to learn lists quickly and easily.

The Modern Language Aptitude Test (MLAT) measures these abilities. Test-takers are taught numbers and words in a language (Kurdish) that they are not likely to have ever studied. They are then tested. They are taught some phonetic notation and then are tested by being asked to listen and underline the best transcription of the word. They are also shown two sentences. One word is underlined in the first sentence; in the second, test-takers are to underline the word that has the same function as the underlined word in the first sentence.

The correlation of scores on aptitude tests to success in foreign language courses tends to be between .40 and .60. Like IQ tests, however, aptitude tests may measure cognitive/academic skills more than language ability per se.

13.6.3 Motivation

Traditionally, **motivation** has been separated into integrative and instrumental. **Integrative motivation** reflects a desire to become part of the second language speech community, while **instrumental motivation** comes from the need to pass a test or learn a language for a job. Motivation consists of effort, desire, and favorable attitudes. Here are some factors in integrative motivation:

- attitudes toward L2 speakers
- interest in foreign languages
- integrative orientation
- attitudes toward courses and teachers
- desire to learn the L2
- attitudes toward learning the L2

Initially, integrative motivation was seen as more powerful than instrumental motivation. To really learn a language, it was thought you needed to have sympathy for, or even want to belong to, the group that speaks that language. However, some studies have found different results. In one, Mexican-American women who rated Anglos more negatively on a questionnaire about various personal attributes actually were more successful at learning English than those who rated Anglos positively. Another study found a negative correlation between Chinese university students' English ability and their desire to study in the United States.

The problem with these studies is that they tend to be based on self-reporting questionnaires. We never see the actual effort. Still, it makes intuitive sense that those who score high on integrative motivation also speak out more in class and that those who drop out of language courses tend to be unmotivated.

Two other types of motivation are resultative and intrinsic. **Resultative motivation** comes about as learners get better at languages; they then want to study more. **Intrinsic motivation** is also important: students need to be interested and challenged by the lessons.

13.6.4 Attitude

We have seen that **attitude** is a component of motivation. Parental attitudes influence their children's attitudes in school. Peers influence each other in their choice of variety of target language. Language learning goes more smoothly when teachers and learners have the same agenda, and teachers' attitudes are very important (they sometimes, for example, have an effect on who gets called on to practice). Feelings of ethnic solidarity may have an influence; in one study, French Canadians with strong ethnic feelings had poorer English pronunciation than peers without strong ethnic feelings. Clearly, teachers need to be sensitive to their students' motivation and attitudes.

13.6.5 Personality Factors

Extroversion/Introversion

Teachers tend to rate personality highly (along with IQ and memory) as important in language learning. They seem to especially value extroversion in language learning. This is different from findings in first language education in general. Extroverts tend to be more easily distracted, while introverts have good study habits. In language learning, however, extroversion is seen as good for seeking out contact, for negotiation, and for maximal output. There have been mixed results in the studies. Studies done naturalistically have found a positive correlation between extroversion and success in language learning. When researchers use tasks or questionnaires, correlation seems to be negative. There is some evidence that **extroversion** is related to academic success in general before puberty and **introversion** to success after puberty.

Risk Taking

Most language teachers would say that **risk taking** is helpful in language learning. Risk takers tend to volunteer more and tend to get more practice. Risk taking might be a factor in tolerance of ambiguity.

Tolerance of Ambiguity

Tolerance of ambiguity seems to be an important factor in language learning success. It can be defined as the capacity to avoid worrying about new situations or situations in which there are mixed messages. To be a good language learner, you obviously need a certain capacity to get past initial anxiety at these situations.

Empathy

Empathy has been studied in relationship to pronunciation. Empathy is related to ego permeability, the ability to change, so the hypothesis is that empathic people have more flexible identities and potentially a better L2 accent.

Inhibition

Inhibition is related to anxiety. Researchers speak of facilitative and debilitative anxiety; learners need to know how to make anxiety work for them. Anxiety can come out of competition; students become anxious when they compare themselves to their peers. What of things that lower inhibition? In one study, drinking alcohol first had a positive effect on pronunciation of L2 Thai, then a negative one; hypnosis and Valium have had no effect.

13.6.6 Learning Styles and Strategies

Educational theorists talk a lot about the necessity for recognizing that different learners get their information in different ways. Some people are quite analytical, while others think holistically. Some people learn aurally and others visually. Teachers need to become aware of the styles of their individual students and try to accommodate as many styles as they can in lessons. Styles are probably part of our makeup and cannot readily be changed. We can learn different strategies for learning, however. Strategies can help people learn and use language more effectively. An influential model of strategies breaks them down into metacognitive, cognitive, and social strategies. Metacognitive strategies help students plan or organize their learning. An example is paying attention to particular words or structures one has questions about. A cognitive strategy is an individual's way of making learning easier. Flash cards are a cognitive strategy. An example of a social strategy is the forming of study groups. Good language learners use a mix of strategies and know when to use the most appropriate one; they are very aware of their own learning.

Educational Implications
It is rare that a teacher has no second language speakers in class. A basic knowledge of second language acquisition is thus useful for all teachers.

13.7 EXERCISES

13.7.1 Words to Know

bilingual	multilingual	interlanguage
silent period	formula	unpacking
simplification	foreigner talk	output hypothesis
integrative motivation	instrumental motivation	second language acquisition
motivation	resultative motivation	intrinsic motivation
introverts	extroverts	risk taking
false friend		

13.7.2 Review

1. Why are errors part of L2 learning?

2. What are some typical stages L2 learners go through?

3. Is L2 learning the same as L1 learning?

4. What is the monitor hypothesis?

5. How is FT like CDS?

6. Why do people have differential success with L2 learning?

7. What sorts of motivation do L2 learners have?

8. What personality factors play a part in L2 learning?

13.7.3 Research Projects

1. Find a nonnative speaker of English on your campus. The International Student Association is a good place to start. Interview the student about his or her language learning history and the ways he or she likes to learn. Use concepts from this chapter and write a report.

2. If you are taking a foreign language now, keep a journal of your language learning. Use concepts from this chapter.

13.8 FURTHER READINGS

General introductions to second language acquisition are Larsen-Freeman and Long (1991), Ellis (1994), and Gass and Selinker (2001).

Doughty and Long (2003) is a collection of state-of-the-art articles that requires some background. Selinker (1972) defined "interlanguage." Selinker (1992) is a source that reflects his current thinking. Corder (1981a) collects some very influential papers, including groundbreaking discussions of mistake and error.

On silent periods, see Hakuta (1976) and Saville-Troike (1988). Weinert (1995), Hakuta (1976), Krashen and Scarcella (1978), and Schmidt (1983) address the idea of formulas. Ellis (1984) has examples of simplification. Corder (1981b) objected to the use of the term *simplification.*

Dulay, Burt, and Krashen (1982) summarizes the morpheme studies. Larsen-Freeman (1976) was an influential critique of some of the early morpheme studies.

Bley-Vroman (1989) has argued that first and second language processes are fundamentally different. On theories of SLA in general, see McLaughlin (1987). Krashen's theory is laid out best in his 1985 book, but see his 2003 book for the latest version. The implications of the theory are discussed in Barasch and James (1994). On incomprehensible input, see White's (1987) article.

The ZISA Project has resulted in numerous papers. Broad outlines of the project are found in Ellis (1994) and Larsen-Freeman and Long (1991). See also Pienemann (1984). Long summarized the benefits of instruction in Beebe (1988). Ellis (1990) is another good summary. For Lightbown's studies, see the summary in Larsen-Freeman and Long (1991).

Ferguson (1971, available in Ferguson [1996]) was one of the first articles to discuss foreigner talk. Larsen-Freeman and Long (1991) have a good summary of the research. Gass and Varonis (1985) is a good collection of articles on input in SLA. Long and Porter (1985) made the case for students working in groups. Chaudron (1988) reports on a number of studies of classroom interaction. Gass (1997) surveys the roles in input and interaction in SLA. Swain's thoughts on output are nicely summarized in an article in Cook and Seidlhofer (1995).

The best book overall about individual differences in SLA is Skehan (1989). Robinson (2002) is more recent but not as complete. Skehan (1998) puts research on individual differences into a wider context. Carroll (1990) is a look back at aptitude from the late 1980s. Gardner (1985) is a now not-so-recent summary of research on attitudes and motivation. For more recent developments, see Ellis (1994) and Skehan (1998). For personality factors, Skehan (1989) remains useful.

Chapter 14

Language and Literature

When studying literature we face challenges that are, if not unique to this field, at least quite different from the rest of the fields we have considered in this text. To begin with, there is little agreement on what literature is. Does literature limit itself to the "great authors" that have withstood the test of time (i.e., are still popular after many years), the so-called **canon?** Or does literature embrace all forms of expression, including, for example, diaries, private correspondence, newspaper articles, small self-edited magazines, newsletters, and other small "marginal" (i.e., outside of the mainstream) forms of publishing? And how about visual media, such as film, television, cartoons, comics, and websites? Needless to say, we will not attempt any such definition, but we will focus our attention on noncontroversial clear-cut cases, without making any claim that our choices of examples represent anything other than an expedient choice.

14.1 CASUAL VS. ELABORATED LANGUAGE

A very significant distinction, which may shed some light on the question of definition presented in the previous paragraph, is that surrounding the idea that literary, artistic use of language is qualitatively different from that of regular, run-of-the-mill use of language for nonaesthetic purposes. This idea goes back to the **Russian formalist** movement and has found one of its most significant expressions in the work of Roman Jakobson.

Essentially, this idea boils down to the claim that artistic use of language differs in that the speaker is (more or less) consciously manipulating the form (i.e., the *way* things are said) of the language rather than focusing exclusively on the content that he or she is trying to convey. By "form" we mean, at the simplest level, the sounds that make up the words.

Similar distinctions might be between rehearsed and unrehearsed language or between everyday use of language and sophisticated or artificial (in the etymological sense, i.e., done with art) use of language. We have chosen to use the pair **casual** and **elaborated language** to indicate the distinction.

A further caveat is necessary: many scholars radically disagree and argue that it is impossible to draw any distinction between casual and elaborated uses of language. We will return to their concerns later.

14.1.1 Arrangement of Sounds

Let us start our analysis of elaborated language by focusing on the way that sounds can be manipulated for aesthetic effects. In traditional literary theory these are called **figures of speech.** The basic principle at play in this context is that of repetition, as was highlighted by the work of Jakobson. Consider the electoral slogan *I like Ike,* used in the 1952 presidential campaign of Dwight Eisenhower. In phonetic transcription, this looks like

[aylaykayk]

Note that there are no spaces between the words, since there are no pauses when we pronounce the sentence. Moving on to the analysis of the slogan, we can see that it follows a very straightforward organization, consisting of three "units" (syllables, actually), each of which begins with the diphthong [ay] and is concluded by a consonant. This looks like

(14.1) ayC-ayC-ayC

where C stands for a consonant. Note the three-way repetition of [ay]. Furthermore, the second and third consonants ([k]) are also repeated. The pleasant, or at least clever, effect of the slogan is thus explained by the very high degree of repetition that we find in its parts.

Naturally, there are many ways that repetition may manifest itself. Let us look at some of the most common ways that simple repetition of sounds is exploited in poetry.

Alliteration

Alliteration is the repetition of consonants. Some authors distinguish between repetition of consonantal sounds at the beginning of the words (alliteration) and at the end of the words (consonance). A good example of alliteration can be found in Shakespeare's *Sonnet 88*. The alliterating sounds have been bolded.

> When **th**ou shalt be disposed to set me *light,*
> And place *my* merit in **th**e eye of scorn,
> Upon **th**y *side* against *my*self I'll *fight,*
> And prove **th**ee virtuous **th**ough **th**ou art forsworn.

Assonance

Assonance is the repetition of vowel sounds. You may find an example in the previous stanza, in the repetition of the [ay] sound (the syllables have been italicized).

Rhyme

Rhyme (or rime) is the repetition of both the vowel and the consonantal sound at the end of a word. We can distinguish two types of rhyme: masculine, which involves only one syllable (e.g., *supp***ort**—*ret***ort**), and feminine, when it involves more than one syllable (e.g., *sp***itefully**—*del***ightfully**).

Slant or approximate rhymes need not have an exact match but accept similarities of sound, rather than identity. Internal rhymes occur in the middle of the line, rather than at the end. Consider the beginning of Samuel Taylor Coleridge's famous *Kubla Khan*, which uses a very nice internal rhyme:

> In Xanadu did Kubla Khan
> A stately pl**easure**-dome decree:
> Where Alph, the sacred river, ran
> Through caverns m**easure**less to man
> Down to a sunless sea.

Visual Effects

When we speak of arranging the sounds of the words, we run the risk of forgetting that, unless it is recited aloud, poetry is very often read in written form. Poets can exploit the written form of language, just as much as they exploit its sound. The next two sections will consider some such effects.

Eye Rhyme

Eye rhyme consists of two rhyming words that are spelled the same (vowel sound and final consonant) but pronounced differently (e.g., *great—meat*). This causes the reader to be somewhat taken aback and can be used for humorous purposes or just as a license (i.e., an imperfection) if the poet could not come up with anything better.

Enjambment

Enjambment can be defined as the lack of a pause at the end of a line. Consider the following lines, from Shakespeare's *The Winter's Tale:*

... stopping the career
of laughter with a sigh (a note infallible
of breaking honesty)? ...

where both the first and the second line are enjambed.

Meter

Sounds are not the only area in which we find repetition. Repetition of syllables and/or stresses is called **meter.** A very broad field of literary analysis is based on the concept of **syllable.** For our purposes, a syllable is a vowel preceded and/or followed by up to three consonants. It is customary to represent the vowels by "V" and the consonants by "C." So the following are some of the possible syllables configurations:

CV	no
CCCVC	split
CCCVCC	splits
VC	on
VCC	orb
VCCC	irks
CCVCC	spits

Note that if two vowels occur within one syllable, one of them has to lose its "syllabic" nature, i.e., it is no longer regarded as a vowel. So in [boi] (*boy*) the syllabic structure is CVC, not CVV. Some linguists will represent nonsyllabic vowels with "glides" ([y] or [w]), so that *boil* would be transcribed as [boyl].

Stress

Words are made up of syllables. A word like *dog* has only one syllable, but *concrete* has two (don't let spelling mislead you; the last *e* is not pronounced!) and *tomorrow* three; *responsible* and *apostrophe* have four.

A syllable may be pronounced with more or less **stress** (i.e., louder or softer). There are different levels of stress, but for metrical purposes we only distinguish between stressed (strong) and unstressed (weak) syllables.

Scanning

Scansion is the process of determining stressed and unstressed syllables for a line of verse. Traditionally, strong syllables are marked with an accent (á), while weak syllables are marked with a small arc (ă). So the word *cat* would be scanned as cát and *purpose* as púrpŏse (note again that the last *e* is silent). If we scan an entire line, we get the following:

(14.2) Týgĕr! Týgĕr! búrnĭng bríght

Repetition of some of the structure of syllables, in terms of combinations of stressed and unstressed syllables, are called **metric feet.** Thus, for example, in the William Blake line in (14.2), we note the repetition of the pattern "stressed-unstressed" three times. This foot is called, with a reference to ancient Greek poetry, a **trochee.** So, the line in (14.2) consists of three trochees, followed by a single stressed syllable.

The most common foot, in English poetry, is the **iamb,** which consists of ˘´ (unstressed-stressed), such as in the famous

(14.3) Tŏ bé ŏr nót tŏ bé

Other commonly used feet are **anapests,** which consist of ˘˘´ (the word *intervene* is an anapest) as in

(14.4) Ărchĭtéctŭrăl pláns hăve thĕ ríght to bĕ blúe

and **dactyls,** which consist of ´˘˘ (*yéstĕrdăy*).

Needless to say, poets may bend the rules to fit the words to their poetic vision. For example, Blake's poem continues

(14.5) Týgĕr! Týgĕr! búrnĭng bríght

    ĭn thĕ fórĕsts ŏf thĕ níght,

and technically the second line does not follow the pattern established in the first line. However, it seems clear that the poet meant the second line to scan

(14.6) ín thĕ fórĕsts óf thĕ níght,

This is an example of what is commonly called "poetic license."

14.1.2 Figures of Thought

As we mentioned before, along with figures of speech, which focus on the sounds of the words, we have **figures of thought,** which focus on the meaning. Under this heading traditionally we deal with similes, metaphors, and metonymies, which are known as "figurative language."

Figurative Language

The basic idea behind figurative language is to talk about something in terms of something else.

Metaphors

An influential definition of metaphor sees it as involving a **tenor** and a **vehicle.** The tenor is the thing that we want to talk about, say *Mary.* The vehicle is the image, that is, the other term that we use to refer to the tenor, say *a peach.* Thus we get the metaphor

(14.7) Mary is a peach.

and the simile

(14.8) Mary is like a peach.

Basically, **metaphors** and **similes** only differ in the presence or absence of an explicit comparison (*like, as*). A more recent approach to metaphors considers them as examples of flouting the cooperative principle (see 3.2.3).

Metonymies

Metonymies are similar to metaphors, in that they entail the use of one thing to talk about another one, but differ in that the vehicle is not a different object or idea but a related object or idea. So, for example,

(14.9) Admission to the museum is $5 a head

does not refer to a museum where decapitated people only are admitted but is an example of the "part-for-the-whole" pattern of metonymy. Similarly, when we

(14.10) Drink a cup of coffee

we are using a "container-for-the-contained" metonymy (you cannot drink cups!).

Cognitive Linguistics on Metaphors

Starting around 1980, a new approach to the study of language, known as cognitive grammar (see 18.2.3), has emphasized the significance of metaphors in language. Far from considering metaphors exceptional (figurative, as opposed to literal language), cognitive linguistics notes that metaphors and metonymies are in fact pervasive. We speak of the legs of a table, the head of a line of people waiting for a bank teller, and potatoes that grow eyes. In addition, we keep our eyes on someone, and we have heads of a company. These metaphors are so common that we forget that they are there at all, but it is clear that a large part of language is built around metaphors.

As the previous examples suggest, metaphors are not randomly chosen either. On the contrary, they are organized along the lines of mappings from one "conceptual domain" to another. A conceptual domain is similar to a frame (see 3.2.2) in that it is a broad concept, based on experience, such as the body of a person. Thus, for example, we map (transfer) from the domain of the body to the domain of objects, such as tables and mountains. Once we see things in this light, it is easy to see how the head of the body being the place where the brain is located can be seen as the decision-making controlling center of the body and how that transfers to companies (or lines). Cognitive linguistics has analyzed large numbers of these metaphors, such as an argument is a war (e.g., *he shot down my arguments, she won the argument*) or life is a day *(the twilight of his years).*

It is now easy to understand why many scholars reject the idea of a radical distinction between casual and elaborated language: if metaphors underlie all forms of language, even those that we would think of as literal, then the grounds for the distinction all but disappear. Needless to say, other scholars argue that the distinction can still be drawn, only on different grounds.

Other Figures of Thought

Naturally, metaphors and metonymies are not the only ways that we can say one thing and mean another. In fact, as you will recall from the previous discussion of the cooperative principle (see 3.2.3) that is roughly how we defined the concept of flouting. Some types of floutings are commonly used in literature (but also outside of it).

Overstatement

Overstatement (aka **hyperbole**) is essentially an exaggeration. When we say to a child in exasperation *I have told you a million times to leave the dog alone,* we do not expect that anyone will take us literally. The purpose of the hyperbole is to stress our fatigue. Consider the following:

> (14.11) I loved Ophelia: forty thousand brothers
>   could not, with all their quantity of love,
>   make up my sum. (*Hamlet*, act 5, scene 2)

which is a very nice example of a literary use of hyperbole.

Understatement

Understatement, or **litotes,** is the opposite of hyperbole. The following, also from Shakespeare, is a beautiful example of the poignant restraint that can be expressed through understatement. Mercutio is talking about the wound that will kill him:

> (14.12) 'Tis not so deep as a well, nor so wide as a church-door, but 'tis
>   enough, twill serve. (*Romeo and Juliet*, act 3, scene 1)

Irony

Irony is commonly defined as saying the opposite of what one means. For example, if someone spills wine on your new jacket, you may say *That* *was smart!* and count on your tone of voice and on the context (namely, that the other person just spilled wine on you) to lead your interlocutor to the inference that you actually mean that it was rather stupid. **Sarcasm** is usually taken to be a bitter, darker type of irony. A well-known example of irony is Swift's *A Modest Proposal* in which the author suggests that a way to alleviate the effects of the potato famine in Ireland is to eat children. The problem with irony, as Swift learned, is that often people will not get it and take the ironist to the letter.

The definition of irony as "saying the opposite of what one means" has been challenged on the grounds that under- and overstatement can be used to be ironical, and therefore one is not saying the opposite of what one means but rather something different. Consider the following example:

(14.13) I am a little upset by your totaling my new car

where the speaker believes that totaling his or her car is upsetting, but the irony lies in the *little* modifier. The problem with this new definition (saying something different than what one means) is indistinguishable from the definition of flouting, which is of course a problem.

Another issue with irony is whether it is necessarily negative, i.e., whether one can use irony only to express a negative judgment or feeling toward something. Some have argued that this is the case and point to the fact that irony is aggressive and mocking. Others have argued that irony can be used to express positive feelings and judgments, such as in an utterance *These American-made cars that last only 100,000 miles* where the speaker of the utterance is clearly pleased with the state of affairs, in contrast with the (now obsolete) stereotype that American-made cars were of bad quality.

Symbols and Allegory

A **symbol** is something that implies or vaguely alludes to something else. Thus, in T. S. Eliot's "The Love Song of J. Alfred Prufrock,"

(14.14) I grow old... I grow old...

      I shall wear the bottoms of my trousers rolled

      Shall I part my hair behind? Do I dare eat a peach?

the trivial questions are symbolic of Prufrock's emotional and intellectual pettiness.

An **allegory** is the extended use of a symbol, possibly throughout an entire work. The *Divine Comedy* and *Pilgrim's Progress* are allegorical works, where the entire plot of the text is symbolic of a moral narrative (the soul's salvation) within a set of religious beliefs.

Allusions and Intertextuality

Allusions are references to other, usually well-known, texts or events that the speaker does not have to repeat in detail but can leave implicit. As such, allusions fall under the banner of **intertextuality,** which can be simply defined as all the references among texts and/or parts thereof.

For example, T. S. Eliot's "The Love Song of J. Alfred Prufrock" starts with a **citation** (in Italian) from Dante's *Divine Comedy* and specifically from the *Inferno*. A citation is an explicit form of intertextual relationship (the author of a text "borrows" a part of another text), which in this case also works as an allusion (it is not explicitly identified as being Dante's text) and moreover as a symbol of the "hellish" situation in which Prufrock finds himself.

Other forms of intertextuality are less obscure, and include footnotes, references, and other scholarly forms of citation of sources. Yet other forms of intertextuality have been codified as **genres** (literary forms that share a given set of characteristics, both formal and content based), such as **parody,** which consists in taking a text and rewriting it keeping either the form or the content unchanged (or minimally so) and introducing changes (again, either formal or related to the content of the text) that ridicule the work or the author. Thus, for example, Samuel Richardson published in 1740 a book called *Pamela*, which became very popular. In 1741 Henry Fielding published *Shamela*, which is a parody of it (as the title, with its allusion to *shame* or *sham* shows) and makes fun of the moralistic purposes of Richardson.

14.2 NARRATIVE

Whereas it can be argued that poetry tends to focus on the form of language, narrative tends to focus more on the contents (needless to say, these are at best general trends, if not downright oversimplifications).

Several approaches have been proposed for the analysis of narrative texts, known as the field of **narratology,** under which falls novels, novellas, short stories, jokes, anecdotes, and letters but not plays (because they are not narrated, they are acted by actors who say what the characters say). We will consider some of the best-known approaches and issues in narratology.

14.2.1 Narrative Functions

The analysis of narrative may be considered to start with the Russian folklorist Vladimir Propp's analysis of a set of fairy tales in which he found a number of **functions,** i.e., minimal narrative units of the kind "the hero leaves the village" and "the hero slays a dragon," which were repeated in all the fairy tales he was analyzing.

Despite Propp's warnings, many scholars took the very specific functions that Propp had found in the Russian fairy tales and tried to apply them to other types of text with predictably disappointing results. Other scholars instead tried to come up with more abstract analyses, in which the concept of function is no longer tied to any specific content but is expressed in terms of whether an action (any action) is performed or not.

This led eventually to the formulation of the concept of **minimal narrative,** i.e., the simplest possible narrative, in the sense that it consists of one action/event. An event is defined as a "change of state." An event may be brought about by an agent or by other forces (e.g., nature). Events may or may not be significant from the point of view of the plot. However, even events and other background parts, such as descriptions, which do not make the story advance, are still meaningful.

From there on, inspired by contemporary research in generative grammar, narratologists tried to write "grammars" of narrative texts. These attempts have had mixed results, due primarily to the fact that it has proven impossible to account for all the significant things in the text and to account for the relative levels of significance of the parts of the text. For example, how does one decide what is the background of a text, as opposed to the central plot? This decision is to a certain extent based on the interpreter's feelings and beliefs, which, needless to say, make writing a "grammar" of the text nearly impossible.

14.2.2 Narrator, Narratee, and Their Implied Relatives

One of the best results in narratology has been the analysis of the role and significance of the "person" doing the telling of the narrative. This fictional character has been called the **narrator** and is emphatically distinguished from the author of the text (a real person, breathing and eating). The presence of a narrator implies that the story is told to someone, just as fictional as the narrator (called the **narratee**) and also emphatically not to be confused with the real audience who lives in the real world, buys the books, and reads them.

A narrator may be explicitly present in the text, as is the case in many 18th-century novels in which the narrator addresses the narratees directly, or may have to be inferred from the text, in which case we speak of an **implied narrator.** An implied narrator is always present in the text, if for nothing else, because tenses and other deictic forms (see 3.2.1) presuppose a speaker in relation to whose location and time of speaking tenses and deictics are determined. This is not the case with the explicit narrator, obviously, as many novels and short stories are written without the narrator directly addressing his or her narratees. This leads to the following graphic:

Author → Narrator → Text → Narratee → Reader

where the extreme left and right are the only "real" people, and the central characters are fictional.

14.2.3 Point of View

Another very significant issue in narratology is that of **point of view.** We may define it as the perspective from which the story is narrated, including the psychological, ideological, and even spatial and temporal aspects of this perspective. In particular, this has often taken the form of deciding which kind of point of view the narrator has in the text.

Types of Narrator

An elaborate typology of the types of authorial perspective has been developed. We will examine only a few of the many possibilities.

Omniscient Narrator

When the story is told from the point of view of a narrator who has access to the unexpressed inner thoughts of all the characters, knows exactly what everyone is doing, and possibly knows how the story will end, we refer to this type of narrator as **omniscient** (i.e., one who knows everything). This is the type of narrator used by the great realist novelists of the 19th century, such as Gustave Flaubert, Charles Dickens, or Leo Tolstoy.

Homodiegetic Narrator

A narrative may be told from the point of view of one of its characters (e.g., Nick Carraway in F. Scott Fitzgerald's *The Great Gatsby*). This type of narrator usually has a limited knowledge: for example, typically he or she only can report on his or her feelings and thoughts. Thus, an **homodiegetic narrator** is a narrator who appears within the narrative he or she tells.

The degree to which the narrator's knowledge is limited may vary, depending, among other things, on the distance from the events narrated (both temporal and emotional). Consider the difference between relating events that just happened and events that happened 30 years before.

A particular type of homodiegetic narrator is that in which the hero of the narrative happens to be the narrator. This is called an autobiographical narrative (**autobiography**). When the narrator and the main characters do not coincide, we speak of third person narrative (because it uses the third person pronouns *he/she/it*). Naive readers often confuse the narrator who says *I* in the narrative with the real author of the text, forgetting that the narrator is a fictional character who may or may not be a faithful representation of the author's beliefs.

Stream of Consciousness

The ultimate development of the limited point of view of the homodiegetic narrator is the **stream of consciousness** in which (parts of) the narrative consist entirely of reporting the thoughts of a particular character. Some chapters of James Joyce's *Ulysses* and Virginia Woolf's *Mrs. Dalloway* are written in this technique.

Unreliable Narrators

An interesting problem, which arises primarily with modern literature, is that of the degree of reliability of the narrator. To put it simply, why should we believe what the narrator is saying? Or, how do we know that the narrator is saying all he or she knows? The problems with the reliability of the narrator are very clear in Henry James's *The Turn of the Screw:* what are we to make of the story as told by a character whose mental stability is at stake? In other words, in a narrative with an unreliable narrator, the reader is invited to "read between the lines" and to find discrepancies between what the narrator says and what the reader can figure out about the story. Examples of unreliable narrators are Mark Twain's *Huck Finn* (a child), the self-apologetic pedophiliac narrator of Vladimir Nabokov's *Lolita*, and the mentally retarded narrator (Benjy) in William Faulkner's *The Sound and the Fury*.

Free Indirect Discourse

An interesting issue, related to the narrator's point of view, comes into being when the narrator mentions someone's speech. There are two ways to do so: quoting it literally, indicating this by quotation marks (direct discourse) or paraphrasing it (indirect discourse). Indirect discourse may be explicitly marked (tagged) by expressions such as *she said* or may be free of any such marker; in the latter case, it is called **free indirect discourse.**

Consider the following examples

Direct speech	*"When do we eat in this place?" said Mary.*
Tagged indirect speech	*Mary asked when lunch would be served.*
Free indirect speech	*Mary wondered when people ate in that place.*

where it is clear how indirect speech may not be a literal representation of the words used by a character, and the typical shifts of tenses and deictics are shown in the free indirect discourse example (*we* becomes *people, eat* becames *ate,* and *this* becomes *that*).

Other Issues Related to Point of View

The way the narrative is presented by the narrator also contributes to the establishment of the point of view. We turn now to a few examples of significant issues in this domain.

Temporal Arrangement

The pace of the narrative is intuitively compared to the pace of the events narrated within it. Thus, the pace of the narrative may match that of the events or be faster or slower. Analogies from film may be easier to grasp than other examples: slow motion sequences are examples of narrative pace that is slower than the action (examples are numberless; think of an action movie that shows the impact of bullets or punches in gory detail); fast motion sequences are obviously the opposite, i.e., the narrative is faster than the events (examples are much rarer; one is the sex scene in Alex's bedroom in *A Clockwork Orange*). The general case, however, is that the narrative pace matches that of the events unfolding.

The time of the narrative may be significantly different than that of the events, needless to say. Descriptive passages in novels imply no passing of time at all, while it is possible to have 20 years summarized in the sentence, *Twenty years went by,* which takes less than a second of narrative time. Furthermore, "montage" (i.e., the way sequences of narrative events are organized) may affect the organization and the perception of the narrative. The most common effects, again using cinematic examples, are flashbacks, flash-forwards, and juxtapositions. In a flashback, the narrative goes back to events that took place before the time of the narrative. Joseph Conrad's *Heart of Darkness* is one long flashback. Flash-forwards are much rarer and consist in the narrative's anticipating events that have yet to happen at the time of the narration. An example can be seen in the movie *Easy Rider* in which images of the main characters' deaths appear in the middle of the story. Juxtapositions have the effect of speeding up the narrative by jumping from one event to the other.

Spatial Arrangement

Just like the way the temporal aspect of the narrative is significant, so is the spatial arrangement. Spatial arrangement may refer to characters' sight, hearing, or even touch. Consider again an example from film: the position of the camera and the type of shot (wide-angle versus close-up) will determine to a large extent the effect a given image has on the viewer.

In narrative, the detail of a description will cause the reader's attention to be focused on a given small object, or even a detail, or conversely to ignore all detail and focus on the broad picture. The incredibly detailed, meticulous, and apparently irrelevant descriptions of the objects on a table by French avant-garde novelist Alain Robbe-Grillet are probably an extreme example of this focalizing aspect of spatial arrangement. The descriptive passages of realist novels are good examples of more common uses of spatial focalization.

Ideology

The political or moral standpoint from which the narrator tells his or her story is crucial to the evaluation of the events and to the passing of judgment toward the motivations of the characters. The standpoint of the narrator may be expressed explicitly, as when the narrator comments on his or her narrative, or is evinced by the use of such evaluative terms as *luckily, unfortunately,* or *heroically.*

For instance, the profoundly sympathetic portrait of the homeless farmers driven to abject poverty by the greed of speculators in John Steinbeck's *Grapes of Wrath* is integral to an understanding of the plot.

Likewise, the antitotalitarian anti-Stalinist satire in George Orwell's *1984* is the basis of the meaning of the novel. In J. D. Salinger's *Catcher in the Rye,* unless one sympathizes with the rebellious main character, his existential angst is hard to fathom.

Educational Implications
This chapter was addressed to secondary teachers of the language arts. It offered a linguistic look at literature.

14.3 EXERCISES

14.3.1 Words to Know

casual language	elaborated language	rhyme
assonance	alliteration	repetition
syllable	scansion	stress
metric foot	trochee	iamb
anapest	dactyl	figurative language
tenor	vehicle	metaphor
allusion	intertextuality	citation
metonymy	overstatement	hyperbole
understatement	litotes	irony
sarcasm	symbol	allegory
genre	parody	narratology
function	minimal narrative	narrator
narratee	implied narrator	point of view
eye rhyme	enjambment	simile
omniscient narrator	homodiegetic narrator	stream of consciousness
unreliable narrator	free indirect discourse	figure of speech
figure of thought	Russian formalism	canon
meter	autobiography	citation

14.3.2 Review

1. What is the difference between casual and elaborate language?

2. What is the difference between alliteration and assonance?

3. What is figurative language? List a few examples and explain how they work.

5. What is a homodiegetic narrator? Can he or she be omniscient?

6. What is an implied narrator? Can you think of an example?

14.3.3 Research Projects

1. Pick a poem written in meter and scan 20–30 lines of it. Do you find any irregular feet? Can you find an explanation for their presence?

2. Pick a poem and try to identify as many figures of speech as you can.

3. Analyze part of a novel or part of a film using the concepts in this chapter.

4. Read George Lakoff and Mark Johnson's book *Metaphors We Live By* (it's easy, don't worry), and choose a metaphor schema to work with (e.g., time is money); list as many metaphors based on that schema as you can find.

5. Write your own poem or short story, using any number of the figures and techniques we describe in the chapter. If you produce a (short) piece that includes all the techniques, send it to us (c/o our publisher).

14.4 FURTHER READINGS

A good general introduction to the field of language and literature is lacking, but students may want to check out Traugott and Pratt (1980). Useful, but partial, texts are Fowler (1986), Leech (1969), and Toolan (1988). Handbooks of literature contain excellent definitions of literary terms and often examples.

The Coleridge example comes from Leech (1969). On scansion, meter, and rhyme, see also Fussell (1979). On the traditional theory of metaphor, see Leech (1969, 150ff.). The terms *tenor* and *vehicle* come from Richards (1936). The groundbreaking Lakoff and Johnson (1980) work remains one of the best introductions to the analysis of metaphors in cognitive linguistics. A little more complex, but very rewarding, is Ungerer and Schmid's (1996) book, which is a general introduction to cognitive linguistics but has a chapter focused on metaphors. The Shakesperian examples of hyperbole and litotes are from Leech (1969).

On narratology, see Bal (1985, now in a second edition) and Prince (1987), which is in the form of a dictionary but is quite readable anyway. On "minimal story/narrative," see Bremond (1973), Prince (1973), and Labov (1972a). The definition of "event" is from Chatman (1978, 44). The significance of background elements is noted forcefully by Barthes (1968). On unrealiable narrators, see Booth (1961). On point of view, see Fowler (1986, Chapter 9) and Bal (1985).

Chapter 15

Linguistics in the Professions

You will recall that we defined applied linguistics as the application of the insights of theoretical linguistics to problems that emerged from other disciplines, such as sociology, psychology, and so forth. Naturally, this does not mean that applied linguistics did not develop its own set of research methods and problems.

In this chapter, we will explore some areas of applied linguistics that have a direct and immediate application to professional concerns, i.e., some areas in which applied linguistics is directly useful to people in a variety of professions, such as lawyers, doctors, teachers, translators, and interpreters.

That (applied) linguistics may have practical applications should not really be a surprise, despite the abstract nature of most linguistic theorizing, if one considers that most professional activities involve communication at one level or another and that communication is largely a linguistic affair.

15.1 LANGUAGE AND THE LAW

Think about lawyer, judge, and police shows you've watched on television. How would you characterize "the language of the law"?

15.1.1 Legal Language

It's generally agreed that legal language has a number of special characteristics. In the law, everyday words have specialized meanings.

Papers detailing the orders of the court are *served.* We speak of legal *instruments* when we mean forms or other documents. The law uses words from Old and Middle English like *aforesaid* and *forthwith* and words from Latin like *nolo contendere,* which means *I do not contest (that).* It also uses words from Old French like *voir dire,* which means roughly jury selection and more modern jargon like *order to show cause, cease and desist,* and *pursuant to stipulation.* Some would say that because law has a special language, it wraps itself in a cloak of mystery. This mysteriousness in turn adds an element of prestige to the law.

Recall our discussion of jargon (see 6.3); among the functions of jargon was certainly that of being obscure to the noninitiated, but there is also the need for precision. By using these traditional collocations *(cease and desist),* lawyers and judges make sure that they know exactly what they mean and therefore reduce the risk of litigation. The downside of jargon is that, as we said before, it makes legal language virtually incomprehensible to the noninitiated.

Since the 1970s, however, the plain language movement has developed. This movement urged that legal documents be written in a language closer to spoken language and therefore be simpler and more understandable. There is evidence that this movement has indeed been successful.

However, on the negative side, we should consider the fact that judges often force the interpretation of the language of the law to push their agenda. For example, a study of U.S. Supreme Court decisions showed that the justices often claim that the meaning of a given law is clear, whereas it is, in fact, ambiguous.

15.1.2 Language in Court

Think back on our discussion of language and gender. Recall how words and phrases like *so, kind of,* and *you know* were seen as examples of powerless speech, while straightforward, unadorned speech (like that of the cowboy heroes in the movies) was considered powerful. Think how powerful speech might be perceived in the courtroom. As more believable, right? First of all, if you speak directly, you're less likely to be seen as sneaky or dishonest. You're telling *the truth and nothing but the truth.* Also, if you don't use hedges or softeners, you sound more "professional" and of higher status. Related to this is the attempt on the part of attorneys to break down witness responses into a question/answer pattern. Short responses tend to sound less authoritative.

The issue of language in the courtroom is an important and practical one. Experiments have been done on word choice in attorneys' questions. People viewed a film of an accident and then were asked a variety of questions. If an experimenter asked, *How fast was the first car going when it smashed into the other car?* people tended to give a faster speed than when asked *How fast were the cars going when they bumped into each other?* In fact, if an experimenter asked, *Did you see the broken taillight?* people were apt to say *Yes* even when there was no broken taillight in the filmed accident they saw.

A further issue involves the use of interpreters and translators, when one of the parties is not a native speaker. While this would seem obvious (how can one defend oneself if one does not understand fully what is being said?), the evidence is that courts fail to use interpreters, although the use of Spanish interpreters in U.S. courts is better than one might expect. One study found that in Australia only one in ten situations that would call for the use of an interpreter received one. In general, the legal system essentially still assumes monolingualism.

15.1.3 Legislation on Language

In the United States, the First Amendment (freedom of speech) has essentially prevented any legislation against language crimes. In many countries, however, there are legal constraints on what can be said. For example, in Italy there used to be a crime called *apology of crime,* which made it illegal to praise a crime. Many countries have banned *vilification,* i.e., the use of offensive language on racial, sexual, and religious grounds. Naturally, there are other types of crimes that are accomplished by saying something (i.e., by the use of a performative speech act, cf. 3.2.3), such as threats and incitement (convincing someone to commit a crime).

A special case of legislation on language is copyright law. Copyright law protects the intellectual ownership of the author of a text while, at the same time, permits the discussion of ideas, teaching, and so forth, via the "fair use" doctrine (i.e., that one may quote small parts of someone else's text without having to pay copyright, while if one reproduces significant parts of the text, one has to pay the author).

Copyright infringement cases often focus on trademarks. A case in point is the McDonald's® legal action against the McSleep hotel chain in 1988. The McSleep owners argued that the prefix *Mc* had become generic (like Kleenex® or Xerox®) and that therefore they were not infringing on McDonald's trademark. However, the judge ruled against McSleep.

15.1.4 Forensic Linguistics

Forensic linguistics is mainly concerned with the use of linguistic features as evidence in trials, although some use the term *forensic linguistics* to indicate the entire field of language and the law. The following sections review some of the principal uses of forensic linguistics. A general caveat should be presented, namely, that the very admissibility of linguistic evidence in court has been challenged and/or has met with difficulties.

Voiceprints and Handwriting

Voiceprints is the term used to indicate the fact that the acoustic analysis of the phonetics of speech may be used to identify speakers. The same goes for handwriting and typing, although there the features are graphic, obviously.

Stylometry

The idea is to identify authorship on the basis of the style of the writing of a text. The style of a text covers everything from word choice to errors. Stylometry is fairly controversial because it is unclear how reliable the various techniques are. In some cases, things are fairly clear cut; for example, in one case the language the police claimed to be that of a nonnative speaker of English was shown to be someone else because the nonnative speaker's language did not have that level of morphological complexity. In another case, the accent of a New York speaker proved that he could not have made bomb threats to an airline, since the caller had a Boston accent.

Stylometry became quite popular in the 1990s because it contributed to the arrest of the Unabomber, after a linguist connected his *Manifesto* with an essay by Theodore Kaczynski that his brother had given to the FBI.

An area in which the use of linguistic clues is very important is the unmasking of fabricated confessions: at times, the police will coerce an accused person into signing a confession that he or she has not really made. Confessions are supposed to be a verbatim transcript of the accused's words. Because of this, it has been possible, in some cases, to unmask the fabricated confession because it was shown that the speaker could not possibly have used the language that was attributed to him or her.

In 1996, a satirical book on the Clinton administration, titled *Primary Colors*, was published. The author of the book was listed as "Anonymous." Many guesses were made as to the identity of Anonymous as the book became a best seller. In February 1996, *New York* magazine hired Donald Foster, a linguist who specializes in stylometry, and he determined that the author was *Newsweek* journalist Joe Klein. Klein initially denied this claim, but when a manuscript that included handwritten corrections turned up in July and Klein's writing was shown to match that of the manuscript, he came clean. The use of the same adverbs (e.g., *reflexively*), of adjectives ending in -*y* (e.g., *talky*), and of words ending in -*ish* were among the evidence Foster used to unmask Klein. Errors are also a good identifier; for example, both Anonymous and Klein use *riffle* to mean *rifle*. Foster was also the linguist who helped identify the Unabomber.

15.2 LANGUAGE AND MEDICINE

Think about times you've spoken with your physician. What happened? Who spoke? How?

The same argument presented for legal language as a jargon is valid for the medical language. Medical language is largely built out of Latin and Greek terminology. Thus, the morpheme -*tomy* indicates the cutting off of some body part (e.g., *appendectomy* means the removal of the appendix); the morpheme *gastro-* indicates the stomach; and *onco-* is a tumor (cancer). The effect of the use of this technical terminology is to make it very hard to understand what is being said, unless one is familiar with these terms. In fact, studies have shown that up to 50 percent of patients may not understand what they are told by the doctors. Naturally, the requirements of precision and lack of ambiguity are also present in medicine and are a motivation for using this technical terminology. The same goes for the use of the metric system, which for U.S. patients is further disorienting.

Nurses' jargons exist as well, which are used as in the more general medical language for precision but also to avoid discussing potentially upsetting topics (such as vomit and feces) in front of patients and visitors. For example, vomit is often referred to as *a spill.*

15.2.1 Discourse

A number of commentators have remarked that physician-patient conversations share a number of characteristics. Indeed, in some sense, it's hard to call doctor-patient encounters "conversations" at all. The topic of the conversation is the patient's body and wellness. The doctor asks most of the questions, and some physicians may even become irritated if the patient asks questions or interrupts. Neither patients nor physicians are completely forthcoming, in the case of the patients perhaps because they "know their place" and in the case of the doctors because sometimes it is felt best for the truth to be sugarcoated or even delayed.

Physicians typically begin with a question like *What's the problem?* and go on to ask a lot of questions. Some critics of doctor-patient communication consider the doctor's typical use of a chain of questions to be a device to control the conversation and thereby the patient. In normal conversations, *Um hm* and other backchannel devices (see 2.6.2) are used to show interest in the others' ideas, to let conversation partners know that we're listening, and to encourage further talk. The use of *Um hm* in doctor-patient conversations tends to be limited to *I heard that.* Other ways that doctors seem to control patients' conversation is by validating or invalidating the patients' responses (e.g., by reformulating them in medical jargon or by ignoring them).

One very specific way that physicians convince patients that they have their best interests at heart is by using *we* or *let's* (let us). How many times has your doctor or nurse said, *Why don't we take off our clothes?* or *Let's get on the table?* Who actually took off their clothes? Who got on the table?

15.2.2 Social Factors

A significant issue that complicates the issue of doctor/patient interplay is social status. Traditionally, doctors have been male (though this is changing) and belonged to the upper class, while their patients often belonged to the lower classes.

The differences in status between the doctors and the patients are reinforced by the institutional settings (the patients wait for the doctor, for example); by the use of title, last name forms of address (see 4.2.2); by the discourse strategies of the doctors, such as asking questions, as we saw previously; and by the generally stressful situation of the medical encounter in general (after all, we tend to see a physician if we are *not* feeling well).

Medical diagnoses and procedures may also be affected by the conversations that take place during consultations. It may be in the patient's best interest, for example, to appear informed when the doctor asks about the patient's knowledge of various procedures. Simply asking,

Is that necessary? or *Is there another way?* for example, may steer a doctor away from a preferred procedure and toward another one. Some studies have suggested that poor people tend to be less informed or at least less aggressive in their questioning of physicians and may therefore receive different treatment than those who are better informed.

15.3 TRANSLATION

Gardeners have an expansive plant vocabulary. Mechanics know the names of many types of wrenches. Things that are important to people are named and subdivided so that they may talk about those things easily and precisely (see 6.3). When members of one group need to talk to members of other groups, translation occurs. Our mechanics need to talk to us in ways that we understand if they expect to be trusted and paid. Though this notion of translation (aka paraphrase) is fundamental and important, most of what people regard as translation is the switching of one language into another.

The word **translation** actually is an umbrella term for two activities: interpreting (of spoken language) and translation (of written language). Interpreting is further divided into consecutive interpreting, in which the speaker waits while sections of his or her remarks are interpreted, and simultaneous interpretation, in which there are no breaks. The interpreter must listen and produce a translation as the speaker speaks. Most translators work from a foreign language into their mother tongue, while interpreters often must go in both directions. Interpretation is a very difficult and complex field.

Anecdotes about mistranslations are plenty. Once Ronald Reagan was listening to a speech in Russian when the interpreter translating for the Soviet dignitary said that the Soviets intended to spank the Americans on their bare bottoms. Needless to say, consternation ensued. It turned out later that the original was much closer to *kick butt.*

15.3.1 Quality of Translation

To return to our mechanic example, someone trying to convey a car repair question may choose to give a very broad definition of the problem *(Your engine is shot),* which is not very helpful, or may choose to be more precise *(You need a ring job)* at the risk of not communicating with the customer who will ask, *What's a ring job?*

When working with literature, translators must face a number of problems. One is cultural. Someone translating a European novel into an

Asian language might face the problem of conveying the central symbols of Christianity to a readership that has not grown up with them. American readers of translated poetry written in Arabic will probably miss allusions to Islam. This is sometimes handled through the use of notes, which can make for a tedious reading experience. Another problem is linguistic. How can a translator convey figures of language like puns or metaphors? (See 3.1.2.)

There are a number of tests of good translation. Different purposes demand different tests. A translation should be accurate. This is necessary for all translations, for who wants to read something that is just wrong? Translations must be accurate linguistically and in terms of knowledge. A number of legends have arisen over the issue of translation in marketing. One says that the Chevrolet® automobile known as the Nova® in the United States was very unpopular and did not sell well in Latin America because *No va* in Spanish means *It doesn't go.* In China, the slogan *Come alive with Pepsi®* was supposedly mistranslated as *Pepsi® brings your ancestors back from the dead.* Neither mistake actually happened, but the point of the examples (care must be taken in international marketing) is a good one.

Another requirement for a good translation is aesthetics. Ideally, especially in a work of art, the beauty of one language should be mirrored in the other. This requirement is obviously not as important in translations of technical manuals and laws.

Perhaps the most difficult requirement is that of cultural accuracy or at least resonance. This is often a problem with biblical translations. In one Native American translation, *ass* was translated in a circumlocution as *a small animal with large ears* so that Jesus was pictured riding into Jerusalem on a rabbit. Translation of the Bible has been an emotional issue throughout history. The very idea of putting it into the vernaculars of Europe so that average people, not just priests, could read it was a central idea of the Reformation.

> Some Americans forget that the Bible was not written in English. Miriam "Ma" Ferguson, the first woman governor of Texas, once said, *If English was good enough for Jesus Christ, it's good enough for me.* Of course, Jesus spoke Aramaic, a Semitic language, and the Bible was introduced to Europe in Greek and Hebrew.

Here are two versions of the first lines of the Sermon on the Mount:

Blessed are the poor in spirit: for theirs is the kingdom of heaven.
Blessed are they that mourn: for they shall be comforted.
Blessed are the meek: for they shall inherit the earth.
   King James Bible (1611)

How blest are those who know their need of God;
the kingdom of Heaven is theirs.
How blest are the sorrowful;
they shall find consolation.
How blest are those of a gentle spirit;
they shall have the earth for their possession.
    New English Bible (1961)

The older version adopts the phrasing *Blessed are...* while the newer begins with *How blest...* with the former plainer in tone than the more rhetorical *how blest*. There is also a difference in the first line: *the poor in spirit* and *those who know their need of God* are seemingly different individuals. The word *meek* has taken on some negative connotations since the first translation, so the more recent translators use the phrase *those of a gentle spirit*. There are other differences in vocabulary and syntax: *they that mourn* versus *the sorrowful; be comforted* and *find consolation*. The King James version is often seen as needing modernizing, while others accord it primacy of place because of its age, beauty of language, and place in Western culture. Like other translations, biblical translations should be judged on their accuracy, beauty, ability to convey the culture of the ancient Middle East, and comprehensibility to readers.

A famous case of culture clashing in translation was the remark made by a Japanese prime minister. When asked for trade concessions by American negotiators, he said, *I'll think about it.* This phrase is used routinely by Japanese among themselves as a soft way of saying something like, *I'm sorry, but I can't help you on that point.* The Americans took the phrase at its face American value and accused the Japanese of duplicity when they did nothing at all.

15.3.2 Testing Translation

How do you test a translation? One time-consuming way is to back-translate the document and see if the two versions agree. A document originally translated from French to English gets translated back into French and the two are compared. Computers can do this now, in a manner of speaking. Here is the first few lines of Mark Twain's *Life on the Mississippi*, translated by a computer program from English to Spanish and back to English again.

Original:

(15.1) The Mississippi is well worth reading about. It is not a commonplace river, but on the contrary is in all ways remarkable. Considering the Missouri its main branch, it is the longest river in the world—four thousand three hundred miles. It seems safe to say it is also the crookedest river in the world, since in one part of its journey it uses up one thousand three hundred miles to cover the same ground that the crow would fly over in six hundred and seventy-five.

English to Spanish to English translation:

(15.2) The Mississippi is well worthy of the reading around. It is not an ordinary river, but in the opposite it is of all the remarkable ways. Considering the Missouri his main ramification, it is the longest river of the world—four thousand three hundred miles. It looks like that safe to say it twisting of the world is also the river more, since in a portion of his trip it uses upon thousand three hundred miles to cover the same earth that the crow would fly above in six hundred and seventy and five.

Another way to test translations is performance testing, in which speakers of two languages use technical manuals, the original and the translation, to perform the procedures described. If it takes them approximately the same amount of time, the translation is efficient, and if they both accomplish the task, it is accurate. Knowledge tests are sometimes given on the two versions to see if people score similarly.

15.3.3 Problems with Translation

Transliteration

Translators must decide how to write proper names and loan words. This becomes a problem if different scripts are used. Sometimes a language will have several conventions for **transliteration,** the representation of the characters or letters of one language with the characters or letters of another. Perhaps the most prominent example has been the systems for transliterating Chinese. The older system transliterated the capital as Peking, while the now preferred system has it as Beijing, which is closer to how northern Chinese actually say it. The following are two examples. The first is the two Chinese characters for Bei Jing/Pei King; the transliteration changes, but the characters remain the same. The second example is *hoteru*, the Japanese loan word for hotel; it consists of three syllabic characters: ho, te, and ru.

Figure 15.1: Bei Jing/Pei King

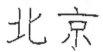

Figure 15.2: Ho te ru = hotel

False Friends

Beginning translators must contend with words that look like they should mean the same thing in another language but do not. These are called **false friends.** Examples are *demander* in French, a verb that means not *demand* but *request. Sensible* in French should be translated *sensitive.* Finally, the Spanish *constipado* means *congested,* as in having a head cold. (See 13.1.)

Imperfect Knowledge

Often the translator has only a limited grasp of the target language. The results may be unclear, or meaningless, but are at times unwittingly funny. The following are a few examples taken from the Internet. They are probably not authentic, but they are cute.

Rome hotel: Fire! It is what can doing, we hope. No fear. Not ourselves. Say quickly to all people coming up down everywhere a prayer. Always is a clerk. He is assured of safety by expert men who are in the bar for telephone for the fighters of the fire to come out.

Polish tourist brochure: As for the tripes serves you at the Hotel Monopol, you will be singing its praise to your children as you lie on your deathbed.

French hotel: A sports jacket may be worn to dinner, but no trouser.

French swimming pool: Swimming is forbidden in absence of the Savior.

Madrid restaurant menu: Tarts of the house.

Madrid hotel: Peoples will left the room at midday of tomorrow in place of not which will be more money for hole day.

15.3.4 Machine Translation

With the invention of the computer, the idea of having a machine that could translate from one language into another took hold. This was one of the central ideas of the field of artificial intelligence. Unfortunately, as example (15.2) shows, computers have a major drawback: they are stupid. It soon became apparent that word-by-word translation was essentially worthless and that anything more sophisticated than that was very complicated. Today, more than 30 years later, sophisticated statistical approaches try to guess the meaning of words from their collocations (i.e., other words with which they typically occur; see 3.1.3), while pioneering approaches are trying to actually analyze the meaning of the text and then render it in the target language.

15.4 LANGUAGE IN EDUCATION

Education takes place largely within the linguistic domain. It makes sense that linguistic issues would be crucial. We have already considered several issues related to the recognition of nonfavored varieties, such as African-American Vernacular English (AAVE) (Chapter 8), or dialects of English (Chapter 5), or gender (Chapter 10). Other issues that have great significance are the proper way of teaching children how to read and write (the "phonics" issue, cf. 11.2.4) and how and when to teach foreign languages (Chapter 13). Incidentally, this is why a course in linguistics is often (and should always be) required of future teachers, in any discipline, but especially language(s).

15.4.1 Teacher Talk as a Register

You will recall the definition of register, from Chapter 6, as a language variety defined by subject matter, setting, and purposes of the interaction. Teachers, especially in the lower grades, address their students with a register close to that of caregivers (aka motherese or CDS; see 12.1.3); this register is marked by clearly enunciated speech, with exaggerated intonation, by simplified sentence structure, and by the obvious power structure of the classroom in which the teacher decides who is given the floor, for how long, etc.

A typical teacher-student exchange involves three phases:

1. **Initiation:** The teacher asks a question to a student.

2. **Response:** The student selected by the teacher answers.

3. **Evaluation:** The teacher evaluates the response (either positively or negatively).

Needless to say, none of these phases needs to be explicitly present; for example, a negative evaluation may be conveyed simply by ignoring the student's response.

15.5 LEXICOGRAPHY

Lexicography, or the science of writing dictionaries, is probably the field of linguistics most people are familiar with, since a dictionary is the result of linguistic research most likely to be owned by an average person.

Some English dictionaries include:

Title	Notes
Oxford English Dict. (see 17.4.4)	Monolingual
Webster's Third New International Dict. (see 17.5.1)	Monolingual
Longman's Dict. of Contemporary English	Monolingual
Collins COBUILD English Language Dictionary	Learners' dictionary
Cambridge Dictionary of American English	Learners' dictionary
Oxford Advanced Learner's Dict. of Current English	Learners' dictionary
Oxford Dictionary of Current Idiomatic English	Dict. of idioms
Longman Dictionary of English Idioms	Dict. of idioms
The BBI Combinatory Dictionary of English	Collocations

15.5.1 Dictionaries

The common conception of dictionaries is that they give the meaning of words. In fact, much more information is available besides meanings. Information found in a typical dictionary entry may include:

- **pronunciation:** Information on the pronunciation of the word is given, often using the IPA (see 2.2.1) (e.g., *COBUILD*), although some dictionaries, notably *Webster's*, use their own systems.

- **grammatical information:** Information about the part of speech is given minimally; often augmented with further detail, such as transitive/intransitive, in the case of verbs, or mass/count, in the case on nouns. Also, idiomatic and phrasal constructions are given (e.g., *get + away = escape*). Irregular morphology and alternative forms are also indicated (e.g., *dive*, past: *dove, dived*).

- **syllabification:** The word is broken into syllables, which is useful to determine where they can be broken in writing at the end of a line (e.g., *in-def-i-nite*). Sometimes a break in morphemes is also provided.

- **etymology:** The history of the word (see 17.6.1).

- **senses:** The various senses of the word are distinguished and listed separately (see 3.1.4 and 15.5.3).

- **meaning(s):** The meanings of the various senses of word are paraphrased. Often a restricted vocabulary is used (see 15.5.3).

- **collocational information:** Information about the collocation(s) (see 3.1.3) of the word is given, often using examples.

- **stylistic information:** Information about the stylistic level or register is provided (see 6.2).

- **usage information:** Information about usage (i.e., what uses are considered acceptable and in what context) is provided, often as "flags" such as **archaic** (= no longer used); **colloquial** (= acceptable only in informal language); *taboo* (= offensive, see 6.4); *slang* (see 6.4); **regionalism** (i.e., a word used only in a given region, e.g., the southern United States).

- **examples and quotations:** Often the best way to show how a word is used is to examine some example of use. In some dictionaries, e.g., the *Oxford English Dictionary (OED),* considerable effort is expended in presenting the first documented use of a word in writing. This establishes uncontrovertibly (attests) the presence of the word in the language at that time.

Usually, a good dictionary will have a preface in which the abbreviations and the kind of information provided are explained in detail.

15.5.2 Types of Dictionaries

Dictionaries can be monolingual or bilingual. A monolingual dictionary contains the information described previously, while a bilingual dictionary provides a translation of the word in another language, as well as some grammatical and collocational information. In language teaching, a significant issue is that the learners' reliance on bilingual dictionaries may retard the onset of fluency, although students seem to prefer them. On the other hand, it is obvious that a bilingual dictionary can be very useful, especially at more advanced levels and in specialized fields.

Concordances and Corpus-Based Dictionaries

Recently, with the advent of computer-based lexicography, which has lowered the cost of acquiring and processing enormous amounts of text, corpus-based dictionaries have begun to appear, such as the *COBUILD* (1995) and the *Longman Dictionary of American English* (2002), based on a corpus of 110 million words. Concordances, which list all occurrences of a word in a corpus in context, are used to establish the meanings and collocations of words. Concordances look like this:

need to	**deal**	with major problems this year
salesman put the	**deal**	through and
has been a great	**deal**	of concern over the news
makes a great	**deal**	of money
learn to	**deal**	with other people

Concordances show the environments that words exist in. Here, we can see that *deal* tends to pair with certain prepositions, like *with* and *of*. This information is potentially useful to both lexicographers as well as to teachers and learners.

Corpus Linguistics

The trend toward using large corpora, often including several millions of words, has become a subfield of the study of language called **corpus linguistics.** For example, the Collins Birmingham University International Language Database has been used as the basis for the *COBUILD* dictionary (1987, 2d ed. 1995) but also for the *Collins COBUILD English Grammar* (1990). Along the same lines, a grammar (Biber et al. 1999) based on a large corpus of texts has been produced, which incorporates register information (see 6.2).

Learners' Dictionaries

An important consideration in the writing of a dictionary is that an advanced learner, or a translator, does not need the same kind of information that a beginning learner does. It makes sense to design dictionaries that cater to the (beginning) learner. *Longman's Dictionary of Contemporary English (LDOCE), COBUILD,* and *Oxford Advanced Learner's Dictionary of Current English (OALDCE)* are all learners' dictionaries that have been designed specifically with learners of English in mind. Learners' dictionaries tend to be much smaller than comprehensive monolingual dictionaries, but they still include 50,000 to 70,000 words. There exist smaller, even pocket-sized dictionaries, but these tend to be bilingual dictionaries, are very limited, and have simplistic one-to-one word correspondences that make them unsuitable for anything beyond the most basic usages. There are even dictionaries for children.

Dictionaries of Idioms and Collocations

Learners need much more than mere word-to-word correspondences or definitions. They need to have information about collocations and multiword units (idioms and phrasal verbs, for example). Dictionaries will try to accommodate such information, but the vastness of the task has led to the creation of dictionaries of idioms (e.g., *The BBI Combinatory Dictionary of English [BBI], Oxford Dictionary of Current Idiomatic English [ODCIE], Longman Dictionary of English Idioms [LDEI]).* A significant issue with idioms is to specify the degree of freedom allowed by the idiom. For example, *spill the beans* can refer to any point in time and can occur with any aspect *(John spilled the beans, will spill the beans, is spilling the beans)*, whereas *bark up the wrong tree* tends to occur in the progressive (cf. *Mary is barking up the wrong tree* versus *Mary barked up the wrong tree*, where the latter expression is questionable).

Dictionaries of Word Relationships

Under this heading we can list a number of types of dictionaries that do not define or translate words but rather provide the user with information about the relationships between a given word and the rest of the words in the lexicon. The most common of these is the dictionary of synonyms and antonyms (cf. 3.1.2), which provides one with words that have a similar or identical meaning to the target words and with words than mean the opposite.

Thesauri are dictionaries that provide users with words that are related (often synonyms, but not necessarily) to the target word. They may be alphabetical or arranged according to conceptual categories, as is the case with *Roget's Thesaurus*, probably the most famous of the kind (first published in 1852). There exist thesauri for learners, for example, the *Longman Lexicon of Contemporary English* (McArthur 1981), and the *Word Routes* series from Cambridge University Press, which presents the grammatical information on the words in the target language (Italian, French, and Spanish) rather than in English.

Specialized Dictionaries

There exist specialized dictionaries of slang, jargon, and other specialist domains, including technical dictionaries in such diverse fields as law, chemistry, linguistics, and wines.

There are even rhyming dictionaries for poets; inverse dictionaries, in which the words are spelled backwards (useful for research in linguistics); spelling dictionaries, in which words are spelled in the regular fashion but also spelled phonetically (e.g., *knight* would be found under *k* but also under *n* and flagged as wrong in that case; these are useful for people with learning disabilities such as dyslexia); dictionaries of common spelling errors; dictionaries of false friends (cf. 15.3.3); dictionaries of quotations.

15.5.3 Issues in Lexicography

The writers of dictionaries face many problems. Some are practical, as dictionaries are very expensive to produce and publishers impose restrictions on the size of the book. For example, the publisher of *Webster's Third* imposed a one-volume limit, which forced the authors to cut some 50,000 words. Other problems are more interesting theoretically.

How to Distinguish the Senses of a Word

In 15.5.1 we mentioned that one of the bits of information provided by dictionaries is the discrimination among the various senses of a word. However, this is far from trivial. Let us consider an example (from *Webster's Third*): the noun *dog* has 13 (!) principal meanings (some with several submeanings) including: the basic animal that barks and wags its tail; a "mean worthless fellow"; a tool for fastening things; various animals (e.g., *prairie dog*); "ostentatious display"; fur; "something inferior of its kind"; a hot dog; an ugly woman (slang); a prostitute (slang); as well as many others. How does one decide that a "mean worthless fellow" is a different sense from "something inferior of its kind"? The answer is that there are no hard and fast rules. The questions can be phrased more technically as when are two words homonyms rather than different senses of the same word and when is a sense of a word a distinct one?

A rule of thumb is that if the speakers do not perceive the words as being related etymologically, then they are separate words (homonyms):

this is the case with (river) *bank* and *bank* (financial institution). The other question is trickier: take *eat.* Is eating soup a different meaning than eating steak?

Restricted Vocabulary

Another problem is called the circularity of the definitions. This can be exemplified by an old lexicographer quip: *sea: where the land ends; land: where the sea ends.* In other words, in order to understand the definitions of the dictionary, often users need to be familiar with words that are as complex (or more) as the words they are checking. In order to address this problem, lexicographers use restricted vocabularies to write the definitions. A **restricted vocabulary** (or defining vocabulary) is a (small) set of words out of which all the definitions have to be written. The most famous of restricted vocabularies is **basic English,** invented in 1930 by C. K. Ogden, which consists of 850 words and had some success outside of lexicography. Some dictionaries use their own restricted vocabularies: for example, *LDOCE* uses a 2,000-word one, listed in the dictionary.

Ideology

A significant issue is the fact that people tend to give dictionaries a degree of confidence that is perhaps excessive. Dictionaries are taken as the ultimate authority on language. *It's in the dictionary* is the kind of argument that is seen as decisive in discussions about the propriety of a word. However, dictionaries are written by people who have their biases and prejudices. People may try to keep their biases at bay, but since the prejudices are often unconscious, they end up surfacing anyway.

Dr. Johnson (cf. 17.4.4), and to a lesser degree Noah Webster (cf. 17.5.1), were quite personal in their definitions, and today's dictionaries are much more objective. However, gender biases are still quite obvious. To use an example, a study of several dictionaries found differences in definitions and uses of examples that clearly showed the sexist biases of the authors. Other areas in which ideological biases show themselves are, for example, which variety gets labeled as vulgar or colloquial or which words are included and which are left out.

15.6 SPEECH PATHOLOGY

Another area of obvious importance in the application of linguistics is in the diagnosis and therapy of the pathologies of language. Speech pathologists and audiologists undergo a serious training in linguistics, mostly in phonetics and phonology, as well as in the specifics of therapy, diagnosis, rehabilitation, and management of the pathologies of language (see 12.3).

Educational Implications
This chapter has addressed the uses applied linguistics has in "the real world," including the world of the classroom.

15.7 EXERCISES

15.7.1 Words to Know

language crimes	forensic linguistics	voiceprints
translation	interpreting	initiation
response	evaluation	lexicography
colloquial	regionalism	thesaurus
restricted vocabulary	basic English	false friend
legal language	handwriting	stylometry
transliteration	corpus linguistics	

15.7.2 Review

1. List all the reasons why patients may have a hard time understanding doctors.

2. What are the reasons lawyers and judges use legal language?

3. What are voiceprints, and how are they used in legal cases?

4. Why is awareness of linguistic issues crucial in the formation of a teacher? List specific issues in which knowledge of linguistic facts is helpful.

5. Why is machine translation difficult to achieve?

15.7.3 Research Projects

1. Task: Here are three examples of translations of the first lines of *The Iliad*. Compare them. Even though you probably don't know ancient Greek, you should be able to notice the differences in the versions and have an opinion on which you would like to continue reading.

Rage—Goddess, sing the rage of Peleus' son Achilles,
murderous, doomed, that cost the Achaeans countless losses,
hurling down to the House of Death so many sturdy souls. . .
    (Robert Fagles)

Sing, goddess, the anger of Peleus' son Achilleus and its devastation,
which put pairs thousandfold upon the Achaians,
hurled in their multitudes to the house of Hades strong souls of heroes...
    (Richard Lattimore)

Sing for me, Muse, the mania of Achilles
that cast a thousand sorrows on the Greeks
and threw so many huge souls into hell...
    (Robert Lowell)

2. Recall the discussion of language in the courtroom (see 15.1). Why do
   you think that people may agree that a taillight was broken even if there
   was none in the film? [Hint: reread the section on presupposition.]

3. Pick three dictionaries and compare the entry for a word of your
   choice. What are the differences?

4. If you have access to the second and third editions of *Webster's*, pick
   a few words and compare their treatment. Can you understand why
   there was so much uproar about the third edition?

5. According to a survey of translators worldwide, here are the ten English words most difficult to translate. Consult several dictionaries for
   each word and write a good definition. Why do you think the words
   are considered so difficult?

      1. plenipotentiary
      2. gobbledegook
      3. serendipity
      4. poppycock
      5. googly
      6. Spam
      7. whimsy
      8. bumf
      9. chuffed
      10. kitsch

15.8 FURTHER READINGS

On the subject of language in the professions, the basic text is Oaks's (1998) anthology of essays, which covers all the topics dealt within this chapter and then some. Older but also interesting texts are Bjarkman and Raskin, *The Real-World Linguist* (1986) and Di Pietro, *Linguistics and the Professions* (1982).

The classic on the language of the law is Mellinkoff (1963). Recent surveys on legal language can found in Gibbons (1999, 2003); Eades (2003); and the works of Shuy (1993, 1998, 2001, 2002). The bomb threat case in Labov's piece is in Oaks (1998). The morphological complexity case is in Gibbons (1999). On the U.S. Supreme Court decisions, see Solan (1993). On the McDonald's case, see Lentine and Shuy in Oaks (1998). On the Unabomber case, Crain (1998) is an entertaining article in *Lingua Franca*. On Foster's unmasking of Klein, see *The Economist* (Feb. 24, 1996), and Foster's own (2000) account.

For a recent survey of research on medical language, see Ong et al. (1995) and Hydén and Mishler (1999). On patient-doctor interaction see Bonvillain (1993, 375–80); Chaika (1994, 388–94); and the papers in Oaks (1998, Chapter 2). The study of social factors in consultations is in Fisher (1982, 1983); the latter is anthologized in Oaks (1998).

On translation, a classic is Steiner (1975). Examples of mistranslation are from *http://www.fuzzydog.com/main.htm.* Sources for machine translation on the Web can be found at *babelfish.altavista.com* or at *shortbus.net.* On urban myths about marketing, see Wilton (2004).

On teacher talk, Heath (1978) is anthologized in Oaks (1998). The other papers in Oaks (1998, Chapter 5) are all interesting selections that address many of the issues on language and education discussed in the text.

On lexicography, see Svensén (1987), English translation (1993). The concordance example comes from Biber, Conrad, and Reppen (1998), which is a good introduction to corpus linguistics. On dictionaries, see Hartmann (1983). On dictionaries in the United States and Britain; Béjoint (1994, Chapter 2) has a useful survey. The *barking* example is from McCarthy (1990, 135). McCarthy (1990, Chapter 10) has a useful comparison of different dictionaries with several examples. Carter (1987, Chapter 6) discusses central issues of lexicography as they relate to teaching. The preference of students for bilingual dictionaries is reported in Hartmann (1983). On basic English, see Crystal (1997).

On the *BBI*, see Benson, Benson, and Ilson (1986, Chapter 6); on *COBUILD*, see Sinclair (1987). Cowie (1999) is a good history of learner dictionaries. The study of sexism in dictionaries is Nilsen (1977). Further readings on dictionaries, especially *OED*, will be found in Chapter 17.

Chapter 16

The Nature of Language

16.1 FEATURES OF LANGUAGE

All languages of the world, or Language (with a capital "L" to indicate that it is an abstraction), share some design features. We are not talking about universal grammar's parameters (see 2.5.2) or language universals, although there is a certain degree of overlap. What we mean here is the fact that languages share some general organizational mechanisms that distinguish them from other forms of communication, such as the systems of communication developed by animals and insects (**zoosemiotics**). In what follows, we will review some of the main design features of language. As you will notice, you will be already familiar with most of them from previous chapters.

16.1.1 The Double Articulation of Language

In 2.4.1, we considered the very important fact that languages use a relatively small inventory of sounds to build a larger but still finite and reasonably contained number of morphemes, which in turn are used to build a potentially infinite number of sentences. This has been nicely summed up as the fact that language makes infinite use of finite elements. The double articulation of language is also called **duality.**

16.1.2 Productivity

Language can be used to produce novel sentences, sentences that have never been uttered before. For example, the sentence *Dr. Strangelove, your strawberry octopus salad is ready* has never been uttered before, and with a modicum of luck, never will; however, you did not have a problem understanding it. This is the biggest problem of all approaches to language based on corpora (see 15.5.2): in principle it is always possible to come up with a new sentence that is *not* in the corpus. Note the closeness of **productivity** to the concept of generation in transformational-generative grammar (see 2.4.2).

16.1.3 Arbitrariness

In 3.1, we introduced the principle of the arbitrariness of the sign. This boils down to the idea that there is no necessary connection between the meaning "dog" and the English word *dog*, as proven by the existence of the word *chien* in French, which expresses roughly the same meaning. Arbitrary signs are opposed to **iconic signs,** which instead have some degree of connection between the sign itself and what it represents. For example, a picture of Fido looks like Fido insofar as it has a physical resemblance to the pooch.

Language is not entirely arbitrary, as proven by **onomatopoeias** (i.e., words that sound like what they mean), such as *crash, bang, hiss, swing, plop, drip, clap,* etc. However, by and large languages are arbitrary.

16.1.4 Interchangeability

This feature refers to the fact that an individual person can both be a speaker and a hearer. While **interchangeability** may strike you as obvious, it is not always the case with animal communication systems, as we will see below.

16.1.5 Displacement

Languages can be used to talk about things that are not here and now, or to be a bit more precise, things that are not present at the time and place of the utterance. This includes the possibility of talking about past and future events but also about possible and even impossible events and/or things (e.g., a square circle). Finally, the **displacement** feature of language makes it possible to have the metalinguistic function of language. Somewhat dramatically, another way that the displacement function of language has been defined is the capacity to lie.

16.1.6 Discreteness

Language uses **discrete,** all or nothing differences between units: thus a [p] is not a [b] and there is no such thing as an *almost* [b] sound. Suppose you produce a sound acoustically exactly between [p] and [b]. The given sound will be heard as either [p] or as [b]. On the same line: a [pit] is not a [bit] slightly changed. Iconic signs, on the other hand, are continuous. For example, the redness of the skin that indicates one is hot goes through a continuum, a gradient of reds, ranging from a very minor reddening to purple. Increased redness means increased heat.

16.1.7 Specialization

Specialization is the property of human language to require only a relatively small part of the behavior of the speaker and to be context-independent: we can talk about yesterday's television program while we are driving a car, for example.

16.1.8 Cultural Transmission

By **cultural transmission,** we mean the fact that not all of the aspects of language are innate (see Chapter 12): for example, a child reared in China will learn Chinese; the same child reared in France would have learned French.

16.2 THE BIRDS AND THE BEES

Now that we have reviewed some of the features that characterize language, we can put them to work in distinguishing between animal communication and human language.

The conclusion we will arrive to is fairly clear: despite the unquestionable feats of communication of animals and insects, there seems to be a uniqueness to human language, which is probably the result of our genetic endowment.

16.2.1 The Bees' Dance

As is well known, bees can signal to other bees the location of good sources of food. For example, by moving along a figure-eight pattern, the bee indicates the direction of flight, in relation to the position of the sun;

the intensity of the dance indicates the quantity of food (more food is indicated by more intense movements). Distance is indicated by choosing different types of dance:

round	less than 5 meters
figure eight	up to 20 meters
tail wagging	beyond 20 meters

While this is impressive, the bees can be fooled very easily, for example, by putting the food source on a tall pole. There is no bee-language word for "up there," apparently. Furthermore, the bee that is doing the dance is completely involved in it (lack of specialization). The bee's "language" is completely genetically determined, is not discrete (since the intensity of the dance parallels the amount of food), is not arbitrary (since the angle of the dance parallels the angle of the flight path), and does not allow bees to talk about the food that was in a given place yesterday.

16.2.2 Birds' Vocalizations

Birds' vocalizations (i.e., sounds produced with the phonatory organs) are divided into calls and songs. Calls are short and have very specific uses (warning of predators, flocking, flight regulation, aggression, and others). Songs are longer and more elaborate. They usually occur only in the mating season. Birds' songs are made of smaller units that can be recombined, but there is no evidence that any meaning is attributed to these. Birds' songs are to some extent transmitted culturally (i.e., learned). However, often male birds are the only ones to sing, while female birds don't. Therefore, birds' songs lack the feature of interchangeability.

16.2.3 Apes

Apes are evolutionarily our closest relatives in the animal kingdom. Chimps, gibbons, and orangutans have calls, up to 16 different kinds. It appears that there may be some cultural transmission. Like birds, apes' calls lack double articulation and displacement (although there are examples of uses of calls when there are no predators, for example, which could be construed as lying).

However, what has by far attracted more attention have been attempts by humans to teach sign language (see 16.4) and other forms of symbolic communication to apes. After attempts at teaching chimps to speak (which is impossible; their vocal tract is too different from humans'), researchers tried to teach them sign language. Washoe was a female chimpanzee who was taught about 130 signs, which she started combining into sentences. Other experiments included the amusingly named Nim Chimpsky; Sarah, who was taught a form of language that involved the manipulation of little plastic figures on a magnetic board; and the famous Koko, a gorilla who was said to have made creative uses of her language (e.g., *potato apple fruit* for *pineapple*).

Critics of the attempts to teach apes sign languages argue that it all boils down to subtle cues to the animals and self-delusion on the part of the experimenters. However, even in the most favorable interpretation of the results, the language level of the apes never went beyond what a two-year-old human baby can do.

16.3 LANGUAGE AND CULTURE

16.3.1 Language and Thought

Can you think without language? The answer to this question, and a good many others in linguistics, is "It depends." Psychologists make a distinction between rational or propositional thought and emotions, which are also, of course, a kind of mental operation. You feel a response to a work of art or a piece of music, and this is clearly a kind of thought without language. But perhaps all kinds of rational thought are not the same either. Psychologists also talk about two kinds of knowledge, declarative knowledge and procedural knowledge. Knowledge of the rules of driving is declarative knowledge, while the actual process of driving, a highly automatic process in experienced drivers, is procedural knowledge. That is, you are not likely to be able to explain just exactly when to push in the clutch or when you start braking.

> Think of your bedroom or the place where you sleep. Is there a window? Think about it.
>
> Now, did you use language at all?

Another example that is often given is the thinking that goes on when you visualize the directions to some place you go often. You are not likely to be putting that visualization into words as you construct it. So, in that sense, there can be thinking without language.

If thinking and language can be separated, is one prior to the other? Which happens first, thought or language? Well, we all know people who seem to speak without thinking, but that's another matter. For many scholars in the middle of the 20th century, it was taken as a given that language determines the way we speak. The **Sapir-Whorf hypothesis,** named for anthropologists Edward Sapir and Benjamin Lee Whorf, had two parts. The first was linguistic determinism, the idea that a people's language dictated the way they spoke. The second was linguistic relativity, the idea that translating ideas from one language to another was extremely difficult and perhaps impossible.

Language helps us make sense of the world. Few would argue that. Those who believed the Sapir-Whorf hypothesis went further and said that members of a culture can see the world in no way other than their language allows. We probably have all heard that the Inuit (Eskimo) (see 17.6.6) language has dozens of words for snow. This is actually not true; there may be a dozen at most. English has almost as many: *powder, sleet, slush,* and *blizzard* come easily to mind. Franz Boas, an American anthropologist, observed that languages like English use free roots (see 2.3.2) to talk about, for example, water *(puddle, rainfall, shower)* where other languages use derivational morphemes (see 2.3.4). That is, part of the word would indicate water (water that stands, water that falls). Boas said that Inuit behaved like English in this regard. *Aput* was snow on the ground, and *gana* was falling snow. Whorf took the work of Boas and its extension by Sapir and promulgated the strong version of what came to be known as the Sapir-Whorf hypothesis or the linguistic relativity hypothesis: language determines thought. People think a certain way, he said, and can think only that way because of their language. As Whorf's claims have been more closely investigated, it seems that the strong version of the theory cannot stand.

If the linguistic relativity hypothesis were correct, color categories would be arbitrary. Different languages would "see" color differently. Much has been made of the fact that some cultures have only two color words: black and white. Others have three: black, white, and red. English has 11 basic color words. When we use the expression **basic color term,** we are not talking about hyphenated words like yellow-green or blue-green, or even turquoise. We are interested in one-word terms that most speakers of the language know (not *magenta, chartreuse,* or *periwinkle*) and words that apply to a wide class of items (not *blond,* for example, which can be used only for hair color).

The anthropologists Berlin and Kay (1969) investigated the claim of linguistic relativity in colors. They studied almost 100 languages and found that there was great agreement on color terms. They worked with speakers of 20 languages in an experiment. People were asked for the color terms in their languages and then shown color chips much like those you would look at to choose a paint color for your house. People within languages agreed on the "best" examples of colors. For example, English speakers, if asked to select the "best" red among many, would agree on a darker red. Interestingly enough, speakers of the other 19 languages also agreed on that red. It seems that colors have a universality. Follow-up experiments have confirmed this view. In addition to casting doubt on linguistic relativity, Berlin and Kay's work was important for work on the theory of prototypes (see 18.2.3).

Where do we stand on linguistic relativity, then? Most people seem to accept what is called the weak version of the Sapir-Whorf hypothesis: language and culture influence each other. This is really not very satisfactory in terms of a theory, but the idea seems to pervade most people's beliefs. Most people agree that there is an interaction between language and culture, that language influences, but does not determine, culture. Culture is also reflected in the language. In Japan, the terms *uchi* (inside) and *soto* (outside) are very important for understanding Japanese culture. Everyone knows what is inside and what is outside to them. They speak of their *haha* (my/our mother) but of someone else's *o-ka-san* (someone else's mother). The word for mother changes depending on whose mother it is, and that change has to do with the concept of inside/ outside, which is culturally determined.

The Sapir-Whorf hypothesis was connected to a view of culture as knowledge. Culture, in this view, is all that is learned and transmitted from generation to generation. It is the knowledge of how to be Japanese or Brazilian. That culture is concerned with knowledge and is not "natural" is clear from the example of children raised by others. Any child will learn the culture she or he grows up in. An American child taken to Mexico at a young age and raised in the culture will be Mexican. That child will also, assuming his or her playmates are Spanish-speaking Mexicans, likely grow up speaking Spanish. Genes have nothing to do with language or culture. However, there are, some believe, certain natural kinds or categories. People are likely to know what a living thing is without being able to describe what makes it living (children are able to do this long before they take any science courses). We all know what a dog is, though we might be hard pressed to give an exact, watertight definition. In this sense, some argue that there is something like a culture competence.

16.3.2 Critical Discourse Analysis

Culture and language interact also in other ways. A very significant issue is the interplay of language and power. We know that languages are socially stratified (see 6.1.1), but there are other ways in which socioeconomic disparities are manifested in language.

The subtler way in which this happens is by the creation of an **ideology,** i.e., a system of beliefs that reinforce one another and are usually put forward by a group (social class) in power. Consider, for example, a racist ideology, such as the Nazi belief in the supremacy of the "Aryan race." By referring to Jews as *vermin,* the Nazi racist discourse achieves the effect of dehumanizing the victims of the Holocaust, i.e., it challenges the fact that the people who were dying in the concentration camps were human beings, just like their killers. This removal of the humanity of the victims makes it easier for the people carrying out the killings to do so (since, for example, one would not empathize with a cockroach).

The most perverse effect of ideology is arguably the naturalization of power imbalance: what is essentially a partial and skewed point of view becomes so hidden in the ideology of the discourse/culture as to become common sense. For example, research in the racist discourse against immigrants in the British and Dutch press showed that the most frequent subjects that were treated in the press matched the common stereotypes of racist discourse: immigration is an invasion; immigrants are freeloaders, criminals, and violent.

Ideology manifests itself pervasively. For example, see 15.5.3 about the ideological biases of dictionaries or see 3.1.3 for differences in connotations in lexical choice. A further example may be found in the use of the passive voice (see 19.2.2). Consider the following headlines about riots in Zimbabwe:

(16.1) RIOTING BLACKS SHOT DEAD BY POLICE AS ANC
        LEADERS MEET

(16.2) POLICE SHOOT 11 DEAD IN SALISBURY RIOT

In (16.1), the use of the passive puts the rioting blacks in evidence and deemphasizes the role of the police. In (16.2), the opposite is true.

Because teachers, teaching materials, and the very institutions in which they teach are steeped in the ideologically biased culture in which they operate, education perpetuates ideology. Therefore, critical discourse analysis has a political commitment (for which it has been criticized) to making students and educators aware of their ideological biases.

16.4 SIGN LANGUAGE

16.4.1 Introduction

Sign language is a visual and gestural form of communication with features considered unique to natural languages. The symbols of sign languages appear as signs composed of handshapes, locations, movements, and palm orientations. Despite much linguistic research, several misconceptions exist about sign languages. What follows are a few basic myths about sign language systems.

- Myth 1: Because sign is a gestural form of communication, it is merely a series of hand gestures or pantomime.

- Myth 2: Sign language is universal.

- Myth 3: Symbols used within systems of sign language are just visual representations of the words of a spoken language.

- Myth 4: Sign is a "deviant" form of language or a slang.

16.4.2 Sign vs. Gesture

It is necessary to distinguish between sign languages and other forms of gesture. Language and gesture are very different forms of communication. Sign languages are highly developed, rule-governed systems of language. Gesture, on the other hand, is used somewhat randomly and symbols are few, whereas sign languages are used systematically and feature several thousand symbols. Nearly all users of language are capable of gesturing, though certainly not all are able to sign.

16.4.3 Universality of Sign Language

Sign languages come into existence and evolve through the communities who use them. As a result, a particular sign language cannot necessarily be understood universally. Like spoken languages, political borders may not specify the locations where a given sign language is used. A country may have one sign language or several, depending on the history of its deaf communities. The sign language used primarily in North America is American Sign Language (ASL), though many others exist including British and Chinese, to name just a few.

16.4.4 Arbitrariness of the Sign

As in other linguistic systems, the signs of sign language are arbitrary. In other words, though sign languages are similar to other systems of language in that they may include **iconic** symbols that are representative of real-world objects, people, and events, they feature, for the most part, arbitrarily assigned symbols. Consider, for example, **onomatopoeic** words in English. These are words that are mimetic of the sounds they represent such as *splash, fizz, pow,* and *screech.* They are referred to as iconic because they are not symbols that have been arbitrarily assigned. To the untrained eye, sign language may appear to be made up of iconic symbols. This is not to say that sign language is not at all iconic. For example, the sign for banana is conveyed by an action that resembles the peeling of a banana. Like spoken language, however, the majority of signs in modern sign languages such as ASL are arbitrary.

16.4.5 Sign as a System of Language

A common misconception about **sign languages** is that they are deviant forms of language or that they are slang. Some believe that sign languages are not natural forms of language and that they do not contain the mechanics fundamental to all languages, such as systems of phonology, morphology, syntax, semantics, and pragmatics. As we will see, this view is mistaken. Sign languages are languages.

Phonology

In spoken languages, sounds or phonemes are combined in systematic patterns. Although sign languages do not generally identify phonemes as units of sound, there is an analogous organization of elements. In sign languages every sign is defined by the following parameters: handshape, location, movement, and palm orientation. A change in any one of these, much like a change in the phonemes of a word, alters the meaning of the sign. For example, the signs FATHER and MOTHER are identical in handshape, movement, and palm orientation but differ in location.

Just as native speakers of a language intuitively know that certain combinations of sounds are not possible, signers are able to judge the acceptability of certain composites without a conscious knowledge of the rules that inform them. An example of this in ASL is called *symmetry condition.* The rule states that in a two-handed sign where both hands are moving, both hands will have the same handshape and movement.

Morphology

Sign languages also have morphology. Agreement verbs in ASL use beginning location and ending location of a sign to determine subject and object. If the sign GIVE begins close to the signer and ends toward the person she or he is talking to, then the meaning is *I give it to you.* Another word-level change is the use of prefixes, suffixes, or infixes. ASL features a suffix referred to as the agent marker. *Work* + AGENT means *worker,* whereas *sing* + AGENT means *singer.*

Syntax

Spoken languages such as English rely in part on word order to convey information about the arguments of the sentence. Subjects and objects are made clear in English sentences because of word order. ASL, in contrast, is considered to have a relatively free word order (though this is somewhat controversial). In simple sentences with plain verbs, there are three possible structures. Thus, the sentence *The cat is sleeping* could be signed three ways:

- CAT SLEEP (**Subject-Verb**)
- SLEEP IT (**Verb-Pronoun**)
- CAT SLEEP IT (**Subject-Verb-Pronoun**)

Word order and vocal intonation are also necessary for hearers of English to differentiate among various kinds of sentences, questions, and statements. Sign languages tend to rely on **nonmanual signals** such as facial expression and posture to show the difference between various types of utterances.

Semantics

Sign languages are typically independent of the spoken languages of the same region though lexical borrowing does take place. Lexical borrowing from spoken languages occurs generally by encoding the writing system of the spoken language into a manual form. For ASL, the borrowing of words from English is accomplished through the manual alphabet. The manual alphabet consists of 26 one-handed signs corresponding to the

26 letters of the English alphabet. **Fingerspelling,** the spelling of words manually, is chiefly reserved for the spelling of proper nouns that have not developed conventional signs. ASL signs sometimes have no single-word cognate in English. Spelling out a word manually on the forehead means roughly *to obsess about,* hence spelling out F-O-O-D on the forehead would mean "to obsess about food" or "to have food on the brain." ASL provides additional vocabulary, when the occasion warrants, to account for differences in meaning. For example, there are two lexical items for *to tease.* They reflect the semantic differences of *to harass, to mock,* and *to joke with.* These semantic differences reveal how language is fused with culture; so much so that words that are clearly borrowed do not necessarily maintain their full original range of meaning. This situation is not unlike spoken languages. Borrowed items are adapted to suit the dynamics of the new tongue.

16.4.6 Language Variation

Language variation occurs from one region to another, among various social classes, between genders, and among various age groups. There exist, for example, *regional accents* in sign language. This is to say that there are signs that are unique to specific regions. The ASL signs EARLY, PICNIC, BIRTHDAY, and SOON are among the signs that vary greatly from region to region. Another example of regional differences can be seen in RABBIT, LEMON, and PEACH. These signs tend to be made on the face in the eastern and midwestern areas of the country but are made on the hands in some regions of the South. As in spoken language, Italian Sign Language seems to have significant variation due, most likely, to geographic isolation. The deaf communities in various Italian cities have only recently begun to interact with communities in other cities. Variation in sign languages can also be the result of differences in social class and ethnicity. This type of variation can be illustrated by the fact that African-American signers use unique signs for SCHOOL and BUS, differences that may have been the result of segregated education.

16.4.7 Language Acquisition

The acquisition of sign language is similar to the acquisition of spoken language. Deaf parents and their children interact similarly to hearing parents and their children. Deaf children learn quickly that certain movements are meaningful and learn sign language through interaction with their caregivers. Hearing children of deaf parents, on the other hand, usually grow up bilingual using the sign language of their parents and the spoken language of the larger community. For deaf children born to hearing parents, language acquisition takes a different course. If these children acquire a natural sign language, it is likely that they have learned it from other deaf people. Method of education usually determines the primary language of deaf children. In many countries debates are still going on as to the best approach to educate deaf students.

16.4.8 Conclusion

As we have seen, sign languages are visual and gestural forms of communication composed of handshapes, locations, movements, and palm orientations. Sign languages are not merely forms of pantomime, nor are they simple gestures that are meant to represent words or objects visually. Sign languages are rule-governed, structured languages complete with the fundamentals unique to natural languages, such as systems of phonology, morphology, syntax, semantics, and pragmatics. Sign languages vary as significantly as spoken languages. Variations may be regional, social, gender based, or age based. Thus, there is certainly no universally understood sign language system. Finally, the sign language acquisition process is similar to that of the acquisition of spoken languages.

Educational Implications
This chapter provided a slightly more theoretical look at what language is. Teachers will be able to use the information on sign language to better understand issues in deaf education.

16.5 EXERCISES

16.5.1 Words to Know

zoosemiotics	iconic	onomatopoeia
duality	productivity	interchangeability
displacement	specialization	discreteness
bird calls	bird songs	Sapir-Whorf hypothesis
basic color term	ideology	cultural transmission
sign	gesture	American Sign Language
agent marker	fingerspelling	nonmanual sign

16.5.2 Review

1. What is the difference between the strong and the weak versions of the Sapir-Whorf hypothesis?

2. What are basic color terms, and why are they significant in relation to the linguistic relativity issue?

3. List at least three reasons why animal communication differs from human language.

4. What is the displacement feature of language? What does it show about human languages?

5. Is stuttering a physical problem? What are its origins?

16.5.3 Research Projects

1. Read George Orwell's *1984* and his celebrated essay *Politics and the English Language,* which has been widely anthologized. Is Orwell a proponent of the strong version of the Sapir-Whorf hypothesis?

2. Read some essays from Whorf (1956). Are you convinced that the Hopi Indians have a different worldview than you do?

3. Read Trew's analysis of the press coverage of the riots in Salisbury (in Fowler et al. 1979), perhaps using Toolan's (1988, Chapter 7) summary. Compare the treatment of the same event in different newspapers (preferably from different political, social, or even national perspectives). What differences can you see?

4. Check out a movie (or videotape) featuring ASL (e.g., *Children of a Lesser God*). Can you identify any of the ASL features we list in this chapter?

5. (Advanced) What are the ideological biases of the authors of this book? Send your answers in a sealed envelope to the authors in care of our publisher.

16.6 FURTHER READINGS

Brown and Eisterhold (2004) offer an overview of language and culture. The features of language come from Hockett's (1958) *A Course in Modern Linguistics*. In the original, there are seven features. We have added, from further research, discreteness. Discussions used in the text, besides Hockett's, are from Wardhaugh (2002) and Crystal (1997). On animal communication there are numerous sources. Most introductory textbooks of linguistics will have a chapter on animal communication. Sebeok (1968) is a mastodontic classic on the subject. Whorf's work has been collected in a book (1956) that is not for beginners. There is an enormous literature on the Sapir-Whorf hypothesis. Berlin and Kay (1969) is likewise fairly technical. A serious but rewarding discussion of the research on basic color terms can be found in Ungerer and Schmid (1996). The myth of the hundreds of Inuit's words for snow is debunked in the hilarious Pullum (1991).

On critical discourse analysis, Wodak (1995) is a short, sophisticated introduction, with good references. Toolan (1988, Chapter 7) has a useful discussion. Van Dijk (1991) reports on the anti-immigrant racist discourse. Among the classics are Fairclough (1989), Mey (1985), and Fowler et al. (1979), from which the example about the riots has been borrowed (from Trew's 1979 work).

Good places to start reading about the deaf are Padden and Humphries (1988) and Lucas (2001).

Chapter 17

Historical Linguistics

You will recall (from 1.2.2) the distinction between the synchronic and the diachronic (or historical) study of language. In this book, we have mainly been concerned with the synchronic view of language. This chapter, on the contrary, is concerned with the history of languages and in particular of the English language.

A fundamental issue, which is often ignored or forgotten, is that languages are constantly changing, like living creatures. The only languages that do not change are the dead ones (for example, ancient Greek). Consider, for example, neologisms and archaisms (see 1.2.2): new words come into use constantly as new concepts arise and old ones disappear, due to changes in the lives of the speakers. For example, do you know what a *pair of snuffers* are? Probably not, because they are a tool used to snuff a candle (i.e., to cut out the charred part of the wick). The reason why you probably were unaware of the existence of this word is simply that very few people who are likely to read this book use candles for lighting since the mass adoption of electric light. Similarly, what use would Queen Victoria have had for a *modem*? Needless to say, many words merely change; witness the evolution of the word *car,* which entered English from the Old French verb *carier* "to carry" in the period between A.D. 1150 and 1500, with the meaning of *baggage* or *transport* (i.e., something that was carried). From there the meaning was extended to the tool used for transport, i.e., a carriage, in the sense of horse-drawn carriage or buggy. With the invention of the steam engine and then of the internal combustion engine, carriages begun to be self-propelled, which led to the term *horseless carriage;* once horseless carriages became the norm, the *horseless* part was dropped (and in some cases replaced by *automobile carriage,* i.e., a carriage that goes by itself) and the term was eventually shortened to *car.* Consider how little a Ferrari Testa Rossa and a horse-drawn carriage have in common, and you will realize how far the meaning has shifted.

17.1 THE HISTORY OF ENGLISH

The following section will focus on the history and development of the English language. English is a **Germanic** language, i.e., it descends from the continuous evolution of some variety of a language (Germanic) spoken in continental Europe between 1000 B.C. and around A.D. 100 around the Elbe region (see Figure 17.1).

Figure 17.1: The Area Inhabited by the Anglo-Saxons

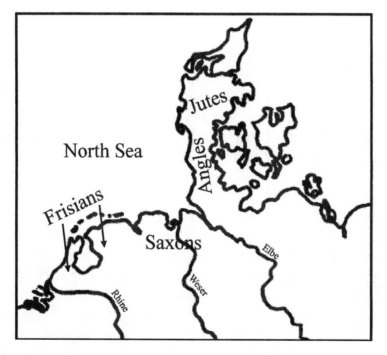

We have no written records of Germanic, but we have a translation of the Gospel written by a missionary (Ulfilas, who lived 311–383 A.D.), which attests **Gothic,** aka East Germanic, one of the languages into which Germanic evolved. There are two other branches of Germanic: one is North Germanic, which includes Icelandic and Norwegian (West), and Danish and Swedish (East). There are a few runic (i.e., written in **runes,** the alphabet in which some Germanic languages were written)

inscriptions in Scandinavia that predate Ulfilas's translation, but otherwise his is the earliest document of a Germanic language. The third branch of Germanic is West Germanic, and it is divided in two branches: High and Low German. High German is the language into which Luther translated the Bible, which eventually became modern German. Low German evolved into Plattdeutsch (a dialect of German spoken on the North Sea); Dutch, spoken in the Netherlands; Flemish (spoken in northern Belgium); Frisian (spoken in the islands off the coast of northwestern Germany; see Figure 17.1); and English. Together all these languages are said to form the Germanic family (see Fig. 17.2 plus 17.6.1 and 17.6.2).

Figure 17.2: The Germanic Language Family

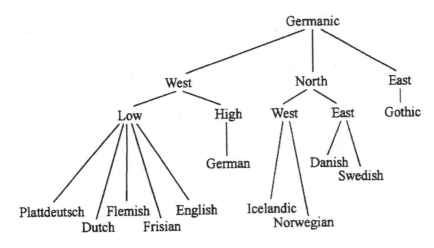

The English that we speak today is of course the result of a long history, which we will trace. Despite the strong identification between the British islands and English, the history of the language begins in Germany and Denmark. That is where the Jutes, the Angles, and the Saxons lived.

17.2 OLD ENGLISH (OE): AD 450 TO 1100

The Jutes, Angles, and Saxons began invading England around the middle of the 4th century. England was inhabited at the time by Celtic people, the descendents of which are the Welsh and the Bretons in France. The Celts had resisted the Roman invasion and conquest (first by Julius Caesar, in 55 BC, but not permanently until a century later) but Britain had been Romanized, but these events had little effect on the language (unlike what happened in France or Spain, in which Latin superseded the languages spoken by the conquered people). Around the 4th century the

Roman legions were withdrawn, leaving the island open to the invasion of the Germanic bands (Angles, Saxons, and Jutes), whose language became Old English.

17.2.1 OE Phonology

The consonants of Old English (OE) were roughly the same as present-day English, with the addition of [x] (a velar fricative; cf. the German sound at the end of the word *Bach*) and [ɣ] (the voiced counterpart of [x]). The vowels were radically different, because they had still their "continental" value, as the Great Vowel Shift (see 17.4.2) had not yet taken place.

The Vowel System of OE

	Front	Central	Back
High	[i] [I]		[u:] [u]
Mid	[e] [ɛ]		[o] [ɔ]
Low	[ae]		[a:] [a]

Long (see 2.2) vowels are indicated either by the colon following them or by a different IPA symbol (the left vowel of each pair is long). OE had also a high front rounded vowel [y:] [y] (cf. French *u* as in *lu*). In OE vowel length was distinctive (i.e., phonemic), unlike in present-day English.

17.2.2 OE Morphology and Syntax

The most significant difference between OE and present-day English is probably the fact that OE had a very rich inflectional morphology, more similar to German or Latin than to present-day English. The following is the declension[1] of the noun *cyning* (king):

Singular		Plural
se cyning	*the king* (Subj)	þā cyningas
þone cyning	*the king* (DO)	þā cyningas
þæs cyninges	*of the king* (Gen)	þāra cyninga
þǣm cyninge	*to the king* (Dat)	þǣm cyningum
þȳ cyninge	*with the king* (Inst)	þǣm cyningum

---

[1]See 19.3.3 on case. The labels used in this chart are the following: Subj: = subject: DO = direct object; Gen = genitive; Dat = dative; Inst = instrumental.

Note that þ = [ð] and c = [k]. The thorn symbol [þ] is a rune. As you can see from the chart, articles and nouns had inflectional endings and so did adjectives and pronouns (see the following verb chart for the personal pronouns). The bar above some vowels, such as in þā, indicates that the vowel was long.

The verbal system was similarly much more complex than present-day English (although considerably simpler than the Indo-European one described later). It had, like present-day English, only two tenses (past and present) but a full-fledged subjunctive mood besides the indicative and imperative ones. To give you an idea of the complexity of the inflections, we reproduce the present indicative of the verb drīfan (drive):

1 sing.	ic drīfe	*I drive*
2 sing.	þu drīfst	*you drive*
3 sing.	hē(o)/hit drīfð	*s/he/it drives*
1 plur.	wē drīfað	*we drive*
2 plur.	gē drīfað	*you drive*
3 plur.	hī drīfað	*they drive*

OE had two classes of verbs, as far as the past tense formation goes: the so-called strong and weak verbs (the remnants of the strong verbs are known in present-day English as "irregular verbs"). **Strong verbs** indicate the change of tense by **ablaut** (i.e., a change in the vowel of the root), e.g., *sing, sang, sung.* **Weak verbs** indicate past tense by adding [-t], [-d], or [əd] (spelled -*ed*), e.g., *walk, walked.* These two classes are common to all Germanic languages.

Needless to say, OE was not uniform. We have evidence for four OE dialects: Kentish, West Saxon, Mercian, and Northumbrian (see Figure 17.3), although most of the texts that have been preserved from this epoch are in West Saxon. Among the texts in OE are *Beowulf,* an alliterative (see Chapter 14.1.1) epic poem, and several religious poems, including four by Cynewulf, one of the few OE poets whose name has been preserved. He insured that this would be the case, by spelling his name in runic alphabet in the text. Prose works tend to come later than poetry. Two of the greatest writers of this period are King Alfred the Great (871–899), who translated (mostly himself), among other works, Bede's (673–735) *Ecclesiastical History of the English Nation,* and Ælfric (circa 995–1020), author of many sermons and lives of saints.

Figure 17.3: OE Dialects

Source: Baugh 1957.

A very significant influence on English was the Danish invasions, which eventually led to the settlement of significant number of Scandinavian speakers. The influence of Scandinavian speakers on OE can be seen by **doublets.** Doublets are words that originally had the same meaning but have come into English from different sources and, once in English, generally differentiated their meanings. Consider for example

(17.1) OE scyrthe [ʃirte] > shirt vs. Old Norse scyrta > skirt

which shows the results of the evolution of the Germanic sounds [sk] that become [ʃ] in OE but remain [sk] in Scandinavian (note the > symbol that indicates the direction of linguistic evolution). An even more significant borrowing (cf. 2.3.5) from the Scandinavian languages is that of the set of plural pronouns, which was adopted in OE originally in the north of the country (where the Scandinavian influence was greatest) and then spread to the rest of the country. This shows a quite significant degree of Scandinavian influence, because it is fairly rare for a language to borrow pronouns; usually languages limit borrowings to nouns, adjectives, adverbs, and verbs.

The end of the OE period is marked by a very significant event in the history of the language, namely the Norman conquest of the island, in 1066. Needless to say, Norman influence on England had been significant before that date. The result of the shift in power was that French became the language of the court, of the upper class, and of instruction. Because of this fact, French became the official language of England for nearly three centuries, while English was relegated to the status of "dialect" spoken by the lower classes.

The social stratification of the diglossic situation (see 9.1.3) can be seen from the borrowing pattern of words. Since French was the "high" language, a large amount of vocabulary was borrowed into English from French and from Latin, via French. For example, consider food: when the servants raised pigs and sheep, they were called precisely that; when they were butchered and eaten by the rich they acquired their Norman names, borrowed from French. This is why today we have the following alternations, unique to English:

Anglo-Saxon word	Norman word	French word
pig	pork	< porc
sheep	mutton	< mouton

Note that fish and chicken do not have alternate names because they were peasant food, and thus the nobles did not eat them.

17.3 MIDDLE ENGLISH (ME): AD 1150 TO 1500

The Middle English period is characterized by the return of the English language as the tongue of the English nation. The Normans had kept their lands in France when they invaded England. Between 1200 and 1250, they lost them and that led to a loss of motivation to use French; the Hundred Years' War (1337–1453) further led to hostility toward the language of the enemy. However, the relative stability of French in England was due to the fact that French was seen across Europe at the time as the language of culture and learning.

French left a massive trace in English: an estimate puts the number of French words borrowed into ME to more than 10,000, of which 75 percent are still in use. In general, French words borrowed into English tend to be perceived as sophisticated and more refined, for example, compare

(17.2) smell (< ME *smellen*) vs. perfume (< French *parfum*)

17.3.1 The Grammar of ME

The two main grammatical phenomena of this period were the loss of inflectional endings and the loss of a large number of the strong verbs.

Loss of Inflectional Endings

The most significant change was without doubt the loss of inflectional distinctions in nouns and verbs. In the nouns, when the sound /m/ appeared at the end of the word, it changed first into /n/ and eventually disappeared altogether; endings in /-a/, /-u/, and /-e/ also weakened into /-e/ and by the 14th century had also disappeared. This reduced the system of inflections to a two-way distinction, carried by the ending [-s] that indicated both the genitive and the plural. Eventually, only the plural sense remained, as is the case in today's English (as well as the 's of the possessive).

The significance of the loss of inflections cannot be underestimated. Essentially, in OE the position of words in the sentence was rather loose, as one could rely on the endings to tell which was the subject and which was the direct object. When the inflectional system was lost, it was up to syntax to signal the subject, direct object, etc., of the sentence. This led to the fairly rigid word order of modern English, which prescribes that the subject (S) comes first, is followed by the verb (V), and then by the direct object (O); this is called an SVO language.

Loss of Strong Verbs

About a third of the strong verbs of OE were no longer used in ME. This pattern continued in the following periods, until by the present time, strong verbs were no longer productive, i.e., they no longer can create new forms (cf. 2.3.5; so if we invent a new verb, it will not be a strong one, e.g., *fax, faxed*). Furthermore, the principle of **analogy** led to the application of the simpler, more common pattern of the weak verbs to the strong verbs, causing a further reduction of the strong verbs. Examples of originally strong verbs that have been regularized are *burn, climb, help, walk,* etc. This is also called **leveling.**

17.3.2 The Literature of ME

As a general rule, medieval English literature imitated French and Italian sources. However, the Anglo-Saxon tradition of alliterative poetry of *Beowulf* was continued in *Piers Plowman* (circa 1370) and *Sir Gawain and the Green Knight* (written in West Midland around the end of the 14th century), which combined alliterative and rhyming techniques.

Geoffrey Chaucer (c1340–1400), the author of *The Canterbury Tales,* was the most significant author of this period. Chaucer was influenced by French medieval poetry and by Italian early Renaissance prose (e.g., Boccaccio). The influence of his language on modern English has been significant, as people have imitated his writing. His dialect shows a Southern influence (see 17.3.3). Here is a short section, the beginning of the "The Nun's Priest's Tale" in *The Canterbury Tales:*

A poure widwe somdel stape in age
Was whilom dwellyng in a narwe cotage
Besdie a grove, stondying in a dale

This can be rendered in modern English as: A poor widow somewhat advanced in age was once living in a small cottage that stood beside a grove, in a dale.

17.3.3 Dialects of ME

There were four main dialects of ME: the Southern (which corresponded to the West Saxon area of OE), the Northern (which corresponded to the Northumbrian area of OE), and the West and East Midland (which corresponded to the western and eastern areas of the Mercian dialect of OE). Kentish retained its distinctiveness in this period as well. See Figure 17.4.

Figure 17.4: ME Dialects

Source: Baugh 1957.

By the end of the 14th century the Midland dialect of ME was on its way to becoming the "Standard," which would eventually become "Standard English." The following were the main reasons for this phenomenon:

- The fact that the Midland variety was intermediate between the more extreme forms of the Northern and Southern dialects.

- The fact that the Midland dialect had the largest base of speakers.

- The presence of the universities of Cambridge and Oxford, at a time when the care of learning passed from the monasteries to the laical institutions.

- The influence of London, which became the capital of England, both politically and economically.

- The influence of the printing press: in 1476, Caxton began publishing books using the new technology; he adopted the London dialect, which thus acquired authority by the very fact of appearing in print.

17.4 MODERN ENGLISH: AD 1500 TO PRESENT

The invention of the moving-type printing press was a very significant event in the history of the language because it allowed a much wider spread of books by reducing their cost. The spread of literature in turn affected the language significantly.

17.4.1 Additions to the Lexicon

The Renaissance period (1450–1650), which included the Elizabethan Age (1558–1603), introduced a large number of words into English in an effort to "enrich" its vocabulary, mainly from Latin, Greek, Italian, French, and other languages. These were primarily learned words, which were therefore called **inkhorn** words (as they were originally used only in writing). There was a controversy over inkhorn words, in which many opposed the widespread borrowing (see 2.3.5), but eventually the use of these words spread. An estimate is that some 10,000 words entered the language in this period. Shakespeare used large numbers of inkhorn words, for example. The situation was so serious that dictionaries of "hard words" began appearing (e.g., Cawdrey [1604], Bullokar [1616], Cockeram [1623]). See also 18.1.4.

17.4.2 The Great Vowel Shift

The most significant event in the history of English at the phonemic level is probably the **Great Vowel Shift** (see Figure 17.5). This phenomenon took place between the end of the 14th century and the end of the 15th, although some of its changes were still taking place into the 18th century! It affects only long vowels (i.e., stressed vowels). Essentially, it consisted in the change of the quality (i.e., the sound) of the long vowels ([a] became [e], [e] became [i], etc.). The following figure illustrates the overall pattern:

Figure 17.5: The Great Vowel Shift

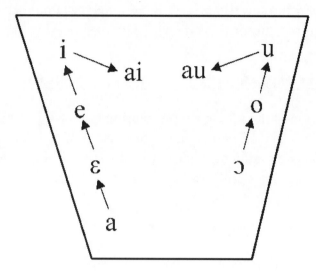

Note the diphthongization (cf. 2.2.1) of [i] > [ai] and [u] > [au]; this stage of the process was not yet complete in Shakespeare's time.

Explanations of the Great Vowel Shift

There are two traditional explanations of the Great Vowel Shift: the so-called "push" and "pull" theories. Both depend on where the change started and assume that the phonetic system tends to preserve the distance between the various phonemes.

The Push Chain

In the push explanation, the [a] vowel started moving front and high, thus displacing (pushing up) the [ɛ] that in turn affected the [e] sound, eventually leading to the diphthongization of [i]. The problem for this approach is that the back vowels would have no reason to move, and yet we know that they did, just like the front ones.

The Pull Chain

The alternative explanation is that the diphthongization of the high vowels started first, leaving a gap in the high region of the system that attracted (pulled up) the vowels below, so [u] > [au] and pulls up [o] > [u]. This explanation has the advantage of explaining the movement of the back and front vowels at the same time.

Mixed Explanation

Another possibility is that the Great Vowel Shift involved both push and pull phenomena, i.e., that [a] started the movement for the front vowels and that [ɔ] moved up as a result of a pull mechanism. Other more recent theories even deny that there was any "great" vowel shift at all and see the various movements as unrelated.

Effects of the Great Vowel Shift

One of the side effects of the Great Vowel Shift is that the spelling of the vowels, which had become standardized before it took place, no longer corresponds to their phonetic value.

Another effect is that, since the Great Vowel Shift only affected long vowels, words that are related morphologically such as *serene* [sɛrin] and *serenity* [sɛrɛniti] have different pronunciations for what is historically the same vowel.

Perhaps the most dramatic effect of the Great Vowel Shift is that while Chaucer's English looked and sounded widely different from modern English, Shakespeare's (1564–1616) English is essentially identical to ours.

17.4.3 Morphology in the Renaissance Period

By this period the great changes of the loss of inflectional endings were over, and so what we see are smaller phenomena. For example, the disappearance of the *thou* pronoun (now only used by the Quakers) was complete by the 16th century. The *-eth* ending for the third person singular (*telleth*), which was the norm in the Southern dialect, was replaced by *-s*, which was common in the Northern dialect. Also, we note a sharp increase in the use of the continuous *(-ing)* forms.

17.4.4 The Augustan Age and the Move toward Standardization

The period that goes from 1650 to 1800, and includes the Augustan Age (1700–1750), is chiefly notable because of the attempts to regulate and "improve" the language. For example, Jonathan Swift (1667–1745), the author of *Gulliver's Travels*, in 1712 wrote *A Proposal for Correcting, Improving and Ascertaining the English Tongue*, in which he condemned the practice of **clipping** (cf. 2.3.5) and the use of monosyllabic words. He also advocated the creation of an English academy, following the Italian and French models (cf. 18.1.4). Along the same lines, Dr. Johnson's dictionary (1755) (cf. 18.1.4) had the purpose of standardizing the language. This period saw also the beginning of prescriptive grammars (see 18.1.4).

The *Oxford English Dictionary* (cf. 15.5.1), which is the ultimate achievement of the trend toward standardization and codification of the language, appeared between 1884 and 1928, in 12 volumes, followed by various supplements.

17.4.5 Recent Morphological and Lexical Developments

As we have seen, by Shakespeare's time, English was roughly set in present-day patterns. This is not to say that there have not been developments in the last 300 hundred years. For example, a very large number of words covering new technological advances, such as radio, television, computers, and medicine, have entered the vocabulary. English has been borrowing words from many languages, as a result of increased travel and awareness of other cultures, such as, limiting ourselves to the food domain, *sushi, kebob, taco, pizza, gefilte fish, tahini,* and *hummus.* (See the following sections for other domains.)

In morphology, the subjunctive has all but disappeared and is now exclusively used in frozen expressions *(be that as it may)* or to indicate unreality *(If I were you).* The 19th century witnessed the creation of a new construction, *get* passive, as in *get hired.* Possibly the most significant phenomenon has been the increase in the use of **phrasal verbs** such as *get on, get away, put off,* and *stand up,* which are associated primarily with American English (see 17.5.1).

Another significant phenomenon, in the 19th and 20th centuries, was the beginning of the British Empire in America, Asia, and Africa, which eventually led to the spread of English worldwide.

17.5 ENGLISH AS A WORLD LANGUAGE

Today English is well on its way to becoming a world language. The number of people worldwide who use English is somewhere between 1½ and 2 billion, although only about 350 m.[2] of that number are actually

---

[2]To avoid repetition, we will abbreviate *million* to m.

native speakers of English. English is the official language (or plays an important role) in about 60 countries. To put things in perspective, it should be remembered that however widespread English may be, it remains a distant second to Chinese, which is spoken by more than 1 billion native speakers.

Such a widespread use has significant effects on the language. A new dictionary records a large number of words and usages, which are not common in either the United States or England. For example, *tea* can mean, besides the beverage and the plant, a meal. In the United States, it is a light meal, eaten in the afternoon. In England, Scotland, Australia, and New Zealand, it means for some the main meal of the day. In Guyana, it means breakfast.

What is Standard English then? As we said elsewhere (see 5.2), nobody owns English. Social and political factors determine what is considered "standard" across the English-speaking world.

17.5.1 American English

Do you think there is an "American language"? If so, what are some examples of this language?

American and Canadian Englishes are not usually considered "new Englishes," but in fact these were the first places, with India, where English took a solid hold outside of England. It is a widely known fact that American English (AmEngl) and British English (BrEngl) differ, in matters of pronunciation, spelling, and lexical choices.

Settlement in North America by English speakers began in 1607, in Jamestown, Virginia. In 1620, a settlement of Puritans (aboard the famous *Mayflower*) arrived in what is now Massachusetts. By 1640 some 25,000 immigrants had arrived. By 1790 the English-speaking population had swelled to 4 m. and was limited to the East. Settlement in Canada was initially contested by the French-speaking colonists. After a series of wars with France, in the second half of the 17th century, settlement of English speakers began in Nova Scotia. After 1776, British loyalists moved to Canada in great numbers. The settlement patterns of the immigrants, and their English dialects, naturally affected the English they spoke (see 5.1.1). By 1830 there were more than 13 m. English speakers on the American continent. By 1890 the number was around 50 m. and spread throughout the continent.

In the earliest colonies, especially in New York, the linguistic situation was very fluid, with Dutch, French, and other languages being spoken as well. For political and economical factors, English relegated French to Quebec and Spanish and Portuguese to southern and Central America. Traces of Dutch, for example, remain in such words as *cruller* (a type of doughnut) from Dutch *krulle.*

The "Melting Pot"

Once English asserted its dominance in North America, the paradigm for new immigrants was that of assimilation. This has been called the "melting pot" since the idea was that the immigrants would lose their original ethnic identity and become Americans. Typically, the first generation immigrants would be nonnative speakers of English with their children growing up to be native speakers of English and bilinguals in their parent's language to varying degrees; the third generation would be monolingual in English, with possibly a few residual traces of the grandparents' language.

One of the central factors of the differentiation between AmEngl and BrEngl was the influx of the non-English speaking immigrants. Only about 30 percent of the population of the United States traces its roots back to the British immigrants. It stands to reason that the influence of the non-English-speaking majority would have affected the language of the "melting pot." Consider, for example, the influence the Native Americans; the African-Americans; the Pennsylvania Dutch (Amish and Mennonite, who speak German, or German-influenced English) communities; the Yiddish-speaking Jewish settlements in New York; the Italians in New York and California; the Japanese; the Chinese; the French and Spanish contacts (e.g., the Southwest, the Cajun in Louisiana); and many other communities, most notably the Scottish and Irish, which preserved their linguistic roots well beyond the three-generation assimilatory pattern of the melting pot.

Colonial Lag

Under the term colonial lag, Marckwardt summed up the observation that AmEngl seems to have retained a number of archaisms in relation to BrEngl. For example, BrEngl pronounces *cart* [kaht] (*r*-less pronunciation); this is an innovation: Shakespeare's contemporaries pronounced it just like contemporary Americans would, [kart] (Boston-type [kahrt] pronunciations in the United States are due to British influence). This is not surprising, as we know from historical linguistics that peripheral areas are more conservative linguistically.

Conversely, AmEngl has evolved independently of BrEngl as well, as for instance in the creation of many new phrasal verbs (see 17.4.5).

American Dialects

The English-speaking areas of North America show a broad dialectal differentiation (see 5.1.1), which reflects the patterns of settlement in the eastern United States: when the colonists expanded westward, they followed routes that, generally speaking, went east to west, thus maintaining the division in north, central, and south regions found in the eastern United States. It is worth noting that it took some 200 years for the colonists to expand west of the Appalachians and that some regions of the United States have been peopled by English-speakers for about a century at the most.

American Linguistic Identity

Around the time of the Revolutionary War, Americans began to realize that there were differences between AmEngl and BrEngl. While initially they felt defensive about them, they finally embraced them and made them into part of a nationalistic sentiment.

Noah Webster published *An American Dictionary of the English Language* in 1828. His greatest achievement was writing the definitions of the words, which were more accurate and precise than any preceding dictionary. He also included many Americanisms. The *Webster* was first published in 1864 (cf. 15.5.1) and then revised in 1890 (when it acquired its current name) and then again in 1909 and 1934 (the so-called "second edition"). It was further revised in 1961 (the so-called *Webster's Third*) amid outrage at the descriptive approach used (cf. 1.2.1). Webster was very keen about language reform, which he associated with political independence, as did Thomas Jefferson and Benjamin Franklin, for example. Webster introduced such AmEngl spellings as *color, humor, tire* (for BrEngl *tyre*), and *fiber* (for BrEngl *fibre*).

In 1919, H. L. Mencken published *The American Language*, which from the title itself made a very clear case for the autonomy of AmEngl from British (in fact, he claimed that they no longer were the same language, which is commonly taken to be somewhat of an overstatement). From the very beginning, American culture was almost obsessed with the question, "What is an American?" Intellectuals felt a need to weigh in on the question of how different Americans were from Europeans in general and the British in particular. Ralph Waldo Emerson's "American Scholar" essay made a connection between the rugged new American, the culture of freedom, and a new language. "We have listened too long to the courtly muses of Europe," Emerson declared. Dialect humorists, such as Augustus Longstreet and George W. Harris (Sut Lovengood) used the new language they heard on the frontier to satirize the young nation. Samuel Clemens (Mark Twain) extended this tradition and made it art.

By the end of the 19th century, the fact that AmEngl was clearly diverging from BrEngl was a source of pride to some writers like Twain and William Dean Howells and a source of worry and irritation to others. Henry James avoided the whole issue by moving to England.

The early decades of the 20th century seemed to settle the literary debate, as departments of American studies began to be organized at universities to study American history and literature as something distinct and even worthy. American writers like Scott Fitzgerald, Gertrude Stein, and Ernest Hemingway still felt they needed to travel to Europe to pursue their muse, however. Today, the theme of "What is an American?" is not often addressed in literature. It is much more common for writers to explore their personal and group identities than a national identity.

AmEngl has been the direct source of some of the varieties of world Englishes. Figure 17.6 illustrates this fact, distinguishing between American- and British-influenced new Englishes, as well as how the diffusion of English is widespread worldwide. Of late, the role of AmEngl in the diffusion of English has increased due to the growing importance of the economical ties between the United States and the rest of the world (which include business but also the export of movies, rock music, and fast food).

17.5.2 World Englishes

Australia/New Zealand

Settlement of Australia began in 1788 as a penal colony of about 700 prisoners and 300 guards. By 1838, 130,000 prisoners had been taken to Australia. Free settlers also began to arrive, and by 1850 the English-speaking population numbered 400,000. By 1900 it was close to 4 m. Recent figures are over 18 m. New Zealand was colonized in 1840 by whalers. By 1850, 25,000 colonists had arrived; by 1900, 750,000. In 1995 the population was above 3.5 m.

Figure 17.6: The Global Diffusion of the English Language

Source: Kachru 1992.

New words were created to describe the different Australian landscape and way of life. Differences in pronunciations have developed as well, such as British *she* pronounced [səɪ] (with the schwa longer than in BrEngl). Influences from aboriginal languages and Maori (in New Zealand) have been limited: *kookaburra, dingo,* and *tui* (a bird), to name a few.

Jamaica

Jamaica was settled by English speakers in 1655. Its main crop was labor-intensive sugar cane, which meant that a large population of slaves was brought in from Africa to work in the plantations. There has been a constant presence of English as an official language (2.5 m. speakers), but the presence of a large African population has given rise to a Jamaican creole (2 m. speakers). Jamaican English shows some differences in pronunciation, e.g., *stomach* [tomok] and *strong* [troŋ]. Jamaican creole has even stronger differences, e.g., *sit down* [sidoŋ] with assimilation (i.e., loss) of the [t]. More significantly, Jamaican creole does not always follow the subject-verb-object word order of British or Jamaican English.

South Africa

In 1795 Britain invaded the Dutch colony of South Africa and by 1806 took full control; soon English and Dutch (Afrikaans) coexisted. Early on, a variety of "African English" spoken by some native Africans developed. South African English had strong ties to BrEngl; a variety of Afrikaans derived from Dutch and a variety of Black/African English continue to coexist with several Bantu languages spoken by native Africans. The Black/African English variety is more closely related to Afrikaans than to BrEngl. An example of pronunciation difference is [ke:] (the : marks a long vowel) for *care*. South African innovations in the lexicon include *apartheid, aardvark,* and *trek.*

West Africa: Gambia/Ghana/Cameroon/Nigeria/Liberia

These West African states have all inherited English from the dismantling of the colonial system (with the exception of Liberia, which was set up as an independent state). English coexists with large numbers of other languages. For example, in Ghana there are speakers of the following languages: Ada, Ewe, Ga-Adangme, Fante, and Nzema on the coast, and moving inland, Twi, Guang, Tem, Senufo, Vagale, Dagbane, Mampele, and Dagare to name a few. It is common for people to be tri- and even quadrilingual. English is used in this complex array of languages as an auxiliary language among speakers of mutually incomprehensible languages and as a language of culture, research, and business. For example, in Nigeria all the national newspapers are printed in English.

In most cases, the role of English as a language of higher education and of government has led to adoption of English as the official language of a state as in Gambia, Ghana, and Nigeria. While English has ties with the colonial past of these countries that many speakers are uncomfortable with, it is generally recognized that there is no clear alternative to the use of English, since none of the other languages used in the country has an "above the parts" status, and thus the adoption of one language would displease the rest of the country. For example, in Nigeria the three largest languages are Hausa (25 m. speakers), Yoruba (20 m.), and Igbo (13 m.). But it is estimated that there are more than 400 languages used in that country! Therefore, English is the most effective way for speakers of different languages to communicate. Or at least it is one effective way to communicate, according to Nigeria's military government, which in 1998, for reasons of geopolitics, added French as a second official language.

Figure 17.7: English in Africa (ESL = Engl. as a second language, ENL = Engl. as a national language, EIL = Engl. as an international language)

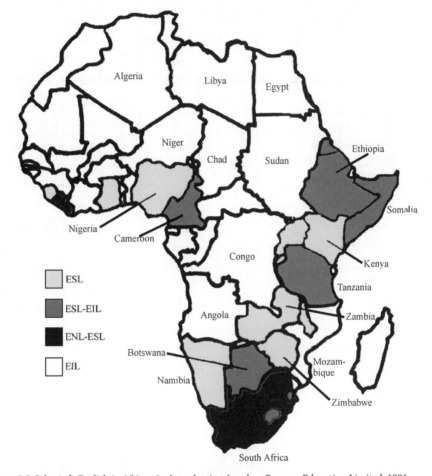

Source: J. J. Schmied, *English in Africa: An Introduction.* London: Pearson Education Limited, 1991.

To further complicate matters, most of these countries have developed "pidgin" varieties of English used as lingua francas. Finally, we should also mention that some writers have produced highly acclaimed literary works incorporating into their English some aspects of the local varieties of English (Chinua Achebe and Amos Tutuola, among others).

To gather a more in-depth idea of the kind of variation that occurs in these societies, consider Table 17.1. The symbols mean respectively: + = English used regularly, * = English only used sometimes, – = English not used.

Table 17.1: Use of English in Some East African States

	Zambia	Zimbabwe	Malawi	Uganda	Kenya	Seychelles	Somalia	Tanzania	Ethiopia
Local court	+	+	+	+	+	+	−	+	−
Local court	*	*	*	*	*	*	−	−	−
Parliament	+	+	+	+	+	+	−	−	−
Civil service	+	+	+	+	+	+	+	−	−
Primary school	+	+	+	+	+	*	−	−	−
Secondary school	+	+	+	+	+	+	+	+	+
Radio	+	+	+	+	+	+	+	+	+
Newspaper	+	+	+	+	+	+	+	+	+
Local novels	+	+	+	+	+	*	*	+	+
Local records	+	+	+	+	+	−	−	−	−
Local plays	+	+	+	+	+	*	*	−	−
Films	+	+	+	+	+	+	+	+	−
Traffic signs	+	+	+	+	+	+	+	−	−
Advertising	+	+	+	+	+	+	+	*	−
Business letters	+	+	+	+	+	+	+	+	+
Private letters	+	+	+	+	+	+	*	−	*

Source: J. J. Schmied, *English in Africa: An Introduction.* London: Pearson Education Limited, 1991.

Asia: India/Singapore/Malaysia/Papua New Guinea

Arguably, the influence of English has been strongest in India. Dating back to 17th-century British rule, the role of English is well entrenched in such public affairs as the higher court system and higher education. The linguistic diversity of the Indian subcontinent has assured that English be kept as a language of wider communication. India has Hindi as its official language and English as its "associate" official language as well as 14 other regional languages. Four to five percent of Indians use English on a regular basis.

Indian English has developed to a large extent on its own in terms of phonetics, lexicon, and semantics. Consider the following examples, which are perfectly acceptable in Indian English and yet sound "strange" in AmEngl: *I would like to have bed tea every day,* or *May I know your good name, please?* There are many varieties of Indian English, some of which are closer to BrEngl than others.

Singapore-Malay English differs from varieties of world English that developed via pidginization, such as West African, Caribbean, and New Guinean (as discussed in the next paragraph), insofar as its origin is almost entirely to be found in the school system where it was also influenced by teachers from India. The effect of language-planning decisions can be seen clearly in the differences between the Singaporean and Malay situations. In 1956 Singapore started bilingual education. Instead, in 1970, Malaysia switched to Malay as its primary medium of schooling. As expected, the functions for which English is used in Malaysia decreased, while they increased and are steadily increasing in Singapore. Recently, Malaysia has re-evaluated the place of English in society, and English has become a compulsory subject in secondary schools. Singapore-Malay English shows marked pronunciation differences from BrEngl or AmEngl. For example, long vowels tend to be shortened (lowered) as in the American *see* [siy] becoming [sI].

The linguistic diversity of Papua New Guinea (PNG) is staggering. More than 700 languages are spoken in PNG. Also, the local English-based pidgin **Tok Pisin** or "pidgin talk" has developed into a full-fledged independent language used for most functions. More than half the population of PNG, or 2 m. people, speak Tok Pisin. As a general rule, English has been used in formal situations, while Tok Pisin was used in informal ones, although Tok Pisin is gaining wider acceptance and may eventually replace English in its formal functions.

China/Japan/Continental Europe

Finally, we turn briefly to those countries where English has primarily an international use.

In China, English is the most widely studied foreign language. The primary motivation is access to Western science and technology (and more recently business opportunities). English has no auxiliary language functions in China though Esperanto is also widely studied.

The same is true of Japan and continental Europe, where English is widely studied for its role as the medium of technology and science, with some interest in music, television, and drama originating in England and the United States. The interest in U.S. technology and culture manifests itself in heavy borrowing of select lexical fields like computers and pop music. Some countries, such as France, are actively resisting what they perceive as "cultural imperialism." For example, software is *software* in Italian but *logiciel* in French; *computer* is *computer* in Italian and *ordinateur* in French.

17.6 DIACHRONIC LINGUISTICS

In section 17.1, we said that English derives from a language spoken anywhere between 2,000 and 3,000 years ago. Short of having a time machine, how do we know? Remember that there are no written documents for any Germanic language prior to about AD 300. Linguists have developed a number of techniques to recontruct languages of the past. **Reconstruction** is the term that indicates all methods used to figure out what a language was like when documents are missing. Reconstructed forms are indicated by a * preceding the form. This is potentially confusing, since the * also indicates a nongrammatical sentence. However, the star for reconstructed forms usually applies only to single words. The most important tool used for reconstruction is the **comparative method.**

17.6.1 The Comparative Method

The comparative method consists in finding regular and systematic (i.e., nonrandom) correspondences between sounds among languages. The languages for which these systematic correspondences are found are then said to form a **language family** (see 17.6.2).

Consider the following examples, all meaning *father:*

French	Spanish	Portuguese	Catalan	Italian	Sicilian
père	padre	pai	pare	padre	patri

It does not take a linguistic genius to see that the forms all resemble one another. Based on this similarity, we would consider hundreds of examples of similar sounds in words and eventually establish the fact that all the forms in the previous example are derived from Latin (Lat.) *pater* (all the languages in the example are **Romance** languages). Consider French, one of the most divergent forms, since it loses the [t], which is preserved unchanged in Sicilian and voiced in Italian and Spanish. By comparing the form [mɛr] < Lat. *mater* (cf. It. *madre,* Sic. *matri*), we can conclude that a Latin [t] in that position disappears. Notice also the regular pattern, whereby Lat. [t] > [d] in Italian, and remains unchanged in Sicilian. Note that in this example, since Lat. *pater* is attested we cheated a little (we already knew the answer), but the point remains that the method is valid also for unattested languages.

Consider now the following examples,

ancient Greek	Latin	Sanskrit	Gothic	Old Irish
pater	pater	piter	fadar	athir

where the Latin form we "reconstructed" previously is compared with words from other languages, roughly from the same period (about 2,000 years ago). Applying the same comparative method, linguists have reconstructed the form *pətèr (the bar indicates that the vowel was long). But what language was this form spoken in? It is the common ancestor of Latin, Greek, Germanic, the Celtic languages, Sanskrit, and many others. It is commonly called **Indo-European** (IE) (see 17.6.3).

We already mentioned that similarities across languages need to be systematic. In other words, we must find regularities (laws) that are (more or less) without exceptions and that involve more than one word and/or sound at a time (i.e., a system of sounds). A good example is **Grimm's law,** named after Jacob Grimm, the linguist who formulated it. Simplifying a little, Grimm's law states that IE voiceless stops (see 2.2.2 for the phonetic description of sounds) became fricatives in the Germanic languages, whereas they underwent no change in the other branches of IE. IE voiced stops became voiceless, and finally IE voiced aspirated stops lost their aspiration. As before, these changes were limited to the Germanic branch. Compare OE *heorte* > ME *hert* > English *heart* to Latin *cor* (cf. *cordial*) and Greek *kardia* (whence *cardiology*, i.e., the branch of medicine concerned with the heart), all of which derive from IE *kerd*. Schematically Grimm's law gives us:

IE	p	t	k	b	d	g	b^h	d^h	g^h
Germ.	f	θ	h	p	t	k	b	d	g

Note how the sounds of the phonological inventory of the IE stops behave differently depending of the **natural class** to which they belong (a natural class is a group of sounds that share some phonological feature, e.g., all voiced stops are a natural class). Note also how Grimm's law applies to all IE words having stops. Or does it? In fact several exceptions were noted. **Verner's law** was designed to account for these: Verner's law states that all voiceless fricatives that are the result of Grimm's law become voiced stops, unless the preceding vowel is stressed (again, we simplify a little). For example, IE *pətèr > Germ. *faθar* (per Grimm's law) and then OE *fæder* (per Verner's law).

Once we have laws of language change, we can establish the history of words, i.e., their **etymology.** One takes a word and reconstructs the forms from which it came, going back as far as possible. For example, the word *foot* can be traced back to ME *fot* and further back to OE fōt. The earliest Germanic form (Gothic *fotus*) can then be compared to the Latin root *ped-* (whence *pedestrian*), to the Greek root *pod-* (whence *podiatrist*, i.e., foot doctor), and to Sanskrit *pad* to reconstruct the IE root **ped.* This is where the etymology of the word stops because many linguists believe that we cannot reconstruct any further. However, some linguists disagree (see 17.6.8).

17.6.2 Language Families

In what follows we will try to give an overview of some of the language families of the world. Keep in mind that there are some 6,700 languages currently spoken in the world and that there are many language families. Some languages have hundreds of millions of speakers, such as Chinese, while others have only a handful and are on the verge of disappearance (the so-called **endangered languages**).

17.6.3 The Indo-European Family

We have seen that English is a Germanic language and that Germanic is one of a set of other families of languages that taken together form the Indo-European family (i.e., all the languages ultimately derived from IE). Now is time to take a look at the other families in the IE family.

Italic

The Romance languages, mentioned previously, include Italian (and all its "dialects"), French (and all its dialects), Spanish, Catalan, Portuguese, Rhaeto-Romansh (spoken in Switzerland (see 9.2.1), Romanian, and Provençal. The Romance languages derive from vulgar Latin, i.e., Latin as it was spoken by the people during the early Middle Ages. However, Latin was not the only Italic language. There were other languages, among which the best known are Oscan and Umbrian, which were also spoken in Italy around 400 BC but were overtaken by the spread of the Latin people.

Hellenic

Hellenic is the family of ancient Greek from which modern Greek (12 m. speakers) is derived. There were several dialects of Greek, with fairly different phonological systems (Attic, from which modern Greek derives; Doric; Eolian; Ionian; and others).

Slavic

The Slavic family is divided in three areas: eastern, western, and southern. The eastern branch includes Russian (170 m. speakers), Ukrainian (41 m.), and Belorussian (10 m). The western branch includes Polish (44 m.), Czech (12 m.), Slovak (5 m.), and Sorbian (spoken by about 70,000 in Germany). The southern branch includes Bulgarian (9 m.), Macedonian (2 m.), Slovenian (2 m.), Serbian and Croatian (21 m.); Serbian and Croatian are the same language, except Serbian is spelled in the Cyrillic alphabet and Croatian in the Roman alphabet. The Cyrillic alphabet was invented by Cyril and Methodius in the 9th century AD to write Old Church Slavonic, which is the earliest Slavic language recorded.

Indo-Iranian

As the name *Indo*-European tells you, some of the speakers of IE ended up in the Indian subcontinent. Sanskrit is in a position similar to Latin in that it spawned a number of prakrits (Sanskrit for *natural, vulgar*), among which are Hindi-Urdu, which has more than 200 m. speakers, in India (Hindi) and Pakistan (Urdu); Bengali (spoken by 200 m. people in India and Bangladesh); Punjabi; Mahrati; Gujarati; Bihari; Nepali; and Orya (32 m. speakers). To these we add Romany (or Gypsy), the language spoken by the Rom people (aka Gypsies). The second branch of Indo-Iranian includes Farsi (Persian), spoken in Iraq, and Pashto, spoken in Afghanistan and Pakistan. Overall, there are more than 300 Indo-Iranian languages.

17.6.4 The Language Families of Africa

Afro-Asiatic

This family comprises the extremely widespread Semitic family (including Arabic and Hebrew), which extends throughout North Africa, the Arabic peninsula, and the Middle East. Arabic has more than 200 m. speakers, but it is a learned language, often learned as a second language. Hebrew is spoken by about 5 m. people, primarily in Israel. The Afro-Asiatic family also includes the following subfamilies: Cushitic, Berber, Omotic, and Chadic. Hausa, spoken primarily in Nigeria, by a total of 38 m. people, is a major Chadic language.

Niger-Kordofanian

The Niger-Kordofanian (aka Niger-Congo) family is probably the largest African language family (more than 1,400 languages), with some 150 m. speakers. It covers an area ranging from Senegal (West Africa), where Wolof is spoken, to East Africa, where Swahili is spoken, and to South Africa, where Zulu is spoken.

Khoisian

This is a smaller language family, with about 35 languages. These languages are spoken primarily by the Nama (spoken by less than 75,000 speakers) and the Hai or San (Bushmen; about 100,000 speakers) around the Kalahari Desert in Southwest Africa.

Nilo-Saharan

This language family is spoken in Central Africa, as the name indicates, and comprises about 200 languages, spoken by about 10 m. people. It includes Massai, spoken by more than 1 m. people in Tanzania and Kenya; Dinka, spoken in Sudan by more than 1 m. people; and Nubian, spoken by about 0.5 m. speakers in Egypt and Sudan. This latter language has a written history dating back to the 8th century AD.

17.6.5 Asia and the Pacific

Sino-Tibetan

Sino-Tibetan comprises two subfamilies: Tibeto-Burman and Chinese. Tibetan includes the Himalayan languages and the Burmese-Lolo family, among which stands out Burmese, spoken by more than 20 m. people in Myanmar (formerly Burma). Chinese comprises 14 more or less different dialects, the largest of which is Mandarin, spoken by more than 885 m. people.

Austronesian

Austronesian is a very large family (more than 1,200 languages) that covers an equally large geographical area: it extends from the island of Madagascar (Malagasy, more than 10 m. speakers) to the Easter Island (Rapa Nui, about 2,500 speakers) and as north as Taiwan (where a small subfamily of 23 Formosan languages is spoken) and the Hawaiian Islands and as far south as New Zealand. The larger subfamily is the Malayo-

Polynesian family. This includes Malay (more than 25 m. speakers in Indonesia and Malaysia); Javanese (more than 75 m. speakers, mostly in Indonesia); Tagalog (or Filipino), the national language of the Philippines, with 15 m. speakers, and Cebuano, with roughly the same number of speakers, also are spoken in the Philippines. The eastern side of the Malayo-Polynesian family is primarily represented by such Oceanic languages as Fijian, Marquesan, Tahitian, Samoan, and Hawaiian.

Austro-Asiatic

The Austro-Asiatic family comprises about 180 languages. It is divided in two subfamilies: the Munda languages, spoken in northern India, with about 7 m. speakers, and the Mon-Khmer languages, a subfamily of about 150 languages, including Mon, spoken by about 1 m. people in Myanmar; Khmer (Cambodian), spoken by about 7 m. people, mostly in Cambodia; and Vietnamese, spoken by more than 65 m. people in Vietnam. Some linguists gather the Austronesian; Austro-Asiatic; Miao-Yao (or Hmong-Mien: Miao, or Hmongic, is a family of languages spoken in China and Southeast Asia; Yao, or Mien, is closely related); and Daic (to which belongs Thai, the official language of Thailand with about 25 m. speakers) families in the Austric family.

Australian

All the aboriginal languages of Australia belong to a family of about 250 languages. Most of them are extinct or nearly so; around 100 Australian languages are still spoken. One estimate has the total number of Australian languages speakers as low as 30,000. A famous Australian language is Dyirbal, because of its mother-in-law language (a special variety of the language speakers have to use when addressing their mother-in-law). Dyirbal has about 40 speakers.

Dravidian

A language family comprising about 80 languages, spoken primarily in southern India. It includes Telegu, Kannada, and Tamil. It is spoken by more than 190 m. people.

Altaic

Altaic languages cover large areas of Asia, ranging from Turkey (Turkish) to Mongolia (Mongolian, 2.5 m. speakers). The Turkic subfamily comprises some 40 languages, among which are Turkish, Azerbaijani, Kazakh, Tatar, and Uzbek.

Japanese and Korean

These two languages present somewhat of a riddle. Japanese is spoken by 125 m. speakers. It borrowed the Kanji writing system from Chinese but is not related to this language. It seems that Japanese is related to Korean (75 m. speakers). Korean uses the *hangul* alphabet, which was created in the 15th century. The hypothesis that Korean may be related to the Altaic family has been advanced.

17.6.6 The Americas

There are at least 59 different *families* of languages in the Americas. It is impossible to do justice to the extreme variety of American languages, a large number of which is in an endangered status. We will have to content ourselves with listing a few representative languages for some representative families.

The Eskimo-Aleut family includes Aleut, which is spoken in Alaska and in Russia by about 150 people, and Eskimo. Eskimo includes Inuktikut (the language of the Inuit people, about 26,000 speakers) and Yupik (about 17,000 speakers). Eskimo languages are spoken in Greenland, Canada, Alaska, and Russia.

Algic includes the Algonquian subfamily and two other languages, Wiyot and Yurok. Algonquian includes Cree, Ojibwa, Menomini, Miami, Potawatomi, Shawnee, MicMac, Arapaho, Cheyenne, and Blackfoot.

The Na-Dene family includes Tlingit, spoken in Alaska by about 1,300 people; Apache (13,000 in Arizona); and Navaho (150,000 in Arizona, New Mexico, and Utah). Navaho is the Native American language with the largest number of speakers.

Siouan includes Dakota, Winnebago, Lakota, Crow, Biloxi, and 13 other languages. It is spoken in the central part of the United States and Canada.

The Muskogean family includes Alabama, Muskogee, Choctaw, and Chickasaw. The Salishan family includes 27 languages among which are Bella Coola, Salish, Lushootseed, and Coeur D'Alene, which had 40 speakers in 1990. This is the language of the tribe of the main character in the film *Smoke Signals.*

Uto-Aztecan is one of the American language families that is not in danger of extinction. Nahuatl (Aztec) is spoken by over 1.5 m. people in Mexico. Uto-Aztecan includes also Hopi (made famous by Whorf), Comanche, Shoshoni, Painte, and Luiseno. Mayan includes the Mayan language with more than 700,000 speakers in Mexico and Belize; Quich'e, spoken by more than 600,000 speakers in Guatemala; Tzotzil (265,000 speakers in Mexico); and Tzeltal (215,000 speakers in Mexico).

The Quechuan family includes 47 languages with more than 6 m. speakers in the Andean region. The Tupi family includes 70 languages, among which is Guarani, spoken in Argentina, Brazil, and Paraguay by about 12,000 people.

A controversial proposal by Joseph Greenberg in 1987 reduces all the families of languages of the Americas to just three: the Eskimo-Aleut, the Na-Dene, and a proposed macrofamily of Amerind.

17.6.7 Isolates

There are languages that do not seem to belong to any family. They are called **isolates.** Basque is probably the best known. It is spoken by some 580,000 people in Spain and about 80,000 in France. Ainu, in Japan, and Zuni, in the United States, are other examples.

17.6.8 Nostratic/Proto-World

Along the lines of the Amerind and Austric hypotheses, some linguists have made bold proposals for finding macrofamilies. The most famous one is the Nostratic family, proposed by Illich-Svitych in 1967, which includes Afro-Asiatic, Indo-European, Dravidian, Uralic (a family of languages including Hungarian and Finnish), Altaic, and possibly others as well. Finally, some linguists have proposed to reconstruct the original language spoken by the first humans (proto-world), which would be the common ancestor of all languages. Interestingly enough, evidence from DNA studies seems to support this bold hypothesis.

Educational Implications

Teachers who teach the history of English will have found basic information in this chapter. All teachers will have received information on English as it exists around the world today and information on language families.

17.7 EXERCISES

17.7.1 Words to Know

second language	foreign language	official language
melting pot	colonial lag	Tok Pisin
Old English	Middle English	Modern English
strong verb	weak verb	ablaut
analogy	leveling	language family
Indo-European	Germanic	natural class
Grimm's law	Verner's law	etymology
endangered language	Gothic	doublet
inkhorn	Great Vowel Shift	clipping
phrasal verb	reconstruction	comparative method
isolate language		

17.7.2 Review

1. What were the effects of the loss of inflectional endings in ME?

2. What are the theories that have been advanced to explain the Great Vowel Shift?

3. Where does Standard English (RP) come from?

4. What is a strong verb? How do strong verbs differ from weak ones?

5. What is the primary reason for worldwide acceptance of the English language?

6. What are the three major classifications that describe the importance of English to a particular culture? Briefly define each.

7. Discuss several ways that English has been altered by the numerous cultures that have adopted it.

8. List some of the advantages and disadvantages of nonnative speakers adopting English as a national language.

9. Why is English one of the most popular choices for study as a foreign language?

17.7.3 Research Projects

1. An impressive list of words borrowed from French can be found in Baugh and Cable (2001). Amuse yourself by making a list of words

with Anglo-Saxon parallels, such as the example in the text *(smell/perfume)*. What does your list tell you about the relative social status of the French borrowings?

2. Research the various calls for an English academy. Why do you think they never succeeded?

3. Using a novel, magazine, Web site, etc., written in a variety of English different from the one you speak (or were taught in school), make a list of features in which it differs from yours.

17.8 FURTHER READINGS

There are many histories of the English language. A very readable one with a lot of illustrations is McCrum, Cran, and MacNeil (1986), which is the companion book to the PBS series *The Story of English*. Crystal (2004) is also very readable. Fennell (2001) has a sociolinguistic focus. Crystal's (2003) *Encyclopedia* is full of information and illustrations. Baugh and Cable (2001) is excellent and deals a lot with the literary aspects of the language. More technical is Strang (1970). On OE, Quirk and Wrenn (1955) remains a basic reference. Mitchell and Robinson (1992) is more recent. On ME, see Burrow and Turville-Petre (1996) or Wright and Wright (1979). Clark (1957) covers both OE and ME.

On the OED and its connections with the creation of the literary canon, see Crowley (1989), which is, however, not for beginners. Much more readable are Murray (1977) and Winchester (1998, 2003).

The three definitions of *tea* are taken from the *Encarta World English Dictionary* (Soukhanov 1999). On the spread of English, see the many publications by Kachru (1982, 1992); Crystal (1997); and Trudgill and Hannah (1994). For Australia/New Zealand, see Eagleson (1982) and Blair and Collins (2001). References for Jamaica (Bailey 1982), the Caribbean (Lawton 1982), South Africa (Lanham 1982), West Africa (Todd 1982), India (Kachru 1982), Singapore (Platt 1982), and Papua New Guinea (Muhlhausler 1982) are in Bailey and Görlach (1982). For Asian Englishes, see Kachru (1982) and Foley (1988). For Singapore English, see Ling and Brown (2003).

On AmEngl, see Mencken (1919), which went through four editions but is more easily available in the one-volume abridgement edited by McDavid (1979); Marckwardt (1958) significantly revised by Dillard in Marckwardt and Dillard (1980); Laird (1970); Dillard (1975, 1992); and Wolfram and Schilling-Estes (1998).

The r-less example is from Wolfram and Schilling-Estes (1998), which has an extensive discussion with a map of the distribution of this feature in the east of the United States. Marckwardt (1958) and Marckwardt and Dillard (1980) have an extensive list of words borrowed from various languages in AmEngl. On colonial lag, see Marckwardt (1958, Chapter 4); on leveling, see Dillard (1975) and Bailey (1991, Chapter 6). On Webster's spelling reform and nationalism see Simpson (1986, Chapter 2); on his dictionary, see Laird (1970, Chapter 15). On the *Webster's Third*, see Marckwardt (1963) and the collection of articles in Sledd and Ebbitt (1962). More recently a monograph by Morton (1994), which sums up the controversy, has appeared.

There are many discussions of the comparative method and historical linguistics. Any introduction to linguistics will have a more advanced discussion. Hock (1991) is very thorough and links historical considerations with social ones. Arlotto (1972) unites a discussion of the comparative method with language families, very much along the lines of the exposition in the text.

The figure of the number of languages, as well as much of the information on language families, comes from Grimes, Grimes, and Pittman's (1996) *Ethnologue*, which is conveniently available on the Internet (http://www. sil.org/ethnologue/). Accessible overviews of the main language families, suitable for beginners, are to be found in Crystal (1997); Finegan (1994); and O'Grady, Dobrovolsky, and Aronoff (1997). Katzner (1995) has useful sketches of many languages and data on language families. The data on numbers of speakers and languages in a family are often vastly divergent. Most of the time, we have adopted *Ethnologue* as the authority. On Austric, the Amerind hypothesis, and Nostratic and proto-world, see Ruhlen (1994), which is very readable.

Chapter 18

Pedagogical Grammar

18.1 HISTORY OF GRAMMAR

It is impossible to understand normative or traditional grammar without a clear understanding of the historical roots of that body of knowledge/beliefs. As is the case with much of our culture, the roots of grammar are in the Greek civilization. The following extremely sketchy outline gives an idea of the origin of some of the central categories of grammar.

The broad picture that we see is somewhat surprising. Essentially the grammatical tools that are used today to describe language were invented roughly 2,000 years ago by people who were describing languages radically (although not completely) different from modern English. This is akin to practicing medicine using the tools and techniques employed by Greek and Roman doctors, something few of us would even consider! In the following sections, we will review some of the research in grammar, throughout the ages, with an eye to the advances (or lack thereof) in the analysis.

18.1.1 The Greeks

The earliest contributions to grammar within the Western tradition are those of the Sophists (5th century B.C.) who catalogued figures of speech and types of sentences. The interest of the Sophists about language was purely instrumental. They were interested in persuading their audience, much like lawyers nowadays. However, they started an interest into the "mechanics" of language.

With Plato begins the debate on the nature of the connection between the word and its signifier (see the **arbitrariness of the linguistic sign, 3.1**). In Plato's words, the two theories are called *fusei* versus *thesei* (nature versus convention). Plato distinguishes within the *logos* λόγος (discourse) an *onoma* (noun) and a *rhema* (verb). Needless to say, the correspondences between modern categories and Greek ones are approximate.

Plato's student Aristotle accepts the definitions of onomata, rhemata, and logos. He adds the *syndesmoi* (which are linking particles, e.g., *men ... de, on the one hand ... on the other*) and *ptosis* (inflections). However, he gives somewhat formal definitions, e.g., a noun does not have tense. In his *Categories* he lists the following semantic classes, which remind us of several terms still used in grammar today; for example, adjectives are said to describe "qualities," nouns are defined as "things" (i.e., substances):

substance	quantity	quality
relation	place	time
position	state/condition	action
affection (cf. passive)		

The Stoics (4th century BC to first century AD) introduced a distinction between the *semainon* = signifier, the semainomenon or *lekton* = signified, and the *pragma* or *tugkanon* = referent.

They distinguish five parts of speech: nouns, verbs, syndesmoi, articles, and pronouns. The syndesmoi are further divided in:

1. uninflected *(syndesmoi)*

2. inflected *(arthra)*

They use some syntactic/distributional criteria. They distinguish the three voices of Greek (active, passive, and middle). They introduce the distinction between words that mean something by themselves *(kategoremata)* and those that need to be used with other words *(synkategoremata)*. The Stoics further distinguish between *ptosis* and *klisis*: *ptosis* corresponds to nominal declension, while *klisis* is verbal inflection.

The Alexandrian Period is characterized by the division of the Alexandrine Empire into two states having each its own capital: Alexandria and Pergamon. They are the location of two schools:

- Alexandria (Aristotelian)—analogists = grammar is orderly and therefore laws that describe the regularities can be found.

- Pergamon—anomalists = grammar is basically random; therefore no rules can be given. One has to list exceptions.

Dionysius Thrax (1st century BC) is the author of the *Tekne Grammatike (Art of Grammar)*. This book is essentially the model that is still used in normative grammar. Dionysius distinguishes eight parts of speech: noun, verb, participle, article, pronoun, preposition, adverb, and conjunction. He uses formal and semantic criteria. His grammar was vastly successful.

18.1.2 The Romans

The first Latin grammatical treatise is Varro's (first century BC) *De Lingua Latina* (The Latin Language). He introduced the term *declinatio* for morphological processes. Declinatio (declension) is subdivided as:

1. naturalis = inflectional

2. voluntaria = derivational

Varro further introduced a classification, within inflectional morphology *(naturalis),* among parts of speech based on the presence or absence of nominal or verbal inflectional morphology, summed up in the following chart. Thus, for example, a participle can be defined as having both nominal and verbal inflection.

Varro		Nominal Morphology	
		+	−
Verbal M.	+	participles	verbs
	−	nouns/adjs	adverbs

The most successful grammar of antiquity was Aelius Donatus's (4th century AD). It was the textbook used to teach grammar for a large part of the Middle Ages. It was so popular that, for a while, a "Donat" was any book.

Also vastly influential was Priscianus's (6th century AD) Latin grammar in 18 books. Priscianus's (Priscian) grammar has eight parts of speech just like Dionysius but the article (which Latin lacks) is replaced by the interjection.

The parts of speech according to Priscian are the following:

nomen	=	noun/adjective
verbum	=	verb
participium	=	participle
pronomen	=	pronoun
adverbium	=	adverb
praepositio	=	prepositions (+ some derivational morpheme)
interiectio	=	interjection
coniunctio	=	conjunction

18.1.3 The Middle Ages

In the Arab grammatical tradition, grammatical thinking arises out of the need to teach classical Arabic in order to read the Quran. The most famous grammarian is Sibawaih from Basra (modern Iraq) who wrote *Al Kitab* (The Book; 8th century AD).

During the Middle Ages grammar becomes largely interested in the problem of the universals, e.g., Bacon (1214–94). The Modistae (13th to 14th century AD) (so-called because a very common title of grammatical work was *De modis significandi* [The ways of meaning]) believed that a common "structure" underlies all languages, which are then essentially all the same and differ only in the ways in which they express these common principles. The modes of being and signifying are described using Aristotle's categories, listed previously. They have been ridiculed for centuries, but lately they have become eerily modern (cf. Chomsky's universal grammar).

From a linguistic point of view, the Middle Ages are "dark ages." Most of the work of the *Modistae* is speculation not grounded in any factual data. However, there are two exceptions: the (pseudo-) Snorri Sturluson (ca. 1100), who discovers the concept of the minimal pair, and Dante Alighieri (1265–1321), who argues that the Romance languages come from Latin and describes various Italian dialects.

18.1.4 The Renaissance

This period also marks the beginning of the grammatical study of the "vulgar" languages (those spoken by the people) derived from Latin. For example, the first grammars of Italian and Spanish are published in the 15th century. Other grammatical work includes Pierre Ramée (1515–72) who writes grammars of Greek, Latin, and French.

Latin grammars are also quite numerous, for example, J. C. Scaligero's *De causis linguae Latinae* (1540) and W. Lily's Latin grammar (influenced by Priscian), which has the distinction of having been prescribed by Henry VIII for school use in 1540.

With the Renaissance and the increase in travel, we see a new interest in languages, translations, the appearence of dictionaries, and of the academies (*Accademia della Crusca*—1582, *Académie Française*—1635). Although an English academy was never instituted, there were numerous appeals for the creation of such a body, e.g., in 1698 by Daniel Defoe (1660–1731) and by John Dryden (1631–1700). This is the beginning of normatism (prescriptivism), for instance, Robert Lowth's grammar (cf. 1.2.1) is published in 1762. Another influential grammar was Lindsey Murray's (1794) *English Grammar*.

The first English dictionary is Robert Cawdrey's (1604). By far the most significant one is Samuel Johnson's *A Dictionary of the English Language* (1755) (see 17.4.4).

The Renaissance and the Enlightenment ushered in the heyday of rationalistic grammar, i.e., language as the expression of reason (e.g., the grammar of Port-Royal [Arnauld and Lancelot, *Grammaire Generale et Raisonnée* (1660)]) and of "philosophical grammar," i.e., the idea that philosophers should fashion a perfectly logical language (Descartes, Leibniz, Spinoza, and Locke).

18.1.5 Scientific Linguistics

At the beginning of the 19th century with the "discovery" of Sanskrit, we have the beginning of historical linguistics and the comparative method. The need for the British to understand and translate laws in Sanskrit and other Indian languages sparked interest and studies in the languages. Sir William Jones (1746–94) in his third *Anniversary Discourse of the Bengal Asiatic Society* (1786; publ. 1788) notes that Sanskrit, Latin, and Greek are descendents of the same language, now no longer spoken (i.e., Indo-European).

The great achievement of historical linguistics (dominated by German scholars, such as Bopp, Schlegel, Schleicher, the Grimm brothers, and Paul) was the establishment of the comparative method (see 17.6.1), which allowed the reconstruction of extinct languages and led to the "discovery" of Indo-European. The historical linguists worked out the "laws" of language change, and in doing so they faced the problem of describing the linguistic structures that changed.

Ferdinand de Saussure addressed this problem in his *Cours de Linguistique Generale* (1916, posthumous), where he distinguished between synchronic and diachronic linguistics (see 1.2.2). While the diachronic description of language follows its laws, synchronically languages are governed by other laws. Saussure recognized that these laws are essentially relational, i.e., that it does not so much matter what a given sound or meaning is, but what is important is the relationship between the two. Thus, for example, the allophones of two phonemes may in fact be the same sound (consider an unreleased [p] and unreleased [t], which are effectively silence), but relationally the sounds are allophones of different phonemes (cf. 2.2.3). In this concept are the seeds of the structuralist approach to linguistics, which is based on relationships and which eventually came to reject the use of meaning as part of linguistic analysis, thus ushering in the formalist/distributional approach.

With Saussure we are into modern linguistics, which by and large rejects normative grammar as unscientific. Saussure is the "father" of modern scientific linguistics and one of the central figures in the structuralist movement.

Structuralism spread throughout Europe in France and Switzerland but also with Hjelmslev in Denmark and more broadly with Trubetzkoy and Jakobson, who founded the Moscow school and later the Prague school. Structuralism also flourished in the United States, although the focus was more on the description of Amerindian languages and on descriptivism. Boas and Bloomfield were the principal exponents of American structuralism. Bloomfield was a proponent of the methodological approach that tried, under the influence of positivism and behaviorism (cf. 12.1.1), to use meaning as little as possible. Among Bloomfield's students were many important scholars including Hockett, Hall, and Harris, Noam Chomsky's teacher.

With Chomsky (see 2.5.2) we enter a new paradigm called generative in which the traditional categories of grammar that have developed through history are rehabilitated (although in later work, Chomsky abandons them).

Grammatical Description

The inherent limitations of these tools in describing languages different than those in which they were developed have been pointed out repeatedly and yet they persist because of tradition and resistance to change. Whether these are the best tools available is a matter of debate, but certainly modern linguistics has developed better tools that, however, have not acquired the broad recognition that would make it possible that they be used for pedagogical purposes, although some of them are slowly filtering down.

An important consideration that arises directly from the history we just examined is that the grammatical categories are, to a certain extent, arbitrary, and fitting words into them a matter of "opinion." Therefore, students should not put too much faith into grammatical analysis. Grammatical analysis is a tool for the understanding of language. The purpose of analyzing language is to understand how it works and whatever tools happen to work should be used. Often students (and their teachers) have a somewhat reverential attitude, if not outright fear of grammatical description. Grammarians are human beings, and their descriptions are going to differ to a certain extent.

In fact, we can look at different linguistic theories and find that they have different approaches to grammatical description. There are many different ways of describing language. A few of particular significance are the following:

1. configurational

2. functional

3. case grammar

Configurational

A configurational definition relies only on the relative position of syntactical elements of the sentence within a tree diagram. For example, within the syntactic trees that we saw in Chapter 2, a configurational definition of the subject is the "NP immediately below S," while a definition of direct object would be the "NP immediately below VP." Significantly, configurational definitions ignore all semantic information (see 2.4.2).

Functional

A functional definition, as the name indicates, looks at the function of the different parts of a sentence. So, for example, in the sentence

(18.1) Mary likes to keep up on biochemistry

Mary is considered to be the known information, that which the sentence is about, while *biochemistry* is considered the new information, that which the sentence tells us. The part in between is considered a transitional area.

Case Grammar

In case grammar the sentence revolves around the verb, and the nouns are the verb's arguments. The basic idea is that in a sentence such as

(18.2) John broke the window with a rock

we have the following semantic "cases" (after the Latin and Greek case system) of nominative (subject), accusative (direct object), etc. (see 19.3.3).

1. agent: *John*

2. patient: *window*

3. instrument: *rock*

18.2 PEDAGOGY OF GRAMMAR

18.2.1 Types of Grammars

It is necessary to define the term **grammar** more carefully. There are at least three different meanings of the word grammar, and it is important to keep them separate:

1. **Normative grammar:** This is prescriptive grammar (see 1.2.1).

2. **Internalized grammar:** This is the knowledge that speakers have in their brains (see 1.2.3).

3. **Descriptive grammar:** These are the grammatical systems designed by grammarians/linguists.

   a. **Descriptive grammars:** These are broad and very detailed descriptions of the phenomena in a given language often worded in fairly traditional terminology. They often include lengthy lists of exceptions to any rule that they propose.

   b. **Theoretical grammars:** These are highly technical, extremely advanced descriptions meant for the specialist, and they often focus on fragments of the language and do not even try to be comprehensive.

c. **Pedagogical grammars:** As the name implies, these are grammars used for the purpose of teaching students. As such they make no claims at comprehensiveness (as do descriptive grammars), and while they assume some theory of grammar, it is not their focus. Sadly, in an effort to simplify the subject matter for pedagogical purposes or given the necessity to use terminology and methodologies that teachers are familiar with, they often end up presenting a distorted and even erroneous view of the subject. A case in point is the still popular Reed-Kellogg diagramming system (see 18.3).

Normative grammars are not very useful for language pedagogy. However, they have very significant social prestige. So it may be important to the students, if not to the teacher, that they be exposed to them. Internalized grammars are obviously not accessible to either teachers or students and thus may be disregarded. Descriptive grammars are quite useful as they provide large amounts of data, although they can be overwhelming. Theoretical grammars are too advanced for classroom use but can be useful for the teacher.

18.2.2 Grammar Pedagogy

Whether it takes place for L1 or L2, language learning can take place at two different levels:

1. Formal

2. Informal

Formal language learning is focused on rules of language and is metalinguistic (i.e., it has language as its focus), while informal language learning is based on direct participation in speech and on implicit observation. A parallel distinction can be made between explicit and implicit knowledge. Explicit knowledge is knowledge about the system; implicit knowledge is the ability to use the system. An example may clarify things: most of you will know how to ride a bicycle; that is implicit knowledge. If you were asked to write a manual on how to ride a bicycle, that would be explicit knowledge, and you would find it enormously harder. For example, if you are falling to the left, in which direction should you turn the steering wheel? (The answer is to the left, incidentally).

The teaching of grammar is obviously a formal, explicit activity. The big question as far as the teaching of grammar goes is: is the teaching of grammar necessary, desirable, and if so, to what extent? To put it differently, does one *have* to teach grammar? And supposing that the answer is positive, how useful is it to teach grammar? We can consider this issue from the point of view of native speakers being taught to write and read in their language (L1) and that of native speakers of another language being taught a second language (L2).

L1 Speakers

There is very little work on the effect of teaching grammar on first language acquisition. Obviously, children learn their first language without any overt teaching of grammar. Several studies in the 1960s and 1970s showed that the teaching of grammar had no effect or even negative effects on children learning how to write. The possibility of a negative effect is due to the fact that one has to use time to teach grammar, which could be used to teach other subjects. In any case, no positive effects on writing of grammar teaching were reported.

Based on these results, a school of thought has emerged that advocates avoiding the teaching of grammar, declaring it nothing more than a waste of the students' time. A more moderate approach, which shares the negative outlook on the effect of grammar instruction, claims that the main problem of grammar instruction is that it is done in abstract and that if it is integrated with the actual writing of the students, it will produce more positive effects.

Recently, a different approach has been taken, mainly concerned with the fact that many students have nonstandard varieties of English in their writing and/or cannot master the basics of the written register of English. Since these students end up suffering in the marketplace and in the world at large, it is clear that remediation should be offered. However, since, as we saw before, teaching grammar has no positive effects, it seems that we are condemned to either let the students fail or advocate one-on-one tutoring (which is financially problematic). The way out of this dilemma is to identify the most damaging errors (either because they are stigmatized forms or because they affect understanding of the text) and to teach a subset of the grammar, designed to address specifically these errors. Some theorists (Noguchi, Weaver) claim that by using their native speakers' intuition, students need not know any grammatical metalanguage but may be taught transformation-like manipulations that will let them, for example, identify the subject of a sentence.

There are some flaws with these approaches:

- The studies were done using traditional grammar, which has been entirely discredited, and Chomskian generative grammar, which is vastly too abstract for teaching purposes. Hence, the conclusion that no teaching of grammar may help writing is unwarranted: the only conclusion that can be drawn from the available studies is that traditional grammar and generative-transformational grammar are inadequate factually or pedagogically, respectively. No one can say that a new approach to grammar would not prove beneficial (see, for example, cognitive grammar in 18.2.3).

- There is no evidence that a subset of English grammar is isolable, besides one that includes all the parts of speech and the types of clauses, which is a much larger set of phenomena that these theorists are willing to accept.

- These approaches work only for native speakers.

- With the exception of the observation about grammar in context, these approaches ignore the issue of motivation. Perhaps the biggest problem is that students (and often teachers) are afraid of grammar, which is often taught in boring and irrational ways (for example, if it confuses prescriptive and descriptive issues or if it uses traditional concepts).

L2 Speakers

The remaining discussion will be based on second language acquisition data. However, it stands to reason that one can extrapolate L2 data to L1 since we are ultimately dealing with the same cognitive structures.

Historically, for thousands of years, the teaching of grammar was, together with translation, the sole pedagogical tool for language teaching. It is only in this century that we have seen serious and concentrated effort against this pedagogical mode. In fact, a broad characterization of recent pedagogical thought would be that of moving away from formal teaching of grammar. The basic idea behind this move away from grammar is that children (L1 acquisition) outperform adults (L2 acquisition) by several orders of magnitude. The reason is that children are not taught formally, and they have access to LAD (language acquisition device). Thus, it makes sense to try to "reactivate" LAD in adults (see Chapter 13) and, consequently, not to teach grammar.

However, recent research has shown that L2 students who receive formal instruction in grammar outperform those students who have not received formal instruction. The second conclusion has been that, by and large, students who have been exposed to formal instruction and students who have not been exposed to formal instruction follow the same acquisition sequence in L2 and that formal instruction cannot change this sequence (interlanguage; see Chapter 13). A direct consequence of this finding is that a given grammatical structure may not be taught until the students are ready for it (i.e., their interlanguage has developed to that point). A further finding has been that, in some cases, the teaching of a given grammatical feature triggers other "implicated" structures that are presupposed by the feature. For example, teaching word order in English (subject, verb, object, etc.) allows students to know where to place relative clauses even if they have received no direct instruction in that particular rule. This triggering is called *projection.*

Besides these results, which clearly show that the teaching of grammar is useful although not necessary, there are other reasons why one would want to teach grammar. The main reason is **metalinguistic awareness.** Metalinguistic awareness is the explicit knowledge on the part of the speaker of how his or her language is organized. Metalinguistic awareness is useful because it provides the speaker with a tool to talk about his or her language. This gives the learner confidence and the possibility to make explicit generalizations that would be otherwise unavailable to him or her. It is also possible that metalinguistic awareness favors retention since it stands to reason that recall of a given notion is enhanced by having a "label" for it.

18.2.3 Cognitive Grammar

The approach known as **cognitive grammar** (CG) has flourished since the late '80s. Its main approach is semantic, and, although it has an elaborate formalism, the analyses proposed by CG are analyses based on meaning. CG differs from the traditional grammatical analyses based on meaning in that it is (a) clearly defined and (b) abstract enough so as not to fall in the trap of defining, say, *subject* as *a thing* or *person.*

CG takes its focus on semantics so far as to deny the existence of purely formal elements in grammar. In fact, CG considers only meaning-to-sound relationships. Traditional "grammatical" concepts, such as *direct object,* are handled as particularly abstract (schematic) meanings. CG posits that all grammatical concepts lie along a continuum ranging from the semantically very concrete (e.g., lexical items) to the semantically very abstract (morphology and syntax).

An area of great interest for CG is the domain of **conceptualization,** i.e., how people organize their perception of reality. Conceptualization includes categorization and the construal of events. Categorization is the abstraction from repeated experience of a given event of a common set of semantic features (cf. the concept of frame or script; see 3.2.2). By considering what all cats you've experienced have in common, you abstract the category of cat. An interesting aspect of categorization is that membership in a category is not a yes-or-no question but rather is based on the concept of **prototypicality.** A prototype is the "best example" of a category. To use a well-known example, a sparrow is a prototype bird, whereas a chicken is not (it is flightless, for starters). Nevertheless, a chicken is a bird. In other words, membership in a category is a matter of degree. Interestingly, grammatical categories are also organized prototypically: for example, a prototypical transitive verb would be *kick (John kicked the ball)*, while a less prototypical example would be *have something (John has a ball)*. Note how a prototypical transitive verb involves a physical action.

As far as construal goes, one can look at a house and a tree and see the house to the left of the tree or the tree to the right of the house. The thing focused on is called the trajector; the backgrounded one is the landmark; so in *Mary is in front of the main Tokyo train station, Mary* is the trajector, and the *main Tokyo train station* is the landmark.

Another very significant domain of conceptualization is the metaphorical construal of reality. A very significant part of our language is metaphorical. Metaphors are organized around schemas, such as *time is money;* consider *Don't waste my time!* or *Can you spare a minute?* (see 14.1.2 for more on CG and metaphors).

The strong points of CG are spatial relations and concepts. The CG analyses of the meanings of prepositions are justly famous (and have influenced mainstream treatments). Thus, in the preposition *to,* the trajector moves toward the landmark, while in *from* it moves away from it. Note that prepositions are taken to have basic spatial meanings that are then extended metaphorically to temporal and other abstract meanings.

CG starts by noting a first, very general, distinction between linguistic expressions that refer to *things* (think of objects) as opposed to *relationships* (think of connections between objects). Relationships are further subdivided into atemporal and temporal (aka processes). Nouns describe things, adjectives and adverbs atemporal relationships, and verbs processes. Things and processes can be further categorized according to the *bounded* feature. Something is said to be bounded if it has a clear boundary: thus a rock has a clear boundary, whereas flour doesn't. This distinction is known in traditional grammar as the count/mass opposition. Consider now the distinction between perfective and imperfective aspect in traditional grammar. It is completely unrelated to the mass/count distinction. However, CG can handle it simply by applying the bounded/unbounded feature distinction to processes: a bounded process is perfective, an unbounded one imperfective. This kind of elegant analysis gives clear insights and seems to offer great promise for the future of CG.

18.3 THE REED-KELLOGG DIAGRAMMING SYSTEM

The so-called Reed-Kellogg sentence diagramming system is an invention peculiar to the American educational system. It is virtually unknown outside of it. It was presented in 1877 by Alonzo Reed and Brainerd Kellogg, who were themselves adapting a similar system developed in 1851 by Stephen C. Clark. It has remained fairly popular, despite its obvious limitations.

18.3.1 The Diagramming System

The Reed-Kellogg (RK) system distinguishes between central elements in the sentence and peripheral ones. The central elements (subject, verb, complements) are placed on a horizontal line; the peripheral elements (modifiers, broadly intended) are placed under the element they modify. RK diagramming does not pay attention to the order of constituents, so a sentence such as *Yesterday I went to the store* and *I went to the store yesterday* would be diagrammed the same way.

The subject and the predicate of the sentence are divided by a vertical line that extends below the main line, as in the following example:

(18.3)   Mary | laughs

The modifiers of each element are placed below the main line:

(18.4)   boys | ate | pizza
                the   *the*   *free*

Embedded sentences are placed above the main line, on "stilts" (see example 18.5):

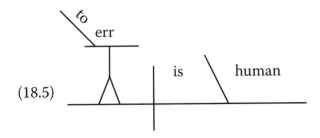

(18.5)

A detailed treatment of the RK diagramming system is unnecessary because we suggest using it with extreme caution in the classroom, if at all. Our skepticism is motivated by the following reasons:

- RK diagramming is, by admission of its very proponents, only a partial system. There are many types of constructions that simply cannot be diagrammed with it, although, of course, one can invent new conventions to handle this.

- RK diagramming deals inadequately with the linear order of constituents.

- RK diagramming deals inadequately with compound and complex sentences.

- RK diagramming is structurally unable to distinguish significant differences in certain syntactic constructions, which makes it useless for the analysis of those differences.

We will exemplify this last problem with a fairly simple example. Consider the sentences

(18.6) John is easy to please.

and

(18.7) John is eager to please.

RK diagramming would be as follows:

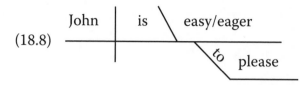

(18.8)

with both sentences having the same structure. This misses entirely the point that in (18.6) the person being pleased is John, while in (18.7) John is doing the pleasing. The existence of a difference can be easily seen by doing a clefting transformation on the sentences, which yields the following:

(18.9) It's easy to please John.

and the nonsensical

(18.10) *It's eager to please John.

The difference is instead clearly captured by the standard linguistic tree diagramming presented in this book (and elsewhere, of course). The word "someone" is introduced in parentheses to show that it is an implied argument not openly realized in the sentence:

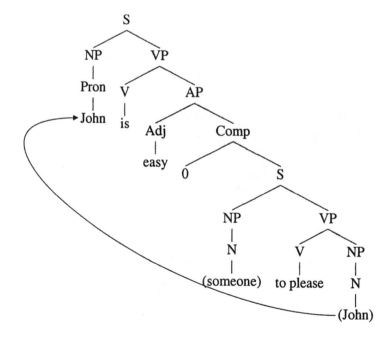

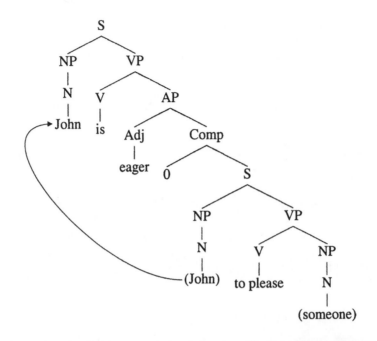

Educational Implications
As George Santayana said, "Those who cannot remember the past are condemned to repeat it." Knowledge of the methods of the past puts current practice into perspective.

18.4 EXERCISES

18.4.1 Words to Know

noun	verb	main verb
auxiliary verb	modal verb	infinitive
participles	gerund	active voice
passive voice	tense	mood
subjunctive mood	aspect	number
gender	case	adjective
adverb	pronoun	proverb
article	conjunction	preposition
particle	interjection	configurational
functional	case grammar	normative grammar
internalized grammar	theoretical grammar	descriptive grammar
metalinguistic awareness	cognitive grammar	conceptualization
categorization	construal	prototypicality
trajector	landmark	

18.4.2 Review

1. When was the grammatical terminology used in our schools invented?

2. How did the increase in travel affect the study of language in the Renaissance?

3. What is the difference between a configurational and a functional description?

4. What is a descriptive grammar?

5. Does the teaching of grammar improve one's writing in L1?

6. Does the teaching of grammar improve one's writing in L2?

18.4.3 Research Projects

1. Read some of the works that purport to show that grammar instruction is ineffective. Are these arguments convincing in your opinion?

2. Research a non-Western grammatical tradition, e.g., Arabic, Indian, Chinese, etc.

3. What are the limitations of using Greek grammar concepts to describe other languages?

18.5 FURTHER READINGS

There is no comprehensive history of grammatical thought. Robins's *Short History of Linguistics* (1997) is a valuable resource, as is the three-volume collection edited by Lepschy (1994). Kelly (1976) and Howatt (1984) survey the history of language teaching and raise many of the issues covered in this chapter. On pedagogical grammar, see the articles in Odlin (1994). Noguchi (1991) and Weaver (1996) are exponents of the "minimal grammar approach." One of the best studies purporting to show the lack of effect of grammar teaching is Elley et al. (1979). Braddock, Lloyd-Jones, and Schoer (1963) is the classical statement of that point. Weaver (1996, Chapter 2) has a survey of the evidence in that area. On cognitive grammar, there is an introduction targeted at students (Ungerer and Schmid 1996), but it is not for beginners. Langacker's work (1987, 1991a, 1991b) is technical but usually clear. The work on metaphors is very accessible: Lakoff and Johnson (1980) and Lakoff and Turner (1989) are good starting points. On CG analyses of prepositions, Vandeloise (1991) is excellent but the examples come from French; Brugman (1983) is a very influential early work but may be harder to find. A *Cognitive English Grammar* by Dirven and Radden is in the works but has yet to appear. Our primary source for Reed-Kellogg diagramming is Gleason (1965, especially Chapter 7). A grammar textbook that still uses Reed-Kellogg diagramming, despite all the evidence against it, is Kolln and Funk (1997).

Chapter 19

English Grammar

19.1 THE BASIC COMPONENTS OF SENTENCES

The two basic building blocks of language are nouns and verbs. When a given unit of language acts like a noun, we call it a nominal. Examples of nominals will be provided in this chapter. There are also other parts of speech, listed in Table 19.1.

Table 19.1: Parts of Speech

Part of speech	Example
Noun	*rock, house, Mary*
Verb	*kick, run, sleep*
Adjective	*pretty, tall, intelligent*
Adverb	*quickly, yesterday, suddenly*
Preposition	*up, down, on, off, over*
Conjunction	*and, but, yet, so, (either) ... or, (neither)... nor*
Article	*the, a, an*
Interjection	*ouch! wow!*

19.2 THE VERB

Verbs may appear in tensed and untensed form. Untensed forms are also called nominal, because the verb is no longer acting as such but is acting more like a noun or an adjective. A tensed form carries inflectional morphemes for tense and person. Tensed forms are called **finite.** Tensed forms include the present *(I sing),* the past *(I sang),* and the continuous form *(I am singing).* Nontensed forms are called **nonfinite** and include **infinitives** *(to go)* and **participles** *(going/gone).*

19.2.1 Types of Verbs

Tensed/Finite Forms

Grammars usually distinguish among three types of verbs:

- **main verbs:** Also known as *full verbs;* these verbs are tensed.

- **auxiliaries (aka helping verbs):** These verbs appear alongside a main verb in the bare infinitive form. The main auxiliaries are *to be, to do,* and *to have* (see Table 19.2). Within auxiliaries, we further distinguish semi-auxiliaries. This type of verb is introduced by either *have* or *be.* Examples include *be able to, be about to, be due to, be going to, be supposed to, have to, be likely to,* and *be bound to.*

- **modal verbs:** A small set of auxiliaries used primarily for distinctions of mood. Modals include the following: *can, may, shall, will, must, could, might, should, would.* It is important to note that *could, might, should,* and *would* are not the past tenses of *can, may, shall,* and *will.* Consider the following examples:

  (19.1) *Will* you open the window?

  (19.2) *Would* you open the window?

- marginal modal auxiliaries include *used to, ought to, dare,* and *need.*

- modal idioms: This category of verbs combines an auxiliary with an infinitive or adverb. It includes the following examples: *had better, would rather, have got to,* and *be to.*

Table 19.2: Forms of the Three Main Auxiliaries

Infinitive	to be	to have	to do
Present 1st person singular	*am*	*have*	*do*
Present 2nd person singular	*are*	*have*	*do*
Present 3rd person singular	*is*	*has*	*does*
Past 1st—3rd person singular	*was*	*had*	*did*
Past 1st—3rd person plural	*were*	*had*	*did*
Past participle	*been*	*had*	*done*

Untensed/Nonfinite forms

The following are the untensed, and hence nonfinite, forms of the verb.

- **Infinitive:** Identified as such because it is preceded by *to* as in *to sing*. Can also be found in the "bare" form, i.e., without the *to*. This is known as the *bare infinitive (e.g., John will sing)*.

- **Participle:** The participle may be defined as a verbal form that functions as an adjective. We distinguish two types of participles: past and present. Both are nonfinite forms, however.

  - **Present:** Aka the *-ing* form: e.g., *breaking, singing, loving*.

  - **Past:** Aka the *-ed* form: e.g., *broken, sung, loved*.

The fact that they are called past and present should not lead you to believe that they refer to past or present actions. Consider the following example

(19.3) I shall be released

in which the *past* participle is used to refer to the future!

- **Gerund:** A present participle in a nominal clause (i.e., which acts as an NP), e.g., *Watching TV is bad for you*. Note that the present participle in a non-nominal clause is not a gerund (e.g., *singing birds woke me up this morning*). Thus, the difference between a gerund and a participle is that a participle is a nonfinite form of a verb used as an adjective, while a gerund is a nonfinite form of a verb used as a noun.

19.2.2 Voice

English features both an active voice and a passive voice.

- Active—a "normal" sentence, e.g., *Mary loves John*.

- Passive—two requirements must be met in order for a sentence to be in the passive voice:

  1. passive always uses the auxiliary verb *to be*

  2. main verb must be in the past participle form

There may be an optional prepositional phrase starting with *by* identifying the agent. (The prepositional phrase may be missing.) Things are complicated by the existence of pseudo-passives, such as *As far as I am concerned...*, which have no corresponding active form. These sentences are not passives.

(19.4) My car was stolen.

This sentence features the passive, without an expressed agent, thus the missing prepositional phrase. Note that *was* is a form of *to be* + past, and *stolen* is a form of *steal* in the past participle.

Compare this to the following example:

(19.5) Someone stole my car.

This sentence is in the active and has an explicit agent.

The purpose of the passive is to shift emphasis from the subject to the direct object of the sentence. Consider the following example:

(19.6) Mary loves John.

Here, we are talking about Mary and the new information is that it is John that she loves. On the other hand, in

(19.7) John is loved by Mary

the emphasis is on John and the new information is that the person who loves him is Mary. This is very useful if, for some reason, one does not want to put emphasis on the agent of the action, which is normally represented by the subject of the active sentence.

19.2.3 TMA System

With the label **TMA,** we commonly indicate the tense, mood, and aspect of the verb.

Tense

The English verb tenses are present and past; there is no future. Instead, we use a modal verb to indicate future time (note the difference between future **time,** i.e., events in the future, and future **tense,** a grammatical category expressed morphologically, e.g., Latin *amabo* where the ending *-abo* indicates future time). For example,

(19.8) John walks. (present)

(19.9) John walked. (past)

(19.10) John will walk. (*will* = modal verb)

The function of tense is primarily to present temporal information, which is done through deictics, i.e., it serves to indicate when the action of the main verb takes place in relation to the time of speaking at which the utterance is produced. The past in this scheme is seen merely as whatever comes <u>before</u> *now*, and the future is obviously what takes place <u>after</u> *now*.

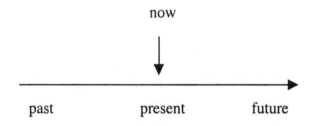

Table 19.3: Traditional Grammatical Terms for the Tenses of English

| Tense | Traditional name of the tense | Aspect | |
		simple	progressive/continuous
Present	simple present	*kicks*	*is kicking*
Past	simple past	*kicked*	*was kicking*
	present perfect	*has kicked*	*has been kicking*
	past perfect	*had kicked*	*had been kicking*
Future	simple future	*will kick*	*will be kicking*
	future perfect	*will have kicked*	*will have been kicking*

Simple Tenses

There are three basic (simple) tenses in English; they are the **present,** the **past,** and the **future.** See Table 19.3. (Recall that the "future" of traditional grammar is really a modal.) Simple tenses present only temporal information, with some exceptions. There are also complex tenses, which combine temporal and aspectual information and refer, for example, to an event that happens before a given event in the past or in the future.

We will examine those later, after we discuss aspect.

Simple present: *Mary sings in the choir.* (habitual event)

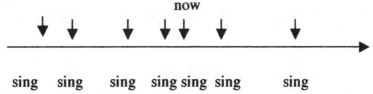

Note the repetition of the event, i.e., its habitual status, but also that crucially the event, the singing, takes place also in the present. Technically, habituality is an aspect, not a tense, but is treated here for simplicity. The present "tense" can in fact have several meanings in English, illustrated in Table 19.4:

Table 19.4: Meanings of the Present Tense Forms

Present	Mary sings right now.
Habit	Mary sings in the choir.
Future	I leave for France on Thursday.
Past	Dante writes the *Divine Comedy* in exile.

The use of the present to indicate a past event is called "historical present" and is not very frequent.

Simple past: *Mary sang in the choir.* (event in the past)

Simple future: *Mary will sing in the choir.* (event in the future)

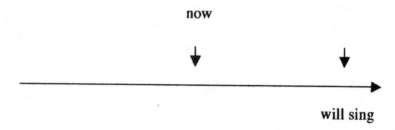

There are several ways of expressing future time in English, shown in Table 19.5:

Table 19.5: Ways of Expressing Future Time

Present tense	*I leave at six.*
Modal verb	*I will leave at six.*
Present continuous form	*I am leaving at six.*
"going to" (gonna)	*I am going to leave at six.*
Periphrastic forms	*I am planning to leave at six.*

Mood

Verbs have mood. **Mood** (aka **modality**) is a term used to describe the indication of whether the action of the verb is necessary, required, intended, possible, advisable, or not. The basic, unmarked modality is that of reality, which is called **indicative.** For example,

(19.11) John *should* love Mary.

Most of the information about modality in English is conveyed by auxiliaries such as the modal verbs discussed previously.

Many languages have moods, such as subjunctive or conditional. The **subjunctive mood** has virtually disappeared from English. It shows a distinction between real and unreal. In the example, *If I were you,* the suggestion is clearly unreal. The subjunctive survives primarily in fixed expressions, e.g., *be that as it may...*

Aspect

Aspect is concerned with the consideration of the verb in an overall perspective, which is not related to tense. Aspect determines:

- whether the action is happening once or a number of times
- whether the action is habitual

- whether the action is completed

- whether the action is beginning or ending

- whether the action is instantaneous or lasts for a period of time

Traditionally, English is analyzed as having two aspects, the perfect and the progressive. These may be marked for either present or past tense and thus may result in any of the following combinations (note that forms involving the future are dealt with in the complex tenses section on p. 350):

- present perfect *(has studied)*

- past perfect *(had studied)*

- present progressive *(is studying)*

- past progressive *(was studying)*

- present perfect progressive *(has been studying)*

- past perfect progressive *(had been studying)*

Perfect

Consider the following examples:

(19.12) Mary lived in Paris for ten years.

(19.13) Mary has lived in Paris for ten years.

In (19.12), Mary no longer lives in Paris, whereas in (19.13) she may still live there. (Let us note that this distinction is lost on many native speakers.)

Progressive

A very important aspectual distinction in English is whether the action lasts for an extended period of time or whether it is instantaneous. The progressive -*ing* form indicates that the action is ongoing either in relation to the time of speaking, i.e., the action has begun before the time of speaking, is ongoing, and will continue for a while after the time of speaking. For example,

(19.14) Mary sings/sang/will sing.

(19.15) Mary is singing/was singing/will be singing.

Complex Tenses

Complex tenses combine the expression of temporality (time) with that of aspectuality (aspect). For example,

(19.16) I had already had breakfast when John came.

In this example, the coming of John takes place before now (past). The having of breakfast takes place before John's coming (past perfect). Similarly, we can have the future in the past:

(19.17) I was going to tell her but I didn't

and the past in the future:

(19.18) I will have had breakfast by the time John comes later.

The following chart presents all the combinations used in English:

	Progressive	Perfect	Perfect Progressive
Present	is sleeping	has slept	has been sleeping
	now ↓ .... sleep	now .... sleep	now .... sleep
Past	was sleeping	had slept	had been sleeping
	now .... sleep	S A N / A = action prior to now / S = sleep	S A N / A = action prior to now (N) / S = sleep
Future	will be sleeping	will have slept	will have been sleeping
	now .... sleep	N S A / A = action posterior to now / S = sleep	N S A / A = action in the future / S = sleep N = now

19.2.4 Number

Every verb has number. **Number** is concerned with how many entities (people and the like) are "doing the action" described in the verb. In English, a verb is singular or plural. However, some languages, such as

Greek, feature a dual (two things). Every number, in turn, corresponds to a person.

- first person—the speaker
- second person—the hearer
- third person—neither the speaker nor the hearer (see 3.2)

19.3 THE NOUN

There are several distinctions made among types of **nouns** in English. Nouns are distinguished according to whether they are common or proper, count or noncount (mass), and concrete or abstract.

Proper nouns are those nouns that have unique reference. In other words, these nouns refer to specific locations *(Manhattan, The Vatican)*, people *(Woody Allen, Pope John Paul II)*, events *(The Academy Awards, Mardi Gras)*, objects *(the Hope Diamond, the Concorde)*, and institutions *(MIT)*.

Common nouns are those nouns that do not feature unique reference. This class might include such nouns as *city, writer, holiday, plane,* and *university.*

Count nouns are used to refer to items that can be counted or measured. Examples of count nouns include *poem* and *papaya.*

Noncount nouns (aka *mass nouns*) are the opposite of count nouns in that they refer to items that cannot be counted or measured. *Poetry* and *music* are examples of noncount nouns. Note how one cannot say **I like a poetry* or **Here are several musics.* It is important to note that there exist in English several nouns that can be identified as both count and noncount. *Pie* is an example of one such noun. A speaker might say *We ate pie for dessert* thus using *pie* as a noncount noun, or he or she might say *There is a pie in the refrigerator,* using the same noun in a countable way.

Concrete nouns are nouns that refer to items that are tangible or can be observed or accessed by the senses. Concrete nouns include *computer* and *flower.*

Abstract nouns refer to those items that are typically not accessible to the senses. Abstract nouns include *happiness* and *idea.*

19.3.1 Number

The grammatical term **number** refers to the requirement that all nouns be either *singular* or *plural.* Singular means that the noun refers to a quantity of one or to a specific proper noun such as *Prague.* Plural refers to a quantity of more than one, to a specific proper noun such as *the Alps,* or to individual items featuring what may be viewed as plural composition (e.g., *stockings, scissors*).

19.3.2 Gender

Nouns can be identified as having **gender**. In English, gender has three classes: feminine, masculine, and neuter.

(19.19) mother: feminine; father: masculine; apple: neuter

Natural and Grammatical Gender

An interesting issue around gender is that not all languages assign gender primarily on the basis of the gendered nature of referents, as is the case in English, where most nouns are feminine if the referent is female (e.g., *woman*), masculine if the referent is male (e.g., *rooster*), and neuter if the referent is not gendered (e.g., *door*). This way of assigning gender is called **natural gender.** However, even in English, there are some examples of nonnatural gender (i.e., **grammatical gender**): *cars, car engines,* and *ships* are often referred to as *she* even though they are not female.

In other languages, gender is assigned much more arbitrarily than from the point of view of sexual dymorphism (i.e., the fact that the male and the female of the species differ in form). In Italian and German, for example, we have plenty of cases of grammatical gender: *porta* (door) is feminine in Italian, as is *tavola* (table), while *soffitto* (ceiling) and *divano* (couch) are masculine; in German, *Mädchen* (young woman) is neuter!

19.3.3 Case

Commonly, grammars of English distinguish between two categories of **case:** common and genitive. The genitive case is also sometimes known as the *possessive.*

(19.20) *Mary* was late for the bus. (common)

(19. 21) *Mary's* bus was on time. (genitive)

The first sentence features an example of the noun, *Mary,* with common case. The second is an example of the same noun marked for the possessive with an *'s.*

There are other cases as well (cf. 18.1.5) (see Table 19.6). Speakers distinguish between the case of the subject and the case of the direct object. This is visible only in the pronouns. For example,

(19.22) *I* am hungry. (subject)

Mary loves *me.* (direct object)

The syntactic role of subject is shown in the pronoun *I* and that of direct object in the pronoun *me.* Usually cases are known by their Latin names, nominative and accusative, respectively.

Other languages, and English itself when it was Old English (see 17.2), have other cases, such as the dative, which indicates the recipient or target of an action; the instrumental which indicates the instrument or tool used to perform an action; the locative, which indicates the position of things; and many others. Finnish, for example, has 16 cases!

Table 19.6: Cases in English Grammar

Traditional name	Latin name	Example (bolded)
Subject	Nominative	**I** am Popeye.
Direct object	Accusative	I love **spinach.**
Indirect object	Dative	I gave **him** a book.
Common	Nominative + accusative	**I** am **Popeye.**
Possessive	Genitive	**Bob's** bike is a Harley.

19.4 MINOR PARTS OF SPEECH

By "minor," we don't mean "unimportant." All parts of speech are important. However, one can have sentences that are just made up of a noun and a verb (e.g., *Tom runs*) but not one that is made of, say, an adjective, a preposition, and a conjunction.

19.4.1 Modifiers

There are two types of **modifiers:**

- Adjectives—modify noun phrases.
- Adverbs—modify verbs and adjectives.

Adjectives

Adjectives can be used either attributively or predicatively:

- Attributive adjectives occur as premodifiers to the noun, as in the following examples: the *yellow* carpet, *strong* coffee.
- Predicative adjectives are used with verbs like *be, seem,* and *appear:* This coffee is *strong.*

Some adjectives may occur in the comparative or superlative degree:

- Comparative adjectives are used to illustrate comparison of objects and are usually marked by the addition of the suffix -er or by the use of the premodifier *more*: *wider* roads, *more* artistic.

- Superlative adjectives are used to describe the highest level that can be achieved and are marked by the suffix -est or by the use of the premodifier *most*: *tallest* building, *most creative.*

Those adjectives that occur in the comparative and superlative are called gradable adjectives (i.e., adjectives that indicate a property or quality that can occur in different quantities). Nongradable adjectives cannot occur in the comparative or superlative, e.g. Italian, as in *I am an Italian linguist* (*Italianer, *Italianest).

Adverbs

Adverbs are modifiers. They may modify sentences and phrases, adjectives, or other adverbs.

(19.23) *Hopefully,* no one will complain about this sentence.

(19.24) The *very* intelligent girl was praised by the teacher.

(19.25) Mary studied grammar *very* successfully.

There are three types of adverbs:

- derivational, which are formed by the addition of the suffix -ly to an adjective: *quick quickly, shrewd shrewdly*

- simple, which do not add a morpheme: *well, only, back, under, here,* etc.

- compound, which are made of more than one morpheme but do not add a derivational morpheme: *somehow, somewhere, somewhat, therefore,* etc.

19.4.2 Pro-forms

Pronouns

A **pronoun** operates like a noun and can replace the noun in sentences. In the following example, *He* replaces the determiner and noun, *The boy.*

(19.26) The boy walked in the room. *He* picked up a toy.

Pronouns differ between the case of the subject and the case of the direct object. A list of all the cases of pronouns is provided in Table 19.7.

Table 19.7: Cases in the Pronouns

Person	Number	Subject	Object	Possessive Pron.	Possessive Det./Adj.
1st		I	me	mine	my
2nd		you	you	yours	your
3rd	sing.	he	him	his	his
		she	her	hers	her
		it	it	its	its
1st		we	us	ours	our
2nd	plur.	you	you	yours	your
3rd		they	them	theirs	their

Note how the object case can work both for direct and indirect objects. Note also that the possessive pronouns occur by themselves, i.e., they are full-blown nominals, whereas the possessive determiners, better known as possessive adjectives, occur in determiner position (hence their name) in noun phrases (NPs), i.e., before a nominal (and hence are not pronouns).

Proverbs

A **proverb** replaces a verb. The term should not be confused with the other meaning of the word proverb, which is that of a popular saying. In the following example, *did* replaces the verb *bought*.

(19.27) Mary bought a house and so *did* John.

19.4.3 Determiners

Three classes of **determiners** can be distinguished in English:

- Central determiners of which the most common are the **articles:** *the, a/an,* zero

  - *the*—determinative in that it refers specifically to things of which the speaker has prior knowledge

  - *a/an*—indeterminative in that it refers to any member of a certain group

- zero—general as it refers to an entire group generically

  (19.28) **Lions** live in the jungle.

- Predeterminers precede central determiners and tend to mark quantity. They include examples such as *half, all,* and *both* (as in *half a bottle of wine*) and what are referred to as multipliers such as *once, twice, three times* (as in *twice the size*).

- Postdeterminers include *first, last, five,* and *many;* they follow central determiners as in the following examples: *the first chapter, the many students.*

19.4.4 Conjunctions

Conjunctions connect sentences or components (i.e., parts) of sentences to make complex sentences. The simplest case is that of conjoining two independent sentences that could stand alone as they are:

(19.29) Mary went to the store *but* Bob stayed home.

The case of conjoining two components is a little more complex. Consider the following:

(19.30) Mary went to the store and to the library.

which can be analyzed as the conjunction *and* joining two prepositional phrases (PPs) *(to the store and to the library)* or as ellipsis (i.e., the deletion of recoverable information), i.e., *Mary went to the store* and *(Mary went) to the library.*

Common conjunctions include *and, or, but,* and *if/then.* Consider the following examples:

- *And*

  - may be used to show union or addition
    (19.31) Mary *and* John came to dinner.

  - may be used to show sequence of events
    (19.32) John woke up *and* took a shower.

  - may be used to show consequence
    (19.33) The child touched the stove *and* burned his hand.

- *But*—may be used to show contrast
  (19.34) Mary didn't study, *but* she passed the exam.

- *Or*—may be used to show exclusivity
  (19.35) You may choose the essay *or* the multiple-choice questions for the final exam.

- *If/then*—may be used to show dependency
  (19.36*) If* you throw a ball in the house, *then* something will be broken.

19.4.5 Prepositions

Prepositions precede NPs and taken together with them create PPs. Prepositions may indicate spatial relationships such as position/direction, e.g., *to, at;* relative position, e.g., *behind, below;* and passage, e.g., *through, across.* They may also be used to refer to temporal relationships such as position in time, e.g., *in, at,* and duration, e.g., *for, throughout.* Other meanings may be conveyed via the use of prepositional phrases, including causes, e.g., *because of, from,* and accompaniment, e.g., *with, without.* See Table 19.8.

Table 19.8: List of Most Common Prepositions

about	above	across	after	against
along	among	around	as	at
barring	before	behind	below	beside
between	beyond	by	concerning	considering
down	during	excepting	excluding	following
for	from	given	going on	in
including	inside	into	less	like
minus	near	of	off	on
onto	opposite	out	out of	outside
over	past	pending	per	plus
regarding	save	through	till	times
to	toward	under	underneath	unlike
until	up	up to	upon	via
vis-a-vis	with	within	without	

19.4.6 Interjections

Interjections don't belong in sentences. They make up sentences of their own. Consider the following examples, each of which would be used alone to form a complete sentence:

(19.37) Wow! Ouch! Oh! Hello! Cowabunga!

19.4.7 Particles

Particles are parts of speech that do not quite belong with any other part of speech, so they are a sort of catch-all category. In English usually we use the word particle to indicate the following (the particles are bolded):

- the second element of a phrasal verb, e.g., put **up,** stand **by,** get **on,** put **off,** get **away with**

- the "to" that marks the infinitive, e.g., **to** go, **to** be, **to** run

- the word "not," as in *Grammar is **not** that hard.*

19.5 PHRASE-LEVEL GRAMMAR

19.5.1 Noun Phrases

The basic structure of the NP in English is as follows:

pre det.	central det.	post det.	pre mod.	mod.	**noun**	post mod.
all	the	many	very	tall	boys	outside

This NP is somewhat of a freak in that all its modifier (mod.) and determiner (det.) slots are filled; most of the time only a few, if any, are. Besides the determiners discussed in 19.4.3 and the modifiers discussed in 19.4.1, it should be noted that PPs and relative clauses may act as modifiers (see 19.5.3):

(19.38) The woman *with the college degree*

(19.39) The woman *who received the Nobel Prize*

19.5.2 Verb Phrases

The basic structure of the verb phrase (VP) in English is as follows:

aux 1	aux 2	aux 3	aux 4	**verb**
modal	*have*	progressive *be* + *-ing*	passive *be* + part.	V

Modals have been discussed in 19.2.1 and in 19.2.3. The *have* is the perfective marker (see 19.2.3), i.e., the element of the VP that indicates that the verb is in the perfect aspect. The first *be* is the form of *be* associated with the continuous aspect (see 19.2.3), while the second one is associated with the passive voice (see 19.2.2). An example of VP with all the slots filled (a very rare case) might be *might have been being helped,* in which *been being* is Amp 3.

19.5.3 Other Phrasal Constituents

The following sections review other types of phrases.

Adjectival Phrase

The basic structure of the adjectival phrase (AdjP) is the following:

pre mod.	**adjective**	post mod.	complement
very	satisfied	indeed	about her work

There are only two postmodifiers for adjectives: *indeed* and *enough* (both are adverbs). Complements may be a PP (see 19.5.3) or a subordinate clause (see 19.6.1).

Adverbial Phrase

The structure of the adverbial phrase (AdvP) is essentially the same of the AdjP:

pre mod.	**adverb**	post mod.	complement
quite	surprisingly	indeed	for her

(as in *Quite surprisingly indeed for her, Mary had not been given a raise that year.*)

Prepositional Phrase

The structure of the PP is different, as it consists of only two elements:

preposition	complement
for	your love

The complement may consist of:

an NP, e.g., for *the boy*

a relative clause, e.g., from *what has transpired*

an -*ing* clause, e.g., after *studying linguistics*

19.6 SENTENCE-LEVEL GRAMMAR

As you will recall from our discussion of syntax (see 2.4.2), sentences are minimally formed by joining an NP and a VP. Each of these constituents may have various modifiers. Traditionally, grammarians distinguish four types of sentences:

1. declaratives: statements

2. interrogatives: questions

3. imperatives: orders

4. exclamatives: expressions of feelings

19.6.1 Complex Sentences

We turn now to cases in which there is more than one sentence. There are two possible configurations: the second sentence may be either a coordinate or a subordinate.

Coordinate Clauses

We discussed coordinate clauses in section 2.5. In a coordination situation, the two clauses are at the same level. Coordinating conjunctions include: *and, or, but, both ... and, (n)either ... nor, not only... but also.*

Subordinate Clauses

We discussed subordinate clauses in section 2.5. In a subordination situation, one of the two clauses is at a higher level (main clause), while the other is at a lower level (subordinate clause). Subordinating conjunctions include: *if ... (then), although, where, while, as, since, because, before, after,* etc.

> How can you distinguish a subordinating conjunction (such as *before*) from a preposition? A subordinating conjunction introduces a finite clause (sentence), while a preposition introduces a phrase (NP, a relative clause, or an -ing clause) (cf. 19.5.3).

Types of Subordinate Clauses

There are three kinds of subordinate clauses:

- **Finite:** Mary knows linguistics is the most interesting subject.
- **Nonfinite:** *Barely missing the house,* the plane landed in the field.
- **Verbless:** *However confident in her work,* the neurosurgeon checked it one more time.

Relative Clauses

Relative clauses (aka adjective clauses) are, in their prototypical form, subordinate clauses that modify a nominal. Relative clauses are introduced by a relative pronoun.

The following are all the relative pronouns of English (those in parentheses are not accepted by all grammarians): *who, whom, whose, which, that, (when, where, why). Who, whom,* and *whose* differ only in case, as can be seen in Table (19.9).

Table 19.9: Cases of the Relative Pronouns (Note: the modified NP is italicized, and the relative pronoun, bolded).

who	subject	*The girl who did this is very smart.*
whom	direct object	*I will marry the girl whom I met at the ball.*
whose	possessive	*I will marry the girl whose shoe I found.*

The well-known usage problems tied to the use of *who, whom,* and *whose* are in fact trivial: *whom* is used when the pronoun is in the direct object case, and *whose* when it is in the possessive case. However, current usage accepts the use of *who* in place of *whom*, which is no longer used in informal speech.

Gender is also indicated by choice of the pronouns: *which* is marked for gender; it modifies neuter referents. *That* is used both for humans and objects, and *who(m)* only for humans (and animals).

The relative pronoun may be omitted if it modifies a noun in object case but not if it modifies a noun in subject case. Thus, we can say *I will marry the girl I met at the ball* (with the relative pronoun *whom* omitted), but not **The girl did this is very smart.* If the pronoun is omitted, grammarians refer to it as a "zero pronoun" and it is indicated by a 0.

The basic structure of a relative clause can be diagrammed as follows:

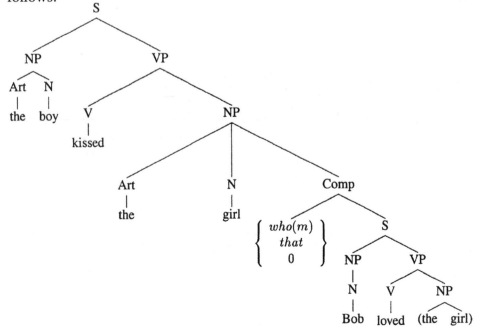

Note how the embedded clause *Bob loved the girl* is "transformed" by the relativization: the direct object moves in comp position and is replaced by the relative pronoun.

There exist other forms of relative clauses. We can distinguish three kinds:

1. supplementary relative (aka non-restrictive)

2. cleft relative

3. fused relative

which are exemplified in the following examples:

(19.40) My mother, who speaks five languages, loves chocolate.

(19.41) It was Mary who was elected treasurer of the club.

(19.42) What is written in this book is all wrong!

(Non-)Restrictive Relative Clauses

Traditional grammars distinguish between **restrictive** and **non-restrictive** relative clauses. A restrictive clause helps identify the referent of the relative clause, whereas a non-restructive one doesn't. Thus, in example (19.40), I obviously have only one mother, and therefore the fact that she loves chocolate does not contribute to identifying her. Conversely, in

(19.43) The girl who did this is very smart.

the presence of the relative clause tells the hearer which of the potentially many girls we are talking about. This is important because restrictive and nonrestrictive clauses are punctuated differently: nonrestrictive clauses are set apart by commas (cf. example 19.40), whereas restrictive ones are not.

Cleft Relative Clauses

Clefting is a process used to emphasize a part of a sentence. It is discussed more fully in (19.6.2). Example (19.41) is an example of cleft relative clause.

Fused Relative Clauses

Fused relatives are relative clauses in which the referent of the relative clause and the relative pronoun are one and the same, as in example (19.42) and in the following examples:

(19.44) a. I enjoyed *what* she said.

b. I go *where* he goes.

c. I'll do *whatever* it takes.

The fused elements are italicized. Note how *what*, in (19.44a), stands for *I enjoyed X* and *She said X*.

19.6.2 Marked Sentential Patterns

The following types of sentences are marked, in the sense that they differ from the more common arrangement of sentences in English and therefore attract attention to parts of the sentence. They are often used for emphasis.

There Sentences

In a sentence of the type

(19.45) There are things a student should know about language.

the subject is postponed. Compare the non-transformed sentence, in which the subject NP has been italicized:

(19.46) *A student* should know (some) things about language.

This has the effect of attracting attention onto the subject itself and on the direct object.

Clefts

Clefts consist in taking the subject of a sentence and putting it between *it + be ... who/that* as in

(19.47) It's Mary who won the race.

The so-called pseudocleft sentences put the emphasis on the second part of the sentence:

(19.48) What I need is a miracle.

It Extraction

Certain kinds of clauses are awkward as the subject of a sentence:

(19.49) *That Marie Curie discovered radium* was well known.

To avoid that, an *it* is inserted in subject position, and the subject (italicized) is postponed:

(19.50) It was well known *that Marie Curie discovered radium.*

Educational Implications
This chapter has given teachers the background knowledge necessary to teach grammar and the language arts.

19.7 EXERCISES

19.7.1 Review

1. What words are mistakenly given as the past tense forms of *can, may, shall,* and *will?*

2. What is the difference between a participle and a gerund?

3. What two requirements must be met for a sentence to be in the passive voice?

4. English verbs have only two tenses, past and present. How do English speakers indicate the future?

5. What is the difference between present perfect and present progressive?

6. Both verbs and nouns have number. What does number mean when applied to each of these categories?

7. In the following sentence, underline the attributive adjective(s) and circle the predicative adjective(s):

   The sleepy woman groped for her cup of strong coffee.

8. What is the difference between the articles *the, a/an,* and zero?

19.7.2 Research Project

Write the number of the definition that most closely matches each grammatical term in the chart that follows.

Definitions:

1. The voice of a "normal" sentence arranged in subject-verb-object order.

2. A closed class of words that may indicate spatial relationships, relative position, temporal relationships, as well as cause and accompaniment.

3. A present participle in a nominal clause.

4. A sentence that uses the auxiliary form *to be* and presents the main verb in the past participle form.

5. A small set of auxiliaries used primarily for distinctions of mood.

6. Adverbs that are formed by the addition of the *-ly* suffix to an adjective.

7. Central determiners, predeterminers, and postdeterminers.

8. Complement the subject of the sentence.

9. Describe the highest level that can be achieved.

10. Follow central determiners.

11. Full verbs that carry inflectional morphemes for person and tense (present, past, and continuous forms).

12. Helping verbs that appear in the bare infinitive form alongside a main verb.

13. Illustrate comparison of objects.

14. Indicates at what time the action took place in relation to "now."

15. Indicates whether the verb is beginning, ending, or continuing.

16. It shows a distinction between real and unreal.

17. Masculine, feminine, or neuter.

18. May be used to lengthen a sentence; show union or sequence of events; or show consequence, contrast, exclusivity, or dependency.

19. Modify noun phrases.

20. Modify verbs and adjectives.

21. Nontensed forms of verbs.

22. Noun gender that equates with biological categories of sexuality.

23. Nouns that do not feature unique reference; general terms that include any of a group.

24. Nouns that have unique reference; in other words, those which refer to specific locations, people, events, objects, institutions, etc.

25. Occur as premodifiers to nouns.

26. Operate like nouns and can replace nouns in sentences.

27. Precede central determiners and tend to mark quantity.

28. Is used in nouns to convey presence of possession (in the genitive form) or absence of possession (in the common form).

29. Single words that are not part of sentences and make up exclamatory sentences of their own.

30. Tensed forms of verbs.

31. The indication of whether the action of the verb is necessary, required, intended, possible, advisable, or real.

32. The requirement that all nouns be either singular or plural.

33. *The, a/an,* and zero.

34. Two types: adjectives and adverbs.

35. Two types: past and present, but they are used to alter the past in relation to the time of the utterance rather than to define the present.

36. Who is doing the action: first person, second person, third person.

37. Replaces a verb in a sentence.

38. Refer to tangible items that can be observed by the senses.

39. Refer to items that can be counted or measured.

40. Refer to items that cannot be counted or measured.

41. Refer to items that cannot be accessed by the senses.

42. Non-tensed form of verbs that are frequently preceded by *to;* the "bare" form stands alone.

abstract nouns	active
adjectives	adverbs
articles	aspect
attributive adjectives	auxiliaries
case	central determiner articles
common nouns	comparative adjectives
concrete nouns	conjunctions
count nouns	derivational
finite verbs	gender
gerund	infinitives
main verbs	modal verbs
modifiers	mood
natural gender	nonfinite verbs
noncount nouns	number (noun)
number (verb)	participles
particles and interjections	passive
postdeterminer articles	predeterminer articles
predicative adjectives	prepositions
pronouns	proper nouns
proverbs	subjunctive mood
superlative adjectives	tense

19.8 FURTHER READINGS

The standard modern reference grammar is Quirk et al. (1973, 1985) condensed, in Quirk and Greenbaum (1973) and Greenbaum and Quirk (1990). Greenbaum (1989) is very clear and directed at students. Celce-Murcia and Larsen-Freeman (1999) is geared toward ESL teachers. Close (1975) is a pedagogical grammar for ESL. Jespersen (1928), in seven volumes, is of historical interest. Biber et al. (1999) is based on a corpus and has register information. Haegeman and Guéron (1999) is based on generative syntax; it is not for beginners. Leech and Svartvik (1975) takes a more communication-oriented approach. Hurford (1994) is a useful reference (but not a comprehensive one).

19.9 ANSWERS TO RESEARCH PROJECT

Matching definitions and grammatical terms:

41.	abstract nouns	1.	active
19.	adjectives	20.	adverbs
7.	articles	15.	aspect
25.	attributive adjectives	12.	auxiliaries
28.	case	33.	central determiner articles
23.	common nouns	13.	comparative adjectives
38.	concrete nouns	18.	conjunctions
39.	count nouns	6.	derivational
30.	finite verbs	17.	gender
3.	gerund	42.	infinitives
11.	main verbs	5.	modal verbs
34.	modifiers	31.	mood
22.	natural gender	21.	non-finite verbs
40.	noncount nouns	32.	number (noun)
36.	number (verb)	14.	participles
29.	particles and interjections	4.	passive
10.	postdeterminer articles	27.	predeterminer articles
8.	predicative adjectives	2.	prepositions
26.	pronouns	24.	proper nouns
37.	proverbs	16.	subjunctive mood
9.	superlative adjectives	35.	tense

Glossary

Cross-references within the glossary are indicated by the symbol (→) following the cross-referenced word, except when used as a note, as in (→ deixis). Different senses of the same word are distinguished by numbers. Antonyms (→) are indicated by the symbol ↔, as in *happy* ↔ *sad*.

∀ A quantifier meaning *for all*.

∃ A quantifier meaning *there exists*.

AAVE. African-American Vernacular English (→ Black English).

Ablaut. The systematic variation of the stem vowel, also called vowel gradation, found especially in strong verbs (→) in a number of Indo-European languages. There are three grades that indicate present, past, and past participle in English such as in *sing, sang, sung*.

Accent. (1) A change in pronunciation in dialectal variation. (2) A synonym for stress (→).

Accent continuum. The degree of variation from standard pronunciation to the most regional accent.

Accommodation theory. A theory whereby a person will conform to the way of speaking of his or her conversational partner.

Acrolect. The most prestigious variety of a dialect (→). Speakers use this to sound sophisticated or in formal situations.

Acronym. A type of word formation in which new words are created by using initials, for example, *NASA*.

Active voice. One of the two voices in English; it puts the emphasis of the sentence on the subject (→ voice, passive voice).

Address form. A linguistic item used to indicate to which speaker an utterance is directed or to attract his or her attention. Forms of address include pronouns, titles (e.g., *Doctor*), names, nicknames, and other specialized forms (e.g., *honey, dear, buddy, sister,* etc.). Forms of address usually indicate familiarity or formality but may also indicate relative age, social status, gender, etc.

Adjacency pair. Two utterances (→) linked together by the fact that the first requires the second one.

Adjective. A modifier of a noun (→), for example, *brilliant* as in *brilliant definition* or *interesting* as in *very interesting lecture*. In English, adjectives precede the noun within a noun phrase (→).

Admixture (language mixing).

Adverb. A modifier of an adjective (→), verb (→), or sentence (→).

Affective connotation. Those aspects of connotative meaning (→) that are influenced by speakers' attitudes and feelings toward the referent (→).

Affix. Bound morpheme (→) classified according to position. Before the root called prefix (→); after the root, suffix (→); root internal, infixes (→).

Affricate. The sound made when air pressure behind a complete closure (stop [→]) is released as a fricative (→).

Age-grading. The fact that speakers change their linguistic habits according to their age. Five-year-olds speak very differently than 10-year-olds, and 40-year-olds speak differently than 70-year-olds. Younger speakers tend to use more slang, for example.

Agglutinative language. In agglutinative languages, morphemes (→) are added to the root (→) of a word, but both keep their original identities.

Airstream. The flow of air in or out of the lungs. Most speech sounds are produced by the airstream.

Allegory. The extended use of a symbol, possibly throughout an entire work.

Alliteration. A poetic device that relies on the repetition of consonants (→). Repetition of consonantal sounds at the beginning of words is known as alliteration; at the end of words, it is known as consonance (→).

Allomorph. The various forms that a morpheme (→) may take. For example, the voiceless *-s* in *caps*, the voiced *-z* in *toys*, and the "irregular" form of *mice* are all allomorphs of the plural morpheme (→).

Allophone. Every way a phoneme (→) can be produced. For example, the phoneme /t/ is usually articulated in an alveolar (→) position as in *eight*, but it can also occur in the dental (→) position as in *eighth*, where it is influenced by the following interdental (→) sound. (→ phone)

Allusion. References to other, usually well-known, texts or events that the speaker does not have to repeat in detail but can refer to implicitly (→ intertextuality, citation).

Alphabetic system. System of writing based on the correspondence between symbols and sounds (as opposed to syllabic systems [→] and logographic systems [→]).

Amalgamation. The process of selecting the compatible meanings of the morphemes (→) in a sentence to arrive at a meaningful interpretation of its sense in Katz and Fodor's model of interpretive semantics (→).

Ambiguity. The property of having more than one meaning.

Analogy. In historical linguistics, the process by which an irregular pattern gets regularized in accordance with the majority pattern, for example, the OE past of *help* is *healp*, which got changed to Modern *helped* (→ past tense). Analogy also applies to elements that are seemingly identical and are thus assigned the same process, for example, in language acquisition (→), where children use the regular plural formation in addition to or instead of the irregular pattern, for example, *mices* or *mouses*.

Anapest. In poetry, a metric foot consisting of two unstressed syllables followed by a stressed syllable (for example, inter'vene).

Anaphor. A pronoun (→) or word in a sentence in place of or in reference to another phrase (→).

Anomia. A feature of aphasia (→), the inability to name things or use nouns.

Antecedent. The unit in a text that is referred to by an anaphor (→) in the text.

Antonyms. Two words with opposite meanings, e.g., *good* and *bad*.

Aphasia. The partial or total loss of language due to damage to the brain. Common forms are dyslexia (→), also called alexia, dysgraphia (→), also agraphia, and anomia (→).

Apology. The expressive speech act (→) used when the speaker feels he or she has hurt the other person and needs to make amends.

Arbitrariness of the linguistic sign. The idea that the connection between the signifier (sequence of sounds) and signified (meaning) of a sign is arbitrary, conventional, without reason.

Archaism. The term used for an old word that has almost gone out of usage through the evolution of the language.

Argot. (French) A restricted language, similar to slang (→), originally used by thieves in the Middle Ages; by extension, a form of slang.

Argument. The entity to which a predicate (→) applies. Each predicate may have one, several, or no arguments.

Article. A class of determiners that marks nouns as either definite, as in *the bird*, or indefinite, as in *a bird.*

Articulation. How sounds are produced by the body's phonatory organs (→), specifically, how the airstream (→) and the voicing (→) or lack thereof are affected by the position of the tongue, lips, teeth, etc.

Aspect. Parts of the semantics of the verb (→) used to describe the duration of the action, its beginning or ending, or its completion. (→ TMA)

Aspirated. A feature in phonetics (→) used to describe the slight puff of air that can be heard in the pronunciation of some sounds, for example, /pʰit/ as in *pit.*

Assimilation. Two sounds articulated (→) closer in the mouth so that they become similar or identical, for example, the bilabial nasal [m] in [tembatls] as in *ten bottles*, which is assimilated to the bilabial plosive [b].

Assonance. A poetic device that relies on the repetition of vowel sounds.

Attitude. In language learning theory, the way in which the learners and their associates approach the task or language learning or even the language or its speakers. Attitude is part of the overall motivation of the student.

Autobiography. A life narrative written by the subject. Autobiographies may be fictive, in which case an author pretends to be writing someone's autobiography.

Autonomy. Existing alone, apart from a larger entity. An autonomous language can exist by itself rather than as a dialect of another language.

Auxiliary. In grammar (→), verbs that "help" the main verb of the sentence, in the sense that they specify its modality (→ mood), tense (→), or aspect (→).

Auxiliary language. A language that has been taken on by other speech communities than those in which it is a native language (→) for the purpose of communication, commerce, or education. (→ language of wider communication, lingua franca, pidgin)

Babbling. Early attempts at communication by children, typically consisting of single vowels or consonants or consonant-vowel combinations.

Backchannel behavior. A type of feedback used in conversation to indicate whether the listener understands, is interested, bored, etc.

Backformation. A word formation technique in which new words are created unconsciously by speakers when they no longer recognize a word's morphemes (→), breaking it down according to perceived or imagined similarity to other words, for example, *burger* from *ham-burger.*

Balanced bilingualism. A type of bilingualism in which the speaker is equally at ease in either language in all domains. (→ bilingual, dominant language)

Basic color term. A set of terms describing basic hues of color, including *black, white,* also *red,* but not *cyan, purple,* or *mauve.*

Basic English. A simplified variant of English with a restricted vocabulary (→) of 850 words, invented by C. K. Ogden and I. A. Richards, intended for international communication and used for the definitions of lexica.

Basilect. The least prestigious form of a dialect (→). This is used when the speakers are speaking in casual situations. (→ mesolect, acrolect)

Behaviorism. A current in scientific thought, now largely discredited, that identifies as the only object of science the study of observable behavior and denies the existence of the mind. It is based on the stimulus-response paradigm and maintains that learning is a purely mechanical matter of reinforcement.

Bidialectalism. The practice of using and being fluent in more than dialect. (→ bilingualism)

Bilingual. Being able to speak two different languages. Also, the ability to read and write two languages. (→ balanced bilingualism, dominant language)

Binary feature. A yes/no feature, for example, male/female. Binary features are marked using +/- signs, corresponding to *yes* and *no,* respectively, for example, [+female], which is equivalent to [-male].

Bioprogram. The theory that ties the origins of pidgins and creoles to the innate universal grammar [→] genetically present in each speaker.

Black English. A variety of American English with strong influences from the pidgin (→) spoken by African slaves in the United States. (→ AAVE)

Blend. A word formation technique of linking two words together and deleting one or more sounds to create new words, for example, *brunch (breakfast + lunch).*

Borrowing. A way to expand a language that involves taking a word or phrase from one language and incorporating it into another.

Bottom-up process. A way of analyzing text that involves processing the sounds, words, or sentences in order to understand the text as a whole. ↩ top-down.

Bound morpheme. The smallest unit in a language with meaning, incapable of standing on its own because it has no independent meaning. An example is the /-s/ morpheme (→), which is used to indicate plurality (aka affixes [→] because it needs to attach to other morphemes).

Brainstorming. Unscrutinized gathering of ideas as a preliminary process to writing, problem solving, etc. (→ mind maps)

Branch. A part of a tree diagram referring to a node (→) and all the nodes that lie below it in the tree.

Bundle of isoglosses. A group of isoglosses (→) forming a dialect boundary.

Calque. A type of direct borrowing (→) from a language where the borrowed word or phrase is translated into the receiving language's literal equivalent, for example, German *Fern-sprecher* from English *tele-phone.*

Camouflage. The fact that certain expressions in AAVE (→) are camouflaged as, i.e., are identical on the surface to expressions of Standard American English (SAE) but different in meaning. For example, the habitual *be* forms in AAVE, as in *This teacher's midterm be easy,* meaning that the midterms are usually easy, which contrast to the *be* forms of the present perfect in SAE, where they could only be used for a subjunctive, as in *This teacher's midterm better be easy or else I'll flunk.*

Caregiver speech. → child-directed speech.

Caretaker speech. → child-directed speech.

Case. Part of the grammar of noun phrases that identifies the grammatical relationships within the sentence. In some languages, case is marked by special endings (Latin, German), while in English case is only apparent in the alternation between subject/direct object pronouns, for example, *I/me.*

Case grammar. In case grammar, the sentence revolves around the verb and the nouns are the verb's arguments. (→ case, grammar, descriptive grammar, theoretical grammar)

Caste. Group of people sharing the same economic and social standing. Unlike for class (→), caste membership is by birth.

Casual language. A distinction made by the Russian formalist movement, it is the regular, everyday use of language for nonaesthetic purposes (→ elaborate language).

Category. A class to which items belong, for example, syntactic categories, such as sentence, noun, verb, or morphological categories, such as root (→) and derivational morpheme (→).

Child-directed speech (CDS). Simplified speech used primarily by adults speaking to children. CDS provides comprehensible input for first language acquisition (aka caregiver speech and caretaker speech).

Citation. An explicit form of intertextual relationship where the author "borrows" part of another text. (→ allusion, intertextuality)

Class. (1) A group of people sharing the same economic level of income, for example, blue collar versus white collar. (2) In grammar, a set of words, usually sharing some grammatical feature (e.g., nouns, verbs). (→ closed class, open class)

Class stratification. Linguistic differentiation, usually dialectal, due to social class status. Working class people speak differently than upper-middle-class people.

Clause. Linguistic unit that can be considered a sentence; it has a subject and a verb (→).

Click. Consonant articulated with the creation of a vacuum chamber in the mouth that is suddenly released producing a characteristic popping or clicking sound. Kisses or the sound one makes to call horses in Western culture are clicks.

Clipping. A word formation technique consisting of shortening longer words to create new words, for example, *(tele)phone, prof(essor).*

Closed class. Word grouping by category (→) where the content of the group usually stays the same, that is, new words are not added to the group (e.g., in English, prepositions and simple and compound adverbs). (↔ open class)

CMC (Computer-mediated communication). Linguistic exchanges that take place through the medium of a computer, as opposed to other technological means, such as the telephone, or no such media, such as face-to-face communication [→].

Coda. The part of the syllable (→) which follows the vowel. It is part of the rime (→).

Coded connotations. The associations attached to certain words that hold true for an entire culture; for example, foxes are considered to be smart animals in the Western culture. Black is considered the color of mourning in the Western culture, while in the Muslim world, white is the color of mourning. (→ connotation, denotation)

Code switching. When a speaker switches between two languages or language styles depending on who he or she is speaking to (e.g., from Spanish to English, *Yo no se what happened*).

Cognitive grammar. An approach to linguistics that has developed in the last quarter of the 20th century in the United States, with a focus on semantic description.

Coherence. In discourse analysis (→), the overall meaning or sense of a text, which ensures that even noncohesive (→) passages may be interpreted as belonging to the text.

Cohesion. The relationship between the parts of the text (such as pronouns, articles, repeated words, etc.), which ensure its being a whole.

Collocations. The linguistic context in which a word usually is found, for example, *serve a prison term*; one cannot *pass* or *spend* a prison term.

Collocative connotation. The connotative (→) meaning carried by the collocations (→) of a given word.

Colloquial speech. Everyday informal speech used without special attention to pronunciation or word choice, as in, *Hey, move your behind over here!* in contrast to the more formal *Could you, please, come here?*

Communication. The process by which ideas and information are negotiated between a speaker and a listener.

Communicative competence. The general competence (→) a speaker has about communication at large. It includes grammatical, lexical, pragmatic, discourse, and social competence.

Communicative dynamism. The analysis of the contribution to the meaning of a sentence by its various parts, in particular its theme (→) and rheme (→).

Community of practice. A group similar to a speech community, →, but of smaller size.

Comp. (→) complementizer.

Comparative method. Technique of comparing forms of two or several languages to determine if a historical relationship connects them. It is used to find characteristics of the ancestor language they are assumed to come from. (→ etymology)

Competence. A person's knowledge of his or her language, the rules he or she must know in order to produce sentences. Competence is abstract, outside of context. (↔ performance) (→ I-language)

Complement. (→ complementizer).

Complementary distribution. The fact that two linguistic items cannot occur at the same time in a given environment (→).

Complementizer. A linguistic item that introduces a subordinate clause (→); e.g., *that* or a zero morpheme in *Mary believes (that) linguistics is fun.*

Compliment. A structured speech act (→) used as a way to foster positive face (→) and to show support or approval to a person.

Compounding. A word formation technique putting two words together to create a new word, for example, *waterfall* from *water + fall.*

Compound bilingualism. Form of bilingualism (→) in which the speaker sees both languages as semantically equivalent but as separate registers in each of which there is a different word for the same thing, in contrast to coordinate bilingualism (→).

Conceptualization. The process of creating concepts and distinguishing among them. The way in which a person conceptualizes the world is his or her worldview.

Configurational definition. Definition of a grammatical term such as subject or direct object exclusively in terms of nodes (→) and their positions in a syntactic tree diagram (→).

Congruence theory. A theory according to which word choice, grammar (→), and phonology (→) are all linked together because a choice at one level implies a similar choice at all other levels, for example, *Yo! Queenie!* as a greeting for the Queen will be anomalous in most usual situations.

Conjunction. Part of speech that connects phrases, clauses, or sentences, for example, *and, if, but, or.*

Connotation. The meaning associations attached to words, beyond their literal meaning. (↔ denotation)

Consonant. Sound produced with either partial or total occlusion of the vocal tract (→). (→ fricative, stop, affricate).

Constituent. The parts that make up the sentence. For example, *Mary loves John* can be broken down into the constituents [Mary], [loves], and [John]. (→ immediate constituent)

Context. The surrounding events in which an utterance is produced or the surrounding sentences in which a sentence occurs in a text.

Context-dependent languages. The class of languages generated by context-sensitive rules (→).

Context-sensitive rules. Rewriting rules that take into account the context of the derivation, for example, a rule that would consider if a verb is transitive (→) to decide whether to generate a direct object.

Contextual presupposition. Background knowledge of contextualization cues (→).

Contextualization cue. Signals such as rising or falling intonation and variance of speed or specific word choice used in speech to signal to the hearer how the utterance is to be understood, for example, *Nice haircut!* said with an ironical intonation is not to be taken literally as a compliment.

Continuum. The gamut of states ranging from one extreme to the other of a phenomenon involving gradual variation.

Contrastive rhetorics. The comparison of writing conventions across cultures and/or writing genres.

Conversation. Verbal interaction between two or more persons.

Conversation analysis. A subdiscipline of sociolinguistics, which focuses on the detailed analysis of conversations that have been recorded and transcribed.

Conversational implicature. (→ implicature)

Conversational maxim. (→ maxim)

Cooperative principle. (aka principle of cooperation) A general set of rules followed by speakers when they communicate. The rules have the purpose of maximizing and streamlining the negotiation of information between the speakers. (→ maxim)

Coordinate bilingualism. Form of bilingualism (→) in which the speaker sees both languages as semantically different and different words in each language as referring to related objects differently, in contrast to coordinate bilingualism (→).

Coordination. A way of joining two sentences together when neither of them is subordinated (→) to the other.

Copula. The verb *to be.*

Copular verb. A verb that behaves like the copula (→) *be* in taking a noun or adjective phrase as adjunct, for example, *become* as in *She became very anxious about the midterm.* Other copular verbs are *appear, feel, get, seem.*

Corpus. A set of sentences, utterances, texts, etc., that are considered as a whole for the purposes of study.

Corpus linguistics. A branch of linguistics (→) that describes and verifies hypotheses about language (→) on the basis of a sufficiently large sample of actual data, a corpus (→) of texts, transcriptions of conversations, etc.

Corpus planning. Type of language planning (→) that focuses mainly on standardizing the grammar (→), spelling, lexicon (→), etc., of a language.

Covert prestige. The respect that is gained by the use of language that is considered to be below standard; use of nonstandard language to identify with or set oneself apart from a group.

Creole. A pidgin (→) that has become the native language (→) of a community. A creole is much richer and complex than a pidgin and is a full-fledged language. (→ decreolization)

Creole continuum. A range of dialectal options ranging from the standard language to the most colloquial.

Creolization. The process whereby a pidgin (→) becomes a creole (→). A pidgin has to acquire grammatical complexity and stylistic variety in order to become a creole.

Critical period. A period of time within which a child will acquire a language with native competence. This period ends between 7 and 12, with some variation. Languages acquired after the critical period are not acquired with native-like competence, at least in the area of phonology, unless great effort is applied.

Cross-cultural communication. Communication that involves people belonging to different cultures, which therefore faces significant problems, as the assumptions and beliefs of the speakers may differ. For example, nodding means "yes" in Western cultures, but a gesture very similar to nodding means "no" in the Arabic world.

Cultural transmission. One of the features of language; it refers to the fact that significant aspects of language (such as the lexicon) are not innate, but need to be learned from other speakers, in a social context.

Dactyl. In poetry, a metric foot (→) consisting of a stressed syllable followed by two unstressed syllables (for example, yésterday).

Decreolization. When a creole (→) loses some attributes usually in favor of its lexifier (→) language or another prestigious language.

Deep structure. An abstract syntactic representation of a sentence before transformations (→) have applied.

Deficit theory. The now discredited idea that children belonging to social or ethnic groups performed poorly in school due to insufficient exposure to language or exposure to ungrammatical or illogical language (aka verbal deprivation).

Deictics. Words that depend on the context of the sentence for part of their meaning; for example, the meaning of *I* depends upon who is speaking. (→ deixis)

Deixis. Refers to the fact that certain words do not really have an independent meaning but function as pointers. Examples are *now, then, here, tomorrow*, etc. The main pointers refer to time, place, and person.

Denominal morpheme. A morpheme (→) that changes a noun to a different part of speech, for example, *haste* to *hasten*.

Denotation. The meaning of a word. (↔ connotation)

Derivation. A type of word formation that results in a new word by adding a derivational morpheme (→). For example, from *nation* to *national*.

Derivational morpheme. A morpheme (→) used to create new words from old ones; for example, *to shop—shopper, to run—runner*. It changes the meaning of the word.

Descriptive grammar. A detailed description of the phenomena in a given language, often worded in traditional terminology. Usually designed by grammarians or linguists. (→ grammar, case grammar, theoretical grammar)

Descriptivism. An approach to the study of language concerned with only the description of linguistic facts and not with how the speakers should or should not use the language. (↔ prescriptivism)

Deverbal. A derivational morpheme (→) that changes a verb to a noun, for example, *run* to *runner*.

Diachronic. The study of language from the point of view of historical development. (↔ synchronic)

Dialect. A variety of language based on geographical or social distribution.

Dialect atlas. A publication that collects dialectological data. Often represented as maps.

Dialect continuum. The gradual passage from one dialect (→) to another (often over a geographical area).

Dialectology. The systematic study of dialect.

Dialogue journal. Students write (→) to a teacher on a given or chosen subject and the teacher replies with an emphasis on communication.

Difference approach. A theory of language variation that see the differences between men and women as resulting from two distinct cultures/backgrounds; (↩ dominance approach)

Diffusion. The process whereby linguistic features from one variety are adopted in another variety, often through contact among speakers.

Diglossia. When two distinct languages, high and low, fully coexist in a community and each is used for different specific purposes.

Diminutive. A linguistic form that differs from another only on the semantic feature [+small]. E.g., *Bill/Billy, book/booklet.* Fairly rare in English, but very common in many other languages, e.g., the Romance languages.

Diphthongs. Two vowels in a syllable, for example, *loud* [lawd]. One of the two vowels turns into a glide; [w] in this case.

Disambiguation. The process of eliminating the ambiguity (→) in a sentence through the choice of the appropriate meanings of the elements that make it up (→ amalgamation) and of context in which the sentence is uttered.

Discourse analysis. The study of units larger than the individual sentence, for example, paragraphs, conversations, texts.

Discourse marker. A word that indicates relationships between linguistic elements greater than the sentence. E.g., *well, then...*, which presupposes a prior argument to which one reacts.

Discreteness. A defining feature of language stating that a unit is sharply distinguished from another in an all or nothing manner, like one word of a minimal pair (→) from the other.

Displacement. The possibility of using language to refer to things that are not here and now, that is, present at the time of utterance, or necessarily possible and real, for example, lying, fiction writing.

Distinguisher. Meaning features necessary to tell apart the various meanings of words in Katz and Fodor's interpretive semantics (→) after the semantic markers (→) have been used.

Ditransitive. A verb that takes two objects, for example, *give* as in *She gave John the book*, where *John* is the indirect object and *book* is the direct object.

Dominance approach. Theory of language variation that sees the differences between men's and women's language as resulting from the distribution of power between the sexes. (↩ difference approach)

Dominant language. In a bilingual situation, the language in which the bilingual speaker is most at ease at any given time. (→ bilingual, balanced bilingualism)

Double articulation. (→ duality).

Double negative. The presence of two negations within one sentence, for example, *I can't get no satisfaction.* (→ first articulation, second articulation)

Doublets. Words that originally had the same meaning, but came into English from different sources and/or at different times, and have taken on different meanings, for example *guard* and *warden*, both from Old French *garden*, with *warden* via the Anglo-Norman variant *wardein.*

Duality. Aka double articulation. The fact that language uses a small inventory of sounds to build a larger number of morphemes, which can form an infinite number of sentences.

Dysgraphia. A form of aphasia (→) that affects the ability to write, corresponding to dyslexia (→).

Dyslexia. A form of aphasia (→) that affects the ability to read, corresponding to dysgraphia (→).

Echolalia. A form of aphasia (→) that consists of the mechanical repetition of all or parts of another speaker's utterances.

Educational linguistics. The application of linguistic insight and methodologies to the solution of problems within the domain of teaching. A prime example of educational linguistic issue is the teaching of English to speakers of AAVE in the United States.

Elaborated code. Style of speaking that makes greater use of certain grammatical items such as adjectives, the pronoun *I*, and more complicated sentence structures. (→ restricted code)

Elaborated pidgin. → extended pidgin.

Elaborate language. The literary, artistic use of language that differs from casual language (→) in that the speaker is consciously manipulating the form of the language rather than focusing exclusively on the content.

E-language. → performance (← I-language).

Embedded sentence. A sentence included in another sentence.

Encyclopedic knowledge. Knowledge of the world (→ frame, script; ↔ lexical knowledge).

Endangered language. A language threatened with extinction, either because it loses in competition with another language in a multilingual situation, as with Plattdeutsch, its use is prohibited politically, as the use of French dialects was, or because it becomes extinct along with its speakers, as with many languages of the Amazon.

English as a foreign language (EFL). The study and teaching of English as a foreign language (i.e., not as a means of everyday interaction).

English as a second language (ESL). The teaching or learning of English in a country in which it is the means of everyday interaction.

Enjambment. The lack of a pause at the end of a line of poetry.

Environment. (1) The context in which a linguistic unit occurs. (2) Specifically, in phonology (→), a position or group of positions in the sequence of sounds. For example, in the word [dog], the vowel [o] is in the following environment: preceded by [d] and followed by [g]. In the word [obo] *(oboe),* the sound [b] is in an intervocalic environment (i.e., surrounded by vowels).

Epicene pronoun. (→ generic pronoun).

Esperanto. An artificial language (→) created by Dr. Zamenhof in 1887.

Estuary English. An accent (→) identified with a group of educated people in an area of London.

Ethnic group. A group of people that share racial, national, or cultural ties. Often a common language is one of the defining elements of ethnicity.

Ethnography of communication. An approach to sociolinguistics that focuses on the sociocultural norms of the community that is studied. For example, who speaks to whom, under which circumstances, using which linguistic forms, etc. This approach tends to focus on cultural differences. (→ communicative competence)

Ethnomethodology. A method in sociology used to describe the way people interact with each other in daily life; see also discourse analysis (→).

Etymology. The study of the origins of words.

Euphemism. A linguistic expression that conveys the same meaning as another but without the nagative connotations of the latter. For example, *be sick to one's stomach* is a euphemism for *vomit.*

Exclusive. The meaning of the pronoun *we* that does not include the hearer, that is, denotes *me and someone else, but not you.* (→ inclusive)

Expanding circle. Nations in which English has not had a central role in the past but is currently used for purposes of business and technology. Examples include China and Japan.

Expressive. A label applied to children whose first words are typically social in nature (for example, *bye-bye*).

Extended pidgin. A pidgin that expands to cover all the domains of everyday life; usually become creoles. (→ pidgin, creole, ↔ restricted pidgin)

Extensive reading. A way to teach reading in which the focus is on reading entire texts.

Externalized language. → E-language, performance.

Extrovert. Psychological category describing people who are outgoing and gregarious. (↔ introvert)

Eye dialect. The representation using spelling of dialectal or nonstandard forms of English. E.g., *dunno, whatsa madda, waddayawant, Mistah Kurtz—he dead* (Conrad).

Eye rhyme. Two rhyming words that are spelled the same (vowel sound and final consonant) but pronounced differently (for example, *great/meat*).

Face. The public image projected by a person. Can be positive face (→) or negative face (→).

Face-to-face interaction. Speech situation in which both parties of the exchange are present and therefore can take advantage of all nonverbal cues that accompany language, as opposed to computer-mediated communication, in which this is not the case.

False friends. Two cognate words, or words that are otherwise similar, that have become differentiated in meaning in their respective languages and are a translation problem, for example, Spanish *embarazada*, which looks like English *embarrassed* but means "pregnant."

Feature. A part of something. (1) Semantic features are the components of the meaning of a word. In structural semantics (→), features help define words by differentiating one word from another; for example, *man* and *woman* are differentiated by the feature [male] or the feature [female]. (→ binary feature) (2) Phonetic features break down the articulatory description of the sounds in distinct features, such as [voice] (→).

Feature analysis. (1) Breaking down the meaning of a word into features (→). (2) Differentiating the words of a lexicon by use of features.

FG. → functional grammar.

Figurative language. The idea behind figurative language is to talk about something in terms of something else. (→ metaphor)

Figure of speech. Elaborate language that is manipulated for aesthetic effect. The most common figures of speech involve sound repetition, such as in alliteration (→), assonance (→), or rhyme (→).

Figure of thought. Figurative language is used to talk about one thing in terms of another thing or to alter language for rhetorical purposes. The most common forms are metaphor (→), metonymy (→), litotes (→), hyperbole (→), irony (→).

Fingerspelling. In sign language (→), the practice of spelling out words using finger signs.

Finite. A verb that is tensed (→) and can exist by itself in a sentence. (↔ nonfinite)

First articulation. The fact that linguistic units can be broken down into morphemes (→).

First language. The language learned by a native speaker (→) in childhood. (→ L1)

Floor. Metaphor in conversation analysis to describe the current turn in a conversation. A speaker may *hold the floor*, that is, not provide the hearer with a transition relevance place (→), or he or she may *yield the floor* and give the hearer a chance to speak.

Flouting. A violation of one of the maxims (→) of the cooperative principle (→) while continuing to follow another maxim. This is used in figurative language (→), for example.

Fluent aphasia. Form of aphasia (→) that does not affect the flow of speech so much as how meaningful or appropriate the utterances are. A fluent aphasic may not hesitate, but make no sense in what he or she is talking about. (→ nonfluent aphasia)

FN. Acronym for *first name*, counterpart to TLN (→). Form of address used by person of higher status (→) to address person of lower status or among people of equal status, for example, *Hey Joe!*

Folk etymology. A case of linguistic change that involves a mistaken analysis on the speakers' part of the morphological structure of the word. For example, the word *hamburger* comes from the name of the German city Hamburg. However, as is evident by compounds such as *cheese-burger* and *veggie-burger*, it was at some point analyzed (erroneously) as *ham + burger*.

Foreign language. An additional language learned in formal/schooled situations. It is generally assumed not to be used on a daily basis in society.

Foreigner talk (FT). The register used by native speakers when addressing nonnative speakers of a language; usually includes slower rate of speech, simplified syntax, and increased volume.

Forensic linguistics. (1) The field of linguistics that deals with the relationships between language and the law. (2) A subfield of the language and law field, dealing specifically with the use of linguistic tools to establish the identity of speakers/writers.

Formula. A linguistic unit, often multiword, that has idiomatic meaning, for example, *How do you do?*, *No thanks*, etc. (→ idiom)

Fossilization. (1) A form or construction is fossilized when its elements can no longer be freely combined, as in idioms (→), for example, *don't cry wolf, okie dokie*. (2) In second language acquisition, fossilization refers to the stabilization of incorrect linguistic features that become a permanent part of the speaker's language (→ interlanguage) and contribute to his or her errors.

Frame. A cluster of information about a lexeme (→) or situation that is stored in our knowledge. (→ script, encyclopedic knowledge)

Free indirect discourse. Literary style in which the narrator switches to the perspective of one of the characters without explicit marking or quoting the character or his or her thoughts directly, for example, *She was looking at the ever so divine flower arrangements*, where the adjective phrase *ever so divine* is in the character's register (→).

Free morpheme. The smallest unit of a language that can stand by itself with its own meaning. For example, /car/, /house/, /garden/. Also called a root morpheme (→) or a stem (→).

Freewriting. A technique to develop ideas; it involves the construction of sentences without regard to grammar (→), sentence structure, standard format, etc.

Fricative. Consonant (→) made when two phonatory organs (→) come close together, without creating complete closure. For example, /f/ in *fin*, /θ/ in *thin*.

Fronting. (1) Moving parts of a sentence to the beginning, usually for emphasis, as *the book* in *The book is what Mary wants.* (2) When one pronounces sounds further forward in the mouth than usual.

Functional grammar (FG). A type of grammar that is based on the idea that language is functionally directed, i.e., it serves a purpose (communication). From this basic fact, the various rules are derived. FG focuses on topics such as how the amount of information available to speakers at a given time affects the way other speakers interact with them.

Functional sentence perspective (FSP). The analysis of sentences in terms of what information their parts give. (→ theme, rheme)

Functions. In narrative analysis, minimal narrative units, for example, *the hero leaves the village, the hero slays the dragon.*

Future tense. A tense (→) which indicates an action taking place after the time of utterance. English does not have a morphologically (→) marked future, and uses modals (→) (e.g., *will*) or periphrastic (→) constructions (e.g., *be going to*) to indicate the future.

Gayspeak. The variety of language spoken by gay, lesbian, and transgendered people.

Gender. In English, one of three grammatical classes (masculine, feminine, neuter). Other languages have up to 12 different classes based on their division of the world into relevant classes. (→ natural gender)

Genderlect. A linguistic variety that is spoken by only one or the other gender.

Generation. In the mathematical theory of languages, combining items according to rules in order to create strings (sequences of items). (→ Σ-F grammar)

Generative grammar. A formal set of rules that creates a set of sentences starting from one atom (S, for *sentence*). (→ Σ-F grammar)

Generative semantics. A theory of semantics that posits that the generation of a sentence is started by the semantic form of the sentence rather than by its syntax. (→ interpretive semantics)

Genre. Discursive forms that share a given set of characteristics, both formal and content based.

Generic pronoun. A pronoun that does not distinguish between masculine and feminine referents. It occurs naturally in some languages (e.g., Finnish), and many "artificial" ones have been proposed for English (aka epicene pronoun).

Germanic. The Germanic languages are a branch of the Indo-European language family (→). Examples of Germanic languages are English, a West Germanic language; Danish, a North Germanic language; and Gothic (→), an East Germanic language.

Gerund. A verb that can function as a noun in a sentence and ends in *-ing.*

Glide. A sound made by articulating a vowel and raising the tongue to a higher position in the mouth, for example, [y] as in [fyum] *(fume).*

Glossolalia. A peculiar linguistic phenomenon in which speakers utter "sentences" in "languages" that they do not speak. The languages and the sentences are constructed subconsciously by the speakers but often resemble "real" languages. Aka speaking in tongues.

Gothic. East Germanic (→) language, now extinct, that was spoken along the western shore of the Black Sea around the 4th century and later spread throughout southern Europe by the Ostrogoths and Visigoths.

Glottal stop. A sound produced by creating an occlusion in the vocal tract using the glottis.

Grammar. (1) A description of a language. (2) The rules that speakers use unconsciously in speaking. (→ case grammar, theoretical grammar, descriptive grammar, internalized grammar)

Grammatical gender. Gender (→) classification of the lexicon that does not coincide with natural gender (→) but signals grammatical relationships. E.g., *sun* is neuter in English, but *le soleil* is masculine in French, and *die Sonne* is feminine in German.

Grammaticality. The idea whether a sentence is considered grammatical according to the grammar (→) of a language.

Great Vowel Shift. This wide-ranging change in the phonemic system of English took place at the turn of the 15th century. It affected the long vowels and diphthongs and changed the pronunciation, for example, of the vowel in *name* from OE [a] to Modern English [e], *shine* from OE [i] to Modern English [ay].

Grimm's law. Jacob Grimm described the systematic sound change that distinguishes the Germanic languages from the other Indo-European languages. The Indo-European voiceless stops *p, t, k* in certain phonological environments became fricatives in Germanic languages and later lost their aspiration, for example, Latin *pes* became English *foot*, while they remained stops elsewhere.

Gullah. A creole close to AAVE (→) spoken on the islands off the coast of Georgia and North Carolina.

Have the floor. In conversation (→), the person who is speaking or is controlling the topic of conversation *has the floor* (→).

Head. The part of a phrase (→) that could replace the entire phrase, for example, in a noun phrase (→), such as in *the red ball,* the noun *ball* is the part that could occur alone as a complete noun phrase.

Heritage language. A language spoken by immigrants of a given ethnic group and their descendents and associates.

Heteronomy. Heteronomous languages are dialects of the same language; they are contrasted with autonomous languages, which are dialects of different languages. (→ dialect, language, autonomy)

Heuristics. Discovery or search procedures used to find the solution to a problem.

High amplitude sucking (HAS). A test used to measure infants' attention. When the baby is interested by a new stimulus, the sucking rate increases; when he or she gets used to a stimulus, the rate slows down.

Homodiegetic narrator. A narrator that appears within the narrative he or she tells.

Homonyms. Words that have the same sound or spelling but different meanings, for example, *bear* as in animal or as in *endure.*

Homophones. Words that sound the same but have different spelling and meaning, for example, [hir] as *hear* or *here.*

Honorifics. Forms used in some languages to denote the levels of politeness in addressing people of a certain status (→). (→ TLN)

Hyperbole. Used in literary studies to describe exaggeration as a figure of thought, for example, *most noble of all warriors.* (↔ litotes)

Hypercorrection. The process of using grammatically incorrect forms when the speaker is afraid to make a mistake by not following a rule, for example, *It is just between you and I,* where the speaker is hypercorrecting the form *you and me,* which is correct in this context.

Hypochoristic. → diminutive.

Hyponymy. A semantic relationship (→) in which something specific is included in some general category, for example, *cat* is a hyponym of *animal*.

Hypotaxis. → subordination.

Iamb. The most common metric foot (→) in English poetry, it consists of an unstressed syllable followed by a stressed syllable, for example, *today*.

Iconic sign. A sign in which there is a nonarbitrary connection between the signifier (→) and the signified (→), like certain handsigns of sign language or a map that resembles the territory it stands for.

Ideology. A more or less systematic set of beliefs that a social group uses to regulate the behavior of people. Usually the term has a somewhat negative connotation (→), in that ideology is seen as artificial or coercive.

Idiolect. An individual variety of language. Every speaker has an idiolect.

Idiom. A phrase or expression that has specific meaning that cannot be derived from the meaning of its parts.

I-language. Chomsky's term for internalized language of individual speakers (→ competence), in contrast to e-language, the externalized actual language (→ performance).

Illocutionary act. In speech act (→) theory, an act performed by a speaker in uttering a sentence (→ locutionary act), for example, promising, baptizing.

Immediate constituent. The constituents in which a phrase or sentence can be subdivided with one division. (→ constituent)

Immersion program. A language teaching situation in which the learner is put in the position of speaking exclusively L2.

Immigrant language. The language spoken by an immigrant community, especially when the immigration is recent or ongoing. With time, immigrant languages become heritage languages. (→)

Imperative mood. The modality (→) concerned with giving orders. E.g., *Get out! Take out the garbage.*

Implicature. Information that can be deduced by a speaker from an utterance and its context and that involves flouting (→) the cooperative principle (→).

Implied narrator. A narrator who is not explicitly present in the text and must be inferred from it. An implied narrator is always present in the text because tenses and other deictic forms presuppose a speaker in relation to whose location and time of speaking tenses are determined.

Inclusive. The meaning of the pronoun *we* that includes both the hearer and the speaker. (→ exclusive)

Indicative mood. The modality (→) concerned with the presentation of facts. *There's a fly in my soup.*

Indirectness. The pragmatic phenomenon whereby the speaker does not say directly what he or she means, but says something that he or she thinks will lead the hearer to understand what the speaker meant, without the speaker having had to explicitly state his or her intention. E.g., Mary is hot, but she does not want to say that she's hot, so she says to Bob: *Aren't you hot?* Presumably Bob will understand that if Mary is concerned about his being hot, she may be hot too. Note how Mary could always deny that she's hot herself.

Indirect speech. (1) Any form of language in which the literal meaning of what is said is not the intended meaning of the speaker. Some forms of indirect speech are very conventional, such as *Can you pass the salt?* which is literally a request for information (about one's physical capacity to perform the action) but indirectly is intended as a request: *Please, pass the salt.* (2) Reported speech.

Individual connotation. The associations people make that are a result of their everyday life and personal experiences (aka restricted connotation).

Indo-European. A language reconstructed by linguists from which most languages of Europe and India ultimately descend.

Inference. Information that can be derived from a sentence's literal meaning.

Infinitive. A nonfinite (→) form of the verb (→) often introduced by *to* in English.

Infix. An affix (→) that is added within a word, for example, *fan-bloody-tastic.*

Inflectional language. A language that does not show separate, independent morphemes (→). For example, in Latin, *amo* can be analyzed as the root (→) *am* and the suffix (→) *-o*, which carries the meanings of *present tense, indicative mood,* and *first person singular.*

Inflectional morpheme. The smallest unit of a language used to mark grammatical categories such as plurality, tense (past or continuous present), adverbs (quick-*ly*), comparatives (tall-*er*), superlatives (tall-*est*), third person singular (talk-*s*), etc. They do not change the meaning of the word and are required by grammatical rules.

Informant. Usually, a native speaker (→) who works with a linguist who does not know a given language and provides linguistic data, translations, and other information. The term "consultant" is preferred.

Inkhorn. A class of words that were added to the English lexicon during the Renaissance. These words were mainly used in written English and stem from Latin as well as Greek, Italian, or French, for example, *illecebrous*: alluring, enticing, attractive; *anacephalize*: to recapitulate.

Innatism. The theory proposed by Noam Chomsky and others that the essential components of language are genetically hardwired in the brain (aka *nativism*).

Inner circle. Nations in which English is spoken as a first language. It includes England, the United States, Canada, Australia, and New Zealand. (↔ outer circle, expanding circle)

Input. The linguistic expressions a speaker is exposed to. (↔ output)

Instrumental motivation. The student is learning an additional language for the purpose of passing a test, getting a job, etc. (→ motivation)

Integrative motivation. The student is learning an additional language in order to become part of the second language speech community. (→ motivation)

Intension. The sense of an expression; the concepts that are conjured up by an expression or word.

Intensive reading. Way of teaching reading by reading small passages and concentrating on the microskills needed to understand them.

Interaction. A factor that is held to be of importance to the acquisition of a first language, most prominently the interaction between mother and child through child-directed speech (→).

Interactional sociolinguistics. Subfield of linguistics (→) that deals with ideas on communication/conversation like code switching (→).

Interactionism. The theory of first language acquisition that finds that speech between caregiver and child is the most important variable in that acquisition.

Interactive-compensatory model. An information-processing model, proposed by Stanovich, according to which speakers use the top-down process (→) until they reach a point of confusion, at which they switch to bottom-up processing (→).

Interchangeability. The fact that the same person can be both the speaker and the hearer in human language.

Interjection. Usually a single word exclamation like *Hey!, Ouch!,* or *Wow!* that denotes some type of emotion.

Interlanguage (IL). The language used by learners of a second language. Interlanguage may differ from both the language of the learner and the target language.

Internalized grammar. Grammatical knowledge that speakers have in their brains. (→ competence)

Interpretive semantics. A theory of semantics that posits the primacy of syntax and in which semantics operates (interprets) on syntactic trees after they have been generated by the grammar. (→ generative semantics)

Interruption. Beginning to speak while another conversational partner has the floor (→).

Intertextuality. All the references among texts and/or parts thereof. (→ allusion, citation)

Intervocalic. Between vowels. The sound [t] in *butter* is intervocalic.

Intonation. Variation of pitch (→) in a sentence (→) or phrase.(→). (→ suprasegmental)

Intransitive. Type of verb that takes a subject only and no direct or indirect object, for example, *die, sleep.*

Intrinsic motivation. The degree to which the student wants to learn an additional language because he or she is interested in the language or the process of learning itself. (→ motivation)

Introvert. Psychological category describing people who are quiet and reserved. (↔ extrovert)

Invention. A word formation technique in which speakers invent new words from scratch, for example, in advertising, *Kodak.*

IPA. International Phonetic Alphabet. (→ phonetic alphabet)

Irony. A form of indirect speech (→) in which the speaker says something that is usually the opposite of what he or she thinks, for example, *King Kong, you are really small!*

Isogloss. An imaginary line drawn on a map to indicate the boundaries of the area in which a particular linguistic feature is used. (→ bundle of isoglosses, dialect)

Isolate language. A language that does not seem to belong to any language family (→), for example, Etruscan, spoken in Italy until the 4th century, or Burushaski, spoken in northwestern India.

Isolating language. A language in which all words are invariable (i.e., do not take affixes), for example, Chinese, Vietnamese.

Jargon. Specific variety of language (→) often connected to an activity or a job; for example, computer jargon.

Journalese. The register (→) of a newspaper language; the style or type of language used in article and headline writing.

Kernel sentence. An active sentence to which no transformations (→) have been applied, for example, *Mary eats corn,* but not *What does Mary eat?* which has been transformed into a question.

Koiné. A form of language that arises from the mixing of several varieties/dialects of a language that result in a common variety/dialect. Originally this happened to classical Greek, from whence the word *koiné* (which means "common") comes.

L1. A speaker's first language. Any language acquired by the speaker before the critical period (→). (→ native language)

L2. A speaker's second language. Any language acquired by the speaker after the critical period (→), thus may in fact be L3, L4, etc. (→ foreign language)

Language. Structured system of sounds, words, and gestures that is used for communication (→).

Language acquisition. The process whereby children learn their native language (→) or children and adults learn a second language (→).

Language acquisition device (LAD). The mental organ facilitating language acquisition postulated by Chomsky and others as genetically endowed with the knowledge of universal grammar (→). LAD, on the basis of observed stimuli, sets the parameters (→) for the child.

Language area. Place where a shared language (→) is spoken.

Language attitudes. The system of positive or negative attitudes that speakers have toward other speakers and/or varieties of their language or other languages. Some language attitudes are unconscious, while others are conscious. Sometimes known as "folk linguistics." An example is the idea that people from the South of the United States have a "drawl."

Language contact. Any situation in which two languages (→) come together, either because of geographical proximity, migration of speakers, travel, or commerce. Usually the contact leads to change in either or both languages. (→ pidgin, language of wider communication, bilingual)

Language death. With the death of the last speaker of a language, the language itself becomes extinct.

Language family. A group of languages that have a historical ancestor and therefore share a number of significant features, for example, the Indo-European language family with its branch of the Germanic language family to which English belongs.

Language maintenance. In a bilingual (→) situation, it is the efforts of speakers to keep their language alive.

Language of wider communication (LWC). Languages that are chosen and used to allow for communication (→) among groups that do not speak the same language; also known as lingua franca (→) or auxiliary language (→).

Language pedagogy. A field of linguistics dealing with teaching languages.

Language planning. Any intervention attempting to regulate or affect the language(s) of a speech community.

Language shift. In a bilingual situation, it is the change of preferred status from one language to another, for example, the language of second-generation immigrants commonly shifts from the language of the old country to that of the new.

Langue. The abstract system of language available to all speakers. Langue is Ferdinand De Saussure's original term. (→ competence ↔ parole)

Lect. Any variety of language (from "dialect" by clipping (→)).

Length. The duration of a sound. How long a sound lasts.

Leveling. In historical linguistics a process by which formerly distinctive forms gradually become identical, for example, former strong verbs with vowel gradation become weak verbs as in *I treaded water* instead of *I trod water*. (→ analogy)

Lexemes. Entities in the lexicon, words. The words *sing, singing, sang,* and *sings* are all manifestations of the same lexeme.

Lexical ambiguity. The ambiguity (→) of words.

Lexical contrast. The theory stating that children learn new words by contrasting them to other words.

Lexical knowledge. All the information connected to a lexeme (→). (↔ encyclopedic knowledge)

Lexicon. All the words in a language.

Lexifier language. The language providing the lexicon (→) for a pidgin (→).

Lingua franca. An auxiliary language (→) originally used during the Crusades in the Mediterranean. By extension, it is used commonly to indicate any language of wider communication (→).

Linguist. Person proficient in the field of linguistics (→).

Linguistic area. → to sprachbund.

Linguistic atlas. → dialect atlas.

Linguistics. The scientific study of a language.

Liquid. The sounds [l] and [r].

Literacy. At one level, the word subsumes reading and writing; at another, the ability to read (→ orality).

Litotes. Litotes (↔ hyperbole) is the term used in literary studies to describe conscious understatement achieved by negation, for example, the ironical *What wonderful weather!* when it is indeed raining and cold, or *Not bad!* for an outstanding achievement.

Locutionary act. In speech act (→) theory the act of uttering a sentence. (→ illocutionary act, perlocutionary act)

Logographic system. System of writing where each character corresponds to a word.

Main clause. Any clause in a sentence that is not enclosed in another clause.

Main verb. The tensed verb of the main clause of a sentence, for example, *wrote* (but not *tickled*) in *I wrote this sentence while I was being tickled.*

Malapropism. A mistake in which a speaker uses a word that sounds like the correct word. E.g., *physical* instead of *fiscal.* After the name of a character (Mrs. Malaprop) in a play by Sheridan.

Manner. A maxim of the cooperative principle (→) requiring that for efficient communication you need to avoid obscurity, ambiguity, unnecessary length, etc., for example, not answer the question *What's the time?* with a Navajo time phrase using semaphore flags to signal it.

Marked. Any occurrence of a linguistic feature that is unusual, unexpected, or just less frequent (↔ unmarked).

Marked received pronunciation (RP). Pronunciation of English used by the British royal family. (→ received pronunciation, unmarked RP)

Marker. A linguistic item that indicates to speakers that a given variety has high or low status or belongs to a certain geographical area, etc. For example, dropping the *g* in the -*ing* forms is a marker of lower-class pronunciation in the United States.

Matched-guise. A technique used to study language attitudes [→]. It involves playing recordings of speakers saying the same things but in different dialects, accents, etc. The subjects are then asked to rate the speaker on various scales (e.g., intelligence) and therefore the subjects' attitudes toward the dialects can be deduced.

Maxim. One of the four "rules" in Grice's cooperative principle (→). The maxims are the source of inferences (→). (→ manner, quality, quantity, relevance)

Meaning. (1) The mental representation of a word or sentence. (2) The truth conditions (→) of a sentence. (→ connotation, denotation)

Mental representation. The ideas or concepts in a speaker's mind that correspond to a word or sentence. (→ semantics, meaning)

Merger. A phonological change, whereby two units that were pronounced differently become indistinguishable. A recent merger in the United States is that between *pen* and *pin.*

Mesolect. A central or middle variety of a dialect, occupying the middle area of the continuum (→) ranging from acrolect (→) to basilect (→). Is used in most situations of daily interaction. (→ dialect)

Metalanguage. Any linguistic expression that has language as its topic, for example, *This sentence has five words.* (→ metalinguistic awareness; ↔ object language)

Metalinguistic awareness. Explicit knowledge on the part of the speaker of how his or her language is organized. Provides the speaker with a tool to talk about his or her own language. (→ metalanguage)

Metaphor. A figure of speech in which a term is transferred from what it literally refers to to something else; as in *This test is a piece of cake.*

Metaphorical code switching. The adoption a style of language different from one's own to convey a certain image. (→ code switching)

Meter. (→ metric foot).

Metonymy. A figure of speech referring to a part for the whole, or from one term to another commonly associated one; for example, *He gave up the bottle* means he quit drinking because the bottle stands for drinking. *She had a glass of water* means that she drank the *contents* of the glass.

Metric foot. In poetry, the repetition of some of the structure of syllables, in terms of combinations of stressed and unstressed syllables, for example, anapest (→), iamb (→), for example the pentameter with five long, stressed syllables in this line of Frost's poem *Design:* I **saw** a **dimp**led **spid**er, **fat** and **white.**

Mind maps. A prewriting technique that involves putting ideas, words, sentences, etc., down on paper in a certain amount of time and then trying to make connections for development of a topic; brainstorming (→).

Minimal narrative. The simplest possible narrative; it consists of one action/ event.

Minimal pair. Two words that have different meanings with only one sound difference, for example, [pin] and [bin].

Minority language. Language spoken by a group of people in an area where the majority of people speaks a different language. Is usually synonymous with subordinate language (→).

Modal verbs. Type of auxiliary verb (→) that comes before a verb and expresses necessity, possibility, or intentionality; for example, *must, might, should.*

Modality. The expression of mood (→) in the semantics of the verb.

Model theoretic semantics. A theory of semantics based on the notion of truth value (→).

Modifier. A syntactic (→) element that is attached to another element and in so doing affects its meaning. Modification may appear before (premodifier) or after (postmodifier). Typical examples of modifiers are adjectives and adverbs. Prepositional phrases and subordinate clauses are also modifiers.

Mood. Part of the semantics of the verb (→). In English it is expressed primarily by modal verbs (→).

Monogenesis. The theory that all creoles derive historically from one pidgin, which was successively relexified (→ relexification).

Monolingual. A speaker or a community speaking only one language. (→ bilingual, diglossia)

Morpheme. The smallest linguistic unit with meaning. They are made of phonemes (→). For example, the phonemes /p/, /u/, and /t/ create the morpheme /put/. Note that the individual sounds have no meaning, while the morpheme does.

Morphology. The branch of linguistics that studies the structure of words.

Mother tongue. The language first learned by a native speaker (→).

Motivation. The reason why a student is learning a second language. (→ integrative motivation, instrumental motivation, resultative motivation, intrinsic motivation)

Multilingual. Being able to speak three or more languages.

Multiple negation. The presence of more than one negative particle in a sentence. E.g., *We don't need no money, no way.* The presence of multiple negations often reinforces the negation.

Multiplex network. Communities in which one person embodies many different roles.

Mutual unintelligibilty. Speakers of different languages or dialects (→) of the same language are unable to understand or communicate with each other.

Narratee. The person to whom the narrative is being told. A fictional character not to be confused with the real audience (readers).

Narratology. The analysis of narrative texts.

Narrator. The person telling the narrative. A fictional character who is distinguished from the author of the text.

Nasalization. A sound's acquisition of nasality (i.e., its being pronounced with an open velum (→) and therefore flow of air through the nasal passage) under the influence of another nasal sound, for example, the [a] in *man* is nasalized.

National language. The language that is considered to be a country's most important, most used language. Often the official language of a country.

Native language. A language spoken by an individual or a speech community learned it as a first language in childhood.

Native speaker. A speaker who learned a given language since early childhood. (↔ nonnative speaker)

Nativism. → innatism.

Natural class. A group of sounds that share a phonological feature, for example, [m], [n], and [ŋ] form the natural class of nasals.

Natural gender. A division of the lexicon in classes based on a match between masculine, feminine, and neuter and the actual gender markings of the objects that are classified, for example, female items are *feminine,* male items are *masculine,* and items unmarked for sex are *neuter.* (→ gender, grammatical gender)

Negation. A linguistic element that means that something is not the case. E.g., *not, no, un-important, im-possible.*

Negative face. The aspect of face (→) concerned with avoiding being imposed upon or inconvenienced. (→ politeness ↔ positive face)

Negative politeness. → face.

Neologism. A new word entering a language through productive (→) word-formation processes.

Networks. A structure of relationships between and among people who share kinship ties, work, or leisure time activities.

Niger-Kordofanian. A language family in Africa that influenced AAVE (→).

Node. The intersection point of two or more branches in a tree diagram (→). The node *S* is at the intersection of the *NP* and *VP* branches (→).

Nonfinite. A verb form that is not finite (→), that is, not marked for person (→), number (→), or tense (→) and cannot exist by itself in a sentence, like an infinitive (→) or a present or past participle (→).

Nonfluent aphasia. Form of aphasia (→) that affects the flow of speech, leads to hesitation, omission of words, mispronunciations (→ fluent aphasia).

Nonmanual signals. In sign languages (→), all aspects of signing not done with the hands (e.g., facial expressions).

Nonstandard. A linguistic form or an entire variety may be called nonstandard if it does not fit a received idea of what the standard variety (→) for that community should be.

NORM. Nonmobile older rural males; informants in most dialect (→) studies.

Normative grammar. Prescriptive (→) grammar based on rules of how speakers should or should not use language.

Noun. A word that is the central element of a noun phrase (→), usually denoting concrete entities like people, places, or things, for example, *landlord, garden, sugar*, or abstract concepts, for example, *freedom*.

Noun phrase. A phrase that can take the place of a noun. The sentence [Mary] [loves] [Bob] could have also been [Mary] [loves] [a tall man], hence [a tall man] is a phrase that can be replaced by a noun [Bob].

NP. noun phrase (→).

Number. Part of the semantics of verbs and nouns concerned with the quality of being singular (one item) or plural (more than one item), in English.

Object language. Language that refers to any object in the world with the exception of language, i.e., is not metalanguage (→).

Occlusion. The closing of the vocal tract during the articulation of a stop (→) (aka occlusive).

Official language. A language that has status conferred on it by the government or a political entity.

Omniscient narrator. A narrator who knows everything, including the unexpressed thoughts of the characters and the end of the story.

Onomastics. The subfield of linguistics that studies names.

Onomatopoeia. A word that sounds like what it means, for example, *buzz*.

Onset. The part of the syllable (→) which precedes the vowel and consists of consonants. Syllables may lack an onset.

Open class. A class of words the number of which is theoretically unlimited because it is open for additions, like the classes of adjectives (→), verbs (→), and nouns (→) in English. (↔ closed class)

Orality. Speech (→ literacy).

Outer circle. Nations in which English is spoken as a second language for purposes of business and education. It includes India, Nigeria, Singapore, and South Africa. (↔ inner circle)

Output. The language produced by the learner. (↔ input)

Output hypothesis. The hypothesis that failure in communication (→ output) leads to improvement in language learning because the speaker, by hearing what he or she says, may notice discrepancies between intention and result.

Overcorrection. → hypercorrection.

Overextension. The phenomenon whereby a child uses a word in a meaning that is broader than the normal meaning, for example, using *ball* to describe any round object, including, for example, the moon or an apple. (↔ underextension)

Overgeneration. In generative grammar (→), the generation of nonsensical (or otherwise ill-formed) sentences, e.g., *The pancakes love flowers*, by a too-powerful grammar.

Overlap. Speaking at the same time as your conversational partner in a helpful, friendly way rather than in a rude, interruptive way. (→ interrruption)

Overlapping environments. Two phones (→) occuring in the same environment (→), or in environments that are partially the same.

Overreporting. A phenomenon whereby speakers believe that they use more prestige forms than they actually do.

Oxymoron. An expression that is a contradiction in terms, e.g., a married bachelor.

Parameter. In universal grammar (→), a rule that determines if a language will allow a certain kind of phenomena. (→ PRO-DROP parameter)

Parataxis. Linking main clauses (→) using coordination (→).

Parody. Rewriting a text, keeping either the form or the content unchanged (or minimally so) and introducing changes (again, either formal or related to the content of the text) that ridicule the work or the author.

Parole. The actual usage by speakers of the linguistic system (→ langue).

Participant observation. A technique of ethnographic and anthropological research whereby the researcher actually takes part in the activities of the group being studied.

Participle. Verb that can function like an adjective in a passive sentence; forms are past and present participle (→).

Particle. Part of speech that includes a variety of uninflected (→) items, e.g., *to* in the infinitive (→) and the nonverbal components of phrasal verbs (→). The particle *around* in the phrasal verb (→) *hang around* cannot clearly be classified as either adverb (→) or preposition (→).

Passive voice. One of the two voices of the English language. It is the opposite of the (↔) active voice and switches emphasis from the subject to the direct object of the active in a sentence (→ voice, active voice).

Past participle. A participle (→) in the past tense (→), in English usually formed by adding *-ed* to the stem (→), for example *listen—listened*, but also *-en*, for example *fall—fallen*, or with irregular forms, for example *build—built*.

Past tense. The past tense (→) is used to refer to an action prior to the moment of utterance. In English, it is formed by adding *-ed* to the stem (→), for example *peek—peeked*, or by changing the stem vowel, for example *sit—sat*. (→ present tense)

Patois. French word meaning "dialect" (→).

Pedagogical grammar. A grammar written specifically for the purpose of teaching. It may contain simplifications or incomplete information so as not to overburden the learners.

Performance. The process of putting to practical use one's competence (↔) of the language. Performance always takes place in a given context. (→ E-language)

Performative speech act. A type of sentence in which an action is performed by merely saying something, for example, *I apologize*, or *Checkmate!* (→ speech act)

Periphrastic. The quality of not being direct, or talking around, which is the meaning of the Greek word, a given subject. Periphrastic constructions are used for euphemisms (→) or for grammatical reasons (e.g., to indicate the future in English).

Perlocutionary act. The aspect of a speech act (→) concerned with the intention to achieve a particular effect, for example, *frighten*. Any of the effects achieved by a speech act (→), whether intended or not.

Person. Deictic grammatical category concerned with distinguishing the speaker (1st p.), the hearer (2nd p.), and others (3rd p.).

Phatic communication. (→ phatic communion).

Phatic communion. Term introduced by anthropologist Bernard Malinowski to indicate the use of language with the goal of establishing social contacts, rather than transmitting information. The term is often misused as "phatic communication."

Phonation. (1) The process of producing speech sounds with the vocal apparatus. (2) Vocal activity in the larynx (for example, voicing).

Phonatory organs. The organs of the body used to produce speech sounds.

Phone. The smallest unit of sound in speech (→ allophone).

Phoneme. (1) A mental image of a sound; the idea of the sound. (2) The smallest distinctive units in language.

Phonetics. The field of linguistics that studies how the sounds of a language are produced.

Phonetic alphabet. Symbols that allow linguistis to represent sounds in languages univocally. (→ IPA)

Phonics. A method of teaching reading that stresses the relationship between symbols (letters) and sounds.

Phonology. The field of linguistics studying how the sound systems of languages are organized.

Phrasal verbs. Construction consisting of a verb (→) and an adverb (→) or a verb and a preposition (→), e.g., *get away, put up with*. The adverb or preposition are also called particles (→).

Phrase. A syntactic unit that is not a full clause (→); in the sentence *Mary loves a tall man*, [a tall man] is a phrase, [Mary] is a phrase, and so is [loves a tall man]. *[loves a] is not a phrase.

Phrase structure rule. The rewriting rules that generate sentences, for example, VP (→) V + (NP) + (PP).

Pidgin. A simplified language originating from the mixture of two or more languages used primarily for trading purposes. A pidgin cannot be a native language. (→ creole, creolization, lexifier language, Black English, restricted pidgin, extended/elaborated pidgin, languages of wider communication)

Pidginization. The process of language contact (→) that results in the creation of a pidgin (→).

Pitch. Whether a sound is acoustically perceived as high or low. From an articulatory point of view, faster or slower vibration of the vocal cords.

Point of view. The perspective from which a story is narrated, including psychological, ideological, and even spatial and temporal ones.

Politeness. In Brown and Levinson's theory, the behavior of speakers as they manage their respective faces (→). Politeness is conceived as positive or negative. Apologies, hedges, deference are all examples of politeness.

Polygenesis. → monogenesis.

Polyglot. Person who is able to speak a number of different languages.

Polysemy. The quality of a word having two or more meanings, for example, *bank* as in *river bank* or the place where one keeps one's money.

Popular etymology. → folk etymology.

Positive face. The aspect of face (→) concerned with boosting the speaker's self image. Compliments increase positive face, for example.

Positive politeness. → face.

Possible world. An imaginary copy of the real world with some significant difference, for example, a possible world in which Richard Nixon was not forced to resign from the presidency of the United States. Possible worlds are sets of presuppositions (→).

Post-creole continuum. → creole continuum.

Postponed preposition. A syntactic construction in which a preposition appears at the end of a sentence: *What do you have to put up with?*

Poverty of stimulus. The argument that the child does not have enough stimuli and well-formed input to learn the language (aka the *logical problem* of language acquisition [→]).

Power. A social factor determining status (→) and accordingly language variety, that is, high or low status speech.

PP. Prepositional phrase (→).

Pragmatic ambiguity. The property of sentences or of larger units of a language, such as paragraphs or texts, to have more than one meaning. It contains no lexical or syntactical ambiguity (→), for example, *I'll be back* can be either a promise or a threat.

Pragmatics. The study of language in context. It deals with how sentences relate to the world around them, most significantly the speakers and hearers.

Predicate. (1) In traditional grammar, the part of the sentence that contains the main verb, as opposed to the subject. (2) In predicate calculus (→), the element of a proposition that provides information about the arguments, for example, John *runs*, Mary *is tall*.

Predicate calculus. A branch of logic used in linguistics to describe the meaning of sentences and to determine their truth value (→).

Prefix. A morpheme (→) that occurs before the root (→) morpheme; for example, *un-believable, pre-determined, in-decisive.*

Preposition. A part of speech used with NPs (→) to form a prepositional phrase (→). Prepositions indicate spatial, temporal, and instrumental relations, for example, *over* as in *One flew over the cuckoo's nest.*

Prepositional phrase. A phrase (→) that has a preposition (→) as its head (→).

Prescriptivism. An unscientific approach to language consisting of formulating rules as to how a language should be used.

Present participle. A participle (→) in the present tense (→), formed by adding *-ing* to the stem (→), for example, *writing* in *I'm writing a glossary entry*, not to be confused with the gerund (→).

Present tense. The present tense (→) is usually used to refer to an action taking place at the moment of utterance but also for general truths, habitual actions, etc. In English, it is not marked morphologically. (→ past tense)

Presupposition. The set of sentences that must be true in order for a sentence to be true or false, for example, *Lunch is ready* presupposes that there exists a lunch.

Principle of cooperation. → cooperative principle.

Principle of falsification. Scientific methodological approach that holds that scientific statements must be falsifiable (i.e., one should have the theoretical possibility to prove them wrong).

Process approach. A theory of writing that focuses on the necessity of putting students through the steps of prewriting, writing, and revising for each assignment.

PRO-DROP parameter. A parameter (→) of universal grammar (→) describing the fact that in some languages, like Spanish or Italian, the subject pronoun can be omitted, whereas in others, like English or German, it can't, for example, Italian *Nevica!* in contrast to English *It snows!*

Product approach. In writing, the idea that the quality of a text is measured by its adherence to certain culturally derived forms (for example, comparison/contrast essay) or grammatical correctness and that the way to teach writing is to teach those forms.

Productive. When a process of language is productive, it can be applied to new elements that enter the language or to elements to which it previously didn't apply. The plural formation by adding the suffix *-s*, for example, *book—books*, is productive in English whereas the plural formation through changing the stem vowel, for example, *goose—geese*, isn't anymore.

Pronoun. A word that can be used in place of a noun (→) or noun phrase (→), for example, *I, her, they.*

Pronouns of power. The *V* pronouns that express a formal relationship—they are based on power (→) and distance.

Pronouns of solidarity. The *T* pronouns that express an egalitarian relationship and are informal, friendly, and intimate.

Prototype theory. A theory that claims that the meaning of words is not based on clear-cut, yes/no distinctions, but rather that there are degrees of membership into a class. For example, there are good examples of the concept of *bird* such as *robins* and *sparrows*, and progressively worse examples ending with flightless birds such as *emus* and *penguins.*

Prototypicality. The semantic phenomenon whereby some members of a class are seen as better examples of the class. A sparrow is a better example of bird than a penguin, despite their both being birds. A sparrow has more features commonly associated with birds (e.g., flight).

Proverb. In grammar, a word that can be used in the place of a verb in a sentence.

Quality. (1) The quality of a sound is its acoustic (→) makeup (→ timbre). In phonetics, the difference between [i] and [e] is a difference of quality. (→ pitch, length, volume) (2) A maxim of the cooperative principle (→) requiring that for efficient communication one must say only what is true and for what one has evidence, for example, not answer the question *What's the time?* by saying *eight-thirty*, when it is really four-thirty.

Quantifier. Words that express quantity, for example, some, all, etc. Used in predicate calculus (→). (→ ∃, ∀)

Quantity. A maxim of the cooperative principle (→) requiring that for efficient communication one needs to be informative and make one's contribution neither too long nor too short, for example, not answer the question *What's the time?* by saying *It is twenty-seven minutes and five seconds after eight on the sixth day of July in the year 1999.*

Reanalysis. → backformation.

Received pronunciation (RP). The standard or accepted accent (→) in Britain, is usually associated with upper-class speakers.

Reconstruction. The methods that are used to reconstruct languages of the past, most importantly the comparative method (→).

Recursion. In generative grammar, (→) a looping application of any of the rules to generate a sentence. Can be an infinite loop, for example, NP = Art + N + PP; PP = Prep + NP; etc.

Referent. Something to which words refer. For example, the referent for *table* is the object you actually touch, see, eat lunch on, etc.

Referential. A label applied to children whose first words tend to be labels for nouns (for example, *kitty, daddy*).

Reflected connotation. Aspects of connotative meaning tied to the meaning of a homophone (→) or to a different meaning of a given word, which are activated regardless of their relevance in a given context, for example, *a whale hump* may bring to mind the slang meaning of *hump.*

Regionalism. A grammatical or lexical dialectal feature that is marked for some (geographical) region. *Yall* is a Southern regionalism.

Register. A variety of language determined by situation and subject.

Relative clause. A subordinate clause that modifies a noun phrase and that is introduced by a relative pronoun *(who/whom, which, that).*

Relevance. A maxim of the cooperative principle (→) requiring that for efficient communication, you need to be relevant and speak on the point, for example, not answer the question *What's the time?* by saying *It's three-thirty in the Pacific time zone*, when speaker and hearer are in Boston, Massachusetts.

Relexification theory. A theory of the origin of pidgins that holds that they all come from Sabir (→) and that the various forms of pidgin all over the world would have replaced the Romance lexicon (→) of Sabir with the lexica of other languages.

Reported speech. A segment of speech in which the speaker relates another speaker's words. (→ indirect speech)

Request. A speech act (→) in which the speaker tries to get the hearer to do something.

Restricted code. Bernstein's term for the variety of language used in informal speech that is simpler and uses more concrete terms, referring to the here and now. (→ elaborated code)

Restricted pidgin. A pidgin that will eventually die out because it does not expand to cover all the domains of everyday life, for example, pidgins spoken in war zones, near military bases, etc. (→ pidgin, creole, extended/elaborated pidgin)

Restricted vocabulary. A vocabulary limited to basic terms in order to facilitate international communication or standardized definitions as in a lexicon.

Restrictive/nonrestrictive clauses. Relative clauses (→) that either help identify the referent of the noun phrase they modify, or do not, respectively. E.g., *the girl who plays the piano is my sister* is a restrictive relative clause if there are more than one girl, but only one who plays the piano. If, however, there is only one girl, then it is nonrestrictive.

Resultative motivation. As the student gets better at learning a second language, he or she is encouraged to continue. (→ integrative motivation, instrumental motivation, motivation, intrinsic motivation)

Reversing language shift. → language maintenance.

Rewriting rule. → phrase structure rule.

Rheme. The part of a sentence that expresses the new part of the meaning (→ functional sentence perspective, theme).

Rhyme. The repetition of both the vowel and the consonantal sound at the end of the word.

Rhotic accents. Accents that preserve the pronunciation of the [r] sound not followed by a vowel, e.g., *car*. Non-rhotic accents delete the [r], such as some Boston accents.

Rime. The part of the syllable (→) that includes the vowel and the following consonants, if any (→ coda)

Risk taking. A psychological category describing people who are willing to accept a high degree of uncertainty in setting out to accomplish a task.

Romance. The group of languages that evolved out of Latin in some of the areas conquered by the Romans. French, Italian, Spanish, Romanian are all romance languages.

Root morpheme. → free morpheme.

Rune. The letters of the alphabet used in certain North Germanic languages from the 3rd century on, for example, by the Vikings. The Runes are derived from either the Greek, Roman, or Etruscan alphabet and were replaced by the Roman alphabet when their users were Christianized in the early Middle Ages.

Russian formalism. A 20th century Russian school of criticism placing emphasis on the medium, the text itself, for its own interpretation and striving for scientific and formal rigor in literary analysis. It became influential in the West through the work of the structuralist (→) linguist (→) Roman Jakobson.

Sabir. A Portuguese-based trade language of the 15th century that is said by relexification theory (→) to be the ancestor of all pidgins (→).

Sapir-Whorf hypothesis. Named after Edward Sapir and Benjamin Lee Whorf and also called linguistic relativity hypothesis, this theory makes two basic claims: language and thinking are interdependent on a fundamental level. Therefore, the language you speak strongly determines the way you perceive the world and cannot fully be translated into another language.

Sarcasm. A type of irony (→), often heavy and/or critical. Current usage however increasingly uses sarcasm to refer to what would have been called irony.

Scansion. The process of determining stressed and unstressed syllables within a line of verse.

Scientific method. Scientific research method that forms a hypothesis based on data that has been collected and continues to check the validity of the hypothesis with new data collected. (→ principle of falsification)

Script. The sum of all the information connected with the meaning (→) of a word. For example, the script for the word *restaurant* has information about the fact that it is a place to go eat; there are servers, cooks, a bill, a tip, etc.

Script network. The representation of how words are connected in the brain. The sum of all links between scripts (→).

Second articulation. The fact that phonemes (→) can be combined into morphemes (→ first articulation).

Second language (L2). Any language not learned as a native speaker, i.e., after roughly the age of 12 (→ critical period, language acquisition, native speaker). *Second* is used at times to imply *third* or *fourth*. L2 is generally used on a daily basis in society.

Second language acquisition. The acquisition of a language other than those acquired by the child before the critical period expires. (→ second language, native speaker, language acquisition)

Semantic feature. Units of meaning into which a given word may be broken. The meaning of a word is said to be the sum of its features, for example, A boy is [+ male], [- adult], etc.

Semantic field. A group of words with related meanings. The meaning of each word is delimited by the meanings of the other words, e.g., furniture.

Semantic relationship. The connection between two or more words in the lexicon. (→ antonymy, synonymy)

Semantics. The field of linguistics studying the meaning in language.

Semiology. The science that studies signs, aka semiotics.

Sentence. A linguistic unit consisting of a subject (NP) (→) and a verb (→), with optional arguments. The largest unit dealt with by syntax (→).

Σ-F grammar. The simplest type of grammar that generates a language.

Sign. (1) In semiotics (→), something referring to something else. Words are signs. (2) In sign languages, the arbitrary symbols that form a highly developed, rule-governed system of that language.

Signified. The mental image of the meaning of a linguistic sign (→).

Signifier. The mental representation of the pronunciation (or spelling) of a linguistic sign (→).

Sign language. A language that uses primarily signs (→) done with the hands to communicate. Sign languages are full blown languages. (→ non-manual signal). American Sign Language is an example of sign language.

Silence. In conversation (→), the absence of speech for any period of time.

Silent period. A period in which the language learner does not produce any output (→). A period of silence is necessary in first language acquisition (→) and encountered also in second language acquisition (→).

Simile. A figure of speech that includes an explicit comparison such as *like* or *as*.

Simplification. A stage in second language acquisition (→) at which the learner uses a simplified form of the language omitting inflectional morphemes and even content words.

Situational code switching. When there are more than two varieties of language in a given community, one variety is used in specific situations and activities and the other variety in other instances. The people of the community alternate varieties as is appropriate. (→ code switching, metaphorical code switching)

Skills (based) approach. In teaching reading, the idea that students should be taught ways to read such as skimming and scanning or should be taught "text-attack" strategies.

Slang. A variety of language used by a subculture (e.g., students) to bolster status. Most slang changes quickly. (→ jargon)

Social connotations. The association attached to different levels of formality. (→ connotation)

Social deixis. Linguistic expressions that include a reference to the social status of the speakers, for example, their respective familiarity, age, power relationships, etc. (→ FN, TLN).

Social stratification. → class stratification.

Sociolinguistics. The branch of linguistics (→) that studies how language is used in all aspects of society.

Solidarity. The security and assurance of belonging to a certain group.

Sound-symbol correspondence. The relationship between the way a word is spoken and its representation through letters.

Spatial deixis. Linguistic expressions that encode references to the position of the speaker(s) in space, for example, *here, there*.

Speaking in tongues. → glossolalia.

Specialization. Human language is specialized in that it is context-independent and requires only part of our attention (in contrast to animal language).

Specific language impairment. Formerly called childhood aphasia, a cluster of language disorders that does not fit any of the other language pathologies.

Speech act. An utterance seen as an action on the part of the speaker; each speech act is seen as consisting of three separate acts: locutionary (→), illocutionary (→), and perlocutionary acts (→). (→ performative)

Speech area. Region where people may not share the same language but their conversational rules are the same.

Speech community. A group of people that differentiate themselves from others by using language in an agreed way.

Split infinitive. An infinitive in which an adverb or adverbial is placed between *to* and the bare verb, for example, *to boldly go*.

Standard English. The standard variety (→) of English. Practically speaking, there used to be a standard variety of British English, known as received pronunciation (→), but there isn't really any standard variety of American English, except in written form.

Standard language. The standard variety (→) of a language.

Standard variety. A variety of language that because of social or cultural prestige is accepted by a community as being more prestigious than others. Standard varieties can arise out of koiné [→] phenomena, or from economic and political prestige (as in the case of the rise of London English), or for cultural reasons, e.g., Luther's bible translation, which becomes standard German.

Status. Status refers to the higher, lower, or equal social position of speakers or speech varieties to each other. Different status relations lead to different speech varieties being used by the speakers, as for example in diglossia (→), the use of basi-, meso- or acrolect (→), or forms of address (→ FN, TLN, honorifics). Status is determined by social factors like prestige, power (→), etc.

Status planning. Type of language planning (→) concerned with people's attitude toward language and dialects (→); often involves deciding which languages will be taught in schools.

Stem. → free morpheme.

Stop. A sound produced with a complete closure (→ occlusion) along the vocal tract (→) and by the subsequent release of the airflow in one short burst.

Stream of consciousness. Narrative technique used to render the uncontrolled mind flow of fragmentary and impressionistic thoughts into words. Its most famous use is in James Joyce's *Ulysses* (1922).

Stress. Emphasis on particular syllables in pronunciation. There are different levels of stress, but for metrical purposes, the distinction is between stressed (strong) and unstressed (weak) syllables.

Strong verb. A verb (→) that uses ablaut (→) instead of inflectional morphemes (→) to form the simple past and the past participle, for example, *eat, ate, eaten.*

Structural semantics. A theory of semantics attempting to define the words of a language through their semantic features (→).

Structuralism. A linguistic (→) term to describe looking at language as a system.

Stuttering. An impairment in the fluency of speech, often consisting in the repetition of syllables in words.

Style. A variety of language that may differ from other varieties in a number of ways, including formality, word choice, situation, etc. [→ register].

Subjunctive mood. Verb form that indicates different degrees of certainty in relationship to the action of the verb such as possibility, hypothetical, untrue situations, etc.

Subordinate language. A language with less prestige than another language used in the same area. (→ superordinate language)

Subordination. A way of joining sentences in which the sentences are on different levels (one is a main clause (→) and the other is contained in it).

Substrate language. A language that provides the grammar of a pidgin (→), usually it is a disempowered language.

Suffix. A morpheme (→) that occurs after the root (→) morpheme; for example, odd-*ly*, love-*s*, laugh-*ed*.

Superordinate language. A language with more prestige than another language used in the same area. (→ subordinate language)

Superstrate language. The language that has power in a given area and imposes its lexicon on the formation of a pidgin (→ lexifier language, pidgin).

Suprasegmental. The part of the pronunciation of a sentence that describes more than one unit (segment). Intonation (→) is a suprasegmental feature.

Surface structure. The syntactic representation of a sentence after the transformations (→) have applied. The closest syntactic structure to how a sentence will actually be uttered.

Syllable. A phonological unit that can be produced in isolation. In English, a vowel preceded and/or followed by up to three consonants.

Syllabic system. A system like Japanese where each syllable corresponds to a written symbol.

Symbol. In literary theory, something that implies or alludes to something else, like the rose that stands for love.

Synchronic. The study of a language from the point of view of how it functions at a given point in time, without reference to its history. (↔ diachronic)

Synecdoche. Figure of speech meaning "part for the whole." E.g., *I will give you a hand moving the sofa* where obviously one does not expect a detached hand.

Synonyms. Two words with similar or identical meanings, for example, *car* and *automobile.*

Syntactic ambiguity. Sentences (→) that are compatible with more than one syntactic analysis.

Syntax. The way words are put together to form constructions, such as phrases (→) and sentences (→). It is based on the idea of grammaticality (→).

T and V pronouns. The pronoun distinction between the polite/formal way to address a person *(tu)* and the formal way *(vous).*

Taboo. Expressions or actions that are discouraged by society.

Tag question. A question that contains an auxilary verb, a negation, and a pronoun at the end of a statement, for example, *It's raining, isn't it?*

Target language. In translation theory, the language into which one is translating. In language teaching, L2 (→).

Tautology. A sentence that is always true, no matter in what circumstances it is uttered, usually because it states something that is true by way of definition (A dog is a dog). In logic, tautologies are believed to convey no information, whereas in natural language tautologies are informative (cf. *boys will be boys* = boys behave in a certain boisterous or reckless way).

Taxonomy. A classification.

Tenor. In the description of metaphor (→), the tenor is the idea or object we want to talk about (→ vehicle).

Tense. Part of the semantics of the verb (→). It indicates the relationship between the event described in the verb and the time of speaking and/or a time of reference. (→ aspect, mood)

Tensed. Verb or clause with an inflectional morpheme (→).

Terminal symbols. In the generation (→) of a sentence, the last units that are generated after all the rules have been applied. Practically, the words of a language.

Text linguistics. A field of linguistics (→) where the focus of study is on written or spoken texts and their construction, organization etc.

Theme. Part of the sentence that presents the old information in the communicative dynamism (→) analysis. It is opposed to the rheme (→), which presents the new information, for example, *Mary* in *Mary is a genius.* (→ functional sentence perspective)

Theoretical grammar. A highly technical, extremely advanced description meant for specialists, often focusing on the fragments of the language, with little attempt to be comprehensive. (→ grammar, case grammar, descriptive grammar)

Thesaurus. A dictionary of synonyms (→) that may be organized alphabetically or on the basis of meaning relationships.

Time deixis. Linguistic expressions that encode reference to the time of speaking, for example, *last year, now.*

TLN. Acronym for *title, last name,* counterpart to FN (→). Form of address used by a person of lower status (→) to address a person of higher status, for example, *Excuse me, Dr. Darwin.* (→ honorific)

TMA. Acronym for tense (→), mood (→), and aspect (→). Roughly, the ways in which the lexical semantics of the verb are modified by the grammar.

Tok Pisin. The English-based pidgin (→) that has become the national language in Papua New Guinea.

Tone. The pitch (→) of a syllable. In some languages differences in tone may convey differences in meaning. Pitches may be level, or rise and/or fall.

Top-down process. Way of analyzing new text that involves using prior knowledge and experience. (→ bottom-up)

Trade language. → LWC.

Transformation. A rule that takes as input a sentence and produces another sentence or structure (and meaning) related to the first one, for example, *Mary sings* becomes *Does Mary sing?* by the application of the *question formation* transformation. (→ deep structure, surface structure)

Transformational-generative grammar. A generative grammar (→) augmented by a set of rules (→ transformation) that can relate different types of sentences, e.g., statements and questions, which are assumed to share the same origin. (→ deep structure)

Transition relevance place (TRP). A point in conversation (→) where it is acceptable to take or relinquish the floor →.

Transitive. A verb that takes only a direct object, for example *drink.*

Translation. The rendering of a source text into a target text in a language different from that of the source text.

Transliteration. To transliterate a word means to use the characters of one language to represent those of another language, for example, to transliterate Arabic or Chinese characters into the Latin alphabet used in English.

Tree diagram. A diagram used to represent the syntactic structure of a sentence. It uses branching lines to show how the sentence is broken down into phrases and words.

Triggering. The setting of a parameter (→) based on input (→ LAD, innatism).

Trochee. In poetry, a metric foot (→) consisting of a stressed syllable followed by an unstressed syllable (for example, fórest).

Truth conditions. What it takes for a sentence to have a truth value (→); the conditions that one needs to check to know if a sentence is true or false.

Truth value. Whether the sentence is true or not is the truth value of the sentence, for example, *Mary is married* is true if and only if Mary happens to be married. If she is not married, then the sentence is false.

Turn taking. The process whereby speakers negotiate who is to speak next.

UG. universal grammar (→).

Underextension. The process by which a child uses a word having a meaning that is narrower than the normal meaning of the word, for example, using *mommy* to indicate only the child's mother and not *any* mother. (↔ overextension)

Underreporting. The phenomenon whereby speakers claim to use less nonprestige forms than they actually do [→ overreporting].

Universal grammar (UG). The very general rules of grammar that are assumed to be common to all languages and are part of the human genetic endowment.

Unmarked. ↔ marked.

Unmarked received pronunciation. A form of pronunciation of English in Britain used by announcers, teachers, secretaries, and educated people in general; considered to be the normal, unexceptional form. (→ received pronunciation, marked RP)

Unpacking. The breaking down of formulaic language into its constituent parts (→ formula).

Unreleased. Term of phonetics (→) for articulating a sound without releasing any airflow.

Utterance. The production of a sentence (→) by a given speaker in a given context.

Variety. Any language system that is distinguishable from another system by linguistic features of any kind.

Vehicle. In the description of metaphor (→), the vehicle is the term we use to refer to the object we are attempting to describe (→ tenor).

Velum. Part of the mouth that opens or closes the connection with the nasal cavity. (→ nasalization)

Verb. A word that is the central element of a verb phrase (→), the predicate that denotes actions, states, or processes. Together with nouns (→) verbs are the principal parts of a sentence.

Verb phrase. A phrase with a verb (→) as its head (→); for example, in the sentence *Mary loves flowers*, [loves flowers] is a verb phrase.

Verbal deprivation. → deficit theory.

Verbal repertoire. The linguistic options available to a speaker or community. For example, the repertoire of forms of address [→] in American English includes first name, title and last name, nicknames, and other options.

Vernacular. Originally, the variety of Latin spoken by the people of the countryside, as opposed to the urban varieties. Then, during the Middle Ages, vernaculars were the various national languages, such as French, Spanish, German, spoken by the people, while learned people spoke Latin. As a result, today vernacular means a nonstandard, popular variety.

Verner's law. Karl Verner described the regular exception to Grimm's law (→), where the Indo-European voiceless stops did not remain fricatives in Germanic but became stops again.

Vocal cords. Aka, vocal folds, larynx. Two bands of muscles at the end of the trachea, which may contract to produce a vibration in the airflow (→ voice).

Vocal tract. The parts of the body used in producing speech sounds.

Voice. (1) In grammar, the way the verb sets up the relationship between the subject and the direct object. In English, there are two voices, active (→) and passive (→). Other languages, such as ancient Greek, have a *middle* voice, which describes actions that the agent does upon him or herself (i.e., reflexive verbs). (2) In phonology, whether the vocal folds are vibrating, in which case a sound is said to be *voiced*. (3) As a nontechnical term, the sounds one makes when speaking, for example, *She spoke with a loud voice.*

Voiced sound. → voice.

Voiceless sound. → voice.

Voiceprint. In forensic linguistics, because the acoustic analysis of someone's speech can be used to identify that speaker, like with fingerprints, it is called a voiceprint.

Volume. The loudness of a sound.

Vowel. Sound produced without any occlusion on the vocal tract. (→ consonant)

Weak verb. In contrast to strong verbs (→), weak verbs use inflectional morphemes (→) to indicate past tense (→) and past participle (→), in English the suffix *-ed* as in *walked.*

Whole language. A type of language instruction in which children read or write texts in their entirety, not in bits or excerpts. The focus is on making language meaningful to students and issues of accuracy in spelling and grammar are played down.

WH-question. A question beginning with *who, what, when, where, why,* or *how.*

Wolof. An African language used as a lingua franca ($\rightarrow$) in West Africa at the time of the slave trade.

Zero copula. The absence of the copular verb *be.*

Zero morpheme. The absence of morpheme that is meaningfully opposed to the presence of another morpheme in a system. E.g., the *-s* marker for the third person singular present of verbs in English and the zero morpheme of the first and second.

Zoosemiotics. The branch of semiotics describing animal communication systems and parts of the human communication system that derive from these through evolution, for example, facial expressions and gestures.

Bibliography

Adams, Marilyn Jager. *Beginning to Read: Thinking and Learning about Print*. Cambridge, MA: The MIT Press, 1990.

Adger, Carolyn Temple, Donna Christian, and Orlando Taylor, eds. *Making the Connection: Language and Academic Achievement among African American Students*. McHenry, IL: Delta Systems, 1999.

Ahulu, Samuel. "Lexical Variation in International English." *English Today* 14, no. 3 (1998): 29–34.

Aitchison, Jean. *Linguistics*, 4th ed. Chicago: NTC Publishing Group, 1992.

Akmajian, Adrian, Richard A. Demers, Ann K. Farmer, and Robert M. Harnish. *Linguistics: An Introduction to Language and Communication*. 5th ed. Cambridge: The MIT Press, 2001.

Allen, Harold B., ed. *Readings in Applied English Linguistics*. 2d ed. New York: Appleton-Century-Crofts, 1964.

Arlotto, Anthony. *Introduction to Historical Linguistics*. Boston: Houghton Mifflin, 1972.

Asher, Ronald E., ed. *The Encyclopedia of Language and Linguistics*. 10 vols. Oxford/New York: Pergamon Press, 1994.

Austin, John L. *How to Do Things with Words*. Oxford: Oxford University Press, 1962.

Bailey, Guy, and Erik Thomas. "Some Aspects of African-American Vernacular English Phonology." In *African-American English: Structure, History and Use*, ed. Salikoko S. Mufwene, John R. Rickford, Guy Bailey, and John Baugh, 85–109. London: Routledge, 1998.

Bailey, Richard W. *Dictionaries of English: Prospects for the Record of Our Language*. Ann Arbor: University of Michigan Press, 1987.

———. *Images of English: A Cultural History of the Language*. Ann Arbor: University of Michigan Press, 1991.

Bailey, Richard W., and Manfred Görlach. *English as a World Language*. Ann Arbor: University of Michigan Press, 1982.

Bal, Mieke. *Narratology: Introduction to the Theory of Narrative*. Translated by Christine van Boheemen. Toronto/Buffalo: University of Toronto Press, 1985.

Barasch, Ronald M., and C. Vaughn James. *Beyond the Monitor Model: Comments on Current Theory and Practice in Second Language Acquisition.* Boston: Heinle & Heinle Publishers, 1994.

Barnes, Susan B. *Computer-Mediated Communication: Human-to-Human Communication across the Internet.* Boston: Allyn & Bacon, 2002.

Baron, Dennis E. *The English-Only Question.* New Haven, CT: Yale University Press, 1990.

Barr, Rebecca, Michael L. Kamil, Peter Mosenthal, and P. David Pearson. *Handbook of Reading Research.* Vol. 2. London: Longman, 1991.

Barsky, Robert F. *Noam Chomsky: A Life of Dissent.* Cambridge, MA: The MIT Press, 1997.

Barthes, Roland. *Elements of Semiology.* Translated by Annette Lavers and Colin Smith. New York: Hill and Wang, 1968.

Baugh, Albert C., and Thomas Cable. *A History of the English Language.* 5th ed. Englewood Cliffs: Prentice-Hall, 2001.

Baugh, John. "Linguistics, Education, and the Law: Educational Reform for African-American Language Minority Students." In *African-American English*, ed. Salikoko S. Mufwene, John R. Rickford, Guy Bailey, and John Baugh, 282–301. London: Routledge, 1998.

———. *Beyond Ebonics: Linguistic Pride and Racial Prejudice.* Oxford: Oxford University Press, 2000.

Beardsmore, Hugo Baetens. "Language Policy and Planning in Western European Countries." *Annual Review of Applied Linguistics* 14 (1993/94): 93–110.

Beebe, Leslie M. "Five Sociolinguistic Approaches to Second Language Acquistion." In *Issues in Second Language Acquistion: Multiple Perspectives*, ed. Leslie Beebe, 43–77. New York: Newberry House, 1988.

Béjoint, Henri. *Tradition and Innovation in Modern English Dictionaries.* Oxford: Clarendon Press, 1994.

Benson, Evelyn, Morton Benson, and Robert Ilson. *Lexicographic Description of English.* Amsterdam/Philadelphia: John Benjamins Publishing Company, 1986.

Berko, Jean. "The Child's Learning of English Morphology." *Word* 14 (1958): 150–77.

Berko-Gleason, Jean. "Fathers and Other Strangers: Men's Speech to Young Children." In *Developmental Psycholinguistics: Theory and Applications*, ed. Daniel P. Dato, 289–97. Washington, DC: Georgetown University Press, 1975.

———. *The Development of Language.* 5th ed. New York: Pearson, 2001.

Berlin, Brent, and Paul Kay. *Basic Color Terms: Their Universality and Evolution.* Berkeley, CA: University of California Press, 1969.

Bernstein, Basil B. *Class, Codes, and Control: Towards a Theory of Educational Transmission.* London: Routledge and Kegan Paul, 1973.

———. *Pedagogy, Symbolic Control and Identity: Theory, Research Critique.* revised ed. Lanham: Rowman and Littlefield, 2000.

Bernstein-Ratner, Nan. "Atypical Language Development." In *The Development of Language*, ed. Jean Berko-Gleason, 369–406. Columbus: Merrill Publishing Company, 1989.

Biber, Douglas. *Variation across Speech and Writing.* Cambridge: Cambridge University Press, 1988.

Biber, Douglas, Susan Conrad, Edward Finegan, Stig Johansson, and Geoffrey Leech. *Longman Grammar of Spoken and Written English.* London: Longman, 1999.

Biber, Douglas, Susan Conrad, and Randi Reppen. *Corpus Linguistics*. Cambridge: Cambridge University Press, 1998.

Bickerton, Derek. *Roots of Language*. Ann Arbor: Karoma, 1981.

Bjarkman, Peter C., and Victor Raskin, eds. *The Real-World Linguist: Linguistic Applications in the 1980s*. Norwood: ABLEX, 1986.

Blair, David, and Peter Collins. *English in Australia*. Philadelphia: John Benjamins, 2001.

Bley-Vroman, Robert. "What Is the Logical Problem of Foreign Language Learning?" In *Linguistic Perspectives on Second Language Acquisition*, ed. Susan Gass and Jacquelyn Schachter, 41–68. Cambridge: Cambridge University Press, 1989.

Blom, Jan-Petter, and John J. Gumperz. "Social Meaning in Linguistic Structures: Code-Switching in Norway." In *Directions in Sociolinguistics: The Ethnography of Communication*, ed. John J. Gumperz and Dell Hymes, 407–34. Oxford: Basil Blackwell, 1986.

Bloomfield, Leonard. *Language*. New York: H. Holt & Company, 1933.

Bolinger, Dwight, and Donald A. Sears. *Aspects of Language*. 3rd ed. New York: Harcourt Brace Jovanovich, 1981.

Bonvillain, Nancy. *Language, Culture, and Communication*. Englewood Cliffs: Prentice-Hall, 1993.

Booth, Wayne C. *The Rhetoric of Fiction*. Chicago: University of Chicago Press, 1961.

Botha, Rudolf P. *The Conduct of Linguistic Inquiry: A Systematic Introduction to the Methodology of Generative Grammar*. Vol. 157, *Janua Linguarum*. Series Practica. The Hague: Mouton, 1981.

Braddock, Richard, Richard Lloyd-Jones, and Lowell Schoer. *Research in Written Composition*. Champaign, IL: National Council of Teachers of English, 1963.

Braine, Martin D. S. "On Two Types of Models of the Internalization of Grammars." In *The Ontogenesis of Grammar: A Theoretical Symposium*, ed. Dan I. Slobin, 153–88. New York: Academic Press, 1971.

Bremond, Claude. *Logique du Récit*. Paris: Seuil, 1973.

Bright, William, ed. *International Encyclopedia of Linguistics*. 4 vols. New York: Oxford University Press, 1992.

Brown, Gillian, and George Yule. *Discourse Analysis*. Cambridge: Cambridge University Press, 1983.

Brown, Penelope, and Stephen C. Levinson. *Politeness: Some Universals in Language Use*. Cambridge: Cambridge University Press, 1987.

Brown, Roger. *A First Language: The Early Stages*. London: George Allen and Unwin, 1973.

Brown, Roger, and Albert F. Gilman. "The Pronouns of Power and Solidarity." In *Language and Social Context*, ed. Pier Paolo Giglioli, 252–82. Harmondsworth: Penguin, 1972.

Brown, Roger, and Camille Hanlon. "Derivational Complexity and Order of Acquisition in Child Speech." In *Cognition and the Development of Language*, ed. John R. Hayes, 11–54. New York: Wiley, 1970.

Brown, Steven. "Gender, Japanese Pronouns, and Social Change: A Preliminary Investigation." *JALT Journal* 16 (1994): 217–24.

Brown, Steven, and Jodi Eisterhold. *Topics in Language and Culture for Teachers*. Ann Arbor: University of Michigan Press, 2004.

Brugman, Claudia. *Story of Over*. Bloomington: Indiana University Linguistics Club, 1983.

Bucholz, Mary. ed., and Robin Tolnach Lakoff. *Language and Woman's Place: Text and Commentaries*. Oxford: Oxford University Press, 2004.

Burrow, John A., and Thorlac Turville-Petre. *A Book of Middle English*. 2d ed. Oxford: Blackwell, 1996.

Bussman, Hadumod. *Routledge Dictionary of Language and Linguistics*. Translated by Kerstin Kazzazi and Gregory Trauth. London: Routledge, 1996.

Butters, Ronald R. *The Death of Black English: Divergence and Convergence in Black and White Vernaculars*. Frankfurt/New York: P. Lang, 1989.

Cameron, Deborah. *Feminism and Linguistic Theory*. London: Macmillan, 1985.

Canagarajah, A. Suresh. *Critical Academic Writing and Multilingual Students*. Ann Arbor: University Michigan Press, 2002.

Carey, Stephen. "Language Management, Official Bilingualism, and Multiculturalism in Canada." *Annual Review of Applied Linguistics* 17 (1997): 204–23.

Carroll, John. "Cognitive Abilities in Foreign Language Aptitude: Then and Now." In *Language Aptitude Reconsidered*, ed. Thomas S. Parry and Charles W. Stansfield, 11–29. Englewood Cliffs, NJ: Prentice Hall, 1990.

Carroll, Tessa. *Language Planning and Language Change in Japan*. Richmond, UK: Curzon, 2001.

Carter, Ronald. *Vocabulary: Applied Linguistics Perspectives*. London: Allen & Unwin, 1987.

Carver, Craig M. *American Regional Dialects: A Word Geography*. Ann Arbor: University of Michigan Press, 1987.

Cassidy, Frederic G., and Joan Houston Hall, eds. *Dictionary of American Regional English*. Vol. 2. Cambridge: Belknap Press of Harvard University Press, 1985.

Catford, John C. *A Linguistic Theory of Translation: An Essay in Applied Linguistics*. London: Oxford University Press, 1965.

Celce-Murcia, Marianne, and Diane Larsen-Freeman. *The Grammar Book: An ESL/EFL Teacher's Course*. 2d ed. Rowley: Newbury House, 1999.

Chaika, Elaine. *Language: The Social Mirror*. 3rd ed. Boston: Heinle & Heinle, 1994.

Chambers, J. K., and Peter Trudgill. *Dialectology*. Cambridge: Cambridge University Press, 1980.

Chatman, Seymour B. *Story and Discourse: Narrative Structure in Fiction and Film*. Ithaca: Cornell University Press, 1978.

Chaudron, Craig. *Second Language Classrooms: Research on Teaching and Learning*. Cambridge: Cambridge University Press, 1988.

Cherny, Lynn. *Conversation and Community: Chat in a Virtual World*. Stanford, CA: CSLI Publications, 1999.

Cipollone, Nick, Steven Hartman Keiser, and Shravan Vasishth, eds. *Language Files*. 7th ed. Columbus: Ohio State University Press, 1998.

Clark, Eve V. *First Language Acquisition*. Cambridge: Cambridge University Press, 2003.

———. *The Lexicon in Acquisition*. Cambridge: Cambridge University Press, 1993.

Clark, John. *Early English*. New York: W. W. Norton & Company, Inc., 1957.

Clark, John, and Colin Yallop. *An Introduction to Phonetics and Phonology*. 2d ed. Oxford: Blackwell, 1995.

Close, Reginald A. *A Reference Grammar for Students of English*. Harlow: Longman, 1975.

Clyne, Michael. "Multilingualism in Australia." *Annual Review of Applied Linguistics* 17 (1997): 191–203.

Coates, Jennifer. "Epistemic Modality and Spoken Discourse." *Transactions of the Philological Society* (1987): 110–31.

———. "Gossip Revisited: Language in All-Female Groups." In *Women in Their Speech Communities: New Perspectives on Language and Sex*, ed. Jennifer Coates and Deborah Cameron, 94–122. London: Longman, 1989.

———. *Women, Men and Language*. 2d ed. London: Longman, 1993.

———. *Language and Gender: A Reader*. Oxford: Blackwell, 1998.

Coates, Jennifer, and Deborah Cameron. *Women in Their Speech Communities*. London: Longman, 1989.

Cohen, Andrew, and Elite Olshtain. "Developing a Measure of Socio-Cultural Competence: The Case of Apology." *Language Learning* 31 (1981): 113–34.

Connor, Ulla. *Contrastive Rhetoric*. Cambridge: Cambridge University Press, 1996.

Conroy, Pat. *The Water Is Wide*. Boston: Houghton Miffin, 1972.

Cook, Vivian James. *Chomsky's Universal Grammar: An Introduction*. 2d ed. Oxford: Blackwell, 1996.

Corder, S. P. *Error Analysis and Interlanguage*. London: Oxford University Press, 1981a.

———. "Formal Simplicity and Functional Simplification." In *New Dimensions in Second Language Acquisition Research*, ed. Roger Andersen, 146–52. Rowley: Newbury House, 1981b.

Cordes, Anne K., and Roger J. Ingham, eds. *Treatment Efficacy for Stuttering: A Search for Empirical Bases*. San Diego: Singular Publishing Group, 1998.

Cowie, A. P. *English Dictionaries for Foreign Learners: A History*. Oxford: Oxford University Press, 1999.

Crain, Caleb. "The Bard's Fingerprints." *Lingua Franca* 8, no. 5 (1998): 28–39.

Crawford, James. *Language Loyalties: A Source Book on the Official English Controversy*. Chicago: The University of Chicago Press, 1992.

Crawford, Mary. *Talking Difference: On Gender and Language*. London: Sage, 1995.

Crowley, Tony. *Standard English and the Politics of Language*. Urbana: University of Illinois Press, 1989.

Cruse, D. A. *Lexical Semantics*. Cambridge: Cambridge University Press, 1986.

Crystal, David. *The Cambridge Encyclopedia of Language*. Cambridge/New York: Cambridge University Press, 1987.

———. *The Cambridge Encyclopedia of the English Language*. 2d ed. Cambridge: Cambridge University Press, 1997.

———. *Language Death*. Cambridge: Cambridge University Press, 2000.

———. *Language and the Internet*. Cambridge: Cambridge University Press, 2001.

———. *A Dictionary of Linguistics and Phonetics*. 5th ed. Oxford: Blackwell, 2003.

———. *The Stories of English*. Woodstock: The Overlook Press, 2004.

Culatta, Richard A., and James R. Tompkins. *Fundamentals of Special Education: What Every Teacher Needs to Know.* Upper Saddle River, NJ: Merrill, 1999.

Culicover, Peter H. *Principles and Parameters: An Introduction to Syntactic Theory.* Oxford: Oxford University Press, 1997.

Curtiss, Susan. *Genie: A Psycholinguistic Study of a Modern-Day "Wild Child."* New York: Academic Press, 1977.

deBoysson-Bardies, Bénédicte. *How Language Comes to Children.* Cambridge, MA: The MIT Press, 1999.

DeFrancisco, Victoria L. "The Sounds of Silence: How Men Silence Women in Marital Relations." *Discourse and Society* 2 (1991): 413–24.

deVilliers, Peter A., and Jill G. deVilliers. *Early Language.* Cambridge: Harvard University Press, 1979.

Dillard, Joey L. *Black English: Its History and Usage in the United States.* New York: Random House, 1972.

———. *All-American English.* New York: Random House, 1975.

———. *A History of American English.* London: Longman Group UK Ltd., 1992.

DiPietro, Robert J., ed. *Linguistics and the Professions: Proceedings of the Second Annual Delaware Symposium on Language Studies.* Norwood, NJ: Ablex, 1982.

Dixon, Robert M. W. *Searching for Aboriginal Languages.* Chicago: University of Chicago, 1984.

Donahue, Thomas S. "On Inland Northern and the Factors for Dialect Spread and Shift." In *"Heartland" English: Variation and Transition in the American Midwest,* ed. Timothy C. Frazer, 49–58. Tuscaloosa: University of Alabama Press, 1993.

Dorian, Nancy C. *Language Death: The Life Cycle of a Scottish Gaelic Dialect.* Philadelphia: University of Pennsylvania Press, 1981.

Doughty, Catherine J., and Michael H. Long, eds. *The Handbook of Second Language Acquisition.* Malden, MA: Blackwell, 2003.

Dressler, Wolfgang. "Language Death." In *Linguistics: The Cambridge Survey Volume IV,* ed. Frederich J. Newmeyer, 184–92. Cambridge: Cambridge University Press, 1988.

Dressler, Wolfgang, and Ruth Wodak-Leodolter, eds. *Language Death: International Journal of the Sociology of Language.* Vol. 12. The Hague: Mouton Publishers, 1977.

Ducrot, Oswald, and Tzvetan Todorov. *Dictionnaire Encyclopedique des Sciences du Langage.* Paris: Editions du Seuil, 1972.

Dulay, Heidi, Marina Burt, and Stephen Krashen. *Language Two.* New York: Oxford University Press, 1982.

Eades, Diana. "Participation of Second Language and Second Dialect Speakers in the Legal System. *Annual Review of Applied Linguistics* 23 (2003): 113–33.

Eagleson, Robert D. "English in Australia and New Zealand." In *English as a World Language,* ed. Richard W. Bailey and Manfred Görlach, 415–38. Ann Arbor: University of Michigan Press, 1982.

Eble, Connie. *Slang and Sociability: In-Group Language Among College Students.* Chapel Hill: University of North Carolina Press, 1996.

Eckert, Penelope. *Jocks and Burnouts: Social Categories and Identity in the High School.* New York: Teachers College Press, 1989.

Eckert, Penelope, and Sally McConnell-Ginet. "Think Practically and Look Locally: Language and Gender as Community-Based Practice." *Annual Review of Anthropology* 21 (1992): 461–90.

———. *Language and Gender.* New York: Cambridge University Press, 2003.

Edwards, James. "Language Planning and Policy in Canada." *Annual Review of Applied Linguistics* 14 (1993/94): 126–36.

———. "Language Minorities and Language Maintenance." *Annual Review of Applied Linguistics* 17 (1997): 30–42.

Edwards, John. *Multilingualism.* Harmondworth: Penguin, 1994.

Eggington, William. "Language Policy and Planning in Australia." *Annual Review of Applied Linguistics* 14 (1993/94): 137–55.

Ehri, Linnea C. "Development of the Ability to Read Words: Update." In *Theoretical Models and Processes of Reading.* 4th ed. Robert B. Ruddell, Martha Rapp Ruddell, and Harry Singer, eds., 323–58. Newark, DE: International Reading Association, 1994.

Ehrlich, Susan. "Gender as Social Practice: Implications for Second Language Acquisition." *Studies in Second Language Acquisition* 19 (1997): 421–46.

Elley, Warwick B., Ian H. Barham, Hilary Lamb, and Malcolm Wyllie. *The Role of Grammar in a Secondary School Curriculum.* Wellington: New Zealand Council for Educational Research, 1979.

Ellis, Rod. *Classroom Second Language Development: A Study of Classroom Interaction and Language Acquisition.* Oxford: Pergamon Press, 1984.

———. *Instructed Second Language Acquisition: Learning in the Classroom.* Oxford: Basil Blackwell, 1990.

———. *The Study of Second Language Acquisition.* Oxford: Oxford University Press, 1994.

Ervin-Tripp, Susan M. *Language Acquisition and Communicative Choice.* Stanford: Stanford University Press, 1973.

Fairclough, Norman. *Language and Power.* London: Longman, 1989.

Fang, Hanquan Q., and J. H. Heng. "Social Changes and Changing Address Norms in China." *Language in Society* 12, no. 4 (1983): 495–509.

Fasold, Ralph H. *The Sociolinguistics of Language.* Vol. 2. Language in Society. Cambridge: Basil Blackwell, 1990.

Fennell, Barbara. *A History of English: A Sociolinguistic Approach.* Malden MA: Blackwell, 2001.

Ferguson, Charles A. "Absence of Copula and the Notion of Simplicity: A Study of Normal Speech, Baby Talk, Foreigner Talk and Pidgins." In *Pidginization and Creolization of Languages,* ed. Dell Hymes, 141–50. Cambridge: Cambridge University Press, 1971.

———. "Diglossia." In *Language and Social Context: Selected Readings,* ed. Pier Paolo Giglioli, 232–51. Harmondsworth: Penguin, 1972.

———. "Sports Announcer Talk: Syntactic Aspects of Register Variation." *Language in Society* 12, no. 2 (1983): 153–72.

———. *Sociolinguistic Perspectives: Papers on Language in Society, 1959–1994.* New York: Oxford University Press, 1996.

Ferris, Dana, and John S. Hedgcock. *Teaching ESL Composition: Purpose, Process, and Practice.* Mahwah, NJ: Lawrence Erlbaum Associates, 1998.

Fillmore, Charles J. *Lectures on Deixis.* Stanford, CA: CSLI, 1997.

Finegan, Edward. *Language: Its Structure and Use.* 2d ed. New York: Harcourt Brace, 1994.

Fisher, Sue. "Doctor Talk/Patient Talk: How Treatment Decisions Are Negotiated in Doctor-Patient Communication." In *The Social Organization of Doctor-Patient Communication,* ed. Sue Fisher and Alexandra Dundas Todd, 135–58. Washington, DC: Center for Applied Linguistics, 1983.

Fishman, Joshua A. *The Rise and Fall of the Ethnic Revival.* Berlin: Mouton, 1985.

———. *Reversing Language Shift: Theory and Practice of Assistance to Threatened Languages.* Clevedon: Multilingual Matters, 1992.

Fishman, Pamela. "Interactional Shitwork." *Heresies* 2 (1980): 99–101.

Foley, Joseph. *New Englishes: The Case of Singapore.* Singapore: Singapore University Press, 1988.

Foster, Donald W. *Author Unknown: On the Trail of Anonymous.* New York: Holt, 2000.

Foster, Susan H. *The Communicative Competence of Young Children: A Modular Approach.* London: Longman, 1990.

Fowler, Roger. *Linguistic Criticism.* Oxford: Oxford University Press, 1986.

Fowler, Roger, Bob Hodge, Gunther Kress, and Tony Trew, eds. *Language and Control.* London: Routledge and Kegan Paul, 1979.

Frank, Francine Wattman, and Paula A. Teichler. *Language, Gender and Professional Writing.* New York: Modern Language Association, 1989.

Frawley, William J. *International Encyclopedia of Linguistics.* 2nd ed. Oxford: Oxford University Press, 2003.

Frescura, Marina Sassu. *Interferenze Lessicali Italiano-Inglese.* Toronto: University of Toronto Press, 1984.

Fromkin, Victoria, Robert Rodman, and Nina Hyams. *An Introduction to Language.* 7th ed. Fort Worth: Harcourt Brace College Publishers, 2002.

Fry, Edward B., ed. *The New Reading Teacher's Book of Lists.* 2d ed. Englewood Cliffs, NJ: Prentice-Hall, 1985.

Funk, Robert, and Martha Kolln. *Understanding English Grammar.* 5th ed. Needham: Allyn & Bacon, 1998.

Fussell, Paul. *Poetic Meter and Poetic Form.* Revised ed. New York: McGraw-Hill, 1979.

Gallaway, Clare, and Brian J. Richards. *Input and Interaction in Language Acquisition.* Cambridge: Cambridge University Press, 1994.

Gardner, Robert C. *Social Psychology and Second Language Learning: The Role of Attitude and Motivation.* London: Edward Arnold, 1985.

Garfinkel, Harold. *Studies in Ethnomethodology.* Cambridge: Polity, 1984.

Gass, Susan M. *Input, Interaction, and the Second Language Learner.* Mahwah, NJ: Lawrence Erlbaum Associates, 1997.

Gass, Susan M., and Evangeline Varonis. "Task Variation and Native/Nonnative Negotiation of Meaning." In *Input in Second Language Acquisition,* ed. Susan M. Gass and Carolyn G. Madden, 149–61. Rowley: Newbury House, 1985.

Gass, Susan M., and Larry Selinker. *Second Language Acquisition: An Introductory Course.* 2d ed. Mahwah, NJ: Lawrence Erlbaum Associates, 2001.

Gee, James P. *An Introduction to Discourse Analysis: Theory and Method.* New York: Routledge, 1999.

Ghadessy, Mohsen, ed. *Registers of Written English.* London: Pinter Publishers, 1988.

Gibbons, John. "Language and the Law." *Annual Review of Applied Linguistics* 19 (1999): 156–73.

———. *Forensic Linguistics: An Introduction to Language in the Justice System.* Malden, MA/Oxford: Blackwell, 2003.

Giglioli, Pier Paolo, ed. *Language and Social Context.* Harmondsworth: Penguin, 1972.

Gleason, H. A. *Linguistics and English Grammar.* New York: Holt, 1965.

Grabe, William, ed. *Language Policy and Planning. Vol. 14. Annual Review of Applied Linguistics.* New York: Cambridge University Press, 1993/94.

———, ed. *Multilingualism. Vol. 17. Annual Review of Applied Linguistics.* New York: Cambridge University Press, 1997.

Grabe, William, and Fredericka L. Stoller. *Teaching and Researching Reading.* Harlow: Longman, 2002.

Grabe, William, and Robert B. Kaplan. *Theory and Practice of Writing: An Applied Linguistic Perspective.* London: Longman, 1996.

Grassi, Corrado. "Deculturalization and Social Degradation of the Linguistic Minorities in Italy." In *Language Death: International Journal of the Sociology of Language*, vol. 12., ed. Wolfgang Dressler and Ruth Wodak-Leodolter, 45–54. The Hague: Mouton Publishers, 1977.

Green, Georgia M. *Pragmatics and Natural Language Understanding.* Hillsdale, NJ: Lawrence Earlbaum Associates, 1989.

Greenbaum, Sidney. *A College Grammar of English.* White Plains, NY: Longman, 1989.

Greenbaum, Sidney, and Randolph Quirk. *A Student's Grammar of the English Language.* Harlow: Longman, 1990.

Grimes, Barbara F., Joseph E. Grimes, and Robert S. Pittman, eds. *Ethnologue: Languages of the World.* Dallas: Summer Institute of Linguistics, 1996.

Grosjean, Francois. *Life with Two Languages: An Introduction to Bilingualism.* Cambridge: Harvard University Press, 1982.

Grundy, Peter. *Doing Pragmatics.* London: Edward Arnold, 1995.

Gumperz, John J., and Dell Hymes, eds. *Directions in Sociolinguistics: The Ethnography of Communication.* Oxford: Blackwell, 1986.

Haarmann, Harald, and Eugene Holman. "Acculturation and Communicative Mobility Among Former Soviet Nationalities." *Annual Review of Applied Linguistics* 17 (1997): 113–37.

Haegeman, Liliane. "Register Variation in English: Some Theoretical Observations." *Journal of English Linguistics* 20, no. 2 (1987): 230–48.

Haegeman, Liliane, and Jaqueline Guéron. *English Grammar: A Generative Perspective.* Oxford: Blackwell, 1999.

Hakuta, Kenji. "A Case Study of a Japanese Child Learning English as a Second Language." *Language Learning* 26 (1976): 321–51.

Hall, Kira, and Mary Bucholtz, eds. *Language and the Socially Constructed Self.* New York: Routledge, 1995.

Hall, Kira, Mary Bucholtz, and Birch Moonwomon. *Locating Power: Proceedings of the Second Berkeley Women and Language Conference, April 4 and 5, 1992.* Berkeley, CA: University of California, 1992.

Hall, Robert A. *Linguistics and Your Language.* 2d, revised ed. Garden City: Anchor Books (Doubleday & Company, Inc.), 1960.

———. *Pidgin and Creole Languages.* Ithaca, NY: Cornell University Press, 1966.

Halliday, M. A. K., and Ruqaiya Hasan. *Cohesion in English.* London: Longman, 1976.

Hamers, Josiane F., and Michael H. A. Blanc. *Bilinguality and Bilingualism.* 2d ed. New York: Cambridge University Press, 2000.

Happe, Francesca. *Autism: An Introduction to Psychological Theory.* Cambridge: Harvard University Press, 1998.

Hartmann, R. R. K., ed. *Lexicography: Principles and Practice.* London: Academic Press, 1983.

Haugen, Einar. "The Implementation of Corpus Planning: Theory and Practice." In *Progress in Language Planning*, ed. Juan Cobarrubias and Joshua Fishman, 269–90. Berlin: Mouton de Gruyter, 1983.

Haviland, S. E., and E. V. Clark. "'This Man's Father Is My Father's Son: A Study of the Acquisition of English Kin Terms." *Journal of Child Language* 1 (1974): 23–47.

Heath, Shirley Brice. *Language in Education: Theory and Practice.* Washington, DC: Center for Applied Linguistics, 1978.

Hedge, Mahabalgiri N. *Introduction to Communicative Disorders.* Austin: PRO-ED, 1991.

Henderson, Edmund H., and Shane Templeton. A Developmental Perspective of Formal Spelling Instruction through Alphabet, Pattern, and Meaning. *The Elementary School Journal* 86, no. 3: 305–16.

Henley, Nancy M., and Cheris Kramarae. "Gender, Power and Miscommunication." In *"Miscommunication" and Problematic Talk*, ed. Nikolas Coupland, Howard Giles, and John M. Wiemann, 18–43. Newbury Park: Sage, 1991.

Herring, Susan C. *Computer-Mediated Communication: Linguistic, Social, and Cross-Cultural Perspectives.* Amsterdam: John Benjamins, 1996.

———. "Computer-Mediated Discourse." In *The Handbook of Discourse Analysis*, ed. Deborah Schiffrin, Deborah Tannen, and Heidi Ehernberger Hamilton. Malden, MA: Blackwell, 2001.

Hock, Hans Henrich. *Principles of Historical Linguistics.* 2d revised and updated ed. Berlin/New York: Mouton de Gruyter, 1991.

Hockett, Charles F. *A Course in Modern Linguistics.* New York: Macmillan, 1958.

Holloway, Joseph E., and Winifred K. Vass. *The African Heritage of American English.* Bloomington: Indiana University Press, 1993.

Holm, John. *Pidgin and Creoles.* 2 vols. Cambridge: Cambridge University Press, 1988–1989.

———. *An Introduction to Pidgins and Creoles.* Cambridge: Cambridge University Press, 2000.

Holmes, Janet. "Hedging Your Bets and Sitting on the Fence: Some Evidence for Hedges as Support Structures." *Te Reo* 27 (1984): 47–62.

———. "Hedging, Fencing, and Other Conversational Gambits: An Analysis of Gender Differences in New Zealand Speech." In *Women and Language in Australian and New Zealand Society*, ed. Anne Pauwels, 59–79. Sydney: Australian Professional Publications, 1987.

———. "Sex Differences and Apologies: One Aspect of Communicative Competence." *Applied Linguistics* 10 (1989): 194–213.

———. *An Introduction to Sociolinguistics.* London: Longman, 1992.

———. *Women, Men, and Politeness.* London/New York: Longman, 1995.

Hornberger, Nancy. "Language Policy and Planning in South America." *Annual Review of Applied Linguistics* 14 (1993/94): 220–39.

Horrocks, Geoffrey C. *Generative Grammar.* London: Longman, 1987.

Howatt, Anthony P. R. *A History of English Language Teaching.* Oxford: Oxford University Press, 1984.

Hudson, Grover. *Essential Introductory Linguistics.* Malden, MA: Blackwell, 2000.

Hurford, James R. *Grammar: A Student's Guide.* Cambridge: Cambridge University Press, 1994.

Hutchby, Ian, and Robin Wooffit. *Conversation Analysis.* Cambridge: Polity Press, 1998.

Hydén, Lars-Christer, and Elliot G. Mishler. "Language and Medicine." *Annual Review of Applied Linguistics* 19 (1999): 174–92.

Hymes, Dell. "Models of the Interaction of Language and Social Life." In *Directions in Sociolinguistics: The Ethnography of Communication,* ed. John J. Gumperz and Dell Hymes, 35–71. Oxford: Blackwell, 1986.

Innes, Gordon. *A Mende-English Dictionary.* Cambridge: Cambridge University Press, 1969.

Jacobs, Greg. "Lesbian and Gay Male Language Use: A Critical Review of the Literature." *American Speech* 71 (1996): 49–71.

Jespersen, Otto. *Language, Its Nature, Development, and Origin.* London: George Allen and Unwin, 1922.

———. *A Modern English Grammar.* Vol. 7. London: George Allen and Unwin, 1928.

Johnson, Robert Keith. "Language Policy and Planning in Hong Kong." *Annual Review of Applied Linguistics* 14 (1993/94): 177–99.

Johnson, Sally, and Ulrike H. Meinhof. *Language and Masculinity.* Cambridge MA: Blackwell, 1997.

Joos, Martin. *The Five Clocks.* New York: Harcourt Brace and World, 1961.

Kachru, Braj. "South Asian English." In *English as a World Language,* ed. Richard W. Bailey and Manfred Görlach, 353–83. Ann Arbor: University of Michigan Press, 1982.

———. *The Other Tongue.* 2d ed. Urbana: University of Illinois Press, 1992.

Kam, Ho Wah, and Ruth Y. L Wong, eds. *English Language Teaching in East Asia Today: Changing Policies and Practices.* Singapore: Eastern Universities Press, 2002.

Kaplan, Robert. "Cultural Thought Patterns in Intercultural Education." *Language Learning* 16 (1966): 1–20.

Katz, Jerrold J., and J. A. Fodor. "The Structure of a Semantic Theory." *Language* 39, no. 1 (1963): 170–210.

Katzner, Kenneth. *The Languages of the World.* New ed. London: Routledge, 1995.

Kelly, Louis G. *25 Centuries of Language Teaching: An Inquiry into the Science, Art, and Development of Language Teaching Methodology, 500 BC–1969.* Rowley, MA: Newbury House, 1976.

Kolln, Martha, and Robert Funk. *Understanding English Grammar.* New York, NY: Pearson, 1997.

Krashen, Stephen D. *The Input Hypothesis: Issues and Implications.* London: Longman, 1985.

———. *Explorations in Language Acquisition and Use.* Portsmouth, NH: Heinemann, 2003.

Krashen, Stephen D., Michael H. Long, and Robin C. Scarcella, eds. *Child-Adult Differences in Second Language Acquisition.* Rowley: Newbury House, 1982.

Krashen, Stephen D., and Robin C. Scarcella. "On Routines and Patterns in Second Language Acquisition and Performance." *Language Learning* 28 (1978): 283–300.

Kreindler, Isabelle. "Multilingualism in the Successor States of the Soviet Union." *Annual Review of Applied Linguistics* 17 (1997): 91–112.

Kulick, Don. "Gay and Lesbian Language." *Annual Review of Anthropology* 29 (2000): 243–85.

Kurath, Hans. *A Word Geography of the Eastern United States.* Ann Arbor: University of Michigan Press, 1949.

Kurath, Hans, and Raven I. McDavid, Jr. *The Pronunciation of English in the Atlantic States.* Ann Arbor: University of Michigan Press, 1961.

Labov, William. "The Logic of Nonstandard English." In *Report of the Twentieth Annual Round Table Meeting on Linguistics and Language Studies*, ed. James E. Alatis, 1–43. Washington, DC: Georgetown University Press, 1969a.

———. *The Study of Non-Standard English.* Washington: ERIC Clearinghouse for Linguistics, 1969b.

———. *Language in the Inner City: Studies in the Black English Vernacular.* Philadelphia: University of Pennsylvania Press, 1972a.

———. *Sociolinguistic Patterns.* Philadelphia: University of Pennsylvania Press, 1972b.

———. "Objectivity and Commitment in Linguistic Science: The Case of the Black English Trial in Ann Arbor." *Language in Society* 11 (1982): 165–201.

———. "The Three Dialects of English." In *New Ways of Analyzing Sound Change*, ed. Penelope Eckert, 1–44. San Diego: Academic Press, Inc., 1991.

———. "The Organization of Dialect Diversity in North America." Paper presented at ICSLP4, the Fourth International Conference on Spoken Language Processing at Philadelphia, Oct. 6, 1996. Available at *http://www.ling.upenn.edu/phono_atlas/ICSLP4.html*

———. "Coexistent Systems in AAVE." In *African-American English*, ed. Salikoko S. Mufwene, John R. Rickford, Guy Bailey, and John Baugh, 110–53. London: Routledge, 1998.

Laird, Charlton. *Language in America.* New York: The World Publishing Company, 1970.

Lakoff, George, and Mark Johnson. *Metaphors We Live By.* Chicago: University of Chicago Press, 1980.

Lakoff, George, and Mark Turner. *More Than Cool Reason: A Field Guide to Poetic Metaphor.* Chicago: University of Chicago Press, 1989.

Lakoff, Robin. *Language and Woman's Place.* New York: Harper & Row, 1975.

Landau, Jacob M., and Barbara Kellner-Heinkele. *Politics of Language in the Ex-Soviet Muslim States.* Ann Arbor: University of Michigan Press, 2001.

Landau, Sidney I. *Cambridge Dictionary of American English.* New York: Cambridge University Press, 2000.

Langacker, Ronald W. *Foundations of Cognitive Grammar: Theoretical Prerequisites.* Vol. 1. Stanford: Stanford University Press, 1987.

———. *Foundations of Cognitive Grammar: Descriptive Application.* Vol. 2. Stanford: Stanford University Press, 1991a.

———. *Concept, Image, and Symbol: The Cognitive Basis of Grammar.* Berlin: Mouton de Gruyter, 1991b.

Lanham, L. W. "English in South Africa." In *English as a World Language,* ed. Richard W. Bailey and Manfred Görlach, 324–52. Ann Arbor: University of Michigan Press, 1982.

Larsen-Freeman, Diane. "An Explanation for the Morpheme Acquisition Order of Second Language Learners." *Language Learning* 26 (1976): 125–34.

Larsen-Freeman, Diane, and Michael H. Long. *An Introduction to Second Language Acquistion Research.* London: Longman, 1991.

Lawton, David L. "English in the Caribbean." In *English as a World Language,* ed. Richard W. Bailey and Manfred Görlach, 251–80. Ann Arbor: University of Michigan Press, 1982.

Leech, Geoffrey N. *A Linguistic Guide to English Poetry.* Harlow: Longman, 1969.

———. *Semantics.* Harmondsworth: Penguin, 1974.

Leech, Geoffrey N., and Jan Svartvik. *A Communicative Grammar of English.* Harlow: Longman, 1975.

Lentine, Genine, and Roger W. Shuy. "Mc-Meaning in the Marketplace." *American Speech* 65, no. 4 (1990): 349–66.

Leonard, Laurence B. *Children with Specific Language Impairment.* Cambridge: MIT Press, 1998.

Lepschy, Giulio, ed. *History of Linguistics.* 3 vols. London: Longman, 1994.

Levinson, Stephen C. *Pragmatics.* Cambridge: Cambridge University Press, 1983.

Lightbown, Patsy M., and Nina Spada. *How Languages Are Learned.* Oxford: Oxford University Press, 1999.

Ling, Low Ee, and Adam Brown. *An Introduction to Singapore English.* Singapore: McGraw Hill, 2003.

Lippi-Green, Rosina. *English with an Accent: Language, Ideology and Discrimination in the United States.* London: Routledge, 1997.

Liria, Anna, and Kira Hall. *Queerly Phrased: Language, Gender, and Sexuality.* Oxford: Oxford University Press, 1997.

LoCastro, Virginia. *An Introduction to Pragmatics: Social Action for Language Teachers.* Ann Arbor: University of Michigan Press, 2003.

Long, Michael. "Instructed Interlanguage Development." In *Issues in Second Language Acquisition: Multiple Perspectives,* ed. Leslie Beebe, 115–41. New York: Newbury House, 1988.

Long, Michael, and Patricia Porter. "Group Work, Interlanguage Talk, and Second Language Acquisition." *TESOL Quarterly* 19 (1985): 207–28.

Lowth, Robert. *Short Introduction to English.* London: J. Hughes, 1762.

Lucas, Ceil, ed. *The Sociolinguistics of Sign Languages.* Cambridge: Cambridge University Press, 2001.

Lyons, John. *Noam Chomsky*. Revised ed. Harmondsworth/New York: Penguin Books, 1977a.

———. *Semantics*. Cambridge: Cambridge University Press, 1977b.

Macaulay, Ronald K. S. "Variation and Consistency in Glaswegian English." In *Sociolinguistic Patterns in British English*, ed. Peter Trudgill, 132–43. London: Edward Arnold, 1978.

———. *The Social Art*. Oxford: Oxford University Press, 1994.

MacNeil, Robert, and William Cran. *Do You Speak American?* New York: Nan A. Talese, 2005.

MacShane, Frank, ed. *Selected Letters of Raymond Chandler*. New York: Columbia University Press, 1981.

Maltz, Daniel N., and Ruth A. Borker. "A Cultural Approach to Male-Female Miscommunication." In *Language and Social Identity*, ed. John J. Gumperz, 195–216. Cambridge: Cambridge University Press, 1982.

Marckwardt, Albert H. *American English*. Oxford: Oxford University Press, 1958.

———. "Dictionaries and the English Language." *The English Journal* 52 (1963): 326–45.

Marckwardt, Albert H., and J. L. Dillard. *American English*. 2d ed. Oxford: Oxford University Press, 1980.

Martinet, Andre. *Elements of General Linguistics*. Translated by Elisabeth Palmer. Chicago: University of Chicago Press, 1966.

Marshall, David F. *Language Planning*. 3 vols. Amsterdam: John Benjamins, 1991.

Matthews, Peter. *The Concise Oxford Dictionary of Linguistics*. Oxford: Oxford University Press, 1997.

———. *Morphology*. 2d ed. Cambridge: Cambridge University Press, 1991.

McArthur, Tom. *Longman Lexicon of Contemporary English*. Harlow: Longman, 1981.

———. *The Oxford Companion to the English Language*. Oxford: Oxford University Press, 1992.

McArthur, Tom, and Roshan McArthur. *The Concise Oxford Companion to the English Language*. Oxford: Oxford University Press, 1996.

McCarthy, Michael. *Vocabulary*. Oxford: Oxford University Press, 1990.

McCrum, Robert, William Cran, and Robert MacNeil. *The Story of English*. New York: Penguin Books, 1986.

McDavid Jr., Raven I. *Dialects in Culture: Essays in General Dialectology*. Alabama: University of Alabama Press, 1979.

McKay, Sandra. "Multilingualism in the United States." *Annual Review of Applied Linguistics* 17 (1997): 242–62.

McLaughlin, Barry. *Theories of Second-Language Learning*. London: Edward Arnold, 1987.

Mellinkoff, David. *The Language of the Law*. Boston: Little, Brown, 1963.

Mencken, H. L. *The American Language*. New York: Alfred A. Knopf, 1919.

Mey, Jacob. *Whose Language: A Study in Linguistic Pragmatics*. Amsterdam/Philadelphia: John Benjamins, 1985.

———. *Pragmatics: An Introduction*. Oxford: Blackwell, 1993.

Milroy, Lesley. *Language and Social Networks*. Oxford: Blackwell, 1980.

———. *Observing and Analyzing Natural Language*. Oxford: Blackwell, 1987.

Mitchell, Bruce, and Fred C. Robinson. *A Guide to Old English*. 5th ed. Oxford: Blackwell, 1992.

Morgan, Marcyliena. *Language, Discourse and Power in African American Culture.* Cambridge: Cambridge University Press, 2002.

Morton, Herbert C. *The Story of Webster's Third.* Cambridge: Cambridge University Press, 1994.

Mufwene, Salikoko, ed. *Africanisms in Afro-American Language Varieties.* Athens: University of Georgia Press, 1993.

———. "Creoles and Creolization." In *Handbook of Pragmatics,* ed. Jef Verschueren, Jan-Ola Östman, and Jan Blommaert, 1–14. Amsterdam: John Benjamins, 1995.

Mufwene, Salikoko, John R. Rickford, Guy Bailey, and John Baugh, eds. *African-American English: Structure, History, and Use.* London: Routledge, 1998.

Muhlhausler, Peter. "Tok Pisin in Papua New Guinea." In *English as a World Language,* ed. Richard W. Bailey and Manfred Görlach, 439–66. Ann Arbor: University of Michigan Press, 1982.

———. *Pidgin and Creole Linguistics.* Oxford: Blackwell, 1986.

Murray, Katharine Maud Elisabeth. *Caught in the Web of Words: James A. H. Murray and the Oxford English Dictionary.* New Haven: Yale University Press, 1977.

Napoli, Donna Jo. *Linguistics: An Introduction.* New York: Oxford University Press, 1996.

Nelson, Katherine. *Structure and Strategy in Learning to Talk.* Society for Research in Child Development. Monograph, Vol. 38, no. 1–2. Chicago: University of Chicago Press, 1973.

Nettle, Daniel, and Suzanne Romaine. *Vanishing Voices: The Extinction of the World's Languages.* New York: Oxford University Press, 2000.

Neustupny, J. V. *Post-Structural Approaches to Language.* Tokyo: University of Tokyo Press, 1970.

Nilsen, Alleen Pace, Haig Bosmajian, H. Lee Gershuny, and Julia P. Stanley. *Sexism and Language.* Urbana: National Council of Teachers of English, 1977.

Noguchi, Rei R. *Grammar and the Teaching of Writing.* Urbana: National Council of Teachers of English, 1991.

Nuttall, Christine. *Teaching Reading Skills in a Foreign Language.* London: Heinemann, 1982.

O'Barr, William, and Bowman K. Atkins. "'Women's Language' or 'Powerless Language'?" In *Women and Language in Literature and Society,* ed. Sally McConnell-Ginet, Ruth Borker, and Nelly Furman, 93–110. New York: Praeger, 1980.

O'Grady, William, Michael Dobrovolsky, and Mark Aronoff, eds. *Contemporary Linguistics: An Introduction.* 3rd ed. New York: St. Martin's Press, 1997.

O'Riagain, Pádraig, and Niamh N. Shuibhne. "Minority Language Rights." *Annual Review of Applied Linguistics* 17 (1997): 11–29.

Oaks, Dallin D. *Linguistics at Work: A Reader of Applications.* Fort Worth: Harcourt Brace College Publishers, 1998.

Obler, Loraine K., and Kris Gjerlow. *Language and the Brain.* Cambridge: Cambridge University Press, 1999.

Ochs, Elinor. *Culture and Langauge Development: Language Acquisition and Language Socialization in a Samoan Village.* Cambridge: Cambridge University Press, 1988.

Ochs, Elinor, and Bambi Schieffelin. "The Impact of Language Socialization on Grammatical Development." In *The Handbook of Child Language*, ed. Paul Fletcher and Brian MacWhinney, 73–94. Cambridge: Blackwell, 1995.

Odlin, Terence, ed. *Perspectives on Pedagogical Grammar*. Cambridge: Cambridge University Press, 1994.

Ong, L. M. L., J. C. J. M. de Haes, A. M. Hoos, and F. B. Lammes. "Doctor-Patient Communication: A Review of the Literature." *Social Science and Medicine* 40, no. 7 (1995): 903–18.

Ong, Walter. *Orality and Literacy: The Technologizing of the Word*. London: Routledge, 1982.

Orton, Harold, Stewart Sanderson, and John Widdowson, eds. *The Linguistic Atlas of England*. London: Croom Helm, 1978.

Padden, Carol, and Tom Humphries. *Deaf in America: Voices from a Culture*. Cambridge: Harvard University Press, 1988.

Partridge, Eric. *Slang, Today and Yesterday*. New York: Macmillan, 1934.

Patthey-Chavez, G. G. "Language Policy and Planning in Mexico: Indigenous Language Policy." *Annual Review of Applied Linguistics* 14 (1993/94): 200–19.

Paulston, Christina Bratt. "Pronouns of Address in Swedish: Social Class Semantics and a Changing System." *Language in Society* 5 (1976): 359–86.

———. *Linguistic Minorities in Multilingual Settings: Implications for Language Policies*. Amsterdam: John Benjamins, 1994.

Paulston, Christina Bratt, and Donald Peckham, eds. *Linguistic Minorities in Central and Eastern Europe*. Clevedon: Multilingual Matters, 1998.

Paulston, Christina Bratt, and G. Richard Tucker. *Sociolinguistics: The Essential Readings*. Malden, MA: Blackwell, 2003.

Pauwels, Anne. *Women Changing Language*. London/New York: Longman, 1998.

Peccei, Jean Stillwell. *Child Language*. London: Routledge, 1994.

Perrine, Laurence. *Sound and Sense: An Introduction to Poetry*. New York: Harcourt, Brace & World, 1956.

Perry, Theresa, and Lisa Delpit, eds. *The Real Ebonics Debate: Power, Language, and the Education of African-American Children*. Boston: Beacon Press, 1998.

Pienemann, Manfred. *Language Processing and Second Language Development: Processability Theory*. Amsterdam: John Benjamins, 1984.

Pierce, Bonny Norton, and Stanley G. M. Ridge. "Multilingualism in Southern Africa." *Annual Review of Applied Linguistics* 17 (1997): 170–90.

Pinker, Steven. *The Language Instinct*. New York: Morrow, 1994.

Platt, John T. "English in Singapore, Malaysia, and Hong Kong." In *English as a World Language*, ed. Richard W. Bailey and Manfred Görlach, 384–414. Ann Arbor: University of Michigan Press, 1982.

Prince, Gerald. *A Grammar of Stories: An Introduction*. The Hague: Mouton de Gruyter, 1973.

———. *A Dictionary of Narratology*. Lincoln: University of Nebraska Press, 1987.

Pullum, Geoffrey K. *The Great Eskimo Vocabulary Hoax, and Other Irreverent Essays on the Study of Language*. Chicago: University of Chicago Press, 1991.

Pullum, Geoffrey K., and William A. Ladusaw. *Phonetic Symbol Guide*. Chicago: University of Chicago Press, 1986.

Quinn, Jim. *American Tongue and Cheek: A Populist Guide to Our Language*. New York: Pantheon Books, 1980.

Quirk, Randolph, and Charles L. Wrenn. *An Old English Grammar*. London: Methuen, 1955.

Quirk, Randolph, and Sidney Greenbaum. *A Concise Grammar of Contemporary English*. New York: Harcourt Brace Jovanovich, Inc., 1973.

Quirk, Randolph, Sidney Greenbaum, Geoffrey Leech, and Jan Svartvik. *A Comprehensive Grammar of the English Language*. London: Longman, 1985.

Radford, Andrew. *Transformational Syntax: A Student's Guide to Chomsky's Extended Standard Theory*. Cambridge: Cambridge University Press, 1981.

———. *Syntax: A Minimalist Introduction*. Cambridge: Cambridge University Press, 1997.

Raskin, Victor. *Semantic Mechanisms of Humor*. Dordrecht: Reidel, 1985.

Reddy, Michael J. "The Conduit Metaphor—A Case of Frame Conflict in Our Language about Language." In *Metaphor and Thought*, ed. Andrew Ortony, 284–324. Cambridge: Cambridge University Press, 1979.

Riagain, Padraig, and Nic Niamh Shuibne. "Minority Language Rights." *Annual Review of Applied Linguistics* 17 (1997): 11–29.

Richards, I. A. *The Philosophy of Rhetoric*. London: Oxford University Press, 1936.

Richards, Jack, John Platt, and Heide Weber. *Longman Dictionary of Applied Linguistics*. 2d ed. Harlow: Longman, 1992.

Rickford, John R. *Dimensions of a Creole Continuum: History, Text and Linguistic Analysis of Guyanese Creole*. Standford: Stanford University Press, 1987.

———. "The Creole Origins of African-American Vernacular English: Evidence from Copula Absence." In *African-American English: Structure, History and Use*, ed. Salikoko S. Mufwene, John R. Rickford, Guy Bailey, and John Baugh, 154–200. London: Routledge, 1998.

———. *African American Vernacular English*. Malden, MA: Blackwell, 1999.

Robins, Robert Henry. *A Short History of Linguistics*. 4th ed. London: Longman, 1997.

Robinson, Peter, ed. *Individual Differences and Instructed Language Learning*. Philadelphia: John Benjamins, 2002.

Romaine, Suzanne. *Pidgins and Creole Languages*. London: Longman, 1988.

———. *Bilingualism*. 2d ed. Oxford/New York: Blackwell, 1995.

Roman, Camille, Suzanne Juhasz, and Cristanne Miller. *The Women and Language Debate: A Sourcebook*. New Brunswick, NJ: Rutgers University Press, 1994.

Ruddell, Robert B., Martha R. Ruddell, and Harry Singer. *Theoretical Models and Processes of Reading*. 4th ed. Newark, DE: International Reading Association, 1994.

Ruhlen, Merritt. *The Origin of Language: Tracing the Evolution of the Mother Tongue*. New York: Wiley, 1994.

Ruiz, Richard. "Language Policy and Planning in the United States." *Annual Review of Applied Linguistics* 14 (1993/94): 111–25.

Rymer, Russ. *Genie: A Scientific Tragedy*. New York: Harper Perennial, 1993.

Safire, William. *On Language*. New York: Times Books, 1980.

Sapir, Edward. *Language: An Introduction to the Study of Speech*. New York: Harcourt, Brace and Company, 1921.

Saussure, Ferdinand de. *Course in General Linguistics.* Translated by Roy Harris, 1983. Paris: Editions Payot, 1916.

Saville-Troike, Muriel. "Private Speech: Evidence for Second Language Learning Strategies During the 'Silent Period'." *Journal of Child Language* 15 (1988): 567–90.

————. *The Ethnography of Communication: An Introduction.* 2d ed. Oxford: Blackwell, 1989.

Schieffelin, Bambi, and Elinor Ochs, eds. *Language Socialization across Cultures.* Cambridge: Cambridge University Press, 1986.

Schiffrin, Deborah. *Approaches to Discourse.* Oxford: Blackwell, 1994.

Schmidt, Richard. "Interaction, Acculturation and the Acquisition of Communication Competence." In *Sociolinguistics and Second Language Acquisition,* ed. Nessa Wolfson and Elliot Judd. Rowley, MA: Newbury House, 1983.

Schneider, Edgar W. *American Earlier Black English.* Tuscaloosa: University of Alabama Press, 1989.

Searle, John R. *Speech Acts: An Essay in the Philosophy of Language.* Cambridge: Cambridge University Press, 1969.

Sebeok, Thomas Albert, ed. *Animal Communication: Techniques of Study and Results of Research.* Bloomington, IN: Indiana University Press, 1968.

Selikowitz, Mark. *Dyslexia and Other Learning Difficulties.* 2d ed. Oxford: Oxford University Press, 1998.

Selinker, Larry. "Interlanguage." *International Review of Applied Linguistics* 10 (1972): 209–31.

————. *Rediscovering Interlanguage.* London: Longman, 1992.

Sells, Peter. *Lectures on Contemporary Syntactic Theories: An Introduction to Government-Binding Theory, Generalized Phrase Structure Grammar, and Lexical-Functional Grammar.* Stanford: CSLI, 1985.

Seymour, Charlena M., and E. Harris Nober, eds. *Introduction to Communication Disorders: A Multicultural Approach.* Boston: Butterworth-Heinemann, 1998.

Shames, George H., Elisabeth H. Wiig, and Wayne A. Secord, eds. *Human Communication Disorders: An Introduction.* 5th ed. Boston: Allyn & Bacon, 1998.

Shaughnessy, Mina P. *Errors and Expectations.* New York: Oxford University Press, 1977.

Shuy, Roger W. *Discovering American Dialects.* Champaign IL: National Council of Teachers of English, 1967.

————. *Language Crimes: The Use and Abuse of Language Evidence in the Courtroom.* Oxford, UK: Cambridge, US: Blackwell, 1993.

————. *The Language of Confession, Interrogation and Deception.* Thousand Oaks, CA: Sage, 1998.

————. Forensic Linguistics. In *The Handbook of Linguistics,* ed. Mark Aronoff and Janie Rees-Miller, 683–91. Malden, MA: Blackwell, 2001.

————. *Linguistic Battles in Trademark Disputes.* New York: Palgrave Macmillan, 2002.

Silva, Tony, and Paul Kei Matsuda. *Landmark Essays on ESL Writing.* Mahwah, NJ: Lawrence Erlbaum Associates, 2001.

Silver, Rita Elaine, Guangwei Hu, and Masakazu Iino. *English Language Education in China, Japan, and Singapore.* Singapore: Nanyang Technological University, 2002.

Simon, John Ivan. *Paradigms Lost: Reflections on Literacy and Its Decline.* New York: C. N. Potter, 1980.

Simpson, David. *The Politics of American English, 1776–1850.* Oxford: Oxford University Press, 1986.

Sinclair, John. *Collins COBUILD (Collins Birmingham University International Language Database) English Language Dictionary.* London: Collins, 1987.

Singh, Ishtla. *Pidgins and Creoles: An Introduction.* London: Arnold, 2000.

Skehan, Peter. *Individual Differences in Second-Language Learning.* London: Arnold, 1989.

———. *A Cognitive Approach to Language Learning.* Oxford: Oxford University Press, 1998.

Skuttnabb-Kangas, Tove, and Robert Phillipson, eds. (in collaboration with Mart Rannut). *Linguistic Human Rights: Overcoming Linguistic Discrimination.* Contributions to the Sociology of Language 67. Berlin: Mouton de Gruyter, 1994.

Sledd, James H., and Wilma R. Ebbitt, eds. *Dictionaries and That Dictionary: A Casebook on the Aims of Lexicographers and the Targets of Reviewers.* Chicago: Scott, Foresman, 1962.

Slobin, Dan. *The Crosslinguistic Study of Language Acquisition.* 5 volumes. Hillsdale, NJ: Lawrence Erlbaum Associates, 1986–1997.

Smith, Frank. *Reading without Nonsense.* New York: Teachers College Press, 1985.

Smitherman, Geneva. *Talkin' and Testifyin': The Language of Black America.* Boston: Houghton Mifflin, 1977.

———. *Talkin That Talk: Language, Culture and Education in African America.* New York: Routledge, 2000.

Snow, Catherine E., and Charles A. Ferguson. *Talking to Children: Language Input and Acquisition: Papers from a Conference Sponsored by the Committee on Sociolinguistics of the Social Science Research Council (USA).* Cambridge: Cambridge University Press, 1977.

Sokolov, Jeffrey L., and Catherine E. Snow. "The Changing Role of Negative Evidence in Theories of Language Development." In *Input and Interaction in Language Acquisition,* ed. Clare Gallaway and Brian J. Richards, 38–55. Cambridge: Cambridge University Press, 1994.

Solan, Lawrence. *The Language of Judges.* Chicago: University of Chicago Press, 1993.

Soukhanov, Anne H., ed. *Encarta World English Dictionary.* New York: St. Martin's Press, 1999.

Spears, Arthur K., "The Black English Semi-Auxiliary 'Come.'" *Language* 58 (1982): 850–72.

Spolsky, Bernard, ed. *Concise Encyclopedia of Educational Linguistics.* Oxford: Elsevier, 1999.

———. *Language Policy.* Cambridge: Cambridge University Press, 2004.

Stanovich, Keith. "Toward an Interactive-Compensatory Model of Individual Differences in the Development of Reading Fluency." *Reading Research Quarterly* 16 (1980): 32–74.

———. *Progress in Understanding Reading: Scientific Foundations and New Frontiers.* New York: Guilford Press, 2000.

Strang, Barbara M. H. *A History of English.* London: Methuen, 1970.

Stavans, Ilan. *Spanglish: The Making of a New American Language.* New York: HarperCollins. 2003.

Steiner, George. *After Babel: Aspects of Language and Translation.* Oxford: Oxford University Press, 1975.

Stewart, Thomas W., and Nathan Vaillette. *Language Files.* 8th ed. Columbus: Ohio State University Press, 2001.

Stubbs, Michael. *Discourse Analysis: The Sociolinguistic Analysis of Natural Language.* Chicago: University of Chicago Press, 1983.

Sunderland, Jane. "Issues of Language and Gender in Second and Foreign Language Education." *Language Teaching* 33, no. 4 (2000): 203–23.

Svensén, Bo. *Practical Lexicography: Principles and Methods of Dictionary-Making.* Translated by John Sykes and Kerstin Schofield. Oxford: Oxford University Press, 1993.

Swacker, Marjorie. "The Sex of the Speaker as a Sociolinguistic Variable." In *Language and Sex*, ed. Barrie Thorne and Nancy Henley, 76–83. Rowley, MA: Newbury House, 1975.

Swain, Merrill. "Three Functions of Output in Second Language Learning." In *Principle and Practice in Applied Linguistics: Studies in Honor of H. G. Widdowson*, ed. Guy Cook and Barbara Seidlhofer, 125–44. Oxford: Oxford University Press, 1995.

Swan, Joan. *Girls, Boys, and Language.* Oxford: Blackwell, 1992.

Talbot, Mary M. *Language and Gender: An Introduction.* Cambridge: Polity Press, 1998.

Tannen, Deborah. *Conversational Style: Analyzing Talk among Friends.* Norwood, NJ: Ablex, 1984.

———. "Gender Differences in Conversational Coherence: Physical Alignment and Topical Cohesion." In *Conversational Organization and Its Development*, ed. Bruce Dorval. Norwood, NJ: Ablex, 1990a.

———. "Gender Differences in Topical Coherence: Creating Involvement in Best-Friends' Talk." *Discourse Processes* 13 (1990b): 73–90.

———. *You Just Don't Understand: Women and Men in Conversation.* New York: Morrow, 1990c.

———. *Gender and Discourse.* Oxford: Oxford University Press, 1994.

———. *The Argument Culture: Moving from Debate to Dialog.* New York: Random House, 1998.

Tharp, Roland G., and Ronald Gallimore. *Rousing Minds to Life: Teaching, Learning, and Schooling in Social Context.* Cambridge: Cambridge University Press, 1988.

Thomas, Jenny. *Meaning in Interaction: An Introduction to Pragmatics.* London: Longman, 1995.

Thomason, Sarah G. *Language Contact: An Introduction.* Washington, DC: Georgetown University Press, 2001.

Todd, Loreto. "The English Language in West Africa." In *English as a World Language*, ed. Richard W. Bailey and Manfred Görlach, 281–305. Ann Arbor: University of Michigan Press, 1982.

———. *Pidgins and Creoles.* 2d ed. London: Routledge, 1990.

———. "Pidgins and Creoles." In *The Encyclopedia of Language and Linguistics*, ed. R. E. Asher, 3177–181. Oxford: Pergamon, 1994.

Toolan, Michael J. *Narrative: A Critical Linguistic Introduction.* London: Routledge, 1988.

Tracy, Karen. *Everyday Talk: Building and Reflecting Identities.* New York: The Guilford Press, 2002.

Traugott, Elizabeth Closs, and Mary Louise Pratt. *Linguistics for Students of Literature.* New York: Harcourt Brace, 1980.

Trew, Tony. "'What the Papers Say': Linguistic Variation and Ideological Difference." In *Language and Control,* ed. Roger Fowler, Bob Hodge, Gunther Kress, and Tony Trew, 117–56. London: Routledge & Kegan Paul, 1979.

Trudgill, Peter. *The Social Differentiation of English in Norwich.* Cambridge: Cambridge University Press, 1974.

———. *Sociolinguistics: An Introduction to Language and Society.* 4th ed. London: Penguin Books, 2001.

———. *A Glossary of Sociolinguistics.* Oxford: Oxford University Press, 2003.

Trudgill, Peter, and Jean Hannah. *International English: A Guide to Varieties of Standard English.* 3rd ed. London: Edward Arnold, 1994.

Turkle, Sherry. *Life and the Screen: Identity in the Age of the Internet.* New York: Simon and Schuster, 1995.

Turner, Lorenzo Dow. *Africanisms in the Gullah Dialect.* Chicago: University of Chicago Press, 1949.

Ullman, Stephen. *The Principles of Semantics.* New York: Barnes and Noble, 1957.

Ungerer, Friedrich, and Hans-Jörg Schmid. *An Introduction to Cognitive Linguistics.* London: Longman, 1996.

Urquhart, Sandy, and Cyril Weir. *Reading in a Second Language: Process, Product and Practice.* Harlow: Longman, 1998.

Van Dijk, Teun A. *Racism and the Press.* London: Routledge, 1991.

Vandeloise, Claude. *Spatial Prepositions: A Case Study from French.* Translated by Anna R. K. Bosch. Chicago: The University of Chicago Press, 1991.

Wallace, William. "How Registers Register: A Study in the Language of News and Sports." *Studies in the Linguistic Sciences* 7, no. 1 (1977): 46–78.

Wardhaugh, Ronald. *An Introduction to Sociolinguistics.* 4th ed. New York: Blackwell, 2002.

Weaver, Constance. *Teaching Grammar in Context.* Portsmouth: Boynton/Cook Publishers, 1996.

Webb, Vic. "Language Policy and Planning in South Africa." *Annual Review of Applied Linguistics* 14 (1993–94): 254–73.

Wei, Li. *The Bilingualism Reader.* New York: Routledge, 2000.

Weinert, Regina. "The Role of Formulaic Language in Second Language Acquisition: A Review." *Applied Linguistics* 16, no. 2 (1995): 181–205.

Weizman, Elda. "Some Register Characteristics of Journalistic Language: Are They Universal?" *Applied Linguistics* 5, no. 1 (1984): 39–50.

West, Candace. "Not Just 'Doctor's Orders': Directive-Response Sequences in Patients' Visits to Women and Men Physicians." *Discourse and Society* 1 (1990): 85–112.

White, Lydia. "Against Comprehensible Input: The Input Hypothesis and the Development of Second Language Competence." *Applied Linguistics* 8 (1987): 95–110.

Whorf, Benjamin Lee. *Language, Thought, and Reality: Selected Writings*. Cambridge, MA: MIT Press, 1956.

Wilton, David. *Word Myths: Debunking Linguistic Urban Legends*. Oxford: Oxford University Press, 2004.

Winchester, Simon. *The Professor and the Madman: A Tale of Murder, Insanity, and the Making of the Oxford English Dictionary*. New York: HarperCollins, 1998.

———. *The Meaning of Everything: The Story of the Oxford English Dictionary*. Oxford: Oxford University Press, 2003.

Wodak, Ruth. "Critical Linguistics and Critical Discourse Analysis." In *Handbook of Pragmatics: Manual*, ed. Jef Verschueren, Jan-Ola Östman, and Jan Blommaert, 204–10. Amsterdam: Benjamins, 1995.

Wolf, Hans-Georg. *Sociolinguistics: English in Cameroon*. Berlin: Mouton de Gruyter, 2001.

Wolfram, Walt. "Reexamining the Development of African American English." *Language* 79, no. 2 (2003): 282–316.

Wolfram, Walt, and Natalie Schilling-Estes. *American English: Dialects and Variation*. Oxford: Blackwell Publishers, 1998.

Wolfram, Walt, and Ralph W. Fasold. *The Study of Social Dialects in American English*. Englewood Cliffs, NJ: Prentice-Hall, 1974.

Wolfson, Nessa. *Perspectives: Sociolinguistics and TESOL*. Rowley, MA: Newbury House, 1989.

Woods, Nicole. "Talking Shop: Sex and Status as Determinants of Floor Apportionment in a Work Setting." In *Women in Their Speech Communities*, ed. Jennifer Coates and Deborah Cameron, 141–57. London: Longman, 1989.

Wright, Joseph, and Elizabeth Mary Wright. *An Elementary Middle English Grammar*. Oxford: Oxford University Press, 1979.

Yamanashi, Masa-aki. "On Minding Your P's and Q's in Japanese: A Case Study from Honorifics." In *Papers from the Tenth Regional Meeting, Chicago Linguistic Society, April 19–21, 1974*, ed. Michael W. La Galy, Robert A. Fox, and Anthony Bruck, 760–71. Chicago: Chicago Linguistic Society, 1974.

Zimmerman, Don, and Candace West. "Sex Roles, Interruptions and Silences in Conversation." In *Language and Sex: Difference and Dominance*, ed. Barrie Thorne and Nancy Henley. Rowley, MA: Newbury House, 1975.

Zwicky, Arnold M., and Ann D. Zwicky. "Register as a Dimension of Linguistic Variation." In *Sublanguage: Studies of Language in Restricted Semantic Domains*, ed. Richard Kittredge and John Lehrberger, 213–18. Berlin: Mouton de Gruyter, 1982.

Index

Æ lfric, 293

AAVE, 4, 112, 119, 126, 129, 132–47, 263
  origins of, 132

aboriginal language, 90, 157, 307, 317

academic discourse, 183

accent, 95, 103–5, 218

acceptability, 87
  social, 88

Accommodation Theory, 105

accusative case, 353

acquisition/learning hypothesis, 222

acrolect, 96, 127, 128

acronym, 30, 189–90

active voice, 44, 324, 344–45

address (forms of) 83–87, 171

adjacency pair, 53–54, 81, 91

adjective, 8, 28, 33, 37, 38, 43, 124, 204, 293,
    295, 335, 342, 353–54, 359
  attributive, 353
  gradable, 354
  predicative, 353

adverb, 28, 34, 37, 43, 51, 124, 295, 325, 335,
    342, 354
  compound, 354
  derivational, 354
  simple, 354

affective filter, 223
  hypothesis, 221, 223

affricate, 21–22

Africa, 134, 151, 153, 302, 307

African languages, 20, 125, 153

African-American, 4, 132–34, 137, 142–43, 304

Afrikaans, 148, 151, 308

Afro-Asiatic, 315, 319

age, 84, 114–16, 221

agent, 244, 345

airstream, 19

Alexandria, 324–25

allegory, 242–43

alliteration, 236

alliterative poetry, 297

allophone, 24, 26, 328

alphabet, 150, 290
  Roman, 175

alveolar, 21–22, 201

alveolar liquid, 218

alveolar stop, 218

alveopalatal, 21

ambiguity, 66, 74, 253, 256
  syntactic, 39–40
  tolerance of, 230

American English, 104, 110, 126, 155–57, 218,
    302–6

American languages, 318–19

American literature, 305

American Sign Language, 208, 282–85

analogy, 202, 283, 297, 325

anaphora, 51

ancient Greek, 289, 314–15

Anglo-Saxon, 8, 297, 321

animal communication, 274–78, 287

Ann Arbor case, 112, 142–44, 147

anomia, 211

antecedent, 51

antonym, 63, 267

anxiety, 223, 227, 231
  debilitative, 231
  facilitative, 231

apes, 277–78
aphasia, fluent and nonfluent, 211
apology, 54, 70–72, 83
aptitude, 228
Arabic, 31, 90, 123–24, 135, 152, 154, 176,
    185, 315, 326
  classical, 151
  colloquial, 151
Arabic grammar, 326
Aramaic, 122, 259
arbitrariness, 176, 277
arbitrariness of the sign, 60, 275, 283, 324
archaism, 7, 289, 304
Aristotle, 50, 324
article, 37–38, 51, 206, 220–21, 225, 324–25,
    342, 355–56
  determinative, 355
  indeterminative, 355
  zero, 356
articulation, 19–20, 209
  manner of, 15
artificial intelligence, 68, 263
aspect, 140–41, 348–49, 358
  imperfective and perfective, 336
aspiration, 24, 313
assimilation, 307
assonance, 236
attitude, 229–30
audience, 69, 183, 244, 323
Australia, 157–58, 254, 303, 306–7, 317
Australian English, 154, 157
Australian languages, 20, 317
authority, 114
autism, 210
auxiliary, 9, 34, 37, 46–47, 206, 209, 221, 343,
    348

babbling, 200–1
Babel (tower of), 123
baby talk, 116
back-channeling, 55, 167–69
backformation, 30–31
background knowledge, 176–77
basilect, 97, 127
Basque, 90, 150, 319
Bede, 293
behaviorism, 181, 194–95, 198, 217, 328
being (mode of), 326
Beowulf, 293, 297
bias, 281
Bible, 4, 6, 50, 123, 130, 259–60, 291
bilabial, 21
bilingual education, 149, 156–57
Bilingual Education Act, 156

bilingualism, 88–90, 148, 150–51, 154–57,
    159, 286, 304
  additive, 90
  balanced, 89
  compound, 89
  coordinate, 89
  maintenance, 157
  passive, 160
bioprogram theory, 127
bird call, 277
Black English, 132
blend, 30
blog, 188, 190
Bloomfield, Leonard, 12, 328
Boas, Frank, 328
borrowing, 31, 294–95, 299, 320–21
bounded, 335–36
brain malfunction, 213
brainstorming, 183
Breton, 90, 159, 161, 291
Britain, 133, 291
British colony, 158
British Empire, 302
British English, 303, 305, 306–8, 310
British isles, 291
Brooklynese, 95
Brown, Penelope, 83, 94
Brown, Roger W., 94, 205, 215
bundle of isoglosses, 99
Burmese, 217, 316
burnout, 114–15

California, 155, 304
calque, 32
Cameroon pidgin, 123, 126, 130
camouflage, 133–34
Canada, 149, 152, 227, 303, 318
Canadian English, 303
canon, 234
Cantonese, 151, 158
caregiver, 196–98
caregiver speech, 168, 196
case, 352–53
caste, 110, 114
Castile, 153
Catalan, 150, 153, 314
Caxton, 299
Celtic, 90, 291, 313
Central America, 149
character (fictional), 243, 245–48
character (Chinese) 175
chat room, 172, 190
chatting (on-line), 188
Chaucer, 154, 297, 301

child-directed speech, 116, 196–98, 214, 225–26, 232, 263
CHILDES Project, 215
China, 88, 151, 158, 311
Chinese, 3, 51, 86, 123, 151, 157–59, 175–76, 220, 229, 276, 303–4, 314, 316, 318
    transliteration of, 261–62
Chomsky, 40, 49–50, 59, 80, 194–95, 326, 328, 333
Christianity, 259–60
chunking, 177
circumlocution, 211
clarification request, 227
class
    semantic, 324
    social, 84, 110–11, 166, 170, 285
    working, 113, 166
classroom, 169–70, 224–25
classroom learning, 221
clause, 8, 36, 140
    adverbial, 43
    coordinate, 360
    infinitive, 6
    main, 45
    nominal, 324
    relative, *see* relative clause
    subordinate, 45, 359–60
    which/when, 174
cleft, 363–64
click, 20
clipping, 30, 302
CMC (computer mediated communication), 186–91
code, elaborated and restricted, 113–14
code switching, 91, 152
codification, 154, 302
Coeur D'Alene, 318
cognitive grammar, 240, 334–36
coherence, 51–53
cohesion, 51–53, 59
collective rights, 153–54
Collins COBUILD, 264, 266
collocation, 32, 253, 263, 265, 267
colonialism, 151, 308
colonization, 127
comics, 234
communication, 222, 226, 252
comparative, 354
comparative method, 6, 312–14, 327
comparison, 354
competence, 2, 7, 8, 80
    communicative, 80, 82, 88, 217
    cultural, 280
competence/performance distinction, 8

complement, 43, 359
complementizer, 45, 47, 49
compliment, 72–73
compounding, 30
comprehension check, 225
comprehension skills, 180
computer mediated communication, *see* CMC
computer translation, 260–61, 263
conceptual domain, 240
conceptualization, 335–36
conditional (mood), 348
conduit metaphor, 80
conferencing, 182
configurational definition, 39
confirmation check, 227
conjunction, 37, 52, 59, 225, 325, 353, 356–57, 360
connotation, 64–66, 78, 281
    affective, 64–65
    coded, 65–66
    collocative, 65
    individual/restricted, 65
    reflected, 65
    social, 65
consonance, 236
consonant, 15, 31, 135, 197, 200, 235–37
    voiceless, 209
consonant cluster reduction, 139
constituent, 34, 35, 36, 41, 47, 359
constitutional amendment, 156
context, 67–68, 74, 81, 117, 207
contextualization cue, 82
contraction, 4, 225
contrastive rhetoric, 51, 185–86
convention, 60
    social, 84–85
conversation, 53–55, 81, 166–69, 171, 172, 199–200, 225, 256–57
cooing, 200
coordination, 45, 46, 174, 207, 360
copula, 4, 206, 220, 221, 225
    zero, 140
copula deletion phenomenon, 137
copyright law, 254
corpus linguistics, 266, 275
corpus planning, 154
correlation coefficient, 227
court of law, 169, 252–54
creole, 122, 125–26, 126–27, 128–29
    origins, theory of, 126–27
creole continuum, 127–28
creole hypothesis, 132, 134, 136–38
critical period, 198
critical period hypothesis, 196

Croatian, 176, 315
crying, 200
Crystal, 11, 121, 216, 272, 288, 321, 322
culture clash, 260
Cyrillic, 150, 154, 315

dactyl, 238
Danish, 290–91, 294
Dante, 97, 154, 243, 326
DARE, 109
data, 9–10
dative, 292, 353
dative movement, 47
deaf education, 157
deafness, 208–9, 285–86
declarative knowledge, 278
declarative sentence, 360
declarative speech act, 70
declension, 292, 324, 325
decreolization, 128–29, 134, 135, 138, 140
deep structure, 44
deference, 84
definition, circularity of, 269
deictics, 67
deixis, 67, 174, 245, 247, 346
    social, 83
democratization, 151
denotation, 64, 66
derivation, 28, 30
description (detail of, in narrative), 248
descriptivism, 2, 3, 10, 305, 328
determiner, 37, 354–56, 358
    central, 355
developmental sequence, 219, 224
diachronic, 6, 7
diachronic linguistics, 312–14
dialect, 4, 88, 91, 95–109, 116, 119, 127–29,
        132–33, 139, 142, 149, 154, 175, 185, 263,
        295
    American, 95–96, 98, 100–5, 305
    British, 99, 103–4, 132–33, 138, 303
    French, 100
    Italian, 97
    Old English, 293–94
    Middle English, 297–98
    social class, 110
    southern (U.S.), 95, 98, 101–2, 133–34,
dialect areas (U.S.), 100–1
dialect boundary, 97–99
dialectologist hypothesis, 126, 132–34, 136,
        138
dialectology, 97, 100, 112, 115, 132–33
dialogue journal, 184
diaphragm, 18–19

diary, 234
dictionary, 32, 152, 154, 171, 264–69, 281, 327
    bilingual, 265–66
    corpus-based, 266
    inverse, 268
    learner, 266–67
    monolingual, 265–66
    of idioms, 267
    of word relationships, 267
    rhyming, 268
    specialized, 268
    spelling, 268
difference approach, 166–69, 172
diglossia, 88, 90, 151–52, 154, 295
Dillard, 146, 321–22
Dimaranan v. Pomona Valley Hospital, 156
diphthong, 18, 236
diphthongization, 300
direct object, 353
disambiguation, 66, 67
discourse, 82, 169, 171, 199, 225, 226
    direct, 247
    elaborated, 226
    free indirect, 247
    indirect, 232
discourse analysis, 51
discourse skills, 180
discourse marker, 180
discourse strategy (of physicians), 257
discreteness, 276, 277
displacement, 275, 277
distance (social), 85, 105
distributional criteria, 324
divergence hypothesis, 138–39, 144
doctor-patient conversation, 257
doctors, language of, 169, 252, 256–58
dominance approach, 166, 172
double articulation, 32, 274, 277
double negative, 3–5
doublet, 294
draft, 182, 185
Dravidian, 151, 317, 319
Dutch, 96, 135, 291, 304, 308
dysgraphia, 212
dyslexia, 211–13, 268
dyslexia/dysgraphia, 212
    deep, 212
    developmental, 213
    phonological, 212
    surface, 212

e-language, 8
e-mail, 187–88, 190
ebonics, 143–44, 147

echolalia, 210
Eckert, Penelope, 114–15, 121, 173
editing, 182, 185, 222
e-mail, 187–88, 190
embedding, 9, 48–49
emoticon, 189–90; see smiley
empathy, 230–31
emphasis, 164
England, 122, 166, 291, 295, 303
English, 3, 4, 6, 51, 87, 91, 103–4, 111, 122–29,
    130, 137, 149–50, 154, 155–59, 175–76,
    185–86, 205–6, 218–19, 224, 229, 260,
    289, 290–311, 313
  acquisition of grammar, 205–7
  as a World Language, 302–3
  history of, 290–302
  informal, 4
  pidgin, 134
  spoken, 4
  written, 4, 5
English academy, 321, 327
English Plus, 156
enjambment, 237
error, 174, 185, 218, 255
error correction, 223
Eskimo-Aleut, 318, 319
Esperanto, 123, 311
ethnicity, 110, 150, 159, 285
ethnography, 167
etymology, 7, 265, 268, 314
euphemism, 120
evaluation, 263
event in narration, 244, 247
exaggeration, 165, 241
Expanding Circle, 104
explicit knowledge, 331
explicitness, 114
expressive (speech act), 70
expressive (children), 201
extroversion, 230

face, 82–83
face-to-face, 188–89, 191
facial expression, 210
fair use, 254
fairy tale, 244
  Russian, 244
false friend, 262
false start, 174, 225
falsification (principle of), 9
familiarity, 83
family resemblance, 202, 204
Farsi, 315
feedback, 169, 182, 184, 219

feminism, 172
figurative language, 239
figure of speech, 235, 239, 323
figure of thought, 239, 241
film, 234, 247
final consonant deletion, 139
final stop (devoicing of), 139
fingerspelling, 285
first articulation, 32–33
first language, 185–86
first language acquisition, 194–208, 221, 225,
    332–33
first words, 201
Fishman, 80, 94, 163, 173
floor, having the, 81–82
flouting, 74, 241
fluency, 185, 222
focus on form, 222
folklinguistic, 165
foreigner talk (FT), 126, 225–26, 232
form (linguistic), 235
formal instruction, 331–32
formal pronoun, 85
formal system, 41
formality, 65, 84, 174
formula, 219, 221
fossilization, 221
frame, 68, 240, 335
France, 99–100, 122, 153, 160, 291, 295, 303,
    311, 319
freedom of speech, 254
freewriting, 183
French, 3, 20, 23, 31, 51, 60, 85, 122, 135, 149–
    52, 154, 159–60, 185, 219, 248, 262, 276,
    292, 295, 299, 304, 311–12, 314, 320
  influence on English, 295
  medieval literature, 297
  medieval poetry, 297
  Revolution, 149
Freud, 50
fricative, 21–22, 201, 313
Frisian, 291
functional distribution, 151–52
future, 344–50

Gaelic, 149, 161, 162
gay speech, 171
gender, 84, 110, 114, 164–71, 191, 207–8, 253,
    352
  grammatical, 352
  natural, 352
General American, 101
generative grammar, 39, 40–41, 244; see also
    universal grammar
Genie, 196

genitive, 292, 352–53
German, 31, 51, 85, 96, 135, 150, 159–60, 224,
    291, 292, 304, 352
  High, 291
  Low, 291
Germanic, 4, 290–94, 312–14
Germany, 82, 122, 150, 224, 291
gerund, 209, 344
gesture, 282, 286
Giglioli, 93, 146, 163
glide, 18, 21–22
glottal stop, 20–21, 139
glottis, 18
government and binding, 50
grammar, 4, 33, 35, 36, 39, 40, 80, 95, 104,
    140, 154, 171, 174, 181, 184, 194–95, 197,
    205–7, 219, 223, 228, 264–66, 323–39,
    342–64
  case, 330
  configurational, 329
  descriptive, 330
  formalist/distributional, 328
  functional, 329
  generative, 39–41, 328, 333
  Greek, 323–25
  history of, 323
  internalized, 8, 330–31
  Latin, 325–26
  normative, 323, 325, 328, 330–31
  pedagogical, 323, 330–34
  philosophical, 327
  rationalistic, 327
  theoretical, 330
  traditional, 323, 332
  transformational-generative, 49–50, 275,
    333
  types of, 330–31
grammar instruction, 330–34
grammatical analysis, 329
grammatical category, 37, 142, 319
grammatical description, 312
grammatical metalanguage, 332
grammatical sensitivity, 228
grammatical structure, 105
grammaticality, 35, 41, 50
grammaticality judgments, 222
Great Britain, 103–4
great vowel shift, 292, 299–301
Greek, 32, 90, 122, 135, 151, 157, 256, 259,
    299, 313–14, 314–15, 327, 330, 351
Grimm brothers, 327
Grimm's law, 313
group identity, 113
groupwork, 226

Guarani, 149, 152, 319
Guiterrez v. Municipal Court, 156
Gullah, 135–36, 145
Gumperz, 81, 93
Guyana, 127–28, 303
Guyanese, 128
Guéron, 367
Gypsy, 315

Haarmann, 163
habit formation, 194
habitual be, 140–41
Haegeman, 121, 367
Hai, 316
Haiti, 151
Haitian creole, 125, 151
Hakuta, 233
Hall, Robert, 12, 130, 328
handwriting, 184, 255
hard palate, 21–22
Hausa, 135, 308, 315
Hawaii, 123, 129, 156, 316
head (of a phrase), 36
hearing impairments, 209
Hebrew, 6, 185, 259, 315
hedge, 164, 168–69, 253
heritage languages, 161
hesitation, 174
heuristics, 182
high amplitude sucking, 199
high variety, 151–52
Himalayan, 316
Hindi, 176, 315, 319
hiragana, 175
historical linguistics, 2
holistic learners, 201
homonym, 66, 175, 268
honorific, 86–87
humility marker, 87
Hundred Years' War, 295
Hymes, 80–82, 93
hyperbole, 165, 241
hypercorrection, 111–12, 164
hypertext, 187
hypnosis, 231
hypotaxis, 45
hypothesis
  validity of, 9
  formulation, 9–10
  testing, 9–10 177, 227

i-language, 8
iamb, 238
iconicity, 259, 267

identity, 84
ideology, 230, 233, 254, 265, 266
idiolect, 97
idiom, 24, 29, 30, 252
illocutionary act, 69, 78
imitation, 194–95
immediate constituent, 36
immigration, 149–50, 153, 155–56, 160, 217, 281, 303–4
imperative, 72, 225, 293, 360
implicature, 52, 73–78
implicit knowledge, 331
incitement, 254
India, 114, 310, 315
Indian English, 310
indicative, 293, 348
Indo-European, 126, 151, 293, 313–15, 319, 327
inductive language-learning ability, 228
industrialization, 103
inference, 52, 74–76
infinitive, 5, 10, 28, 209, 343–44
infix, 28, 87
inflection, 28–29, 34, 293, 296, 324
    nominal, 325
    verbal, 325
inflectional ending, loss of, 296, 301
Inland Northern, 101, 109
innatism, 196–98, 202, 276
input, 197, 199, 206, 223, 225–26
    comprehensible, 223
    hypothesis, 223
    incomprehensible, 223
    simplified, 226
    ungrammatical, 226
    unmodified, 226
insect communication, 274, 276–77
intellectual ownership, 254
interaction, 81–82, 225–26
interactionism, 194, 196–98
interactive-compensatory model, 177, 179
interchangeability, 275, 277
interdental, 21
interjection, 325, 357
interlanguage, 217–19, 226–27, 334
Internet, 162, 186–87, 190
interpretation, 258
interpreter, 252, 254, 258
interrogative, 360
interruption, 55, 167, 169
intertextuality, 243
intonation, 69, 82, 164, 174, 188, 196–97, 200, 207, 263, 284
    rising, 164, 168

introversion, 230
intuition, 222; see also grammaticality
Inuit, 279, 318
inversion (of subject and verb, in questions), 207
IPA, 14–17, 27, 56, 58, 145, 264, 292
Irish, 149, 161, 304
irony, 74, 241–42
Islam, 123, 259
isogloss, 97–100, 108
isoglosses, bundle of, 99–100, 102
isolates, 319
it extraction, 364
Italian, 50–51, 85, 96–97, 124, 135, 157, 159, 185, 243, 299, 304, 311–12, 314, 326, 352
    Renaissance, 297
Italian Sign Language, 285
Italy, 96, 122, 160

Jakobson, 234–35, 328
Jamaica, 127–28, 137, 307
Jamaican, 131
    Creole, 307
    English, 307
Japanese, 31, 86–87, 115–16, 123, 165, 175, 207, 217–18, 260, 262, 280, 304, 318
jargon, 118–19, 253, 256, 268
Javanese, 197, 317
Jespersen, 165, 367
Johnson, Samuel, Dr., 269, 302, 327
joking, 74
judge, 252–53
Jutes, 290–92
juxtaposition, 248

Kachru, 104, 109, 321
kana, 175
kanji, 318
Kaplan, 185–86, 193
katakana, 175
kategoremata, 324
Kathaverusa, 151
Kazakhstan, 150
kernel sentence, 44, 57–58
klisis, 324
Koko, 278
Krashen, 221–23, 233

labio-dental, 21
Labov, 109, 111–12, 115, 121, 138, 143, 146–47, 227, 251, 272
Lakoff, George, 250, 341
Lakoff, Robin, 164–67, 169, 173

Lakota, 318
language,
    ability, 228
    administrative, 158
    aptitude, 228
    aptitude test, 228
    area, 82
    artificial, 123
    artificial use of, 235
    artistic use of, 234–35
    attitude, 95, 105, 165, 229–30
    autonomy, 96
    auxiliary, 123–24, 129, 308, 311
    boundary, 99
    casual, 234–35, 241
    change, 112, 115, 313, 327
    common, 82, 96
    contact, 88, 153–54, 160–61
    conversational, 152
    crime, 254
    dead, 6
    death, 90, 155, 160–61
    dominant, 89, 123, 155, 159
    elaborated, 234–35, 241
    endangered, 149–50, 162, 314, 318
    everyday use of, 235
    evolution of, 3
    externalized, 8
    extinct, 162, 327
    features of, 274–76
    figurative, 74, 239–40
    foreign, 157, 160, 185, 232, 311
    foreign, education, 156
    formal, 149, 152
    heritage, 161
    heteronomy, 96
    human (as opposed to animal), 276
    indigenous, 122, 149, 160
    informal, 152
    laws, 156
    learning, 194–213, 217–31, 331–34
    learning ability, 228
    legal, 165, 252–55
    lexifier, 123–24, 128
    literal, 240
    logical, 327
    maintenance, 90, 153–54, 160–61, 163
    majority, 162
    minority, 148–53, 159–62
    mixing, 91
    national, 103, 148–51, 159, 320
    native, 156
    natural, 282
    nature of, 274–86
    norm, 227
    official, 149, 153, 156, 158–59, 295
    pedagogy, 2, 116, 331
    planning, 6, 90–91, 148, 154–55, 171
    policy, 148–61
    primary, 156
    reform, 305
    regional, 149
    rehearsed, 235
    rights, 153–54
    Romance; see Romance languages
    second, 159, 185,
    second, acquisition, 217–31; see second
        language acquisition
    sexist, 6, 171
    shift, 90, 153–55, 157, 160
    sophisticated use of, 235
    spoken, 54, 188, 253, 258; see orality
    subordinate, 148, 153, 158
    substrate, 126
    superordinate, 148, 153, 158
    superstrate, 123, 126
    target, 226, 268
    teaching, 265
    universal, 274
    unrehearsed, 235
    variation, 95, 97, 110, 112, 175, 285
    women's, 164
    written, 54, 188
language acquisition, 89, 194–213
    order of, 205–7
    stages of, 200
language acquisition device, 196, 198, 333–34
language and medicine, 256–58
language and thought, 278–80
language development
    atypical, 208–13
language family, 312–19
language in court, 253–54
language in education, 263–64
language in the workplace, 156
language of instructions, 117
language of wider communication, 122, 310
Langue d'hoc, 99–100
Langue d'oil, 99–100
larynx, 19, 22
lateral, 22
lateralization, 213
Latin, 3, 4, 7, 51, 90, 122, 135, 154, 253,
    291, 295, 299, 312–14, 316, 325–27,
    330
    terminology, 256
law, 252–54
LDOCE, 269
learning, 222, 224
    collaborative, 184

learning strategy, 231
learning style, 221, 231
learning/acquisition dichotomy, 222
lectal variation, 127
legislation on language, 254–55
letter (alphabetic), 176, 179
leveling, 297
Levinson, 59, 78, 83, 94
lexeme, 26–27
lexical category, 37
lexical contrast, 204
lexical item, 114
lexicography, 32, 264–69
    computer-based, 266
lexicon, 26, 61, 117, 171, 268, 303, 310
license, 237
life experience, 176
limited English proficiency, 157
lingua franca, 122–23, 127, 125, 134, 151, 153,
    309
linguistic analysis, basic tools of, 13
linguistic determinism, 279
linguistic evidence, admissibility of, 255
linguistic marker, 87
linguistic relativity, 279
linguistic relativity hypothesis, 279
linguistic rights, 153–54
linguistics, 1–2
    anthropological, 2
    applied, 252
    cognitive, 240–41, 334–36
    computational, 2
    corpus, 7
    descriptive, 3
    diachronic, 6, 289, 312–14, 328
    forensic, 2, 255–56
    historical, 6, 289–302, 312–14, 328; see
        diachronic
    scientific, 327–28
    synchronic, 7, 289, 328
    text, 2, 51
    theoretical, 49–51, 252
linguistics in the professions, 252–70
liquid, 22–23
listserver, 187
literacy, 174–91
literature, 164, 234–49, 259
loan word, 31–32, 261
Locke, 327
locutionary act, 69, 78
logical problem of language acquisition,
    194
London, 104, 298–99
Long, 232–33
low variety, 151–52

Malay, 158–59, 311, 317
Malayo-Polynesian, 316–17
Malaysia, 151, 311, 317
male identity, 170
Mampele, 308
Mandarin, 158–59
Mandinka, 135
manner, maxim of, 74
manual alphabet, 284–85
Maori, 307
Marckwardt, 304, 322
margin comment, 185
marked sentential patterns, 363–64
Marquesan, 317
marriage, 168, 171
Martinet, 12, 59
Massai, 316
matched guise technique, 105–6
meaning, 5, 13, 23–26, 28–29, 32–33, 35, 52,
        60–69, 74–76, 174–77, 223, 239, 263–64,
        268–69, 328, 334–35
    associative, 66
    connotative, 64–66
    core, 64
    evocative, 66
    illocutionary, 69
    implicature, 74–76
    implied, 63
    inference, 74–76
    intended, 68–69, 74
    intension, 64
    lexical, 60–67, 268–69
    literal, 69, 76
    negotiation of, 210
    nonliteral, 69
    presupposition, 74–76
    relationship, 63
    shift in, 63
    sentence, see utterance
    utterance 67–69
meaning-to-sound relationship, 334
media, 150, 159
medical jargon, 256
medical language, 256–58
melting pot, 304
memory, 177, 230
Mencken, 305, 321
mental representation, 24–25, 60
mental retardation, 209, 212
mesolect, 97, 127
metalinguistic awareness, 334
metalinguistic function, 227, 275
metalinguistic knowledge, 227
metaphor, 63, 74, 80, 239–41, 250–51, 259,
        335

meter, 237–39, 250
Methodius, 315
metonymy, 63, 240
metric foot, 238, 250
metric system, 256
Mexico, 149, 280, 319
Middle Ages, 123, 326
Middle East, 260
Middle English, 253, 295–99, 313
    dialects of, 297–98
    East Midland, 297–98
    Kentish, 297–98
    literature of, 297
    Northern, 297–98
    Southern, 297–98
    West Midland, 297–98
middle voice, 324; see voice
minimal input, 196
minimal narrative, 244
minimal pair, 25–26, 111, 218, 326
minimalism, 50
miscue analysis, 177
modal, 209, 343, 358
modality, 348
Modern English, 296, 297, 299–302, 323
Modern Language Aptitude Test, 228
modifier, 353–54, 358–60
Modistae, 326
monitor, 221–22
monitor hypothesis, 221–22, 232
monolingualism, 88, 155, 160, 304
monophthongization, 139
monosyllabic words, 302
mood, 293, 345, 348
morpheme, 26–29, 32, 35, 50, 57, 124, 175,
        205–6, 220, 223–24, 256, 274, 279, 342,
        354
    bound, 27–29, 175
    definition of, 26
    derivational, 28, 279, 354
    free, 27–29, 175
    inflectional, 28–29, 124, 342
    root, 27–29
morpheme acquisition, 205–6, 220, 224
    order of (in first language English), 205–6
    order of (in second language English), 220,
        223–24
morpheme studies, 223
morpho-syntax, 207, 220
morphology, 1, 50, 124, 155, 180, 204, 206,
        209, 218, 224, 255, 283–84, 286, 292,
        301–2, 334
mother tongue, 125, 159, 258
mother-in-law language, 317

motherese, 116, 196, 263
motivation, 221, 228–30, 232
    instrumental, 228–29
    integrative, 228–29, 214
    intrinsic, 229
    resultative, 229
multilingualism, 148–54, 157, 308
mutual intelligibility, 127, 139, 158
Myanmar, 316–17

Na-Dene, 318–19
naming conventions, 171
narrative, 243–49
    autobiographical, 246
    minimal, 244
    spatial arrangement of, 248
    temporal arrangement of, 247
    third person, 246
narrative functions, 244
narrative time, 247–48
narratology, 243
narrator, 244–48
    explicit, 245
    homodiegetic, 245–46
    ideology of, 248
    implied, 245
    omniscient, 245
    unreliable, 246
nasal cavity, 18–20, 22
nasalization, 19–20, 139
nationalism, 305
nationality/immigration laws, 150
Native American, 259, 304
    languages, 156, 318–19
    language rights, 156
nativism, 194
natural class, 313
natural order hypothesis, 221, 223
negation, 30, 46, 76, 218, 221
negative evidence, 197, 221, 224
negative face, 83
neologism, 7, 115, 289
neurolinguistics, 2
neurosis, 210
new word, 154, 165; see also neologism
New Zealand, 303, 306–7, 316
newspaper, 234
    register in English, 116
Nigeria, 32, 308–9, 316
Nim Chimpsky, 278
nominative, 353
nonmanual signal in sign language, 284
nonnative speaker, 255
nonstandard, 105, 112

Norman conquest, 295
North Carolina, 104, 135
Northumbrian, 293–94
Norwegian, 125, 290–91
noun, 29, 33–42, 124, 201, 221, 292, 295, 296,
        324–25, 330, 335, 342, 351–53, 354, 358,
        361
    abstract, 351
    common, 351
    concrete, 351
    count, 335–36, 351
    mass, 335–36, 351
    noncount, 335–36, 351
    proper, 351
novel, 176, 243, 245, 259
Nubian, 316
number, 206, 350–52

object
    direct, 5, 39, 43, 45, 47, 292, 296, 334,
        352–53
    indirect, 5, 43, 47
Obler, 216
occlusion, 21
occupational groups, 110
occupational status, 84
occupational variety (of speech), 118–19
offensive language, 119–20, 254
Official English, 149, 156–57
Ojibwa, 318
Old English, 253, 291–95, 297, 313–14, 353
Old French, 253, 289
Old Norse, 294
onomatopoeia, 275, 283
output, 223, 226–27
output hypothesis, 226–27
overgeneralization, 185
overlap, 54, 167, 169
overstatement, 241, 242
Oxford English Dictionary, 11, 264, 302

Pacific Pidgin, 124–25
pairwork, 226
palatal, 21
palate, hard and soft, 22
palm orientation in sign language, 283, 286
Papua New Guinea, 123, 130, 197, 311
paragraph, 2, 13, 51, 181–82
parallelism, 52
parameter, 50–51
paraphrase, 225, 247, 258
parataxis, 45
parody, 243
participle, 47, 325, 343–45

particle hopping, 46
passive voice, 5, 44, 47, 207, 281, 302, 324,
        344–45
    irreversible, 207
    reversible, 207
past perfect, 346, 349–50
past tense, 342, 345–48
    acquisition of irregular, 206, 220
    acquisition of regular, 206, 220
patient, 256–58
pause, 174, 196, 225, 235
peer review, 182
Pennsylvania Dutch, 304
perfective marker, 358
performance, 2, 7–9, 80
Pergamon, 324–25
perlocutionary act, 69, 78
perlocutionary force, 70
person, 9, 342
personality factor, 221, 230–32
perspective, 245
persuasion, 323
pharyngeal, 21
pharynx, 19, 22
Philippines, 28, 123, 317
phonation, 19–20
phonatory organ, 14, 18, 24, 277
phoneme, 24–26, 283–84, 300–1, 328
    distinctive definition of, 25
    psychological definition of, 25
phonemic, 292, 299
phonemic coding ability, 228
phonetic alphabet, 14–18; see also IPA
phonetic notation, 228
phonetic system, 300
phonetic transcription, 235
phonetics, 1, 13, 218, 270, 310, 313
    articulatory, 18–23
    in Chinese characters, 175
    in forensic linguistics, 255
phonics, 179–80, 263
phonological inventory, 313
phonology, 1, 31, 50, 98, 124, 135, 139, 142,
        144, 147, 155, 171, 218, 222, 270, 283–84,
        286, 313
phonotactics, 135
phrasal verb, 26, 32, 46, 302, 305
phrase, 34, 36–37
    adjectival, 35, 359
    adverbial, 35, 359
    noun, 34–40, 45–49, 358
    prepositional, 35–40, 46, 48–49, 345, 357,
        359
    verb, 34–37, 39–40, 45–47, 49, 358

phrase level grammar, 358–59
phrase structure grammar, 36–37, 41–42
phrase structure rule, 41
phrase structure tree, 45
physician, 256
Piaget, 208
pidgin, 123–27, 130–31, 134, 219, 225, 226, 309
    elaborated, 125, 129
    restricted, 125, 129
pidginization, 311
Pinker, Steven, 11, 59
pitch, 14, 23, 196
plantation, 123, 126, 127, 134, 136
Plantation Creole, 134, 136
Plato, 50, 324
playacting, 74
playground, 169–70
plot, 244
plural, 206, 220, 351–52
pluralism, 156
plurality, 27–29
plurimorphemic, 27
poem, 250, 293
poetic license, 239
poetry, 235–39, 243, 277, 293
    ancient Greek, 238
    English, 238
point of view, 245–49
police, 252, 281
Polish, 20, 315
politeness, 83, 195, 207–8
polyglot, 1
polysemy, 66, 124
polysyllabic word, 210
portfolio, 185
Portuguese, 20, 123, 125, 127, 135, 304, 314
positive face, 83
positivism, 328
possessive, 206, 220, 296, 353
postdeterminer, 356, 358
postmodifier, 358–359
power, 85, 166, 169, 263, 281
pragmatics, 2, 67, 104, 116, 207–8, 210, 218, 283, 286
Prague school, 328
prayer, 161
precision, 253
predeterminer, 356, 358
    multiplier, 356
prefix, 27–28, 87, 180
premodifier, 358
preposition, 5, 6, 35–40, 46, 48–49, 124, 202–3, 205, 325, 335, 345, 357, 359, 360
prescriptivism, 2–4, 6, 11, 302, 327, 330

present continuous; *see* present progressive
present progressive, 205, 220, 346, 348–50
present tense, 342–48
prestige, 96–97, 101, 111–13, 128, 150, 166, 253, 331
    covert, 105, 166
presupposition, 74–76, 82
    contextual, 82
preverbal stage, 198–99
prewriting, 182–83
principle of cooperation, 52–53, 73–74, 239, 241
    flouting of, 74, 239, 241
    maxims of, 73–74
    violation of, 74
process approach to writing, 182–84
process, in cognitive grammar, 335
processing
    bottom-up, 176–77, 179–80
    top-down, 177, 179–80
productivity, 28–29, 274–75
profanity, 105
progressive, 205, 220, 342–43, 346, 349–50
pronoun, 37, 51, 59, 85–86, 124, 165, 171, 221, 225, 293, 324–25, 352–55
    nonreciprocal, 85
    of power, 85
    of solidarity, 86
    personal, 85–86, 293
    reciprocal, 85
    tu and *vos*, 85–86
pronoun case, 220, 352–53
pronunciation, 16, 58, 104–5, 111–13, 115, 145, 164, 166, 175, 211, 230–31, 237–38, 264, 301, 303–4, 307
prosody, 198
prototype, 204, 222, 280, 335
prototype theory, 204
prototypicality, 335
proverb, 355
pseudocleft, 364
psychoanalysis, 165
psycholinguistics, 2, 177
psychology, 68, 176, 245, 252, 278
    social, 105
psychotherapy, 210
ptosis, 324
pull theory, 300–1
pun, 259
punctuation, 181, 184
Punjabi, 315
push theory, 300–1

quality, maxim of, 73
quantity, maxim of, 73

question, 9, 10, 46, 53, 207, 221, 225, 257, 360
   choice, 225
   clarification, 197
   tag, 164, 168–69
   Wh–, 5, 6, 47
   yes/no, 47
quotation mark, 247

racism, 156, 281
reading, 176–81, 211–13
   extensive, 180, 192
   intensive, 180, 192
reading/writing connection, 184
realism, 248
reanalysis, 30
received pronunciation, 104
receiver, 80
reconstruction, 312–14, 327
recursion, 47–48
referent, 60, 324
regional variety, 132
regionalism, 101
register, 116–18, 188, 263–64, 266, 332
   discursive definition of, 117
   formal, 161
   social definition of, 117
   subject matter definition of, 117
relationship, in cognitive grammar, 335
   atemporal, 335
   temporal, 335
relative (clause), 5, 142, 161, 358–63
   cleft, 362
   fused, 363
   restrictive, 36
relevance, maxim of, 73
Renaissance, 122, 299, 301, 326–27
repetition, 59, 196, 235–37
respect, 83
rhema, 324
rhetorical mode, 180–81, 183
rhyme, 236
   approximate, 236
   feminine, 236
   internal, 236
   masculine, 236
Richards, Jack, 11
Roman, 97, 291–92, 325–26
   alphabet, 315
Roman Empire, 122
Romance language, 122, 185–86, 312, 314, 326
root, 27–29, 293
rote learning ability, 228
rule, 3–5, 9, 41–42, 139–40, 167, 185, 219, 222

rule-learning, 222
Russian, 125, 150, 185–86, 315

Samoan, 124, 317
Samoans, 197
Sanskrit, 313–14, 315, 327
Sapir, 12, 279
Sapir-Whorf hypothesis, 279–80, 287
sarcasm, 242
Saussure, 11–12, 78, 328
Savannah, 135
Saville-Troike, 93, 233
Saxons, 290–92
schema, 177; *see* semantic script
schematic knowledge, 177
schematic meaning, 334
Schilling-Estes, 109, 146, 321
school, 150, 154–55, 157–58 169, 180
schwa, 16, 108
scientific method, 9
Scotland, 303
Scots Gaelic, 149
Scottish, 133, 166, 304
script (semantic), 68, 335
script (orthographic), 154–55, 176
second articulation, 32–33
second language acquisition, 207, 217–32, 333–34
second language learning, 177, 217–18
segregation, 138
semantic feature, 61–63, 203–4
semantic feature analysis, 61–63, 203–4
semantic processing, 226
semantic transfer, 218
semantics, 1, 52, 60–68, 98, 135, 207, 209, 218, 283–84, 286, 310, 329–30, 334
sense, (of a word), 265, 268; *see also* meaning
sentence, types of, 43–49, 359–64
sentence combining, 182
sentence-level grammar, 359–64
Sermon on the Mount, 259–60
sexism, 171–72
Shakespeare, 3, 50, 236–37, 241, 299–301, 304
shibboleth, 3–4
short story, 243, 245, 250
short-term memory, 212
Shoshoni, 318
Shuy, 109, 272
Sierra Leone, 126, 135
sign language, 278, 282–86
   acquisition of, 285–86
signified, 60, 324
signifier, 60, 324

silent period, 219, 221
similarity attraction theory, 105
simile, 239
simplification, 123, 161, 196–98, 221
Singapore, 151, 158–59, 310
singular, 343, 350–52
skills-based approach to reading, 179–80
Skinner, B. F., 194
slang, 115, 118–21, 171, 189, 265, 283
slant rhyme, 236
slavery, 134, 136, 307
slogan, 235
smiley, 190–191; *see* emoticon
Smitherman, 143, 146
social class, 3–4, 110–12, 114
social exchange theory, 105
social group, 110, 115
social networks, 112–13
social stratification, 111, 281, 295
sociolinguistics, 2, 80–93, 115, 154, 170, 174,
    219
  interactional, 81
  quantitative, 112
sociology, 252
soft palate, 20–21
softener, 253; *see* hedge
solidarity, 83, 85–86, 105, 113, 149, 166, 172
Sophists, 323
sound, 13–14, 16, 18–21, 23–25, 33, 175–79,
    198–200, 209, 228, 235–37, 239, 274, 283,
    312, 328
  acquisition of, 184
  smilarity of, 221
  vegetative, 199–200
  voiced, 20
  voiceless, 20
sound wave, 13–14
sound-symbol correspondence, 175, 179
South African English, 154, 308
southern American English, 137, 139
Soviet Union, 150, 154
Spain, 122, 150, 153, 291, 319
spam, 190
Spanglish, 91
Spanish, 51, 91, 137, 149, 152–53, 155, 157, 160,
    218, 220, 254, 260–62, 280, 304, 312, 314
spatial relation, 335
speech, 160, 174, 188, 192, 201, 225, 227
  careful, 112
  casual, 112
  clarity of, 197
  direct, 247
  disconnected, 226
  enunciated, 263

female, 164
  indirect, 247
  male, 164
  powerful, 253
  powerless, 253
  unadorned, 253
speech act, 69–73
  cross-cultural differences, 72–73
  performative, 70, 254
  preconditions for, 70–71, 73
  teaching of, 71
speech community, 82, 112
speech event, 69
speech pathology, 270
speech style, 105
speech therapy, 270
spelling, 14, 154, 176–79, 184, 212, 237–38, 303
split infinitive, 5
spoken language, 14
spontaneous conversation, 227
square bracket, 14
Sranan, 125
standard, 103, 112
Standard American English (SAE), 132–34,
    136–43, 145, 147
Standard English, 103–4, 112, 117, 127–28,
    134, 140–41, 134, 282, 287
standard language, 97, 104, 128
standard theory (Chomsky's), 49
standardization, 103, 152, 154–55, 302
status, 83–88, 166, 172, 253, 257
  class, 84
  occupational, 84
  social, 67, 83–88, 321
status language, 154
status planning, 154, 162
stem, 27
stereotype, 95, 112, 281
stimulus, 199
  poverty of, 194, 198
stop, 15, 21–22
strategy (for SLA)
  cognitive, 231
  metacognitive, 231
  social, 231
stream of consciousness, 246
stress, 23, 200, 225, 238, 313
structuralism, 328
stuttering, 8, 210–11
stylistics, 116
stylometry, 255–56
subject, 34, 36, 38–39, 292, 296, 352–53
  marker, 207
subjunctive, 293, 302, 348

subordination, 45–46, 174, 360–63
substrate, 123, 126–27
substrate theory, 123, 126–27
subtitles, 157
suffix, 27–29, 87, 180, 354
superlative, 354
superstrate, 123
superstrate theory, 123, 126
suprasegmental, 23, 188
surface structure, 39, 42, 46
sustained silent reading, 180
SVO language, 296
Swahili, 3, 151, 153, 316
Switzerland, 122, 159–160, 314
syllabic (writing system), 175
syllabification, 265
syllable, 178–79, 235–38
symbol, 228, 242–43
synchronic, 6–7
syndesmoi, 324
synkategoremata, 324
synonym, 63, 225, 267
syntactic criteria, 324
syntactic processing, 226
syntactic role, 353
syntax, 1, 35–51, 57–58, 98, 117, 123, 142,
    161, 177, 196, 198, 218, 223–26, 260,
    283–84, 286, 292, 296, 329, 334, 359
  acquisition of, 221

taboo word, 116, 119–20
Tagalog, 28, 317
Tannen, Deborah, 166, 173
Tanzania, 151, 153, 317
tap, 24; see flap
target language, 226–27, 247
target vocabulary, 226
teachability/learnability thesis, 224
teacher talk, 263
teaching foreign languages, 263; see second
    language acquisition
technical terminology, 256
technology, 154
teeth, 18, 21–22
telegraphic speech, 205, 211
television, 157, 161, 176, 234
television talk shows, 152
tense, 9, 28, 140, 245, 247, 293, 342–43,
    345–50
territorial rights, 154
text, 2, 13, 52, 176
Thai, 231, 317
Thailand, 317
thesaurus, 267

timbre, 14
TMA, 345–50
Tok Pisin, 123–25, 311
tone, 14, 23
tongue, 18, 20–23
topic, 225–26
  shift, 168, 225
  decay, 189
trachea, 18–19
trademark, 254
transcription, 14, 56–57, 145, 172, 174, 227
transfer, 217–18, 220, 223
transformation, 44, 46–47, 58
translation, 252, 258–63, 265, 333
  (opposed to interpretation), 258
  accuracy of, 258–59
  aesthetics of, 258–59
  Biblical, 259–60
  cultural accuracy of, 258–59
  machine, 263
  performance testing of, 260–61
  word-by-word, 263
transliteration, 261
tree diagram, 37, 39–40, 42, 45, 57–58, 329,
    338
trilingualism, 159
trochee, 238
Trudgill, 93, 96, 109, 147, 173, 321
turn taking, 54–55, 81
two-word stage, 204–5, 214

Unabomber, 255–56
unbounded (feature), 336; see bounded
underextension, 202, 204
understatement, 241–42
UNESCO, 154
Ungerer, 250, 340
United Kingdom, 149–50
United States, 103–4, 122, 134, 149, 153, 155–
    57, 160, 171, 175–76, 303, 311, 318–19
  army bases, 125
  dialectology of, 98, 100–3,
  Constitution of, 156
  Supreme Court, 253
universal grammar, 49–51, 127, 196, 221, 274,
    326
universality, 280
universals, linguistic, 274, 326
Urdu, 176, 315
usage, 265
utterance, 69–70, 64
uvula, 18, 21–22
uvular, 21, 23
Uzbek, 317

Valley Girl, 95
vehicle, 239–40
velar, 21
velar fricative, 292
velum, 18, 20, 22
verb, 5, 10, 28, 32–39, 43–44, 47, 125, 136–37,
        140, 204, 293, 295–96, 324–26, 330, 335,
        342–51, 353, 355, 358, 364
    classes of, 293
    copular, 43
    ditransitive, 43
    finite, 342
    Helping, 343
    intransitive, 43
    irregular, 293
    main, 10, 34, 47, 343–44
    modal, 343, 346, 348
    nominal, 322
    nonfinite, 322, 324
    phrasal, see phrasal verb
    strong, 293, 296–97
    tenses, 345–48
    tensed, 342
    transitive, 43, 335
    weak, 293, 297
verb form, 224
verbal system, 193
vernacular, 154
    African American (AAVE), 132–44
Verner's law, 313
verse, 238
vilification, 254
visual effects, 236–37
visual media, 234
vocabulary, 26, 95, 104, 124–25, 152, 177, 184,
        197, 201, 205, 207, 218, 225, 260, 295
    restricted, 269
    subordinate, 225
    superordinate, 225
    technical, 155
vocabulary acquisition, 197, 202–4
vocal folds, 20–22
vocal tract, 19–22
voice, 44, 344–45, 358
voiced stop, 15, 313
voiceprint, 255
volume, 14
vowel, 16–18, 20, 124, 197, 200, 218, 236–37,
        293, 299–301
    ablaut, 293
    back, 16–17, 300
    front, 17–17, 300
    high, 16–17, 300
    length, 292

    long, 292–93, 299–301
    nonsyllabic, 237
    quality of, 299
    rounded, 292
    syllabic, 237

Wardhaugh, 93, 288
Washoe, 278
we, 67, 355
    exclusive, 124
    inclusive, 124
web page, 187
website, 234
Webster, 11, 154, 264, 268–69, 271, 305,
        322
Welsh, 149, 154, 159, 291
West African pidgin, 134
West Germanic, 291
West Midlands, 95
West Saxon, 293
Western Europe, 217
Western Samoans, 197–98
whole language, 180–81, 192
Whorf, 279, 287, 318
wide-angle shot, 248
Wolfram, 109, 147, 321
Wolof, 134–35, 316
women's discourse, 169
word skills, 180, 169
word choice, 82, 255
word order, 207, 284, 296, 334
world English, 306–11
World War II, 155, 217
World Wide Web, 145, 186, 190, 262; see
        Internet
writing, 174–91, 211–12
process approach to, 182–85
    product approach to, 181–82
    system, 175–76
        alphabetic, 175–76
        logographic, 175
        syllabic, 175
teaching of, 175, 181–85
writing first, 184

Yiddish, 6, 304
Yoruba, 32, 135, 308
Yule, 59

zero copula, 140
ZISA Project, 224–25
zoosemiotics, 274
Zulu, 316
Zuni, 319